PRENTICE HALL MATHEMATICS

ALGEBRA 1

California
ALL-IN-ONE
Student Workbook
Version A

PEARSON

Prentice
Hall

Boston, Massachusetts
Upper Saddle River, New Jersey

ISBN-13: 978-0-13-350115-5
ISBN-10:   0-13-350115-9

17 V011 15 14 13

Daily Notetaking Guide

Lesson 1-1 2
Lesson 1-2 4
Lesson 1-3 7
Lesson 1-4 10
Lesson 1-5 13
Lesson 1-6 16
Lesson 1-7 20
Lesson 1-8 23
Lesson 2-1 26
Lesson 2-2 28
Lesson 2-3 32
Lesson 2-4 34
Lesson 2-5 37
Lesson 2-6 41
Lesson 3-1 43
Lesson 3-2 45
Lesson 3-3 47
Lesson 3-4 50
Lesson 3-5 52
Lesson 3-6 54
Lesson 4-1 57
Lesson 4-2 59
Lesson 4-3 62
Lesson 4-4 64
Lesson 4-5 66
Lesson 4-6 69
Lesson 4-7 72
Lesson 5-1 74
Lesson 5-2 77
Lesson 5-3 80
Lesson 5-4 83
Lesson 5-5 86
Lesson 6-1 88
Lesson 6-2 91
Lesson 6-3 93
Lesson 6-4 96
Lesson 6-5 99
Lesson 6-6 101
Lesson 7-1 104
Lesson 7-2 106
Lesson 7-3 109
Lesson 7-4 112
Lesson 7-5 114
Lesson 8-1 117
Lesson 8-2 120
Lesson 8-3 122
Lesson 8-4 124
Lesson 8-5 127
Lesson 8-6 129
Lesson 8-7 131
Lesson 8-8 134
Lesson 9-1 136
Lesson 9-2 139
Lesson 9-3 141

Lesson 9-4 143
Lesson 9-5 145
Lesson 9-6 147
Lesson 9-7 150
Lesson 9-8 153
Lesson 10-1 155
Lesson 10-2 158
Lesson 10-3 160
Lesson 10-4 163
Lesson 10-5 166
Lesson 11-1 168
Lesson 11-2 170
Lesson 11-3 172
Lesson 11-4 175
Lesson 11-5 178

Practice, Guided Problem Solving, Vocabulary

Chapter 1 Tools of Algebra

Practice 1-1 183
Guided Problem Solving 1-1 184
Practice 1-2 185
Guided Problem Solving 1-2 186
Practice 1-3 187
Guided Problem Solving 1-3 188
Practice 1-4 189
Guided Problem Solving 1-4 190
Practice 1-5 191
Guided Problem Solving 1-5 192
Practice 1-6 193
Guided Problem Solving 1-6 194
Practice 1-7 195
Guided Problem Solving 1-7 196
Practice 1-8 197
Guided Problem Solving 1-8 198
Vocabulary 1A: Graphic Organizer 199
Vocabulary 1B: Reading Comprehension 200
Vocabulary 1C: Reading/Writing Math Symbols 201
Vocabulary 1D: Visual Vocabulary Practice 202
Vocabulary 1E: Vocabulary Check 203
Vocabulary 1F: Vocabulary Review 205

Chapter 2 Solving Equations

Practice 2-1 207
Guided Problem Solving 2-1 208
Practice 2-2 209
Guided Problem Solving 2-2 210
Practice 2-3 211
Guided Problem Solving 2-3 212
Practice 2-4 213
Guided Problem Solving 2-4 214
Practice 2-5 215
Guided Problem Solving 2-5 216
Practice 2-6 217
Guided Problem Solving 2-6 218
Vocabulary 2A: Graphic Organizer 219

Vocabulary 2B: Reading Comprehension 220
Vocabulary 2C: Reading/Writing Math Symbols 221
Vocabulary 2D: Visual Vocabulary Practice 222
Vocabulary 2E: Vocabulary Check 223
Vocabulary 2F: Vocabulary Review 225

Chapter 3 Solving Inequalities

Practice 3-1 227
Guided Problem Solving 3-1 228
Practice 3-2 229
Guided Problem Solving 3-2 230
Practice 3-3 231
Guided Problem Solving 3-3 232
Practice 3-4 233
Guided Problem Solving 3-4 234
Practice 3-5 235
Guided Problem Solving 3-5 236
Practice 3-6 237
Guided Problem Solving 3-6 238
Vocabulary 3A: Graphic Organizer 239
Vocabulary 3B: Reading Comprehension 240
Vocabulary 3C: Reading/Writing Math Symbols 241
Vocabulary 3D: Visual Vocabulary Practice 242
Vocabulary 3E: Vocabulary Check 243
Vocabulary 3F: Vocabulary Review Puzzle 245

Chapter 4 Graphs and Functions

Practice 4-1 247
Guided Problem Solving 4-1 248
Practice 4-2 249
Guided Problem Solving 4-2 250
Practice 4-3 251
Guided Problem Solving 4-3 252
Practice 4-4 253
Guided Problem Solving 4-4 254
Practice 4-5 255
Guided Problem Solving 4-5 256
Practice 4-6 257
Guided Problem Solving 4-6 258
Practice 4-7 259
Guided Problem Solving 4-7 260
Vocabulary 4A: Graphic Organizer 261
Vocabulary 4B: Reading Comprehension 262
Vocabulary 4C: Reading/Writing Math Symbols 263
Vocabulary 4D: Visual Vocabulary Practice 264
Vocabulary 4E: Vocabulary Check 265
Vocabulary 4F: Vocabulary Review Puzzle 267

Chapter 5 Linear Equations and Their Graphs

Practice 5-1 269
Guided Problem Solving 5-1 270
Practice 5-2 271
Guided Problem Solving 5-2 272
Practice 5-3 273
Guided Problem Solving 5-3 274
Practice 5-4 275
Guided Problem Solving 5-4 276

Practice 5-5 277
Guided Problem Solving 5-5 278
Vocabulary 5A: Graphic Organizer 279
Vocabulary 5B: Reading Comprehension 280
Vocabulary 5C: Reading/Writing Math Symbols 281
Vocabulary 5D: Visual Vocabulary Practice 282
Vocabulary 5E: Vocabulary Check 283
Vocabulary 5F: Vocabulary Review Puzzle 285

Chapter 6 Systems of Equations and Inequalities

Practice 6-1 287
Guided Problem Solving 6-1 288
Practice 6-2 289
Guided Problem Solving 6-2 290
Practice 6-3 291
Guided Problem Solving 6-3 292
Practice 6-4 293
Guided Problem Solving 6-4 294
Practice 6-5 295
Guided Problem Solving 6-5 296
Practice 6-6 297
Guided Problem Solving 6-6 298
Vocabulary 6A: Graphic Organizer 299
Vocabulary 6B: Reading Comprehension 300
Vocabulary 6C: Reading/Writing Math Symbols 301
Vocabulary 6D: Visual Vocabulary Practice 302
Vocabulary 6E: Vocabulary Check 303
Vocabulary 6F: Vocabulary Review 305

Chapter 7 Exponents

Practice 7-1 307
Guided Problem Solving 7-1 308
Practice 7-2 309
Guided Problem Solving 7-2 310
Practice 7-3 311
Guided Problem Solving 7-3 312
Practice 7-4 313
Guided Problem Solving 7-4 314
Practice 7-5 315
Guided Problem Solving 7-5 316
Vocabulary 7A: Graphic Organizer 317
Vocabulary 7B: Reading Comprehension 318
Vocabulary 7C: Reading/Writing Math Symbols 319
Vocabulary 7D: Visual Vocabulary Practice 320
Vocabulary 7E: Vocabulary Check 321
Vocabulary 7F: Vocabulary Review 323

Chapter 8 Polynomials and Factoring

Practice 8-1 325
Guided Problem Solving 8-1 326
Practice 8-2 327
Guided Problem Solving 8-2 328
Practice 8-3 329
Guided Problem Solving 8-3 330
Practice 8-4 331
Guided Problem Solving 8-4 332

Practice 8-5 333
Guided Problem Solving 8-5 334
Practice 8-6 335
Guided Problem Solving 8-6 336
Practice 8-7 337
Guided Problem Solving 8-7 338
Practice 8-8 339
Guided Problem Solving 8-8 340
Vocabulary 8A: Graphic Organizer 341
Vocabulary 8B: Reading Comprehension 342
Vocabulary 8C: Reading/Writing Math Symbols 343
Vocabulary 8D: Visual Vocabulary Practice 344
Vocabulary 8E: Vocabulary Check 345
Vocabulary 8F: Vocabulary Review 347

Chapter 9 Quadratic Equations and Functions

Practice 9-1 349
Guided Problem Solving 9-1 350
Practice 9-2 351
Guided Problem Solving 9-2 352
Practice 9-3 353
Guided Problem Solving 9-3 354
Practice 9-4 355
Guided Problem Solving 9-4 356
Practice 9-5 357
Guided Problem Solving 9-5 358
Practice 9-6 359
Guided Problem Solving 9-6 360
Practice 9-7 361
Guided Problem Solving 9-7 362
Practice 9-8 363
Guided Problem Solving 9-8 364
Vocabulary 9A: Graphic Organizer 365
Vocabulary 9B: Reading Comprehension 366
Vocabulary 9C: Reading/Writing Math Symbols 367
Vocabulary 9D: Visual Vocabulary Practice 368
Vocabulary 9E: Vocabulary Check 369
Vocabulary 9F: Vocabulary Review Puzzle 371

Chapter 10 Radical Expressions and Equations

Practice 10-1 373
Guided Problem Solving 10-1 374
Practice 10-2 375
Guided Problem Solving 10-2 376
Practice 10-3 377
Guided Problem Solving 10-3 378
Practice 10-4 379
Guided Problem Solving 10-4 380
Practice 10-5 381
Guided Problem Solving 10-5 382
Vocabulary 10A: Graphic Organizer 383
Vocabulary 10B: Reading Comprehension 384
Vocabulary 10C: Reading/Writing Math Symbols 385
Vocabulary 10D: Visual Vocabulary Practice 386
Vocabulary 10E: Vocabulary Check 387
Vocabulary 10F: Vocabulary Review 389

Chapter 11 Rational Expressions and Equations

Practice 11-1 391
Guided Problem Solving 11-1 392
Practice 11-2 393
Guided Problem Solving 11-2 394
Practice 11-3 395
Guided Problem Solving 11-3 396
Practice 11-4 397
Guided Problem Solving 11-4 398
Practice 11-5 399
Guided Problem Solving 11-5 400
Vocabulary 11A: Graphic Organizer 401
Vocabulary 11B: Reading Comprehension 402
Vocabulary 11C: Reading/Writing Math Symbols 403
Vocabulary 11D: Visual Vocabulary Practice .404
Vocabulary 11E: Vocabulary Check 405
Vocabulary 11F: Vocabulary Review Puzzle 407

A Note to the Student:

This section of your workbook contains notetaking pages for each lesson in your student edition. They are structured to help you take effective notes in class. They will also serve as a study guide as you prepare for tests and quizzes.

Lesson 1-1

Using Variables

Lesson Objectives	California Content Standards
• Model relationships with variables • Model relationships with equations	7AF1.1

Take Note

A variable is _____

_____

An algebraic expression is _____

_____

An equation is _____

_____

An open sentence is _____

Examples

❶ **Writing an Algebraic Expression** Write an algebraic expression for "the sum of *n* and 8."

"Sum" indicates addition. Add the first number, [ ], and the second number, [ ].

n [ ] 8

❷ **Writing an Algebraic Expression** Define a variable and write an algebraic expression for "ten more than twice a number."

Relate | ten more than | | twice | | a number |

Define Let | *y* | = the number.

Write [ ]   [ ]   [ ]

[ ] + [ ]

❸ **Writing an Equation** Write an equation to show the total income from selling tickets to a school play for $5 each.

Relate The | total income | is | 5 | times | the number of tickets sold |.

Define Let | *t* | = the number of tickets sold.

Let | *i* | = the total income.

Write [ ]   =   [ ]   ·   [ ]

[ ] = [ ]

④ Application Write an equation for the data in the table.

Gallons	4	6	8	10
Miles	80	120	160	200

Relate Miles traveled equals 20 times the number of gallons

Define Let m = the number of miles traveled.

Let g = the number of gallons.

Write ☐   =   ☐ · ☐

☐ = ☐

CA Standards Check

1. Write an algebraic expression for each phrase.

a. the quotient of 4.2 and c

b. t minus 15

2. Define a variable and write an algebraic expression for each phrase.

a. 9 less than a number

b. the sum of twice a number and 31

3. Suppose the price of a CD is $15. Write an equation to find the cost of n CDs.

4. Define the variables and write an equation for the data in the table.

amount earned	$15	$20	$25	$30
amount saved	$7.50	$10	$12.50	$15

Lesson 1-2

Exponents and Order of Operations

Lesson Objectives	California Content Standards
• Simplify and evaluate expressions and formulas • Simplify and evaluate expressions containing grouping symbols	25.2

Take Note

Order of Operations

1. Perform any operation(s) [   ].

2. Simplify [   ].

3. [   ] in order from left to right.

4. [   ] in order from left to right.

Simplify means _____

_____

An exponent is _____

A base is _____

A power is _____

_____

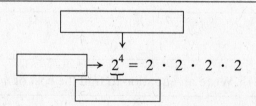

$$2^4 = 2 \cdot 2 \cdot 2 \cdot 2$$

Evaluate means _____

_____

Examples

❶ Simplifying a Numerical Expression Simplify $32 + 6^2 - 14 \cdot 3$.

$32 + 6^2 - 14 \cdot 3 = 32 + \boxed{} - 14 \cdot 3$ Simplify the power: $6^2 = 6 \cdot \boxed{} = \boxed{}$.

$ = 32 + \boxed{} - \boxed{}$ Multiply 14 and 3.

$ = \boxed{} - 42$ Add and subtract in order from left to right.

$ = \boxed{}$ Subtract.

❷ Evaluating an Algebraic Expression Find the total cost of a pair of jeans that costs $32 and has an 8% sales tax.

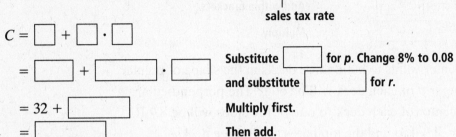

$C = \boxed{} + \boxed{} \cdot \boxed{}$

$= \boxed{} + \boxed{} \cdot \boxed{}$ Substitute $\boxed{}$ for p. Change 8% to 0.08 and substitute $\boxed{}$ for r.

$= 32 + \boxed{}$ **Multiply first.**

$= \boxed{}$ **Then add.**

The total cost of the jeans is $\boxed{}$.

❸ Evaluating Expressions With Exponents Evaluate each expression for $x = 11$ and $z = 16$.

a. $(xz)^2$

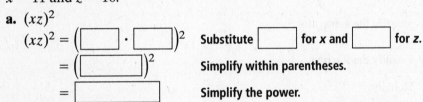

$(xz)^2 = \left(\boxed{} \cdot \boxed{}\right)^2$ Substitute $\boxed{}$ for x and $\boxed{}$ for z.

$= \left(\boxed{}\right)^2$ Simplify within parentheses.

$= \boxed{}$ Simplify the power.

b. xz^2

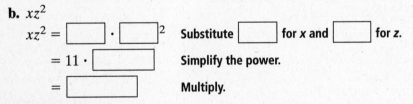

$xz^2 = \boxed{} \cdot \boxed{}^2$ Substitute $\boxed{}$ for x and $\boxed{}$ for z.

$= 11 \cdot \boxed{}$ Simplify the power.

$= \boxed{}$ Multiply.

CA Standards Check

1. Simplify each expression.

a. $6 - 10 \div 5$ **b.** $3 \cdot 6 - 4^2 \div 2$ **c.** $4 \cdot 7 + 4 \div 2^2$

2. Evaluate each expression for $c = 2$ and $d = 5$.

a. $4c - 2d \div c$ **b.** $d + 6c \div 4$ **c.** $c^4 - d \cdot 2$

Name_____ Class_____ Date _____

Examples

④ Simplifying an Expression Simplify $4[(2 \cdot 9) + (15 \div 3)^2]$.

$4[(2 \cdot 9) + (15 \div 3)^2] = 4\left[\boxed{} + \left(\boxed{}\right)^2\right]$ **First simplify $(2 \cdot 9)$ and $(15 \div 3)$.**

$ = 4\left[18 + \boxed{}\right]$ **Simplify the power.**

$ = 4\left[\boxed{}\right]$ **Add within brackets.**

$ = \boxed{}$ **Multiply.**

⑤ Application A carpenter wants to build three decks in the shape of regular hexagons. The perimeter p of each deck will be 60 ft. The perpendicular distance a from the center of each deck to one of the sides will be 8.7 ft. Use the formula $A = 3\left(\dfrac{pa}{2}\right)$ to find the total area of all three decks.

$A = 3\left(\dfrac{pa}{2}\right)$

$ = 3\left(\dfrac{\boxed{} \cdot \boxed{}}{2}\right)$ **Substitute**  **for p and** 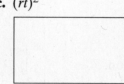 **for a.**

$ = 3\left(\dfrac{\boxed{}}{2}\right)$ **Simplify the numerator.**

$ = 3\left(\boxed{}\right)$ **Simplify the fraction.**

$ = \boxed{}$ **Multiply.**

The total area of all three decks is $\boxed{}$ ft^2.

CA Standards Check

3. Evaluate each expression for $r = 9$ and $t = 14$.

a. rt^2
b. r^2t
c. $(rt)^2$

4. Simplify each expression.

a. $5[4 + 3(2^2 + 1)]$
b. $12 + 3[18 - 5(16 - 13)]$

5. The area of a trapezoid can be found using the formula $\frac{1}{2}h(b_1 + b_2)$. Find the area of a trapezoid with height $h = 300$ ft and bases $b_1 = 250$ ft and $b_2 = 170$ ft.

Lesson 1-3

Exploring Real Numbers

Lesson Objectives	California Content Standards
• Classify numbers • Compare numbers	1.0, 1.1, 24.3, 25.1

Take Note

Real Numbers

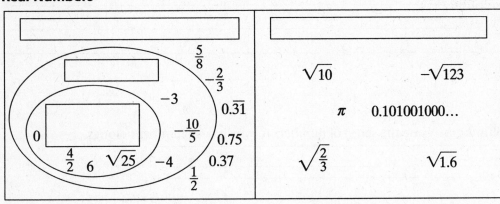

Natural numbers are _____

_____

Whole numbers are _____

_____

Integers are _____

_____

Rational numbers are _____

_____

_____

Irrational numbers are _____

_____

_____

_____

1, 2, 3, ...

0, 1, 2, 3, ...

... −2, −1, 0, 1, 2, ...

$0.101001000...$ π $\sqrt{10}$

**Decimal representations of each of these
are nonrepeating and nonterminating.**

Name_____ Class_____ Date _____

Real numbers are _____

_____

A counterexample is _____

_____

An inequality is _____

_____

Opposites are _____

_____

Absolute value is _____

_____

Examples

① Classifying Numbers Name the set(s) of numbers to which each number belongs.

a. -13 [ ]

b. 3.28 [ ]

② Using Counterexamples Determine whether the statement is true or false.
If it is false, give a counterexample.

All negative numbers are integers.

A negative number can be a [   ], such as $-\frac{2}{3}$. This is not an

integer. The statement is [   ].

③ Ordering Fractions Write $-\frac{3}{4}$, $-\frac{7}{12}$, and $-\frac{5}{8}$ in order from least to greatest.

$-\frac{3}{4} =$ [   ]

$-\frac{7}{12} =$ [   ]   **Write each fraction as a decimal.**

$-\frac{5}{8} =$ [   ]

[   ] < [   ] < [   ]   **Order the decimals from least to greatest.**

From least to greatest, the fractions are [   ] , [   ] , and [   ] .

④ Finding Absolute Value Find each absolute value.

a. $|-2.5|$ -2.5 is [   ] units from 0 on a number line. $|-2.5| =$ [   ]

b. $|7|$ 7 is [   ] units from 0 on a number line. $|7| =$ [   ]

Name_____ Class_____ Date _____

CA Standards Check

1. Name the set(s) of numbers to which each number belongs.

   a. −12

   b. $\frac{5}{12}$

   c. −4.67

   d. 6

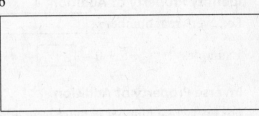

2. Is each statement true or false? If it is false, give a counterexample.

   a. All whole numbers are integers.

   b. No fractions are whole numbers.

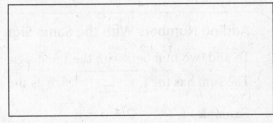

3. Write $\frac{1}{12}$, $-\frac{2}{3}$, and $-\frac{5}{8}$ in order from least to greatest.

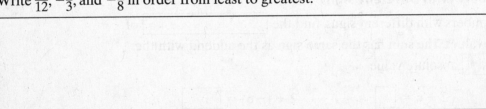

4. Find each absolute value.

   a. $|5|$

   b. $|-4|$

   c. $|-3.7|$

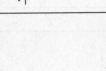

   d. $\left|\frac{5}{7}\right|$

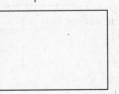

Lesson 1-4

Lesson Objectives	California Content Standards
• Add real numbers using models and rules • Apply addition	1.0, 2.0

Take Note

Identity Property of Addition

For every real number n, [   ].

Examples $-5 + 0 =$ [   ] $0 + 5 =$ [   ]

Inverse Property of Addition

For every real number n, there is an additive inverse $-n$ such that [   ].

Examples $17 + (-17) =$ [ ] $-17 + 17 =$ [ ]

Adding Numbers With the Same Sign

To add two numbers with the same sign, [   ] their absolute values.
The sum has the [   ] sign as the addends.

Examples $2 + 6 =$ [   ] $-2 + (-6) =$ [   ]

Adding Numbers With Different Signs

To add two numbers with different signs, find the [   ] of
their absolute values. The sum has the same sign as the addend with the
[   ] absolute value.

Examples $-2 + 6 =$ [   ] $2 + (-6) =$ [   ]

An additive inverse is _____

The sum of additive inverses is _____

Name_____ Class_____ Date _____

Examples

❶ Using a Number Line Model Simplify each expression.

a. $3 + (-5)$

$3 + (-5) = $ ▢

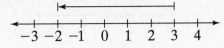

Start at ▢.
Move left ▢ units.

b. $-3 + 5$

$-3 + 5 = $ ▢

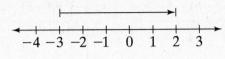

Start at ▢.
Move right ▢ units.

❷ Adding Numbers Simplify each expression.

a. $12 + (-23) = $ ▢   The difference of the absolute values is ▢. The ▢

addend has the greater absolute value, so the sum is ▢.

b. $-6.4 + (-8.6) = $ ▢   Since both addends are ▢, add their absolute values.

The sum is ▢.

❸ Evaluating Expressions Evaluate $6.3 - p$ for $p = -8.5$.

$6.3 - p = 6.3 - $ ▢   Substitute ▢ for **p**.

$= $ ▢ $ - $ ▢   means the opposite of ▢ which is ▢.

$= $ ▢   Simplify.

❹ Application A scuba diver who is 88 ft below sea level begins to ascend to the surface.

a. Write an expression to represent the diver's depth below sea level after rising any number of feet.

Relate | 88 ft below sea level | plus | feet diver rises |

Define Let ▢ r = the number of feet diver rises.

Write ▢ $+$ ▢

▢ $+$ ▢

b. Find the new depth of the scuba diver after rising 37 ft.

$-88 + r = -88 + $ ▢   Substitute ▢ for **r**.

$= $ ▢   Simplify.

The scuba diver is ▢ ft below sea level.

CA Standards Check

1. Use the number line to find each sum.

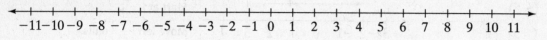

$$-11\ -10\ -9\ -8\ -7\ -6\ -5\ -4\ -3\ -2\ -1\ \ 0\ \ 1\ \ 2\ \ 3\ \ 4\ \ 5\ \ 6\ \ 7\ \ 8\ \ 9\ \ 10\ \ 11$$

a. $-6 + 4$

b. $4 + (-6)$

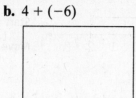

c. $-3 + (-8)$

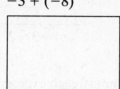

d. $9 + (-3)$

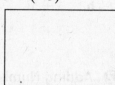

2. Find each sum.

a. $-7 + (-4)$

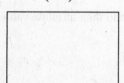

b. $-26.3 + 8.9$

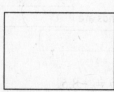

c. $-\frac{3}{4} + \left(-\frac{1}{2}\right)$

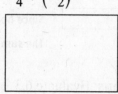

d. $\frac{8}{9} + \left(-\frac{5}{6}\right)$

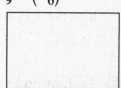

3. Evaluate each expression for $t = -7.1$.

a. $t + (-4.3)$

b. $-2 + t$

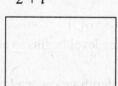

c. $8.5 + (-t)$

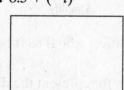

d. $-t + 7.49$

4. The temperature one winter morning is $-14°F$. Define a variable and write an expression to find the temperature after it changes. Then evaluate your expression for a decrease of 11 degrees Fahrenheit.

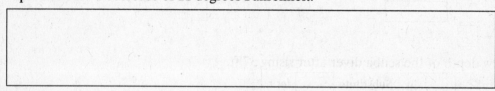

Name_____ Class_____ Date_____

Lesson 1-5   **Subtracting Real Numbers**

Lesson Objectives	California Content Standards
• Subtract real numbers • Apply subtraction	1.0, 2.0

Take Note

Subtracting Numbers

To subtract a number, add [   ].

Examples $3 - 5 = 3 +$ [   ] $= -2$ $3 - (-5) = 3 +$ [   ] $= 8$

Examples

① Absolute Values Simplify $|-13 - (-21)|$.

$|-13 - (-21)| = |-13 +$ [   ] $|$ **The opposite of −21 is** [   ].

$= |$ [   ] $|$ **Add within absolute value symbols.**

$=$ [   ]   **Find the absolute value.**

② Evaluating Expressions Evaluate $x - (-y)$ for $x = -3$ and $y = -6$.

$x - (-y) =$ [   ] $- [-($ [   ] $)]$ **Substitute** [   ] **for x and** [   ] **for y.**

$=$ [   ] $-$ [   ]   **The opposite of −6 is** [   ].

$=$ [   ]   **Subtract.**

③ Application The temperature in Montreal, Canada, at 6:00 P.M. was −8°C. Find the temperature at 10:00 P.M. if it fell 7°C.

Find the temperature at 10:00 P.M. by subtracting [   ] from the temperature at 6:00 P.M.

$-8 - 7 =$ [   ] $+ ($ [   ] $)$ **Add the opposite.**

$=$ [   ]   **Simplify.**

The temperature at 10:00 P.M. was [   ] °C.

Name_____ Class_____ Date_____

CA Standards Check

1. Simplify each expression.

a. $|8 - 7|$

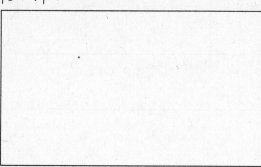

b. $|7 - 8|$

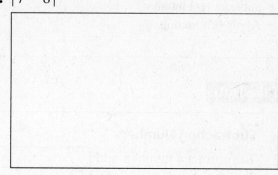

c. $|-10 - (-4)|$

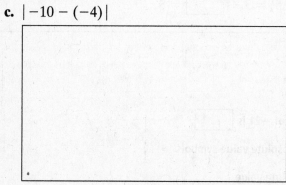

d. $|-4 - (-10)|$

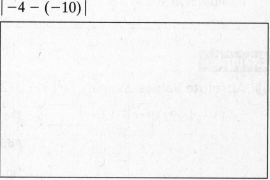

2. Evaluate each expression for $t = -2$ and $r = -7$.

a. $r - t$

b. $t - r$

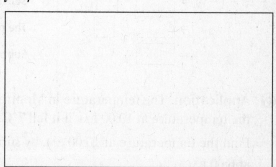

c. $-t - r$

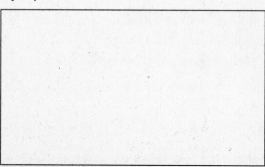

d. $-r - (-t)$

3. The closing price of stock PQR on Thursday was $14.23. It had
fallen $1.23 since the close on Wednesday. Find its closing price
on Wednesday.

Lesson 1-6

Lesson Objectives	California Content Standards
• Multiply real numbers • Divide real numbers	1.0, 1.1, 2.0

Take Note

Identity Property of Multiplication

For every real number n, [ ].

Examples $1 \cdot 5 =$ [ ] $1 \cdot (-5) =$ [ ]

Multiplication Property of Zero

For every real number n, [ ].

Examples $35 \cdot 0 =$ [ ] $-35 \cdot 0 =$ [ ]

Multiplication Property of −1

For every real number n, [ ].

Examples $-1 \cdot 5 =$ [ ] $-1 \cdot (-5) =$ [ ]

Multiplying Numbers With the Same Sign

The product of two positive numbers or two negative numbers is [ ].

Examples $5 \cdot 2 =$ [ ] $-5(-2) =$ [ ]

Multiplying Numbers With Different Signs

The product of a positive number and a negative number, or a negative

number and a positive number, is [ ].

Examples $3(-6) =$ [ ] $-3 \cdot 6 =$ [ ]

Dividing Numbers With the Same Sign

The quotient of two positive numbers or two negative numbers is [ ].

Examples $6 \div 3 =$ [ ] $-6 \div (-3) =$ [ ]

Dividing Numbers With Different Signs

The quotient of a positive number and a negative number, or a negative

number and a positive number, is [ ].

Examples $-6 \div 3 =$ [ ] $6 \div (-3) =$ [ ]

Inverse Property of Multiplication

For every nonzero real number a, there is a multiplicative inverse $\frac{1}{a}$ such

that [ ].

Examples $5\left(\frac{1}{5}\right) =$ [ ] $-5\left(-\frac{1}{5}\right) =$ [ ]

The multiplicative inverse of a nonzero real number a is _____

A reciprocal of a nonzero real number $\frac{a}{b}$ is _____

Examples

❶ Multiplying Numbers Simplify the expression $-6\left(\frac{3}{4}\right)$.

$-6\left(\frac{3}{4}\right) = -\dfrac{\boxed{}}{\boxed{}}$ The product of a positive number and a negative number is $\boxed{}$.

$= -\boxed{}$ Write $-\dfrac{\boxed{}}{\boxed{}}$ as a mixed number.

❷ Application Use the function $t = -5.5\left(\frac{a}{1000}\right)°$F to calculate the change in temperature t for an increase in altitude a of 7200 ft.

$t = -5.5\left(\dfrac{\boxed{}}{1000}\right)$ Substitute $\boxed{}$ for a.

$= -5.5\left(\boxed{}\right)$ Divide within parentheses.

$= \boxed{}°$F   Multiply.

❸ Simplifying Exponential Expressions Use the order of operations to simplify each expression.

a. $-0.2^4 = -\left(\boxed{} \cdot \boxed{} \cdot \boxed{} \cdot \boxed{}\right)$ Write as repeated multiplication.

$= -\boxed{}$ Simplify.

b. $(-0.2)^4 = \left(\boxed{}\right) \cdot \left(\boxed{}\right) \cdot \left(\boxed{}\right) \cdot \left(\boxed{}\right)$ Write as repeated multiplication.

$= \boxed{}$ Simplify.

CA Standards Check

1. Simplify each expression.

a. $4(-6)$

b. $-10(-5)$

c. $-4.9(-8)$

d. $-\frac{2}{3}\left(\frac{3}{4}\right)$

2. a. Use the function $t = -5.5\left(\frac{a}{1000}\right)°$F to find the change in temperature if a
balloon rises 4500 ft from the ground.

b. Suppose the temperature is 40°F at ground level. What is the approximate air
temperature at the altitude of the balloon?

Simplify each expression.

3. a. -4^3

b. $(-2)^4$

c. $(-0.3)^2$

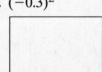

d. $-\left(\frac{3}{4}\right)^2$

Examples

❹ Dividing Numbers Simplify the expression $-54 \div (-9)$.

$-54 \div (-9) = \boxed{}$ The quotient of a negative number and a negative number is $\boxed{}$.

❺ Evaluating Expressions Evaluate $-\frac{x}{y} - 4z^2$ for $x = 4, y = -2$, and $z = -4$.

$-\dfrac{x}{y} - 4z^2 = -\left(\dfrac{\boxed{}}{\boxed{}}\right) - 4\left(\boxed{}\right)^2$ Substitute $\boxed{}$ for **x**, $\boxed{}$ for **y**, and $\boxed{}$ for **z**.

$= -\left(\dfrac{\boxed{}}{\boxed{}}\right) - 4\left(\boxed{}\right)$ Simplify the power.

$= \left(\boxed{}\right) - \boxed{}$ Divide and multiply.

$= \boxed{}$ Subtract.

❻ Division Using the Reciprocal Evaluate $\frac{p}{r}$ for $p = \frac{3}{2}$ and $r = -\frac{3}{4}$.

$\dfrac{p}{r} = \boxed{} \div \boxed{}$ Rewrite the equation.

$= \dfrac{\boxed{}}{\boxed{}} \div \left(\boxed{}\dfrac{\boxed{}}{\boxed{}}\right)$ Substitute $\dfrac{\boxed{}}{\boxed{}}$ for **p** and $\boxed{}\dfrac{\boxed{}}{\boxed{}}$ for **r**.

$= \dfrac{3}{2}\left(\boxed{}\dfrac{\boxed{}}{\boxed{}}\right)$ Multiply by $\boxed{}\dfrac{\boxed{}}{\boxed{}}$, the reciprocal of $-\dfrac{3}{4}$.

$= \boxed{}$ Simplify.

CA Standards Check

Simplify each expression.

4. a. $-42 \div 7$

b. $-8 \div (-2)$

c. $8 \div (-8)$

d. $-39 \div (-3)$

5. Evaluate each expression for $x = 8, y = -5$, and $z = -3$.

a. $3x \div (2z) + y \div 10$

b. $\dfrac{2z + x}{2y}$

6. Evaluate $\dfrac{x}{y}$ for $x = 8$ and $y = -\dfrac{4}{5}$.

Lesson 1-7

The Distributive Property

Lesson Objectives	California Content Standards
• Use the Distributive Property • Simplify algebraic expressions	1.0, 4.0, 10.0

Take Note

Distributive Property

For every real number $a, b,$ and $c,$

$a(b + c) = \boxed{}$ $(b + c)a = \boxed{}$

$a(b - c) = \boxed{}$ $(b - c)a = \boxed{}$

Examples

$5(20 + 6) = \boxed{} + \boxed{}$

$(20 + 6)5 = \boxed{} + \boxed{}$

$9(30 - 2) = \boxed{} - \boxed{}$

$(30 - 2)9 = \boxed{} - \boxed{}$

A term is _____

_____

A constant is _____

A coefficient is _____

_____

Like terms are _____

_____

Examples

❶ Simplifying a Numerical Expression Find the total cost of 4 CDs that cost $12.99 each.

$4(12.99) = 4\left(\boxed{}\right)$ **Rewrite 12.99 as 13 − $\boxed{}$.**

$= \boxed{}\left(\boxed{}\right) - \boxed{}\left(\boxed{}\right)$ **Use the Distributive Property.**

$= \boxed{} - \boxed{}$ **Multiply.**

$= \boxed{}$ **Simplify.**

The total cost of 4 CDs is $\boxed{}$.

❷ **Simplifying an Expression** Simplify $3(4m - 7)$.

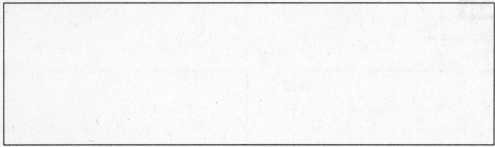

$3(4m - 7) = \boxed{}\left(\boxed{}\right) - \boxed{}\left(\boxed{}\right)$ **Use the Distributive Property.**

$= \boxed{}m - \boxed{}$ **Simplify.**

❸ **Using the Multiplication Property of −1** Simplify $-(5q - 6)$.

$-(5q - 6) = \boxed{}(5q - 6)$ **Rewrite the expression using −1.**

$= \boxed{}\left(\boxed{}\right) - \boxed{}\left(\boxed{}\right)$ **Use the Distributive Property.**

$= \boxed{}q + \boxed{}$ **Simplify.**

CA Standards Check

1. Find the total cost of 6 pairs of socks that cost $2.95 per pair.

2. Simplify each expression.

   a. $2(3 - 7t)$ **b.** $(0.4 + 1.1c)(3)$

3. Simplify each expression.

   a. $-(2x + 1)$ **b.** $(3 - 8a)(-1)$

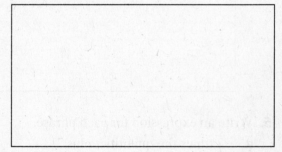

Examples

④ Combining Like Terms Simplify $-2w^2 + w^2$.

$-2w^2 + w^2 = \left(\boxed{} + \boxed{}\right)w^2$ **Use the Distributive Property.**

$= \boxed{}$ **Simplify.**

⑤ Writing an Expression Write an expression for the product of -6 and the quantity 7 minus m.

Relate $\boxed{-6}$ times $\boxed{\text{the quantity 7 minus } m}$

Write $\boxed{}$ · $\boxed{}$

$-6(7 - \boxed{})$

CA Standards Check

4. Simplify each expression.

   a. $7y + 6y$

   b. $3t - t$

   c. $-9w^3 - 3w^3$

   d. $8d + d$

5. Write an expression for each phrase.

   a. -2 times the quantity t plus 7

   b. the product of 14 and the quantity 8 plus w

Lesson 1-8

Properties of Numbers

Lesson Objectives	California Content Standards
• Identify properties • Use deductive reasoning	1.0, 24.1, 25.2

Take Note

Properties of Real Numbers
For every real number a, b, and c,

Commutative Property of Addition

Example $3 + 7 = \square + \square$

Commutative Property of Multiplication

Example $3 \cdot 7 = \square \cdot \square$

Associative Property of Addition

Example $(6 + 4) + 5 = \square + (\square + \square)$

Associative Property of Multiplication

Example $(6 \cdot 4) \cdot 5 = \square \cdot (\square \cdot \square)$

Identity Property of Addition

Example $9 + 0 = \square$

Identity Property of Multiplication

Example $6 \cdot 1 = \square$

Inverse Property of Addition
For every a, there is an additive inverse $\square$ such that $\boxed{}$.
Example $5 + (-5) = \square$

Inverse Property of Multiplication
For every a ($a \neq 0$), there is a multiplicative inverse $\frac{1}{a}$ such that $\boxed{}$.

Example $5 \cdot \square = 1$

Distributive Property
$a(b + c) = \boxed{}$ **Example** $5(4 + 2) = \boxed{} + \boxed{}$
$a(b - c) = \boxed{}$ **Example** $5(4 - 2) = \boxed{} - \boxed{}$

Multiplication Property of Zero
For every real number n, $\boxed{}$.

Example $-35 \cdot 0 = \square$

Multiplication Property of –1
For every real number n, $\boxed{}$.

Example $-1 \cdot (-5) = \square$

Deductive reasoning is _____

Name_____ Class_____ Date _____

Examples

❶ Identifying Properties Name the property each equation illustrates. Explain.

a. $3 \cdot a = a \cdot 3$

[   ], because

_____

b. $p \cdot 0 = 0$

[   ], because

_____

c. $6 + (-6) = 0$

[   ], because

_____

d. $z\left(\frac{1}{z}\right) = 1$ for $z \neq 0$

[   ], because

_____

❷ Application Suppose you buy a shirt for \$14.85, a pair of pants for \$21.95, and a pair of shoes for \$25.15. Find the total amount you spent.

$14.85 + 21.95 + 25.15 = 14.85 +$ [   ] $+$ [   ]   [   ] **Property of Addition**

$= ($ [   ] $+$ [   ] $) +$ [   ]   [   ] **Property of Addition**

$=$ [   ] $+$ [   ]   **Add within parentheses first.**

$=$ [   ]   **Simplify.**

The total amount you spent was \$[   ].

❸ Justifying Steps Simplify $3x - 4(x - 8)$. Justify each step.

$3x - 4(x - 8) = 3x -$ [   ] $+$ [   ]   [   ] **Property**

$= ($ [   ] $)x + 32$ [   ] **Property**

$=$ [   ] $x + 32$ **Subtract.**

$=$ [   ] $+ 32$ [   ] **of Multiplication**

CA Standards Check

1. Name the property that each equation illustrates. Explain.

   a. $1m = m$

   [ ]

   b. $(-3 + 4) + 5 = -3 + (4 + 5)$

   [ ]

   c. $(3 \cdot 8)0 = 3(8 \cdot 0)$

   [ ]

   d. $2 + 0 = 2$

   [ ]

   e. $np = pn$

   [ ]

   f. $p + q = q + p$

   [ ]

2. You buy a package of cheese for $2.50, a loaf of bread for $2.15, a cucumber for $.65, and some tomatoes for $3.50. Find the total cost of the groceries.

   [ ]

3. Simplify each expression. Justify each step.

   a. $5a + 6 + a$

   [ ]

   b. $2(3t - 1) + 2$

   [ ]

Name_____ Class_____ Date_____

Lesson 2-1   **Solving Two-Step Equations**

Lesson Objectives	California Content Standards
• Solve two-step equations • Use deductive reasoning	5.0, 25.0

Take Note

> **Solving Two-Step Equations**
>
> **Step 1** Use the Addition or Subtraction Property of Equality to get the term with a variable alone on one side of the equation.
>
> **Step 2** Use the Multiplication or Division Property of Equality to write an equivalent equation in which the variable has a coefficient of □.

Example

❶ Solving a Two-Step Equation Solve $21 = -p + 8$.

$21 - \boxed{} = -p + 8 - \boxed{}$ **Subtract** □ **from each side.**

$\boxed{} = -p$ **Simplify.**

$\boxed{}(13) = \boxed{}(-p)$ **Use the Multiplication Property of Equality. Multiply each side by** □.

$\boxed{} = p$ **Simplify.**

Check $21 = -p + 8$

$21 \stackrel{?}{=} -\left(\boxed{}\right) + 8$ **Substitute** $\boxed{}$ **for** *p*.

$21 = \boxed{}$ ✓

CA Standards Check

1. Solve each equation. Check your answer.

a. $7 = 2y - 3$ **b.** $\frac{x}{9} - 15 = 12$ **c.** $-x + 15 = 12$

Examples

❷ Application You order iris bulbs from a catalog. Iris bulbs cost $.90 each. The shipping charge is $3.00. If you have $14.00 to spend, how many iris bulbs can you order?

Relate | cost per iris | times | number of iris bulbs | plus | shipping | equals | amount to spend |

Define Let $\boxed{b}$ = the number of bulbs you can order.

Write $\boxed{}$ · $\boxed{}$ + $\boxed{}$ = $\boxed{}$

$$0.9b + \boxed{} = 14.00$$

$$0.9b + 3.00 - \boxed{} = 14.00 - \boxed{} \qquad \text{Subtract } \boxed{} \text{ from each side.}$$

$$0.9b = \boxed{} \qquad \text{Simplify.}$$

$$\frac{0.9b}{\boxed{}} = \frac{11}{\boxed{}} \qquad \text{Divide each side by } \boxed{}.$$

$$b = \boxed{} \qquad \text{Simplify.}$$

Check Is the solution reasonable? You can only order whole iris bulbs. Since 13 bulbs would cost 13 · $.90 = $17.00 plus $3.00 for shipping, which is more than $\boxed{}$, you can only order $\boxed{}$ bulbs.

❸ Using Deductive Reasoning Solve $3 - 5z = 18$. Justify each step.

$$3 - 5z \,\boxed{}\boxed{} = 18 \,\boxed{}\boxed{} \qquad \text{Subtraction Property of Equality}$$

$$-5z = \boxed{} \qquad \text{Simplify.}$$

$$\frac{-5z}{\boxed{}} = \frac{15}{\boxed{}} \qquad \boxed{} \text{Property of Equality}$$

$$z = \boxed{} \qquad \text{Simplify.}$$

CA Standards Check

2. Suppose tulip bulbs are on sale for $.60 per bulb. What number of bulbs can you order?

$\boxed{}$

3. Solve $-9 - 4m = 3$. Justify each step.

$$\boxed{}$$

Lesson 2-2

Solving Multi-Step Equations

Lesson Objectives	California Content Standards
• Use the Distributive Property when combining like terms • Use the Distributive Property when solving equations	2.0, 4.0, 5.0

Take Note

Steps for Solving a Multi-Step Equation

Step 1 Clear the equation of fractions and decimals.

Step 2 Use the Distributive Property to remove parentheses on each side.

Step 3 Combine like terms on each side.

Step 4 Undo addition or [　　　　　　　　].

Step 5 Undo multiplication or [　　　　　　　　].

Example

❶ **Combining Like Terms** Solve $3a + 6 + a = 90$.

$$4a + 6 = 90 \qquad \textbf{Combine like terms.}$$

$$4a + 6 - \boxed{} = 90 - \boxed{} \qquad \textbf{Subtract } \boxed{} \textbf{ from each side.}$$

$$4a = \boxed{} \qquad \textbf{Simplify.}$$

$$\frac{4a}{\boxed{}} = \frac{\boxed{}}{\boxed{}} \qquad \textbf{Divide each side by } \boxed{}.$$

$$a = \boxed{} \qquad \textbf{Simplify.}$$

CA Standards Check

1. Solve $7 = 4m - 2m + 1$. Check your answer. [　　]

Examples

❷ Application You need to build a rectangular pen in your backyard for your dog. One side of the pen will be against the house. Two sides of the pen have a length of x ft and the width will be 25 ft. What is the greatest length the pen can be if you have 63 ft of fencing?

Relate | length of side | plus | 25 ft | plus | length of side | equals | amount of fencing |

Define Let | x | = length of a side adjacent to the house.

Write ☐ + ☐ + ☐ = ☐

$x + 25 + x =$ ☐

☐$x + 25 =$ ☐   **Combine like terms.**

☐ $+ 25 -$ ☐ $=$ ☐ $-$ ☐   **Subtract** ☐ **from each side.**

$2x =$ ☐   **Simplify.**

$$\frac{2x}{\square} = \frac{\square}{\square}$$ **Divide each side by** ☐ .

$x =$ ☐

The pen can be ☐ feet long.

❸ Solving an Equation With Grouping Symbols Solve $2(x - 3) = 8$.

☐ $-$ ☐ $= 8$ **Use the** ☐ **Property.**

☐ $-$ ☐ $+$ ☐ $= 8 +$ ☐   **Add** ☐ **to each side.**

$2x =$ ☐   **Simplify.**

$$\frac{2x}{\square} = \frac{\square}{\square}$$ **Divide each side by** ☐ .

$x =$ ☐   **Simplify.**

Check $2(x - 3) = 8$

$2(☐ - 3) \stackrel{?}{=} 8$ **Substitute** ☐ **for x.**

$2(☐) \stackrel{?}{=} 8$

☐ $= 8$ ✓

④ Solving an Equation That Contains Fractions Solve $\frac{3x}{2} + \frac{x}{5} = 17$.

$$\frac{3x}{2} + \frac{x}{5} = 17$$

$\boxed{}\left(\frac{3x}{2} + \frac{x}{5}\right) = \boxed{}(17)$ **Multiply each side by** $\boxed{}$**, a common multiple of 2 and 5.**

$\boxed{}\left(\frac{3x}{2}\right) + \boxed{}\left(\frac{x}{5}\right) = 10(17)$ **Use the Distributive Property.**

$\boxed{}x + \boxed{}x = \boxed{}$ **Multiply.**

$17x = 170$ **Combine like terms.**

$\dfrac{17x}{\boxed{}} = \dfrac{170}{\boxed{}}$ **Divide each side by** $\boxed{}$**.**

$x = \boxed{}$ **Simplify.**

CA Standards Check

2. A carpenter is building a rectangular fence for a playground. One side of the playground is the wall of a building 70 ft wide. He plans to use 340 ft of fencing material. What is the length of the playground if the width is 70 ft?

Solve each equation.

3. a. $3(k + 8) = 21$

b. $15 = -3(x - 1) + 9$

4. a. $\frac{m}{4} + \frac{m}{2} = \frac{5}{8}$

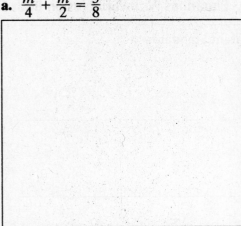

b. $\frac{2}{3}x - \frac{5}{8}x = 26$

Name_____ Class_____ Date _____

Lesson 2-3

Equations With Variables on Both Sides

Lesson Objectives	California Content Standards
• Solve equations with variables on both sides • Identify equations that are identities or have no solution	4.0, 5.0, 25.3

Vocabulary

An identity is _____

Example

1 Application You can buy a skateboard for $60 from a friend and rent the safety equipment for $1.50 per hour. Or you can rent all items you need for $5.50 per hour. How many hours must you use the skateboard to justify buying your friend's skateboard?

Relate | cost of friend's skateboard | plus | equipment rental | equals | skateboard and equipment rental |

Define Let $\boxed{h}$ = the number of hours you must skateboard.

Write $\boxed{}$ $+$ $\boxed{}$ $=$ $\boxed{}$

$$60 + \boxed{}h = \boxed{}h$$

$$60 + 1.5h - \boxed{}h = 5.5h - \boxed{}h \qquad \textbf{Subtract } \boxed{}h \textbf{ from each side.}$$

$$60 = \boxed{}h \qquad \textbf{Combine like terms.}$$

$$\frac{60}{\boxed{}} = \frac{4h}{\boxed{}} \qquad \textbf{Divide each side by } \boxed{}.$$

$$\boxed{} = h \qquad \textbf{Simplify.}$$

CA Standards Check

1. A hairdresser is considering ordering a certain shampoo. Company A charges $4 per 8-oz bottle plus a $10 handling fee per order. Company B charges $3 per 8-oz bottle plus a $25 handling fee per order. How many bottles must the hairdresser buy to justify using Company B?

Daily Notetaking Guide

Example

❷ Identities and Equations With No Solutions Solve each equation.

a. $-6z + 8 = z + 10 - 7z$

$-6z + 8 = -\boxed{}z + 10$ **Combine like terms.**

$-6z + 8 + \boxed{} = -6z + 10 + \boxed{}$ **Add** $\boxed{}$ **to each side.**

$\boxed{} = \boxed{}$ $\boxed{}$ **true for any value of z!**

The equation has $\boxed{}$ solution.

b. $4 - 4y = -2(2y - 2)$

$4 - 4y = -\boxed{}y + \boxed{}$ **Use the Distributive Property.**

$4 - 4y + \boxed{} = -4y + 4 + \boxed{}$ **Add** $\boxed{}$ **to each side.**

$\boxed{} = \boxed{}$ $\boxed{}$ **true!**

The equation is true for every value of y, so the equation is an _____

CA Standards Check

2. Determine whether $9 + 5n = 5n - 1$ is an *identity* or whether it has *no solution.* $\boxed{}$

3. Solve each equation.

a. $-6d = d + 4$

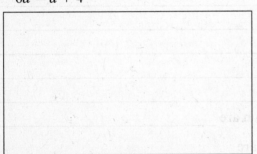

b. $7k - 4 = 5k + 16$

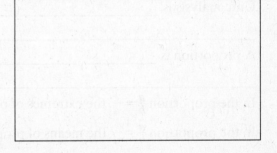

c. $m - 5 = 3m$

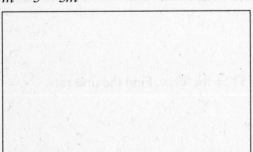

d. $7k - 4 = 5k + 16$

Lesson 2-4

Ratio and Proportion

Lesson Objectives	California Content Standards
• Find ratios and rates • Solve proportions	5.0, 15.0, 25.0

Vocabulary and Take Note

Cross Products of a Proportion

If $\frac{a}{b} = \frac{c}{d}$ then $ad =$ ☐.

Example $\frac{2}{3} = \frac{8}{12}$, so $2 \cdot 12 = 3 \cdot 8$

A ratio is _____

_____

A rate is _____

_____

A unit rate is _____

_____

Unit analysis is _____

_____

A proportion is _____

_____

In the proportion $\frac{a}{b} = \frac{c}{d}$, the extremes of proportion are _____

In the proportion $\frac{a}{b} = \frac{c}{d}$, the means of proportion are _____

In the proportion $\frac{a}{b} = \frac{c}{d}$, the cross products are _____

Examples

① Using Unit Rates A brand of grapefruit juice costs $1.56 for 48 oz. Find the unit rate.

cost → ☐
──────────── = $ ☐ /oz
ounces → ☐ oz

The unit rate is ☐ per oz.

Name_____ Class_____ Date _____

❷ Application In 2000, Lance Armstrong completed the 3630-km Tour de France course in 92.5 hours. Traveling at his average speed, how long would it take Lance Armstrong to ride 295 km?

Define Let $\boxed{t}$ = time needed to ride 295 km.

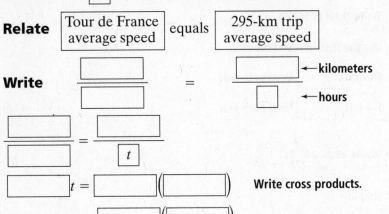

Relate $\boxed{\text{Tour de France average speed}}$ equals $\boxed{\text{295-km trip average speed}}$

Write

$\dfrac{\boxed{}}{\boxed{}}$ = $\dfrac{\boxed{}}{\boxed{}}$ ← kilometers
← hours

$\dfrac{\boxed{}}{\boxed{}}$ = $\dfrac{\boxed{}}{t}$

$\boxed{}t = \boxed{}\left(\boxed{}\right)$ Write cross products.

$t = \dfrac{\boxed{}\left(\boxed{}\right)}{\boxed{}}$ Divide each side by $\boxed{}$.

$t \approx \boxed{}$ Simplify. Round to the nearest tenth.

Traveling at his average speed, it would take Lance approximately $\boxed{}$ hours to cycle 295 km.

❸ Converting Rates The fastest recorded speed for an eastern gray kangaroo is 40 mi per hour. What is the kangaroo's speed in feet per second?

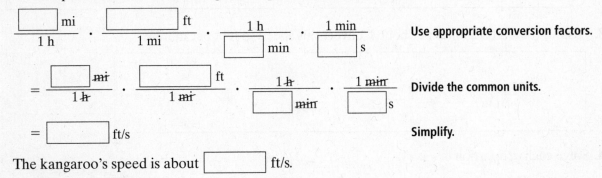

$\dfrac{\boxed{} \text{ mi}}{1\text{ h}} \cdot \dfrac{\boxed{} \text{ ft}}{1\text{ mi}} \cdot \dfrac{1\text{ h}}{\boxed{}\text{ min}} \cdot \dfrac{1\text{ min}}{\boxed{}\text{ s}}$ Use appropriate conversion factors.

$= \dfrac{\boxed{} \text{ mi}}{1\text{ h}} \cdot \dfrac{\boxed{} \text{ ft}}{1\text{ mi}} \cdot \dfrac{1\text{ h}}{\boxed{}\text{ min}} \cdot \dfrac{1\text{ min}}{\boxed{}\text{ s}}$ Divide the common units.

$= \boxed{}$ ft/s   Simplify.

The kangaroo's speed is about $\boxed{}$ ft/s.

CA Standards Check

1. Main Street Florist sells two dozen roses for $24.60. Fresh Flowers sells six roses for $7.50. Find the unit rate for each. Which florist has the lower cost per rose?

Name_____ Class_____ Date _____

Example

❹ **Solving Multi-Step Proportions** Solve the proportion.

$$\frac{z + 3}{4} = \frac{z - 4}{6}$$

$(z + 3)(\boxed{}) = 4(\boxed{})$ **Write cross products.**

$6z + \boxed{} = \boxed{} - 16$ **Use the Distributive Property.**

$\boxed{} + 18 = -16$ **Subtract** $\boxed{}$ **from each side.**

$2z = -\boxed{}$ **Subtract** $\boxed{}$ **from each side.**

$\dfrac{2z}{\boxed{}} = -\dfrac{\boxed{}}{\boxed{}}$ **Divide each side by** $\boxed{}$.

$z = \boxed{}$ **Simplify.**

CA Standards Check

2. Suppose you walk 2 miles in 35 minutes.

   a. Find the average walking speed. Write an equation that relates the distance d you walk to the time t you walk.

   b. Use the equation to find how far you would walk in an hour.

   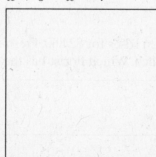

3. A sloth travels 0.15 miles per hour. Convert this speed to feet per minute.

4. Solve each proportion.

   a. $\dfrac{x + 2}{14} = \dfrac{x}{10}$

   b. $\dfrac{3}{w + 6} = \dfrac{5}{w - 4}$

   c. $\dfrac{y - 15}{y + 4} = \dfrac{35}{7}$

Daily Notetaking Guide

Lesson 2-5
Equations and Problem Solving

Lesson Objectives	California Content Standards
• Define a variable in terms of another variable • Model distance-rate-time problems	4.0, 5.0, 15.0

Vocabulary

Consecutive integers are _____

_____

An object in uniform motion is _____

_____

Examples

❶ Consecutive Integer Problem The sum of three consecutive integers is 72. Find the integers.

Define   Let $\boxed{x}$ = the first integer.

         Then $\boxed{x + 1}$ = the second integer,

         and $\boxed{}$ = the third integer.

Relate $\boxed{\text{first integer}}$ plus $\boxed{\text{second integer}}$ plus $\boxed{\text{third integer}}$ is $\boxed{72}$

Write $\boxed{}$ + $\boxed{}$ + $\boxed{}$ = $\boxed{}$

$x + \boxed{} + \boxed{} = 72$

$\boxed{}x + \boxed{} = 72$ **Combine like terms.**

$3x + 3 - \boxed{} = 72 - \boxed{}$ **Subtract** $\boxed{}$ **from each side.**

$3x = \boxed{}$ **Simplify.**

$\dfrac{3x}{\boxed{}} = \dfrac{\boxed{}}{\boxed{}}$ **Divide each side by** $\boxed{}$ **.**

$x = \boxed{}$ **Simplify.**

If $x = 23$, then $x + 1 = \boxed{}$, and $x + 2 = \boxed{}$. The three integers are $\boxed{}$, $\boxed{}$, and $\boxed{}$.

Name_____ Class_____ Date _____

❷ Same-Direction Travel An airplane left an airport flying at 180 mi/h. A jet that flies at 330 mi/h left 1 hour later. The jet follows the same route as the airplane on parallel altitudes. How many hours will it take the jet to catch up with the airplane?

Define Let $\boxed{t}$ = the time the airplane travels.

Then $\boxed{t-1}$ = the time the jet travels.

Relate

Aircraft	Rate	Time	Distance Traveled
Airplane		t	$180t$
Jet	330		$330(t-1)$

Write

$180t = 330\left(\boxed{}\right)$ The distances traveled are equal.

$180t = \boxed{}\,t - \boxed{}$ Use the Distributive Property.

$180t - \boxed{} = 330t - 330 - \boxed{}$ Subtract $\boxed{}$ from each side.

$\boxed{}\,t = -330$ Combine like terms.

$\dfrac{-150t}{\boxed{}} = \dfrac{-330}{\boxed{}}$ Divide each side by $\boxed{}$.

$t = \dfrac{\boxed{}}{\boxed{}}$ Simplify.

$t - 1 = \dfrac{\boxed{}}{\boxed{}}$

The jet will catch up with the airplane in $\boxed{}$ hours.

CA Standards Check

1. The sum of three consecutive integers is 48.

a. Define a variable for one of the integers.

Daily Notetaking Guide

b. Write expressions for the other two integers.

c. Write and solve an equation to find the three integers.

2. A group of campers and one group leader left a campsite in a canoe. They traveled at an average rate of 10 km/h. Two hours later, the other group leader left the campsite in a motorboat. He traveled at an average rate of 22 km/h.

a. How long after the canoe left the campsite did the motorboat catch up with it?

b. How long did the motorboat travel?

Example

❸ Opposite-Direction Travel Two jets leave Dallas at the same time and fly in opposite directions. One is flying west 50 mi/h faster than the other. After 2 hours, they are 2500 miles apart. Find the speed of each jet.

Define Let $\boxed{x}$ = the speed of the jet flying east.

Then $\boxed{}$ = the speed of the jet flying west.

Relate

Jet	Rate	Time	Distance Traveled
Eastbound	x		$2x$
Westbound		2	$2(x + 50)$

Write

$2x + 2\left(\boxed{}\right) = 2500$

$2x + 2x + \boxed{} = 2500$ **Use the Distributive Property.**

$\boxed{} + 100 = 2500$ **Combine like terms.**

$4x + 100 - \boxed{} = 2500 - \boxed{}$ **Subtract** $\boxed{}$ **from each side.**

$4x = 2400$ **Simplify.**

$\dfrac{4x}{\boxed{}} = \dfrac{2400}{\boxed{}}$ **Divide each side by** $\boxed{}$.

$x = \boxed{}$

$x + 50 = \boxed{}$

The jet flying east is flying at $\boxed{}$ mi/h. The jet flying west is flying at $\boxed{}$ mi/h.

CA Standards Check

3. Sarah and John leave Perryville traveling in opposite directions on a straight road. Sarah drives 12 miles per hour faster than John. After 2 hours, they are 176 miles apart. Find Sarah's speed and John's speed.

Lesson 2-6

Mixture Problems

Lesson Objectives	California Content Standards
• Solve mixture problems	4.0, 15.0, 25.0

Take Note

Solving Mixture Problems Mixture problems involve combining two or more quantities.

Step 1 Define a variable and decide which unknown quantity the variable will represent.

Step 2 Express the other unknown quantity or quantities in terms of that variable.

Step 3 Organize the given and unknown quantities in a [ ].

Step 4 Write an equation that represents the situation and solve for the [ ].

Example

① Solving Mixture Problems Raisins cost $2 per pound and nuts cost $5 per pound. How many pounds of each should you use to make a 42-lb mixture that costs $3 per pound?

Define Let r = the number of pounds of raisins.

Then $42 -$ [ ] = the number of pounds of nuts.

Relate

	Amount (lb)	Cost Per Pound	Cost (dollars)
Raisins			$2r$
Nuts			
Mixture	42	$3	

Write $2r + 5(42 - r) = 3(42)$

$2r + 210 - 5r = 126$ Use the [ ] Property.

[ ] $+ 210 = 126$ Combine like terms.

[ ] $+ 210 - 210 = 126 - 210$ Subtract [ ] from each side.

$-3r =$ [ ]   Simplify.

$\dfrac{-3r}{\boxed{}} = \dfrac{-84}{\boxed{}}$ Divide each side by [ ].

$r =$ [ ]   Simplify.

You should use 28 lb of raisins and [ ] of nuts.

CA Standards Check

1. How many of each do you need to make a 50-lb mixture that costs $3.50/lb?

[blank box]

Example

❷ **Solving Percent Mixture Problems** A chemist has one solution that is 40% acid and another solution that is 80% acid. How many liters of each solution does the chemist need to make 400 liters of a solution that is 48% acid?

Define Let a = the number of liters of 40% acid solution.

Then $400 - a$ = the number of liters of 80% acid solution

Relate

	Amount of Solution (L)	Percent Acid	Amount of Acid (L)
40% Solution	a		$0.4a$
80% Solution		80%	
48% Solution			$0.48(400)$

Write $0.4a +$ [ ] $= 0.48(400)$ **The amount of acid in the 40% and 80% solutions equals the amount of acid in the mixture.**

$0.4a + 320 - 0.8a =$ [ ]   **Use the** [ ] **Property.**

[ ] $+ 320 = 192$ **Combine like terms.**

$-0.4a + 320 - 320 = 192 - 320$ **Subtract** [ ] **from each side.**

$-0.4a =$ [ ]   **Simplify.**

$\dfrac{-0.4a}{\boxed{}} = \dfrac{-128}{\boxed{}}$ **Divide each side by** [ ] **.**

$a =$ [ ]   **Simplify.**

The chemist needs 320 L of 40% solution and [ ] of 80% solution.

Check 40% of 320 L is [ ] and 80% of 80 L is [ ]. The total amount of acid in the mixture is [ ], or 192 L. This is equal to 48% of 400 L.

CA Standards Check

2. A chemist has a 10% acid solution and a 60% acid solution. How many liters of each solution does the chemist need to make 200 L of a solution that is 50% acid?

[blank box]

Daily Notetaking Guide

Lesson 3-1

Inequalities and Their Graphs

Lesson Objectives	California Content Standards
• Identify solutions of inequalities • Graph and write inequalities	5.0

Vocabulary

A solution of an inequality is _____

_____

Examples

❶ Identifying Solutions by Evaluating Is each number a solution of $3 + 2x < 8$?

a. -2

$3 + 2x < 8$

$3 + 2\left(\boxed{}\right) < 8$ ← **Substitute for x.** →

$3 - \boxed{} < 8$ ← **Simplify.** →

$\boxed{} < 8$ ← **Compare.** →

-2 is a solution.

b. 3

$3 + 2x < 8$

$3 + 2\left(\boxed{}\right) < 8$

$3 + \boxed{} < 8$

$\boxed{} < 8$

3 is not a solution.

❷ Graphing Inequalities

a. Graph $d < 3$.

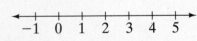

The solutions of $d < 3$ are all the points to the $\boxed{}$ of 3.

b. Graph $-3 \geq g$.

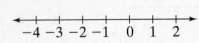

The solutions of $-3 \geq g$ are $\boxed{}$ and all the points to the $\boxed{}$ of -3.

❸ Writing an Inequality From a Graph Write an inequality for each graph.

a. 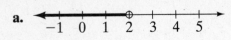 $x < \boxed{}$ Numbers $\boxed{}$ 2 are graphed.

b. 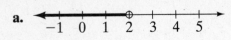 $x \leq \boxed{}$ Numbers $\boxed{}$ -3 are graphed.

CA Standards Check

1. Is each number a solution of $6x - 3 > 10$?

a. 1

b. 2

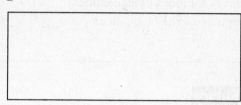

c. 3

d. 4

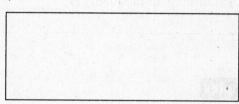

2. Graph each inequality.

a. $a < 1$

b. $n \geq -3$

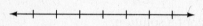

c. $2 > p$

3. Write an inequality for each graph.

a.

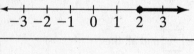

b.

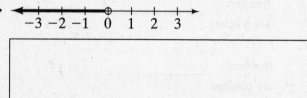

Lesson 3-2

Lesson Objectives	California Content Standards
• Use addition to solve inequalities • Use subtraction to solve inequalities	5.0

Take Note

Addition Property of Inequality

For every real number a, b, and c,

if $a > b$, then [_____];   if $a < b$, then [_____].

Examples

$3 > 1$, so $3 + 2$ [ ] $1 + 2$. $-5 < 4$, so $-5 + 2$ [ ] $4 + 2$.

This property is also true for $\geq$ and $\leq$.

Subtraction Property of Inequality

For every real number a, b, and c,

if $a > b$, then [_____];   if $a < b$, then [_____].

Examples

$3 > -1$, so $3 - 2$ [ ] $-1 - 2$. $-5 < 4$, so $-5 - 2$ [ ] $4 - 2$.

This property is also true for $\geq$ and $\leq$.

Equivalent inequalities are _____

_____

Examples

❶ Using the Addition Property of Inequality Solve $8 \geq d - 2$. Graph the solution.

$8 + \boxed{} \geq d - 2 + \boxed{}$ **Add** $\boxed{}$ **to each side.**

$\boxed{} \geq d$, or $d \leq 10$ **Simplify.**

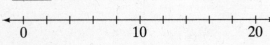

❷ Application To receive a B in your literature class, you must earn more than 350 points of reading credits. Last week you earned 120 points. This week you earned 90 points. Write an inequallity to describe how many more points you must earn to receive a B.

Relate | points earned | plus | points needed | is more than | points required | .

Define Let $\boxed{p}$ = the number of points needed.

Write $\boxed{}$ + $\boxed{}$ $\boxed{}$ $\boxed{}$

You must earn 141 more points.

CA Standards Check

1. a. Solve $m - 6 > -4$. Graph your solution.

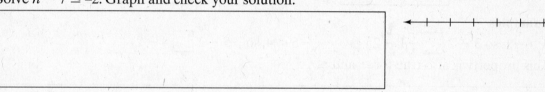

b. Solve $n - 7 \leq -2$. Graph and check your solution.

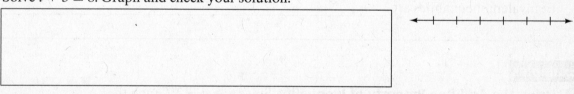

2. a. Solve $t + 3 \geq 8$. Graph and check your solution.

b. Your baseball team has a goal to collect at least 160 blankets for a shelter. Team members brought 42 blankets on Monday and 65 blankets on Wednesday. Write an inequality to describe how many blankets the team must donate on Friday to meet or exceed their goal.

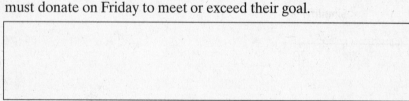

Name_____ Class_____ Date_____

Lesson 3-3

Lesson Objectives	California Content Standards
• Use multiplication to solve inequalities • Use division to solve inequalities	5.0

Take Note

Multiplication Property of Inequality

For every real number a and b, and for $c > 0$,

if $a > b$, then ac ☐ bc;   if $a < b$, then ac ☐ bc.

Examples

$4 > -1$, so $4(5)$ ☐ $-1(5)$. $-6 < 3$, so $-6(5)$ ☐ $3(5)$.

For every real number a and b, and for $c < 0$,

if $a > b$, then ac ☐ bc;   if $a < b$, then ac ☐ bc.

Examples

$4 > -1$, so $4(-2)$ ☐ $-1(-2)$. $-6 < 3$, so $-6(-2)$ ☐ $3(-2)$.

This property is also true for $\geq$ and $\leq$.

Division Property of Inequality

For every real number a and b, and for $c > 0$,

if $a > b$, then $\frac{a}{c}$ ☐ $\frac{b}{c}$;   if $a < b$, then $\frac{a}{c}$ ☐ $\frac{b}{c}$.

Examples

$6 > 4$, so $\frac{6}{2}$ ☐ $\frac{4}{2}$. $2 < 8$, so $\frac{2}{2}$ ☐ $\frac{8}{2}$.

For every real number a and b, and for $c < 0$,

if $a > b$, then $\frac{a}{c}$ ☐ $\frac{b}{c}$;   if $a < b$, then $\frac{a}{c}$ ☐ $\frac{b}{c}$.

Examples

$6 > 4$, so $\frac{6}{-2}$ ☐ $\frac{4}{-2}$. $2 < 8$, so $\frac{2}{-2}$ ☐ $\frac{8}{-2}$.

This property is also true for $\geq$ and $\leq$.

Examples

❶ Multiplying to Solve an Inequality Solve $3 \leq -\frac{3}{5}x$. Graph and check the solution.

$$\left(\boxed{}\,\frac{\boxed{}}{\boxed{}}\right)(3) \geq \left(\boxed{}\,\frac{\boxed{}}{\boxed{}}\right)\left(-\frac{3}{5}x\right)$$

Multiply each side by the reciprocal of $-\frac{3}{5}$, which is $\boxed{}$, and reverse the inequality symbol.

$-5 \geq x,$ or $x \leq -5$ **Simplify.**

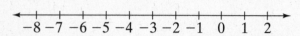

Check $3 = -\frac{3}{5}x$ **Check the computation.**

$3 = -\frac{3}{5}\left(\boxed{}\right)$ **Substitute** $\boxed{}$ **for x.**

$3 = \boxed{}$ ✓

$3 \leq -\frac{3}{5}x$ **Check the direction of the inequality.**

$3 \leq -\frac{3}{5}\left(\boxed{}\right)$ **Substitute** -10 **for x.**

$3 \leq 6 \,\boxed{}$

❷ Dividing to Solve an Inequality Solve $-4c < 24$. Graph the solution.

$$\frac{-4c}{\boxed{}} > \frac{24}{\boxed{}}$$ **Divide each side by** $\boxed{}$. **Reverse the inequality symbol.**

$c > -6$ **Simplify.**

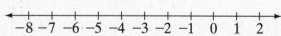

❸ Application Your family budgets $160 to spend on fuel for a trip. How many times can they fill the car's gas tank if it costs $25 each time?

Relate | cost per tank | times | number of tanks | is at most | total fuel budget | .

Define   Let $\boxed{t}$ = the number of tanks of gas.

Write $\boxed{}$ · $\boxed{}$ $\boxed{}$ $\boxed{}$

$25t \leq 160$

$$\frac{25t}{\boxed{}} \leq \frac{160}{\boxed{}}$$ **Divide each side by** $\boxed{}$.

$t \leq \boxed{}$ **Simplify.**

Your family can fill the car's gas tank at most 6 times.

CA Standards Check

Solve each inequality. Graph and check your solutions.

1. a. $\frac{b}{4} > \frac{1}{2}$

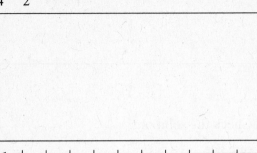

b. $\frac{4}{3}y \le -8$

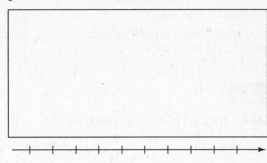

c. $-\frac{k}{4} > -1$

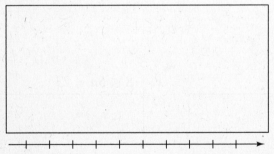

d. $-t < \frac{1}{2}$

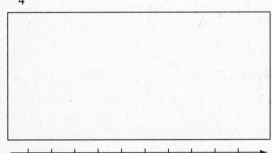

2. a. $-3w \ge 12$

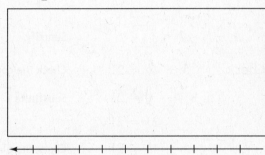

b. $0.6 > -0.2n$

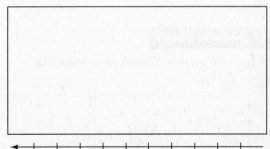

3. Students in the school band are selling calendars. They earn $.40 on each calendar they sell. Their goal is to earn more than $327. Write and solve an inequality to find the fewest calendars they can sell and still reach their goal.

Lesson 3-4

Solving Multi-Step Inequalities

Lesson Objectives	California Content Standards
• Solve multi-step inequalities with variables on one side • Solve multi-step inequalities with variables on both sides	4.0, 5.0

Example

❶ Using More Than One Step Solve $5 + 4b < 21$. Check the solutions.

$5 + 4b - \boxed{} < 21 - \boxed{}$ **Subtract** $\boxed{}$ **from each side.**

$4b < \boxed{}$ **Simplify.**

$\dfrac{4b}{\boxed{}} < \dfrac{16}{\boxed{}}$ **Divide each side by** $\boxed{}$.

$b < \boxed{}$ **Simplify.**

Check $5 + 4b = 21$ **Check the computation.**

$5 + 4\left(\boxed{}\right) \stackrel{?}{=} 21$ **Substitute** $\boxed{}$ **for** *b*.

$21 = 21$ ✓

$5 + 4b < 21$ **Check the direction of the inequality.**

$5 + 4\left(\boxed{}\right) < 21$ **Substitute 3 for** *b*.

$17 < 21$ $\boxed{}$

CA Standards Check

Solve each inequality. Check your solution.

1. a. $-3x - 4 \le 14$ **b.** $5 < 7 - 2t$ **c.** $-8 < 5n - 23$

Examples

❷ Using the Distributive Property Solve $3x + 4(6 - x) < 2$.

$3x + \boxed{} - \boxed{} < 2$ **Use the Distributive Property.**

$\boxed{} + 24 < 2$ **Combine like terms.**

$-x + 24 - \boxed{} < 2 - \boxed{}$ **Subtract** $\boxed{}$ **from each side.**

$-x < \boxed{}$ **Simplify.**

$\dfrac{-x}{\boxed{}} > \dfrac{-22}{\boxed{}}$ **Divide each side by** $\boxed{}$ **. Reverse the inequality symbol.**

$x \boxed{} \boxed{}$ **Simplify.**

❸ Gathering Variables on One Side of an Inequality Solve $5(-3 + d) \le 3(3d - 2)$.

$\boxed{} + \boxed{}d \le \boxed{}d - \boxed{}$ **Use the Distributive Property.**

$-15 + 5d - \boxed{} \le 9d - 6 - \boxed{}$ **Subtract** $\boxed{}$ **from each side.**

$-15 - \boxed{} \le -6$ **Combine like terms.**

$-15 - 4d + \boxed{} \le -6 + \boxed{}$ **Add** $\boxed{}$ **to each side.**

$-4d \le \boxed{}$ **Simplify.**

$\dfrac{-4d}{\boxed{}} \ge \dfrac{9}{\boxed{}}$ **Divide each side by** $\boxed{}$ **. Reverse the inequality symbol.**

$d \boxed{} \boxed{}$ **Simplify.**

CA Standards Check

2. a. $4p + 2(p + 7) < 8$

b. $15 \le 5 - 2(4m + 7)$

3. Solve each inequality. Check your solution.

a. $3b + 12 > 27 - 2b$

b. $-6(x - 4) \ge 7(2x - 3)$

Lesson 3-5   Compound Inequalities

Lesson Objectives	California Content Standards
• Solve and graph inequalities containing *and* • Solve and graph inequalities containing *or*	3.0

Vocabulary

A compound inequality is _____

Examples

① **Writing a Compound Inequality** Write a compound inequality that represents each situation. Graph the solution.

a. all real numbers that are at least −1 and at most 3

$b \geq -1$ and $b \leq$ ☐   ⟵─┼─┼─┼─┼─┼─┼─┼─┼─┼─┼─⟶
                                          −5 −4 −3 −2 −1 0 1 2 3 4 5
$-1 \leq b \leq 3$

b. all real numbers that are less than 31 but greater than 25

31 ☐ n and n ☐ 25   ⟵─┼─┼─┼─┼─┼─┼─┼─┼─┼─┼─⟶
                                          23   25   27   29   31   33
31 ☐ n ☐ 25

② **Solving a Compound Inequality Containing And** Solve $5 > 5 - f > 2$. Graph your solution.

Write the compound inequality as two inequalities joined by 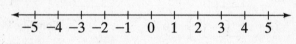 .

$$5 > 5 - f \qquad \boxed{} \qquad 5 - f > 2$$
$$5 - 5 > 5 - f - 5 \qquad\qquad 5 - f - 5 > 2 - 5$$
$$\boxed{} > -f \qquad\qquad\qquad -f > \boxed{}$$
$$\frac{0}{-1} \boxed{} \frac{-f}{-1} \qquad\qquad\qquad \frac{-f}{-1} \boxed{} \frac{-3}{-1}$$
$$0 < \boxed{} \qquad\qquad\qquad f < \boxed{}$$

$$\boxed{} < f < \boxed{}$$

⟵─┼─┼─┼─┼─┼─┼─┼─┼─┼─┼─⟶
−5 −4 −3 −2 0 1 2 3 4 5

③ **Writing Compound Inequalities** Write an inequality that represents the situation. Graph the solution.

all real numbers that are less than 0 or greater than 3

$n <$ ☐ or $n >$ ☐   ⟵─┼─┼─┼─┼─┼─┼─┼─┼─┼─┼─⟶
                                          −5 −4 −3 −2 0 1 2 3 4 5

❹ **Solving a Compound Inequality Containing *Or*** Solve the compound inequality $3x + 2 < -7$ or $-4x + 5 < 1$. Graph your solution.

$$3x + 2 < -7 \qquad \text{or} \qquad -4x + 5 < 1$$

$$x < \boxed{} \qquad \text{or} \qquad x > \boxed{}$$

$$\begin{array}{ccccccccccc} \longleftarrow & \! & \! & \! & \! & \! & \! & \! & \! & \! & \longrightarrow \\ -5 & -4 & -3 & -2 & 0 & 1 & 2 & 3 & 4 & 5 \end{array}$$

CA Standards Check

1. Write a compound inequality that represents each situation. Graph the solution.

   a. all real numbers greater than −2 but less than 9

   b. The books were priced between $3.50 and $6.00, inclusive.

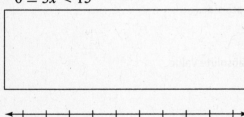

$$\longleftarrow \!+\!+\!+\!+\!+\!+\!+\!+\!+\!+\! \longrightarrow$$

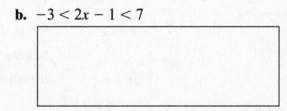

$$\longleftarrow \!+\!+\!+\!+\!+\!+\!+\!+\!+\!+\! \longrightarrow$$

2. Solve each inequality. Graph your solution.

   a. $-6 \le 3x < 15$

   b. $-3 < 2x - 1 < 7$

$$\longleftarrow \!+\!+\!+\!+\!+\!+\!+\!+\!+\!+\! \longrightarrow$$

$$\longleftarrow \!+\!+\!+\!+\!+\!+\!+\!+\!+\!+\! \longrightarrow$$

3. Write an inequality that represents all real numbers that are at most −5 or at least 3. Graph your solution.

4. Solve the compound inequality $-2x + 7 > 3$ or $3x - 4 \ge 5$. Graph your solution.

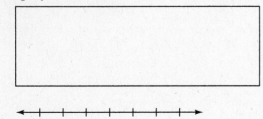

$$\longleftarrow \!+\!+\!+\!+\!+\!+\!+\! \longrightarrow$$

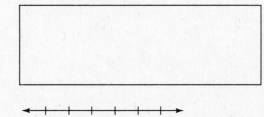

$$\longleftarrow \!+\!+\!+\!+\!+\!+\!+\! \longrightarrow$$

Lesson 3-6

Absolute Value Equations and Inequalities

Lesson Objectives	California Content Standards
• Solve equations that involve absolute value • Solve inequalities that involve absolute value	3.0

Take Note

Solving Absolute Value Equations

To solve an equation in the form $|A| = b$, where A represents a variable expression and $b > 0$, solve _____

Solving Absolute Value Inequalities

To solve an inequality in the form $|A| < b$, where A is a variable expression and $b > 0$, solve _____

To solve an inequality in the form $|A| > b$, where A is a variable expression and $b > 0$, solve _____

Similar rules are true for $|A| \le b$ and $|A| \ge b$.

Examples

1 **Solving an Absolute Value Equation** Solve and check $|a| - 3 = 5$.

$|a| - 3 + \boxed{} = 5 + \boxed{}$ **Add** $\boxed{}$ **to each side.**

$|a| = \boxed{}$ **Simplify.**

$a = \boxed{}$ or $a = -\boxed{}$ **Definition of absolute value.**

Check $|a| - 3 = 5$

$\left|\boxed{}\right| - 3 \stackrel{?}{=} 5$ ← **Substitute** $\boxed{}$ **and** $\boxed{}$ **for a.** → $\left|\boxed{}\right| - 3 \stackrel{?}{=} 5$

$\boxed{} - 3 = 5$ ✓ $\boxed{} - 3 = 5$ ✓

Daily Notetaking Guide

❷ Solving an Absolute Value Equation Solve $|3c - 6| = 9$.

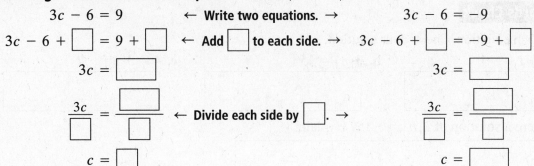

$$3c - 6 = 9 \qquad \leftarrow \text{Write two equations.} \rightarrow \qquad 3c - 6 = -9$$

$$3c - 6 + \boxed{} = 9 + \boxed{} \quad \leftarrow \text{Add } \boxed{} \text{ to each side.} \rightarrow \quad 3c - 6 + \boxed{} = -9 + \boxed{}$$

$$3c = \boxed{} \qquad\qquad\qquad\qquad\qquad 3c = \boxed{}$$

$$\frac{3c}{\boxed{}} = \frac{\boxed{}}{\boxed{}} \quad \leftarrow \text{Divide each side by } \boxed{}. \rightarrow \quad \frac{3c}{\boxed{}} = \frac{\boxed{}}{\boxed{}}$$

$$c = \boxed{} \qquad\qquad\qquad\qquad\qquad c = \boxed{}$$

The value of c is $\boxed{}$ or $\boxed{}$.

❸ Solving an Absolute Value Inequality Solve $|y - 5| \leq 2$. Graph the solutions.

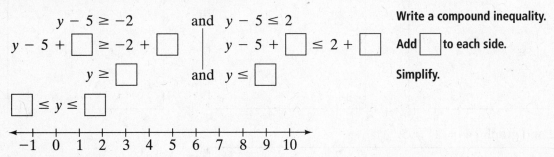

$$y - 5 \geq -2 \qquad \text{and} \quad y - 5 \leq 2 \qquad\qquad \textbf{Write a compound inequality.}$$

$$y - 5 + \boxed{} \geq -2 + \boxed{} \quad \Big| \quad y - 5 + \boxed{} \leq 2 + \boxed{} \qquad \textbf{Add } \boxed{} \textbf{ to each side.}$$

$$y \geq \boxed{} \qquad \text{and} \quad y \leq \boxed{} \qquad\qquad \textbf{Simplify.}$$

$$\boxed{} \leq y \leq \boxed{}$$

$$\overleftrightarrow{\quad\underset{-1}{|}\quad\underset{0}{|}\quad\underset{1}{|}\quad\underset{2}{|}\quad\underset{3}{|}\quad\underset{4}{|}\quad\underset{5}{|}\quad\underset{6}{|}\quad\underset{7}{|}\quad\underset{8}{|}\quad\underset{9}{|}\quad\underset{10}{|}\quad}$$

❹ Application The ideal diameter of a piston for one type of car is 88.000 mm. The actual diameter can vary from the ideal diameter by at most 0.007 mm. Find the range of acceptable diameters for the piston.

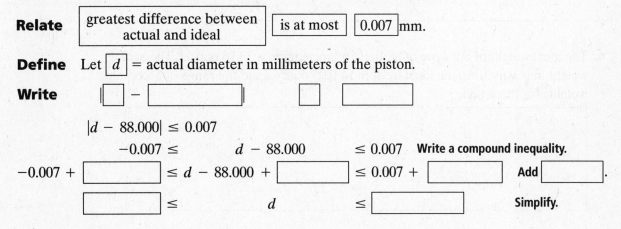

Relate $\boxed{\begin{array}{c}\text{greatest difference between}\\\text{actual and ideal}\end{array}}$ $\boxed{\text{is at most}}$ $\boxed{0.007}$ mm.

Define Let $\boxed{d}$ = actual diameter in millimeters of the piston.

Write $\Big| \boxed{} - \boxed{} \Big| \qquad \boxed{} \quad \boxed{}$

$$|d - 88.000| \leq 0.007$$

$$-0.007 \leq \qquad d - 88.000 \qquad \leq 0.007 \quad \textbf{Write a compound inequality.}$$

$$-0.007 + \boxed{} \leq d - 88.000 + \boxed{} \leq 0.007 + \boxed{} \qquad \textbf{Add } \boxed{}.$$

$$\boxed{} \leq \qquad d \qquad \leq \boxed{} \qquad \textbf{Simplify.}$$

The actual diameter must be between 87.993 mm and 88.007 mm, inclusive.

Algebra 1 Lesson 3-6

Name_____ Class_____ Date _____

1. Solve each equation. Check your solution.

    a. $|t| - 2 = -1$ **b.** $3|n| = 15$ **c.** $4 = 3|w| - 2$

    d. Is there a solution of $2|n| = -15$? Explain.

2. Solve each equation. Check your solutions.

    a. $|c - 2| = 6$ **b.** $-5.5 = |t + 2|$ **c.** $|7d| = 14$

3. Solve and graph $|w + 2| > 5$.

4. The ideal weight of one type of model airplane engine is 33.86 ounces. The actual weight may vary from the ideal by at most 0.05 ounce. Find the range of acceptable weights for this engine.

Lesson 4-1

Graphing on the Coordinate Plane

Lesson Objective	California Content Standards
• Graph points on the coordinate plane	Prepares for 6.0

Examples

❶ Identifying Coordinates

a. Name the coordinates of point P in the graph below.

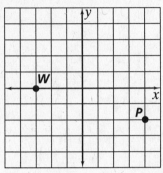

Move ☐ units to the ☐ of the origin. Then move ☐ units ☐.

The coordinates of P are ☐ .

b. Name the coordinates of point W in the graph above.

Since W is 3 units directly ☐ of the origin, the ☐ is ☐ .

The coordinates of W are ☐ .

❷ Graphing Points

a. Graph the point $A\left(1\frac{1}{2}, -2\right)$ on the coordinate plane.

Move ☐ units to the ☐ of the origin.

Then move ☐ units ☐ .

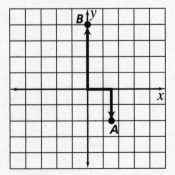

b. Graph the point $B(0, 4)$ on the coordinate plane.

Since the x-coordinate is ☐ , point B is on the ☐ .

Move ☐ units ☐ from the origin.

❸ Identifying Quadrants

In which quadrant or on which axis would you find each point?

a. $(4, -2)$

Since the *x*-coordinate is [____] and the *y*-coordinate is [____], the

point is [____].

b. $(5, 0)$

Since the *y*-coordinate is [__], the point is [____].

CA Standards Check

1. Name the coordinates of each point in the graph below.

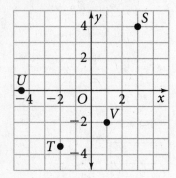

a. *S* [____]

c. *U* [____]

b. *T* [____]

d. *V* [____]

2. Graph the points on the same coordinate plane.

a. $C(2, 2)$ **b.** $D\left(-2\frac{1}{2}, -3\right)$ **c.** $E\left(4, -3\frac{1}{2}\right)$ **d.** $F(0, -4)$

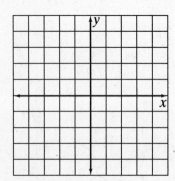

3. In which quadrant or on which axis would you find each point?

a. $(-4, 0)$ [____] **c.** $(-3, 2)$ [__]

b. $(-3, 4)$ [__] **d.** $(4.9, 5.6)$ [__]

Lesson 4-2

Lesson Objective	California Content Standards
• Identify functions	16.0, 17.0, 18.0

Vocabulary

A relation is _____

The domain of a relation is _____

The range of a relation is _____

The vertical-line test says that, on the graph of a relation, _____

_____

_____

A function is _____

_____

Example

1 **Identifying a Function Given a Table** Find the domain and range of the relation. Is the relation a function?

Basketball Players				
Height (inches)	75	78	72	74
Weight (pounds)	204	225	180	197

domain: {[   ]}   **List the values in order.**

range: {[   ]}   **Do not repeat values.**

Each value in the [   ] corresponds to exactly one value in the [   ]. [   ], the relation [   ] a function.

CA Standards Check

1. Find the domain and range of each relation. Is each relation a function?

a.

x	y
−2	3
3	−1
5	0
−4	3

b.

x	y
−3	−5
6	7
−3	4
8	−2

Examples

❷ **Using a Mapping Diagram** Find the domain and range of each relation. Use a mapping diagram to determine whether each relation is a function.

a. {(4, 3), (2, −1), (−3, −3), (2, 4)}

The domain value 2 corresponds to two range values, [ ] and [ ].

The relation [ ] a function.

b. {(0, 5), (−8, 10), (5, 5), (14, 6)}

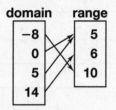

There is no value in the [ ] that corresponds, or maps, to more than one value of the [ ]. The relation [ ] a function.

❸ **Using the Vertical-Line Test** Find the domain and range of each relation. Use the vertical-line test to determine whether each relation is a function.

a. {(0, −2), (1, −2), (−3, 1), (−2, 0), (−1, −1), (3, 2), (2, −3)}

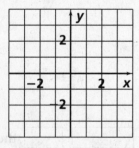

Graph the ordered pairs on a coordinate plane.

[   ]

[ ] vertical line intersects the graph at more than one point.
The relation [ ] a function.

b.

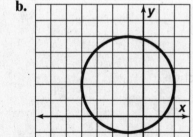

domain: { [   ] }

range: { [   ] }

[ ] vertical line intersects the graph at more than one point. The relation [ ] a function.

Name_____ Class_____ Date _____

2. Find the domain and range of each relation. Use a mapping diagram to determine whether each relation is a function.

    a. $\{(4, -4), (3, 1), (9, 5), (4, 3), (-5, 0)\}$ **b.** $\{(7.5, 2), (9, -1), (6, 3), (5, 6), (8, -1)\}$

3. Find the domain and range of each relation. Use the vertical-line test to determine whether each relation is a function.

    a. $\{(0, 2), (1, -1), (-1, 4), (0, -3), (2, 1)\}$ **b.**

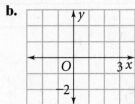

Lesson 4-3

Function Rules, Tables, and Graphs

Lesson Objectives	California Content Standards
• Model functions using rules, tables, and graphs • Identify symbolic expressions as functions	16.0, 17.0, 18.0

Vocabulary

A function rule is _____

Function notation is _____

_____

An independent variable is _____

A dependent variable is _____

Example

① Evaluating a Function Rule

a. Evaluate $f(x) = -5x + 4$ for $x = 3$.

$f(x) = -5x + 4$

$f(3) = -5\boxed{} + 4$ **Substitute** $\boxed{}$ **for x.**

$f(3) = \boxed{} + 4$ **Simplify.**

$f(3) = \boxed{}$

b. Evaluate the function rule $f(g) = -2g + 4$ to find the range of the function for the domain $\{-1, 3, 5\}$.

$f(g) = -2g + 4$ 　　　　$f(g) = -2g + 4$ 　　　　$f(g) = -2g + 4$

$f(\boxed{}) = -2(\boxed{}) + 4$　$f(\boxed{}) = -2(\boxed{}) + 4$　$f(\boxed{}) = -2(\boxed{}) + 4$

$f(\boxed{}) = \boxed{} + 4$　$f(\boxed{}) = \boxed{} + 4$　$f(\boxed{}) = \boxed{} + 4$

$f(\boxed{}) = \boxed{}$　$f(\boxed{}) = \boxed{}$　$f(\boxed{}) = \boxed{}$

The range is $\left\{\boxed{}\right\}$.

CA Standards Check

1. Find the range of each function for the domain $\{-2, 0, 5\}$.

a. $f(x) = 2x + 1$ 　　　　**b.** $y = -x + 2$ 　　　　**c.** $g(t) = t^2 - 4$

Examples

❷ Application At the local video store you can rent a video game for $3. It costs you $5 a month to operate your video game player. The total monthly cost $C(v)$ depends on the number of video games v you rent.

Model the function rule $C(v) = 5 + 3v$ using a table of values and a graph.

v	C(v) = 5 + 3v	(v, C(v))
0	$C(\boxed{}) = 5 + 3(\boxed{}) = \boxed{}$	$(\boxed{}, \boxed{})$
1	$C(\boxed{}) = 5 + 3(\boxed{}) = \boxed{}$	$(\boxed{}, \boxed{})$
2	$C(\boxed{}) = 5 + 3(\boxed{}) = \boxed{}$	$(\boxed{}, \boxed{})$

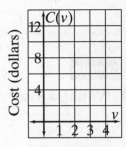

Number of video games

❸ Identifying Functions Find the domain of each relation. Determine whether each relation is a function.

a. $x = 6x + 7$

Multiplication and addition are defined for $\boxed{}$, so the domain is $\boxed{}$. For every real number x, the value of $6x + 7$ is a unique real number, so the relation is $\boxed{}$.

b. $x = 2y^2$

The value of $2y^2$ is always positive or equal to $\boxed{}$, so the domain is $\boxed{}$. The relation assigns two y-values, 1 and -1, to $x = \boxed{}$, so the relation is $\boxed{}$.

CA Standards Check

2. Model the rule $f(x) = 3x + 4$ with a table of values and a graph.

x	f(x)

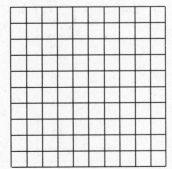

3. Find the domain of each relation. Determine whether each relation is a function.

a. $y = -2x + 1$ $\boxed{}$

b. $y = \dfrac{1}{x - 5}$ $\boxed{}$

Lesson 4-4

Lesson Objective	California Content Standards
• Write a function rule given a table or a real-world situation	16.0

Example

❶ **Writing a Rule From a Table** Write a function rule for the table.

x	y
1	2
2	5
3	10
4	17

Ask yourself, "What can I do to 1 to get 2, 2 to get 5, . . . ?" You multiply

each *x*-value times [   ] and add [   ] to get the *y*-value.

Relate   [y]   equals   [x times itself]   plus   [1]

Write   [   ]   =   [   ]   +   [   ]

A rule for the function is [   ].

CA Standards Check

1. Write a function rule for each table.

a.

x	f(x)
1	−2
2	−1
3	0
4	1

b.

x	y
1	3
2	6
3	9
4	12

c.

x	y
1	4
2	5
3	6
4	7

Example

❷ **Application** The journalism class makes $25 per ad sold in the yearbook. If the class sells *n* ads, how much money will it earn?

a. Write a function rule to describe this relationship.

Relate | money earned | is | 25 | times | number of ads sold |

Define Let | *n* | = number of ads sold.

Let | *P(n)* | = money earned.

Write [   ] = [   ] · [   ]

The function rule [   ] = [   ] describes the relationship between the number of ads sold and the money earned.

b. The class sold 6 ads. How much money did the class earn?

$P(n)$ = 25 · [   ]

$P($[ ]$)$ = 25 · [   ] **Substitute 6 for *n*.**

$P($[ ]$)$ = [   ] **Simplify.**

The class earned $[   ].

CA Standards Check

2. a. A carpenter buys finishing nails by the pound. Each pound of nails costs $1.19. Write a function rule to describe this relationship.

b. How much do 12 lb of finishing nails cost?

c. Suppose you buy a word-processing software package for $199. You charge $15 per hour for word processing. Write a rule to describe your profit as a function of the number of hours you work.

Lesson 4-5

Direct Variation

Lesson Objectives	California Content Standards
• Write an equation of a direct variation • Use ratios and proportions with direct variations	15.0, 16.0

Take Note

Direct Variation

A function in the form $y = kx$, where $k \neq 0$, is a [　　　　　].

The constant of variation k is the coefficient of x. The variables y and x

are said to vary [　　　　] with each other.

Examples

❶ Is an Equation a Direct Variation? Is each equation a direct variation?
If it is, find the constant of variation.

a. $2x - 3y = 1$

$-3y = 1 - [\quad]$ **Subtract** [\quad] **from each side.**

$y = -[\quad] + [\quad] x$ **Divide each side by** [\quad].

The equation [　　　　] have the form $y = kx$. It [　　　　] a direct variation.

b. $2x - 3y = 0$

$-3y = [\quad]$ **Subtract** [\quad] **from each side.**

$y = [\quad] x$ **Divide each side by** [\quad].

The equation [\quad] the form $y = kx$, so the equation [\quad] a direct

variation. The constant of variation is [\quad].

❷ Writing an Equation Given a Point Write an equation of the direct variation
that includes the point $(-3, 2)$.

$y = kx$ **Use the general function form of a direct variation.**

$[\quad] = k([\quad])$ **Substitute** [\quad] **for x and** [\quad] **for y.**

$-[\quad] = k$ **Divide each side by** [\quad] **to solve for k.**

$y = [\quad] x$ **Write an equation. Substitute** [\quad] **for k in $y = kx$.**

An equation of the direct variation is [　　　　].

Name_____ Class_____ Date_____

❸ **Application** The weight an object exerts on a scale varies directly with the mass of the object. If a bowling ball has a mass of 6 kg, the scale reads 59. Write an equation for the relationship between weight and mass.

Relate   The weight varies directly with the mass. When $x = 6$, $y = 59$.

Define   Let = the mass of an object.

Let $\boxed{y}$ = the weight of an object.

Write

$\boxed{} = k\boxed{}$ **Use the general form of a direct variation.**

$\boxed{} = k\left(\boxed{}\right)$ **Solve for k. Substitute** $\boxed{}$ **for x and** $\boxed{}$ **for y.**

$\dfrac{\boxed{}}{\boxed{}} = k$ **Divide each side by** $\boxed{}$ **to solve for k.**

$y = \dfrac{\boxed{}}{\boxed{}}x$ **Write an equation. Substitute** $\dfrac{\boxed{}}{\boxed{}}$ **for k in y = kx.**

The equation $\boxed{}$ relates the weight of an object to its mass.

CA Standards Check

1. Is each equation a direct variation? If it is, find the constant of variation.
   a. $7y = 2x$ **b.** $3y + 4x = 8$ **c.** $y - 7.5x = 0$

2. Write an equation of the direct variation that includes the point $(-3, -6)$.

3. A recipe for a dozen corn muffins calls for 1 cup of flour. The number of muffins varies directly with the amount of flour used. Write a direct variation for the relationship between the number of cups of flour and the number of muffins.

Examples

❹ Direct Variations and Tables For the table at the right, use the ratio $\frac{y}{x}$ to tell whether y varies directly with x. If it does, write an equation for the direct variation.

The ratio $\frac{y}{x}$ is [_____] for each pair of data, so y [_____] vary directly with x.

x	y	$\frac{y}{x}$
−1	2	$\frac{2}{-1} =$ [___]
1	2	$\frac{\square}{\square} =$ [___]
2	−4	$\frac{\square}{\square} =$ [___]

❺ Application Suppose a windlass requires 0.75 lb of force to lift an object that weighs 48 lb. How much force would you need to lift 210 lb?

Relate $\dfrac{\text{force}}{\text{weight}} = \dfrac{\boxed{}}{\boxed{}}$, which is about $\boxed{}$.

Define Let $\boxed{n}$ = the force you need to lift 210 lb.

Write Let w = the weight and f = the force.

$f = 0.0156\,w$ **Write an equation.**

$f = 0.0156\,(\boxed{})$ **Substitute** $\boxed{}$ **for** w.

$f = \boxed{}$ **Simplify.**

You need about $\boxed{}$ lb of force to lift 210 lb.

CA Standards Check

4. For the data in each table, tell whether y varies directly with x. If it does, write an equation for the direct variation.

a.

x	y
−2	3.2
1	2.4
4	1.6

b.

x	y
4	6
8	12
10	15

5. Recall Example 5. Suppose a second windlass requires 0.5 lb of force to lift an object that weighs 32 lb. How much force would you need to lift 160 lb?

Lesson 4-6

Inverse Variation

Lesson Objectives	**California Content Standards**
• Solve inverse variations • Compare direct and inverse variation	15.0, 16.0

Take Note

Direct and Inverse Variation

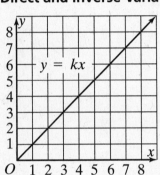

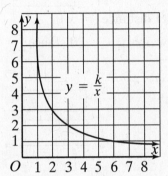

y varies [   ] with x.

y is [   ] proportional to x.

The [   ] $\frac{y}{x}$ is constant.

y varies [   ] with x.

y is [   ] proportional to x.

The [   ] xy is constant.

An equation in the form $xy = k$ or $y = \frac{k}{x}$, where $k \neq 0$, is an [   ].

The [   ] is k.

Examples

❶ Finding the Missing Coordinate The points $(5, 6)$ and $(3, y)$ are two points on the graph of an inverse variation. Find the missing value.

$x_1 \cdot y_1 = x_2 \cdot y_2$ Use the equation $x_1 \cdot y_1 = x_2 \cdot y_2$ since you know coordinates but not the constant of variation.

[   ]([   ]) = [   ]y_2 Substitute [   ] for x_1, [   ] for y_1, and [   ] for x_2.

[   ] = [   ]y_2 Simplify.

[   ] = y_2 Solve for y_2.

The missing value is [   ]. The point $(3, \boxed{})$ is on the graph of the

inverse variation that includes the point $(5, 6)$.

❷ Application Jeff weighs 130 pounds and is 5 ft from the lever's fulcrum. If Tracy weighs 93 pounds, how far from the fulcrum should she sit in order to balance the lever?

Relate   A weight of [   ] lb is 5 ft from the fulcrum.

A weight of [   ] lb is [   ] ft from the fulcrum.
Weight and distance vary inversely.

Define   Let weight$_1$ = [   ] lb.

Let weight$_2$ = 93 lb.

Let distance$_1$ = [   ] ft.

Let distance$_2$ = x ft.

Write   weight$_1$ · distance$_1$ = weight$_2$ · distance$_2$

[   ] · [   ] = [   ] · x **Substitute.**

[   ] = [   ]x **Simplify.**

$$\frac{[]}{[]} = x$$ **Solve for x.**

[   ] ≈ x **Simplify.**

Tracy should sit about [   ] ft from the fulcrum to balance the lever.

❸ Determining Direct or Inverse Variation Decide whether each data set represents a direct variation or an inverse variation. Then write an equation to model the data.

a.

x	y
3	10
5	6
10	3

The values of y seem to vary [   ] with the values of x. Check each product xy.

xy: $3(10) = 30$ $5(6) = 30$ $10(3) = 30$

The product of xy is the same for all pairs of data.

So, this is an [   ] variation, and $k =$ [   ].

The equation is [   ].

b.

x	y
2	3
4	6
8	12

The values of y seem to vary [   ] with the values of x. Check each ratio $\frac{y}{x}$.

$\begin{array}{c} y \rightarrow \\ x \rightarrow \end{array}$ $\frac{3}{2} = 1.5$ $\frac{6}{4} = 1.5$ $\frac{12}{8} = 1.5$

The ratio $\frac{y}{x}$ is the same for all pairs of data. So, this is a

[   ] variation, and $k =$ [   ].

The equation is [   ].

Name_____ Class_____ Date _____

CA Standards Check

1. Each pair of points is on the graph of an inverse variation. Find the missing value.

   a. $(3, y)$ and $(5, 9)$

   b. $(75, 0.2)$ and $(x, 3)$

2. **a.** A 200-lb weight is placed 6 ft from a fulcrum. How far from the fulcrum should a 300-lb weight be placed to balance the lever?

   b. An 90-lb weight is placed 3 ft from a fulcrum. What weight should you put 6 ft from the fulcrum to balance the lever?

3. Determine whether the data in each table represent a direct variation or an inverse variation. Write an equation to model the data in each table.

   a.

x	y
3	12
6	6
9	4

   b.

x	y
3	12
5	20
8	32

4. Explain whether each situation represents a direct variation or an inverse variation.

   a. You are a discount store. All sweaters are on sale for $15 each.

   b. You walk 5 miles every day. Your speed and time vary from day to day.

Name_____ Class_____ Date_____

Lesson 4-7

Inductive and Deductive Reasoning

Lesson Objectives	California Content Standards
• Use inductive reasoning in continuing number patterns • Distinguish between inductive and deductive reasoning	24.1

Vocabulary

Inductive reasoning is _____

A conjecture is _____

Example

1 **Extending Number Patterns** Use inductive reasoning to describe each pattern. Then find the next two numbers.

a. 15, 20, 25, 30, . . .

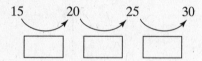

The pattern is "add ☐ to the previous number." To find the next two

numbers, you ☐_____☐: 30 + ☐ = 35 and

35 + ☐ = 40.

b. 1, 3, 9, . . .

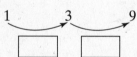

The pattern is "multiply the previous number by ☐." To find the next two

numbers, you ☐_____☐: 9 × ☐ = 27 and

27 × ☐ = 81.

CA Standards Check

1. Use inductive reasoning to describe each pattern. Then find the next two numbers in each pattern.

a. 2, 6, 18, 54, . . .

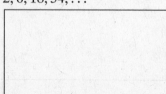

b. 4, 11, 18, 25, . . .

c. 1, −3, 9, −27, . . .

Daily Notetaking Guide

Examples

❷ **Writing a Function Rule to Describe a Pattern** Look at the pattern of sums below. Write a function rule that gives the sum of the first n powers of -2, where n is a natural number. Then predict the sum of the first 10 powers of -2.

$-2^0 = -1 = 1 - 2^1$
$-2^0 + (-2^1) = -1 + (-2) = -3 = 1 - 2^2$
$-2^0 + (-2^1) + (-2^2) = -1 + (-2) + (-4) = -7 = 1 - 2^3$
$-2^0 + (-2^1) + (-2^2) + (-2^3) = -1 + (-2) + (-4) + (-8) = -15 = \boxed{}$

Let $n = $ a natural number.
Let $A(n) = $ the sum of the first n powers of -2.

$A(n) = -2^0 + (-2^1) + (-2^2) + (-2^3) + \ldots + (-2n - 1) = \boxed{}$

The sum of the first 10 powers of -2 is $\boxed{}$

❸ **Determining Inductive or Deductive Reasoning** Explain whether each situation represents inductive reasoning or deductive reasoning.

a. You are given that $5(a + b) = c$. You conclude that $5a + 5b = c$.

Since your conclusion is based on using the Distributive Property of Addition, this is $\boxed{}$.

b. A ski hill has had an increase in sales of 200 season passes for each of the past 4 years. It is concluded that this year there will be 200 more season passes sold than last year.

Since the conclusion is based on the observation of sales for the past 4 years, this is $\boxed{}$.

CA Standards Check

2. Look at the pattern of sums below. Write a function rule that gives the sum of the first n positive even integers, where n is a natural number. Then predict the sum of the first 30 positive even integers.

$3 = 3 = 1(3)$
$3 + 5 = 8 = 2(4)$
$3 + 5 + 7 = 15 = 3(5)$
$3 + 5 + 7 + 9 = 24 = 4(6)$

$\boxed{}$

3. You conclude a person is at least 16 years old because he or she has a driver's license, and you know the legal driving age is 16 years. Explain whether this situation represents inductive reasoning or deductive reasoning.

$\boxed{}$

Lesson 5-1

Rate of Change and Slope

Lesson Objectives	California Content Standards
• Find rates of change from tables and graphs	6.0, 7.0, 8.0
• Find slope	

Take Note

Rate of Change

$$\text{Rate of change} = \frac{\text{change in the } \boxed{} \text{ variable}}{\text{change in the } \boxed{} \text{ variable}}$$

Slope

Slope is _____

$$\text{slope} = \frac{\text{vertical change}}{\text{horizontal change}} = \frac{\text{rise}}{\text{run}} = \frac{y_2 - y_1}{x_2 - x_1}, \text{ where } x_2 - x_1 \neq 0$$

Slopes of Lines

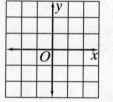 A line with $\boxed{}$ slope slants upward from left to right.

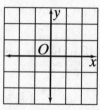 A line with $\boxed{}$ slope slants downward from left to right.

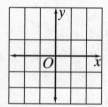 A line with a slope of 0 is $\boxed{}$.

A line with an undefined slope is $\boxed{}$.

Name_____ Class_____ Date _____

Examples

① Finding Rate of Change Using a Table For the data in the table, is the rate of change the same for each pair of consecutive mileage amounts?

Find the rate of change for each pair of consecutive mileage amounts.

$$\frac{\text{rate of}}{\text{change}} = \frac{\text{change in cost}}{\text{change in number of miles}}$$ **Cost depends on the number of miles.**

Fee for Miles Driven	
Miles	**Fee**
100	$30
150	$42
200	$54
250	$66

$$\frac{42-30}{150-100} = \frac{\boxed{}}{\boxed{}} = \frac{\boxed{}}{\boxed{}}$$

$$\frac{\boxed{} - 42}{200 - \boxed{}} = \frac{\boxed{}}{\boxed{}} = \frac{\boxed{}}{\boxed{}}$$

$$\frac{66 - \boxed{}}{\boxed{} - 200} = \frac{\boxed{}}{\boxed{}} = \frac{\boxed{}}{\boxed{}}$$

The rate of change for each pair of consecutive mileage amounts is

$\boxed{}$ per $\boxed{}$ miles. The rate of change is the same for all the data.

② Finding Slope Using a Graph Find the slope of each line.

a.

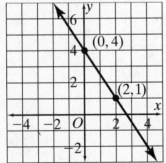

b.

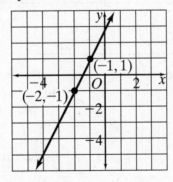

$\text{slope} = \dfrac{\text{rise}}{\text{run}}$

$= \dfrac{\boxed{} - 1}{0 - \boxed{}}$

$= \dfrac{\boxed{}}{\boxed{}} = -\dfrac{\boxed{}}{\boxed{}}$

The slope of the line is $\boxed{}$.

$\text{slope} = \dfrac{\text{rise}}{\text{run}}$

$= \dfrac{-1 - \boxed{}}{\boxed{} - (-1)}$

$= \dfrac{\boxed{}}{\boxed{}} = \boxed{}$

The slope of the line is $\boxed{}$.

❸ Finding Slope Using Points Find the slope of the line through $E(3, -2)$ and $F(-2, -1)$.

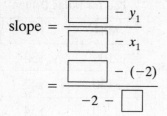

slope $= \dfrac{\boxed{} - y_1}{\boxed{} - x_1}$

$= \dfrac{\boxed{} - (-2)}{-2 - \boxed{}}$ **Substitute** $\left(\boxed{}, \boxed{}\right)$ **for** (x_2, y_2) **and** $\left(\boxed{}, \boxed{}\right)$ **for** (x_1, y_1).

$= \dfrac{1}{\boxed{}} = -\dfrac{\boxed{}}{\boxed{}}$ **Simplify.**

The slope of $\overleftrightarrow{EF}$ is $\boxed{}$.

CA Standards Check

1. a. Using the table in Example 1, find the rate of change using mileage amounts 100 and 200.

b. Critical Thinking Does finding the rate of change for just one pair of mileage amounts mean that the rate of change is the same for all the data? Explain.

2. Find the slope of each line.

a.

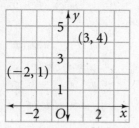

b.

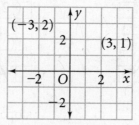

3. Find the slope of the line through $C(2, 5)$ and $D(4, 7)$.

Lesson 5-2

Slope-Intercept Form

Lesson Objectives	California Content Standards
• Write linear equations in slope-intercept form • Graph linear equations	6.0, 7.0

Take Note

Slope-Intercept Form of a Linear Equation

The slope-intercept form of a linear equation is $y = mx + b$.

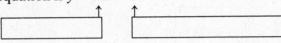

A linear equation is _____

_____

The y-intercept is _____

_____

Example

❶ Identifying Slope and *y*-Intercept What are the slope and y-intercept of $y = 2x - 3$?

$y = \quad mx + \quad b$ **Use slope-intercept form.**

$y = \boxed{}x + \boxed{}$

The slope is $\boxed{}$; the y-intercept is $\boxed{}$.

CA Standards Check

1. a. Find the slope and y-intercept of $y = \frac{7}{6}x - \frac{3}{4}$.

```



```

b. Critical Thinking For the equation in Example 1, what happens to the graph of the line and to the equation if the y-intercept is moved down 3 units?

```



```

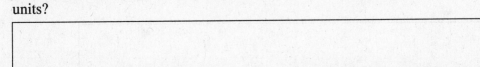

Daily Notetaking Guide

Algebra 1 Lesson 5-2   **77**

Name_____ Class_____ Date _____

Examples

❷ **Writing an Equation** Write an equation of the line with slope $\frac{1}{4}$ and y-intercept 5.

Step 1 Use the slope-intercept form. $y = \boxed{} x + \boxed{}$

Step 2 Substitute $\boxed{}$ for m and $\boxed{}$ for b. $y = \boxed{} x + \boxed{}$

❸ **Writing an Equation From a Graph** Write the equation for the linear function shown in the graph.

Step 1 Find the slope. Two points on the line are $(0, 1)$ and $(3, -1)$.

$$\text{slope} = \frac{\boxed{}}{\boxed{}}$$

$$= \boxed{}$$

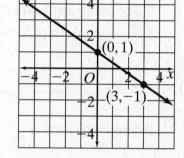

Step 2 Write an equation in slope-intercept form. The y-intercept is $\boxed{}$.

$$y = mx + b$$

$$y = \boxed{} x + \boxed{} \quad \textbf{Substitute } \boxed{} \textbf{ for } \textbf{\textit{m}} \textbf{ and } \boxed{} \textbf{ for } \textbf{\textit{b}}.$$

CA Standards Check

2. Write an equation of a line with slope $m = \frac{2}{5}$ and y-intercept $b = -1$.

3. a. Write the equation of the line using the points $(0, 1)$ and $(2, 2)$.

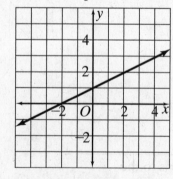

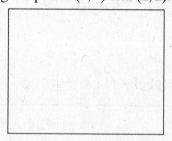

b. Critical Thinking Does the equation of the line change if you use $(-2, 0)$ instead of $(2, 2)$? Explain.

Example

❹ **Graphing Equations** The base pay for a used-car salesperson is $300 per week. The salesperson also earns 15% commission on sales made. The equation $t = 300 + 0.15s$ relates total earnings t to sales s. Graph the equation.

Step 1 Identify the slope and y-intercept.

$$t = 300 + 0.15s$$

$t = \boxed{} + \boxed{}$ **Rewrite the equation in slope-intercept form.**

slope y-intercept

Step 2 Plot two points. First plot a point at the y-intercept. Then use the slope to plot a second point.

The slope is $\boxed{}$, which equals $\dfrac{\boxed{}}{100}$. Plot a second point $\boxed{}$ units above and $\boxed{}$ units to the right of the y-intercept.

Step 3 Draw a line through the points.

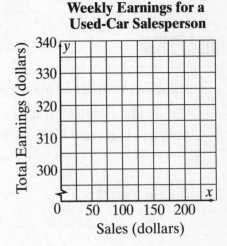

Weekly Earnings for a Used-Car Salesperson

CA Standards Check

4. Suppose the base pay of a delivery person is $150, and his commission on each sale is 30%. The equation relating his total earnings t to sales s is $t = 150 + 0.3s$. Graph the equation.

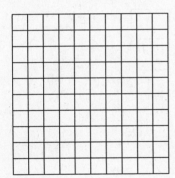

Lesson 5-3

Standard Form

Lesson Objectives	California Content Standards
• Graph equations using intercepts • Write equations in standard form	6.0

Take Note

Standard Form of a Linear Equation

The standard form of a linear equation is [   ], where $A, B,$ and C are real numbers, and A and B are not both zero.

The x-intercept is _____

_____

Example

① **Finding *x*- and *y*-Intercepts** Find the x- and y-intercepts of $2x + 5y = 6$.

Step 1 To find the x-intercept, substitute 0 for y and solve for x.

$2x + 5y = 6$

$2x + 5(0) = 6$

[   ]$x = $[   ]

$x = $[   ]

The x-intercept is [   ].

Step 2 To find the y-intercept, substitute 0 for x and solve for y.

$2x + 5y = 6$

$2(0) + 5y = 6$

[   ]$y = $[   ]

$y = $[   ]

The y-intercept is [   ].

CA Standards Check

1. Find the x- and y-intercepts of $4x - 9y = -12$.

Examples

② **Graphing Lines Using Intercepts** Graph $3x + 5y = 15$ using intercepts.

Step 1 Find the intercepts.

$3x + 5y = 15$

$3x + 5\left(\boxed{}\right) = 15$ **Substitute** $\boxed{}$ **for** *y*.

$\boxed{}x = \boxed{}$ **Solve for** *x*.

$x = \boxed{}$

$3x + 5y = 15$

$3\left(\boxed{}\right) + 5y = 15$ **Substitute** $\boxed{}$ **for** *x*.

$\boxed{}y = \boxed{}$ **Solve for** *y*.

$y = \boxed{}$

Step 2 Plot $\left(\boxed{}, 0\right)$ and $\left(0, \boxed{}\right)$.
Draw a line through the points.

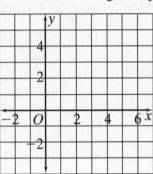

③ **Transforming to Standard Form** Write $y = \frac{2}{3}x + 6$ in standard form using integers.

$y = \frac{2}{3}x + 6$

$\boxed{}y = \boxed{}\left(\frac{2}{3}x + 6\right)$ **Multiply each side by** $\boxed{}$.

$\boxed{}y = \boxed{}x + \boxed{}$ **Use the Distributive Property.**

$\boxed{} + 3y = \boxed{}$ **Subtract** $\boxed{}$ **from each side.**

The equation in standard form is $\boxed{}$.

CA Standards Check

2. Graph $5x + 2y = -10$ using the *x*- and *y*-intercepts.

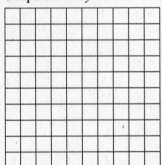

3. Write $y = -\frac{2}{5}x + 1$ in standard form using integers.

Example

④ Application Write an equation in standard form to find the number of hours you would need to work at each job to make a total of $130.

Job	Amount Paid per hour
Mowing Lawns	$12
Delivering Newspapers	$5

Define Let $\boxed{x}$ = the hours mowing lawns.

Let $\boxed{y}$ = the hours delivering newspapers.

Relate $\boxed{\text{\$12 per h mowing}}$ plus $\boxed{\text{\$5 per h delivering}}$ equals $\boxed{\text{\$130}}$

Write $\boxed{}$ + $\boxed{}$ = $\boxed{}$

The equation in standard form is $\boxed{}$.

CA Standards Check

4. Write an equation in standard form to find the number of minutes someone who weighs 150 lb would need to bowl and walk to burn 250 Calories.

Activity by a 150-lb Person	Calories Burned per Minute
Bicycling	10
Bowling	4
Hiking	7
Running 5.2 mi/h	11
Swimming Laps	12
Walking 3.5 mi/h	5

Lesson 5-4

Point-Slope Form and Writing Linear Equations

Lesson Objectives	**California Content Standards**
• Graph and write linear equations using point-slope form • Write a linear equation using data	6.0, 7.0

Take Note

Point-Slope Form of a Linear Equation

The point-slope form of the equation of a nonvertical line that passes through the point (x_1, y_1) and has slope m is [   ].

Linear Equations

Slope-Intercept Form	**Standard Form**	**Point-Slope Form**
$y = $ [ ] $+$ [ ]	$Ax + By = $ [ ]	$\left(y - \boxed{}\right) = m\left(x - \boxed{}\right)$
m is the slope and b is the y-intercept.	A and B are not both 0.	(x_1, y_1) lies on the graph of the equation, and m is the slope.

Examples

$y = -\frac{2}{3}x + \frac{5}{3}$	$2x + 3y = 5$	$y - 1 = -\frac{2}{3}(x - 1)$

Examples

❶ Graphing Using Point-Slope Form Graph the equation $y - 2 = \frac{1}{3}(x - 1)$.

The equation shows that the line passes through $\left(\boxed{}, \boxed{}\right)$ with slope $\boxed{}$.

Start at $\left(\boxed{}, \boxed{}\right)$.

Using the slope, go up $\boxed{}$ unit and right $\boxed{}$ units to $\left(\boxed{}, \boxed{}\right)$.

Draw a line through the two points.

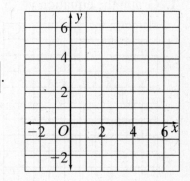

❷ Writing an Equation in Point-Slope Form Write the equation of the line with slope -2 that passes through the point $(3, -3)$.

$y - y_1 = m(x - x_1)$ Use the point-slope form.

$y - \left(\boxed{}\right) = \boxed{}\left(x - \boxed{}\right)$ Substitute $\left(\boxed{}, \boxed{}\right)$ for (x_1, y_1) and $\boxed{}$ for m.

$y + \boxed{} = \boxed{}\left(x - \boxed{}\right)$ Simplify.

The equation is [   ].

❸ Using Two Points to Write an Equation Write equations for the line in point-slope form and in slope-intercept form.

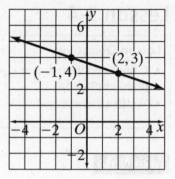

Step 1 Find the slope.

$$\frac{y_2 - y_1}{x_2 - x_1} = m$$

$$\frac{\boxed{} - \boxed{}}{\boxed{} - \boxed{}} = \boxed{}$$

The slope is $\boxed{}$.

Step 2 Use either point to write the equation in point-slope form.

Use $(-1, 4)$.

$$y - y_1 = m(x - x_1)$$

$$y - \boxed{} = \boxed{}\left(x - \left(\boxed{}\right)\right)$$

$$\boxed{}$$

Step 3 Rewrite the equation from Step 2 in slope-intercept form.

$$y - \boxed{} = \boxed{}(x + \boxed{})$$

$$y - \boxed{} = \boxed{}\,x - \boxed{}$$

$$\boxed{}$$

CA Standards Check

1. Graph the equation $y - 5 = -\frac{2}{3}(x + 2)$.

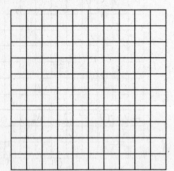

2. Write the equation of the line with slope $\frac{2}{5}$ that passes through the point $(10, -8)$.

Name_____ Class_____ Date _____

Example

❹ **Writing an Equation Using a Table** Is the relationship shown by the data linear? If so, model the data with an equation.

x	y
3	6
2	4
−1	−2
−3	−6

Step 1 Find the rate of change for consecutive ordered pairs.

-1 ($\quad$) $\boxed{}$

-3 ($\quad$) $\boxed{}$

-2 ($\quad$) $\boxed{}$

$$\frac{\boxed{}}{-1} = \boxed{}$$

$$\frac{\boxed{}}{-3} = \boxed{}$$

$$\frac{\boxed{}}{-2} = \boxed{}$$

The relationship $\boxed{}$ linear. The rate of change is $\boxed{}$.

Step 2 Use the slope and a point to write an equation.

$y - y_1 = m(x - x_1)$ **Use point-slope form.**

$y - \boxed{} = \boxed{}\left(x - \boxed{}\right)$ **Substitute** $\left(\boxed{}, \boxed{}\right)$ **for** (x_1, y_1) **and** $\boxed{}$ **for** m.

CA Standards Check

3. a. Write an equation for the line in Example 3 in point-slope form using point $(2, 3)$.

b. Write the equation you found in part (a) in slope-intercept form.

4. Is the relationship shown by the data at the right linear? If so, model the data with an equation.

x	y
−11	−7
−1	−3
4	−1
19	5

Lesson 5-5

Parallel and Perpendicular Lines

Lesson Objectives	California Content Standards
• Determine whether lines are parallel	7.0, 8.0
• Determine whether lines are perpendicular	

Take Note

Slopes of Parallel Lines

Nonvertical lines are parallel if _____

Any two vertical lines are parallel.

Example The equations $y = \frac{2}{3}x + 1$ and $y = \frac{2}{3}x - 3$ have the same slope, $\frac{2}{3}$, and different y-intercepts. The graphs of the two equations are parallel.

Slopes of Perpendicular Lines

Two lines are perpendicular if the product of their slopes is $\boxed{}$.
A vertical and a horizontal line are also perpendicular.

Example The slope of $y = -\frac{1}{4}x - 1$ is $-\frac{1}{4}$. The slope of $y = 4x + 2$ is 4.
Since $-\frac{1}{4} \cdot 4 = -1$, the graphs of the two equations are perpendicular.

Parallel lines are _____

Perpendicular lines are _____

The product of a number and its negative reciprocal is _____

Examples

❶ Writing Equations of Parallel Lines Write an equation for the line that contains $(-2, 3)$ and is parallel to $y = \frac{5}{2}x - 4$.

Step 1 Identify the slope of the given line. The slope of $y = \frac{5}{2}x - 4$ is $\boxed{}$.

Step 2 Write the equation of the line through $(-2, 3)$ using slope-intercept form.

$y - y_1 = m(x - x_1)$ **Use point-slope form.**

$y - \boxed{} = \boxed{}\left(x - \boxed{}\right)$ **Substitute** $\left(\boxed{}, \boxed{}\right)$ **for** (x_1, y_1) **and** $\boxed{}$ **for** m.

$y - \boxed{} = \boxed{}x - \boxed{}\left(\boxed{}\right)$ **Use the Distributive Property.**

$y - \boxed{} = \boxed{}x + \boxed{}$ **Simplify.**

$y = \boxed{}x + \boxed{}$ **Add** $\boxed{}$ **to each side and simplify.**

❷ **Writing Equations for Perpendicular Lines** The line in the graph represents the street in front of a house. The sidewalk from the front door is perpendicular to the street. Write an equation representing the sidewalk.

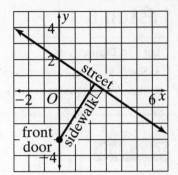

Step 1 Find the slope m of the street.

$$m = \frac{y_2 - y_1}{x_2 - x_1} = \frac{\boxed{} - \boxed{}}{\boxed{} - \boxed{}} = \frac{\boxed{}}{\boxed{}} = -\frac{\boxed{}}{\boxed{}}$$

Points $(0, 2)$ and $(3, 0)$ are on the street.

Step 2 Find the negative reciprocal of the slope.

The negative reciprocal of $-\frac{2}{3}$ is $\boxed{}$, so the slope of the

sidewalk is $\boxed{}$.

The y-intercept is $\boxed{}$.

The equation for the sidewalk is $\boxed{}$.

CA Standards Check

1. Write an equation for the line that contains $(2, -6)$ and is parallel to $y = 3x + 9$.

2. a. Write an equation of the line that contains $(1, 8)$ and is perpendicular to $y = \frac{3}{4}x + 1$.

2. b. Application Using the diagram in Example 2, write an equation in slope-intercept form for a new sidewalk perpendicular to the street from a front door at $(-1, -1)$.

Lesson 6-1

Solving Systems by Graphing

Lesson Objectives	California Content Standards
• Solve systems by graphing • Analyze special types of systems	9.0

Take Note

Numbers of Solutions of Systems of Linear Equations

different slopes

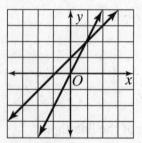

The lines [ ]
so there is
[ ] solution.

same slope
different *y*-intercepts

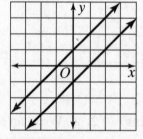

The lines [ ]
so there are
[ ] solutions.

same slope
same *y*-intercept

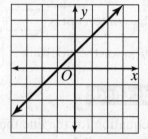

The lines are [ ]
so there are
[ ]
solutions.

A system of linear equations is _____

_____

A solution of a system of linear equations is _____

_____

No solution means _____

_____

A system of equations has infinitely many solutions when _____

_____

Examples

❶ Solving a System of Equations Solve by graphing.

$y = 2x + 10$
$y = 4x$

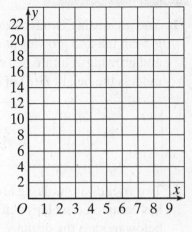

$y = 2x + 10$ **The slope is** ☐ **. The intercept on the**

vertical axis is ☐ **.**

$y = 4x$ **The slope is** ☐ **. The intercept on the**

vertical axis is ☐ **.**

Graph the equations $y = 2x + 10$ and $y = 4x$ on the same coordinate plane.

The lines intersect at (☐ , ☐).

❷ Systems With No Solution Solve by graphing. $y = 3x + 2$
                                                          $y = 3x - 2$

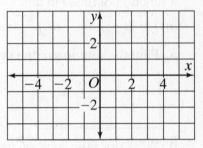

Graph both equations on the same coordinate plane.

$y = 3x + 2$ **The slope is** ☐ **. The y-intercept is** ☐ **.**

$y = 3x - 2$ **The slope is** ☐ **. The y-intercept is** ☐ **.**

The lines are ☐ . There is ☐ solution.

❸ Systems With Infinitely Many Solutions Solve by graphing.

$3x + 4y = 12$

$y = -\frac{3}{4}x + 3$

Graph both equations on the same coordinate plane.

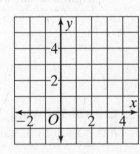

$3x + 4y = 12$ **The y-intercept is** ☐ **. The x-intercept is** ☐ **.**

$y = -\frac{3}{4}x + 3$ **The slope is** ☐ **. The y-intercept is** ☐ **.**

The graphs are the same line. The solutions are an infinite number of ordered pairs (x, y), such that $y = -\frac{3}{4}x + 3$.

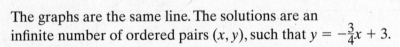

CA Standards Check

1. You are testing two fertilizers on bamboo plants C and D. Plant C is 5 cm tall and growing at a rate of 3 cm/day. Plant D is 1 cm tall and growing at a rate of 4 cm/day. Write a system of equations that models the height $H(d)$ of each plant as a function of days d.

2. Two friends are walking around a quarter-mile track. One person has completed six laps before the second one starts. The system below models the distance $d(t)$ in miles each walker covers as a function of time t in hours.

$$d(t) = 3t + 1.5 \qquad d(t) = 4t$$

   a. Find the solution of the system by graphing.

   b. What does the solution mean in terms of the original situation?

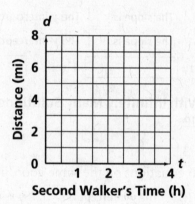

Distance (mi)

Second Walker's Time (h)

3. **Critical Thinking** Without graphing, how can you tell if a system has no solution? Give an example.

4. Solve by graphing. $\quad y = \frac{1}{5}x + 9$

$$5y = x + 45$$

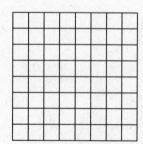

Name_____ Class_____ Date _____

Lesson 6-2

Lesson Objectives	California Content Standards
• Solve systems by graphing • Analyze special types of systems	9.0

Vocabulary

The substitution method is _____

_____

_____

Example

❶ **Using Substitution and the Distributive Property** Solve using substitution. $-2x + y = -1$

$4x + 2y = 12$

Step 1 Solve the first equation for y because it has a coefficient of 1.

$-2x + y = -1$

$y = \boxed{}$ **Add** $\boxed{}$ **to each side.**

Step 2 Write an equation containing only one variable and solve.

$4x + 2y = 12$ **Start with the other equation.**

$4x + 2 \left(\boxed{}\right) = 12$ **Substitute** $\boxed{}$ **for y in that equation.**

$4x + \boxed{} = 12$ **Use the Distributive Property.**

$\boxed{} = \boxed{}$ **Combine like terms and add** $\boxed{}$ **to each side.**

$x = \boxed{}$ **Divide each side by** $\boxed{}$.

Step 3 Solve for y in the other equation.

$-2\left(\boxed{}\right) + y = -1$ **Substitute** $\boxed{}$ **for x.**

$\boxed{} + y = -1$ **Simplify.**

$y = \boxed{}$ **Add** $\boxed{}$ **to each side.**

Since $x = \boxed{}$ and $y = \boxed{}$, the solution is $\left(\boxed{}\right)$.

CA Standards Check

1. Solve using substitution. Check your solution.

 a. $y = 2x$
 $7x - y = 15$

 b. $6y + 8x = 28$
 $3 = 2x - y$

Example

❷ **Application** A class with 26 students is going to the zoo. Five chaperones will each drive a van or a car. Each van seats 7 persons, including the driver. Each car seats 5 persons, including the driver. How many vans and cars will be needed?

Let $\boxed{v}$ = number of vans and $\boxed{c}$ = number of cars.

drivers $\boxed{v} + \boxed{c} = 5$

people $7\boxed{v} + 5\boxed{c} = 31$

Solve using substitution.

Step 1 Write an equation containing only one variable.

$v + c = 5$ **Solve the first equation for c.**

$c = \boxed{} + 5$

Step 2 Write and solve an equation containing the variable v.

$7v + 5c = 31$

$7v + 5\left(\boxed{} + \boxed{}\right) = 31$ **Substitute** $\boxed{}$ **for c in the second equation.**

$7v - \boxed{} + \boxed{} = 31$ **Solve for v.**

$\boxed{} + \boxed{} = 31$

$\boxed{} = \boxed{}$

$v = \boxed{}$

Step 3 Solve for c in either equation.

$\boxed{} + c = 5$ **Substitute 3 for v in the first equation.**

$c = \boxed{}$

$\boxed{}$ vans and $\boxed{}$ cars are needed to transport 31 persons.

CA Standards Check

2. A softball team played 149 games. The team won 8 more than two times the number of games they lost. How many games did they lose?

Lesson 6-3

Solving Systems Using Elimination

Lesson Objectives	California Content Standards
• Solve systems by adding or subtracting • Multiply first when solving systems	9.0

Vocabulary

The elimination method is _____

_____

_____

Examples

1 **Adding Equations** Solve by elimination. $2x + 3y = 11$

$-2x + 9y = 1$

Step 1 Eliminate x because the sum of the coefficients is zero.

$$2x + 3y = 11$$
$$\underline{-2x + 9y = 1}$$

Add the two equations.

$\boxed{} + \boxed{} = \boxed{}$ Addition Property of Equality

$y = \boxed{}$ Solve for y.

Step 2 Solve for the eliminated variable x using either original equation.

$2x + 3y = 11$ Choose the first equation.

$2x + 3\left(\boxed{}\right) = 11$ Substitute $\boxed{}$ for y.

$2x + \boxed{} = 11$ Solve for x.

$2x = \boxed{}$

$x = \boxed{}$

Since $x = \boxed{}$ and $y = \boxed{}$, the solution is $\left(\boxed{}, \boxed{}\right)$.

Check See if $(4, 1)$ makes the equation *not* used in Step 2 true.

$-2\left(\boxed{}\right) + 9\left(\boxed{}\right) \stackrel{?}{=} 1$ Substitute $\boxed{}$ for x and $\boxed{}$ for y into the second equation.

$\boxed{} + \boxed{} \stackrel{?}{=} 1$

$\boxed{} = 1 ✔$

❷ Multiplying One Equation Suppose the school band is selling cans of popcorn for $5 per can and cans of mixed nuts for $8 per can. The band sells a total of 240 cans and receives a total of $1,614. Find the number of each type of can sold.

Define Let $\boxed{p}$ = number of cans of popcorn sold.

Let $\boxed{n}$ = number of cans of nuts sold.

Relate $\boxed{\text{total number of cans}}$ $\boxed{\text{total amount of sales}}$

Write $\boxed{} + \boxed{} = 240$ $5\boxed{} + 8\boxed{} = 1614$

Step 1 Eliminate one variable.

Start with the given system.	To prepare to eliminate p, multiply the first equation by $\boxed{}$.		Subtract the equations to eliminate p.

$$p + n = 240 \quad \rightarrow \quad \boxed{}(p + n = 240) \quad \rightarrow \quad 5p + 5n = 1200$$
$$5p + 8n = 1614 \quad \rightarrow \quad \underline{5p + 8n = 1614} \quad \rightarrow \quad \underline{5p + 8n = 1614}$$

$$\boxed{} - \boxed{} = \boxed{}$$

Step 2 Solve for n.

$$\boxed{}\,n = \boxed{}$$

$$n = \boxed{}$$

Step 3 Solve for the eliminated variable using either of the original equations.

$$p + n = 240 \quad \textbf{Choose the first equation.}$$
$$p + \boxed{} = 240 \quad \textbf{Substitute } \boxed{} \textbf{ for } n.$$
$$p = 102 \quad \textbf{Solve for } p.$$

The band sold $\boxed{}$ cans of popcorn and $\boxed{}$ cans of mixed nuts.

CA Standards Check

1. Solve by elimination.

$$6x - 3y = 3$$
$$-6x + 5y = 3$$

Example

❸ **Multiplying Both Equations** Solve by elimination. $3x + 5y = 10$
$5x + 7y = 10$

Step 1 Eliminate one variable.

| **Start with the given system.** | **To prepare to eliminate *x*, multiply one equation by ☐ and the other equation by ☐.** | **Subtract the equations to eliminate *x*.** |

$3x + 5y = 10$ →   ☐$(3x + 5y = 10)$ → $15x + 25y = 50$
$5x + 7y = 10$ →   ☐$(5x + 7y = 10)$ → $15x + 21y = 30$
   ☐ + ☐ = ☐

Step 2 Solve for *y*.

☐$y = $ ☐
$y = $ ☐

Step 3 Solve for the eliminated variable *x* using either of the original equations.

$3x + 5y = 10$ **Use the first equation.**
$3x + 5($☐$) = 10$ **Substitute** ☐ **for *y*.**
$3x + $☐$ = 10$
$3x = $☐
$x = $☐

The solution is ☐ .

CA Standards Check

2. Suppose a school band sells erasers for $2 per package and pencils for $5 per package. The band sells 220 packages in all and earns a total of $695. Find the number of each type of package sold.

3. Solve by elimination.
$15x + 3y = 9$
$10x + 7y = -4$

Lesson 6-4

Applications of Linear Systems

Lesson Objective	California Content Standards
• Write systems of linear equations	9.0, 15.0

Take Note

Methods for Solving Systems of Linear Equations

Graphing   Use graphing for solving systems that are easily graphed. If the point of intersection does not have integers for coordinates, find the exact solution by using one of the methods below.

Substitution   Use substitution for solving systems when one variable has a coefficient of 1 or -1.

Elimination   Use elimination for solving any system.

Examples

❶ Writing Systems A chemist has one solution that is 50% acid. She has another solution that is 25% acid. How many liters of each type of acid solution should she combine to get 10 liters of a 40% acid solution?

Define Let $\boxed{a}$ = volume of the 50% solution.

Let $\boxed{b}$ = volume of the 25% solution.

Relate volume of solution   amount of acid

Write $\boxed{} + \boxed{} = 10$ $\boxed{}a + \boxed{}b = \boxed{}(10)$

Step 1 Choose one of the equations and solve for a variable.

$a + b = 10$ **Solve for a.**

$a = 10 - \boxed{}$ **Subtract $\boxed{}$ from each side.**

Step 2 Find b.

$\boxed{}a + \boxed{}b = \boxed{}(10)$

$0.5\big(\boxed{}\big) + 0.25b = 0.4(10)$ **Substitute $\boxed{}$ for a. Use parentheses.**

$5 - \boxed{} + 0.25b = 0.4(10)$ **Use the Distributive Property.**

$5 - \boxed{} = \boxed{}$ **Simplify.**

$-0.25b = \boxed{}$ **Subtract $\boxed{}$ from each side.**

$b = \boxed{}$ **Divide each side by $\boxed{}$.**

Step 3 Find a. Substitute $\boxed{}$ for b in either equation.

$a + \boxed{} = 10$ **Solve for a.**

$a = \boxed{}$ **Subtract $\boxed{}$ from each side.**

You need $\boxed{}$ L of 50% solution and $\boxed{}$ L of 25% solution.

❷ **Finding a Break-Even Point** Suppose you have a typing service. You buy a personal computer for $1750 on which to do your typing. You charge $5.50 per page for typing. Expenses are $.50 per page for ink, paper, electricity, and other expenses. How many pages must you type to break even?

Define Let $\boxed{p}$ = the number of pages.

Let $\boxed{d}$ = the amount of dollars of expenses or income.

Relate

| Expenses are per-page expenses plus computer purchase. | | Income is price times pages typed. |

Write $\boxed{} = 0.5\boxed{} + 1750$ $\qquad$ $\boxed{} = 5.5\boxed{}$

Use substitution since it is easy to substitute for d with these equations.

$d = 0.5p + 1750$ $\quad$ **Start with one equation.**

$\boxed{} = 0.5p + 1750$ $\quad$ **Substitute** $\boxed{}$ **for** d.

$\boxed{} = 1750$ $\quad$ **Solve for** p.

$p = \boxed{}$

To break even, you must type $\boxed{}$ pages.

CA Standards Check

1. Suppose a chemist combines a 25% acid solution and a 50% acid solution to make 40 L of 45% acid solution. How many liters of each solution did she use?

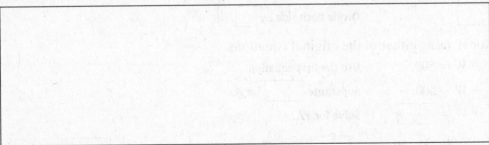

2. Suppose a car club publishes a newsletter. Expenses are $.35 for printing and mailing each copy, plus $770 total for research and writing. The newsletter costs $.55 per copy. How many copies of the newsletter must the club sell to break even?

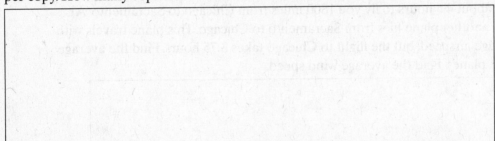

Name_____ Class_____ Date_____

Example

❸ Finding Speed Suppose it takes you 6.8 hours to fly about 2800 miles from Miami, Florida, to Seattle, Washington. At the same time, a friend flies from Seattle to Miami. His plane travels at the same average airspeed, but his flight only takes 5.6 hours. Find the average airspeed of the planes. Find the average wind speed.

Define Let $\boxed{A}$ = the airspeed.   Let $\boxed{W}$ = the wind speed.

Relate   with tail wind   with head wind

(rate)(time) = distance   (rate)(time) = distance

$\boxed{(A + W)}$ (time) = distance $\boxed{(A - W)}$ (time) = distance

Write $\boxed{}\ 5.6 = \boxed{}$ $\boxed{}\ 6.8 = \boxed{}$

Step 1 Solve by elimination. First divide to get the variables on the left side of each equation with coefficients of 1 or −1.

$(A + W)5.6 = 2800 \rightarrow A + W = \boxed{}$ **Divide each side by** $\boxed{}$.

$(A - W)6.8 = 2800 \rightarrow A - W \approx \boxed{}$ **Divide each side by** $\boxed{}$.

Step 2 Eliminate W.

$$\begin{array}{rcr} A & + W = & 500 \\ A & - W = & 412 \\ \hline \end{array}$$ **Add the equations to eliminate W.**

$\boxed{} + \boxed{} = \boxed{}$

Step 3 Solve for A.

$A = \boxed{}$ **Divide each side by** $\boxed{}$.

Step 4 Solve for W using either of the original equations.

$A + W = 500$ **Use the first equation.**

$\boxed{} + W = 500$ **Substitute** $\boxed{}$ **for A.**

$W = \boxed{}$ **Solve for W.**

The average airspeed of the planes is $\boxed{}$ mi/h. The average wind speed is $\boxed{}$ mi/h.

CA Standards Check

3. A plane takes about 4.5 hours to fly you 1800 miles from Chicago to Sacramento. At the same time, another plane flies from Sacramento to Chicago. This plane travels with the same average airspeed, but the flight to Chicago takes 3.75 hours. Find the average airspeed of the planes. Find the average wind speed.

Name_____ Class_____ Date_____

Lesson 6-5

Linear Inequalities

Lesson Objectives	California Content Standards
• Graph linear inequalities • Write and use linear inequalities when modeling real-world situations	6.0

Vocabulary

A linear inequality is _____

_____

Each point in the region is a [_____] of the inequality.

The solutions of an inequality are _____

_____

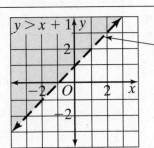

Each point on a *dashed* boundary line is not a solution.

Each point on a *solid* boundary line is a solution.

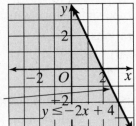

Example

① **Rewriting to Graph an Inequality** Graph $4x - 3y \geq 6$.
Solve $4x - 3y \geq 6$ for y.
$4x - 3y \geq 6$

$-3y \geq \boxed{} + 6$ Subtract $\boxed{}$ from each side.

$y \boxed{} \boxed{} x - 2$ Divide each side by $\boxed{}$. Reverse the inequality symbol.

Graph $y = \boxed{} x - \boxed{}$. The coordinates of the points on the boundary line make the inequality true. So, use a $\boxed{}$ line.

Since $y \leq \boxed{} x - \boxed{}$, shade $\boxed{}$ the boundary line.

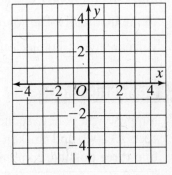

CA Standards Check

1. a. Graph $y \geq 3x - 1$.

b. Graph $6x + 8y \geq 12$.

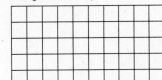

Example

❷ **Application** Suppose your budget allows you to spend no more than $24 for decorations for a party. Streamers cost $2 a roll and tablecloths cost $6 each. Use intercepts to graph the inequality that represents the situation. Find three possible combinations of streamers and tablecloths you can buy.

Relate | cost of streamers | plus | cost of tablecloths | is less than or equal to | total budget |

Define Let ⬚ s = the number of rolls of streamers.

Let ⬚ t = the number of tablecloths.

Write   2⬚   +   6⬚   ≤   ⬚

Graph $2s + 6t = 24$ by graphing the intercepts $(\boxed{}, \boxed{})$ and $(\boxed{}, \boxed{})$. The coordinates of the points on the boundary line make the inequality true. So, use a $\boxed{}$ line.

Graph only in Quadrant I, since you cannot buy a negative amount of decorations.

Test the point $(0, 0)$.

$$2s + 6t \le 24$$

$$2\left(\boxed{}\right) + 6\left(\boxed{}\right) \le 24 \quad \textbf{Substitute (0, 0) for (s, t).}$$

$$\boxed{} \le 24 \quad \textbf{Since the inequality is true, (0, 0) is a solution.}$$

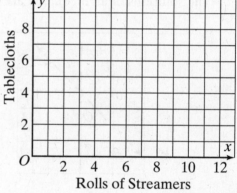

Shade the region containing $(0, 0)$.

Since the boundary line is included in the graph, the intercepts are also solutions to the inequality. The solution $(9, 1)$ means that if you buy $\boxed{}$ rolls of streamers, you can buy $\boxed{}$ tablecloth. Three solutions are $(9, 1)$, $\left(\boxed{}, \boxed{}\right)$, and $\left(\boxed{}, \boxed{}\right)$.

CA Standards Check

2. Suppose you plan to spend no more than $24 on meat for a cookout. Hamburger costs $3.00/lb and chicken wings cost $2.40/lb. Write and graph an equation to find three possible combinations of hamburger and chicken wings you can buy.

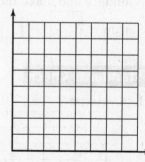

Name_____ Class_____ Date _____

Lesson 6-6

Systems of Linear Inequalities

Lesson Objectives	California Content Standards
• Solve systems of linear inequalities by graphing • Model real-world situations using systems of linear inequalities	9.0

Vocabulary

A system of linear inequalities is _____

_____

A solution of a system of linear inequalities is _____

_____

Example

1 **Writing a System of Inequalities From a Graph** Write a system of inequalities from each shaded region below.

boundary: $y = -\frac{1}{2}x + 2$

The region lies [   ] the boundary line, so the inequality is $y \boxed{} -\frac{1}{2}x + 2$.

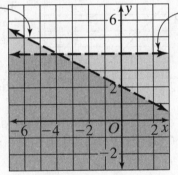

boundary: $y = 4$

The region lies [   ] the boundary line, so the inequality is $y \boxed{} 4$.

system for the darkened region: $y < -\frac{1}{2}x + 2$
$y < 4$

CA Standards Check

1. Write a system of inequalities for the dark region in each of the following graphs.

a. [   ]

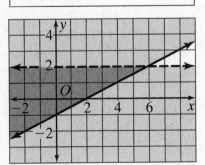

b. [   ]

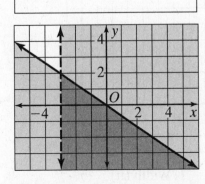

Name_____ Class_____ Date_____

Example

② **Application** You need to make a fence for a dog run. The length of the run can be no more than 60 ft, and you have 136 feet of fencing that you can use. What are the possible dimensions of the dog run?

Relate | the length | is no more than | 60 ft | | the perimeter | is no more than | 136 ft |

Define Let $\boxed{\ell}$ = length of the dog run.

Let $\boxed{w}$ = width of the dog run.

Write $\boxed{}$ ≤ $\boxed{}$ $\quad$ $2\boxed{} + 2\boxed{}$ ≤ $\boxed{}$

Solve by graphing. $\quad \ell \le \boxed{}$

$\qquad\qquad\qquad 2\ell + 2w \le \boxed{}$

$\ell \le 60$

Shade $\boxed{}$
$\ell = 60$.

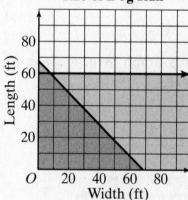

Size of Dog Run

$2\ell + 2w \le 136$

Graph the intercepts

$\left(\boxed{}, \boxed{}\right)$ and $\left(\boxed{}, \boxed{}\right)$.

Test $(0, 0)$.

$2\left(\boxed{}\right) + 2\left(\boxed{}\right) \le 136$

$\qquad\qquad \left(\boxed{}\right) \le 136$

Shade $\boxed{}$ $2\ell + 2w = 136$.

The solutions are the coordinates of the points that lie in the darkened region and on the parts of the lines $\ell = 60$ and $2\ell + 2w = 136$ that border the dark region.

CA Standards Check

2. Suppose you want to fence a rectangular garden plot. You want the length of the garden to be at least 50 ft and the perimeter to be no more than 140 ft. Solve by graphing to show all of the possible dimensions of the garden.

Dimensions of Garden

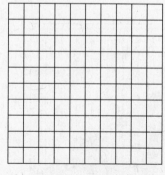

Width (ft)

Name_____ Class_____ Date _____

Example

❸ **Application** Suppose you have two jobs, babysitting for $5 per hour and sacking groceries for $6 per hour. You can work no more than 20 hours each week, but you need to earn at least $90 per week. How many hours can you work at each job?

Relate | the number of hours worked | is less than or equal to | 20 | | the amount earned | is at least | 90 |

Define Let ⬚ b = hours of babysitting.

Let ⬚ s = hours of sacking groceries.

Write ⬚ + ⬚ ≤ ⬚   5⬚ + 6⬚ ≥ ⬚

Solve by graphing. $b + s \leq 20$
$5b + 6s \geq 90$

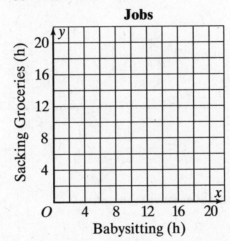

Jobs

The solutions are all the coordinates of the points that are nonnegative numbers in the shaded region and on the lines $b + s = 20$ and $5b + 6s = 90$.

CA Standards Check

3. a. Give two solutions from the graph in Example 3.

b. Critical Thinking Why are the solutions to the problem only nonnegative numbers?

Lesson 7-1

Zero and Negative Exponents

Lesson Objectives	California Content Standards
• Simplify expressions with zero and negative exponents • Evaluate exponential expressions	2.0

Take Note

Zero as an Exponent

For every nonzero number a, [   ].

Examples $5^0 = 1$ $(-2)^0 = 1$ $(1.02)^0 = 1$ $\left(\frac{1}{3}\right)^0 = 1$

Negative Exponent

For every nonzero number a and integer n, $a^{-n} =$ [   ].

Examples $6^{-4} = \frac{1}{6^4}$ $(-8)^{-1} = \frac{1}{(-8)^1}$

Examples

❶ Simplifying a Power Simplify:

  a. $3^{-2} =$ [   ]   **Use the definition of negative exponent.**

           $=$ [   ]   **Simplify.**

  b. $(-22.4)^0 =$ [   ]   **Use the definition of zero as an exponent.**

❷ Simplifying an Exponential Expression Simplify each expression.

  $\dfrac{1}{x^{-3}} = 1 \div x^{-3}$ **Rewrite using a division symbol.**

        $= 1 \div \dfrac{1}{\boxed{}}$ **Use the definition of negative exponent.**

        $= 1 \cdot$ [   ]   **Multiply by the reciprocal of $\frac{1}{x^3}$, which is** [   ] **.**

        $=$ [   ]   **Identity Property of Multiplication**

CA Standards Check

1. Simplify each expression.

  a. 3^{-4} **b.** $(-7)^0$ **c.** $(-4)^{-3}$

  [   ]   [   ]   [   ]

Daily Notetaking Guide

Name_____ Class_____ Date _____

Example

③ Evaluating an Exponential Expression Evaluate $4x^2y^{-3}$ for $x = 3$ and $y = -2$.

$$4x^2y^{-3} = 4\left(\boxed{}\right)^2\left(\boxed{}\right)^{-3}$$ **Substitute** $\boxed{}$ **for x and** $\boxed{}$ **for y.**

$$= \frac{4\left(\boxed{}\right)^2}{\left(\boxed{}\right)^3}$$ **Use the definition of negative exponent.**

$$= \frac{36}{-8} = \boxed{}$$ **Simplify.**

CA Standards Check

2. Simplify each expression.

a. $11m^{-5}$

b. $7s^{-4}t^2$

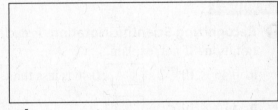

c. $\dfrac{2}{a^{-3}}$

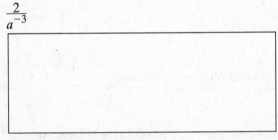

d. $\dfrac{n^{-5}}{v^2}$

3. Evaluate each expression for $n = -2$ and $w = 5$.

a. $n^{-3}w^0$

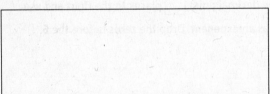

b. $\dfrac{n^{-1}}{w^2}$

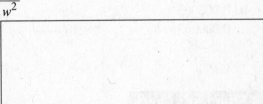

c. $\dfrac{w^0}{n^4}$

d. $\dfrac{1}{nw^{-2}}$

Lesson 7-2

Scientific Notation

Lesson Objectives	California Content Standards
• Write numbers in scientific and standard notation • Use scientific notation	2.0

Take Note

Scientific Notation

A number in scientific notation is written as the product of two factors in the form $a \times 10^n$, where n is an integer and $1 \leq a < 10$.

Examples 3.4×10^6 5.43×10^{13} 2.1×10^{-10}

Examples

❶ Recognizing Scientific Notation Is each number written in scientific notation? If not, explain.

a. 0.46×10^4 ⬚ ; 0.46 is less than ⬚ .

b. 3.25×10^{-2} ⬚

c. 13.2×10^6 ⬚ ; ⬚ is greater than ⬚ .

❷ Writing a Number in Scientific Notation Write each number in scientific notation.

a. 234,000,000

$234{,}000{,}000 = \boxed{} \times 10^{\boxed{}}$

Move the decimal point ⬚ places to the left and use ⬚ as an exponent. Drop the zeros after the 4.

b. 0.000063

$0.000063 = \boxed{} \times 10^{\boxed{}}$

Move the decimal point ⬚ places to the right and use ⬚ as an exponent. Drop the zeros before the 6.

CA Standards Check

1. Is each number written in scientific notation? If not, explain.

a. 3.42×10^{-7}

b. 52×10^4

c. 0.04×10^{-5}

Example

❸ **Writing a Number in Standard Notation** Write each number in standard notation.

a. elephant's mass: 8.8×10^4 kg

$$8.8 \times 10^4 = \boxed{}$$

$$= \boxed{} \text{ kg}$$

A positive exponent indicates a number greater than 10. Move the decimal point $\boxed{}$ places to the right.

b. ant's mass: 7.3×10^{-5} kg

$$7.3 \times 10^{-5} = \boxed{}$$

$$= \boxed{} \text{ kg}$$

A negative exponent indicates a number between 0 and 1. Move the decimal point $\boxed{}$ places to the left.

CA Standards Check

2. Write each number in scientific notation.

a. 267,000

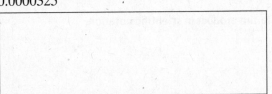

b. 46,205,000

c. 0.0000325

d. 0.000000009

3. Write each number in standard notation.

a. 3.2×10^{12}

b. 5.07×10^4

c. 5.6×10^{-4}

d. 8.3×10^{-2}

Examples

❹ **Using Scientific Notation to Order Numbers** Order 0.0063×10^5, 6.03×10^4, 6103, and 63.1×10^3 from least to greatest.

Write each number in scientific notation.

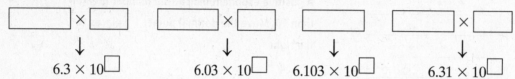

$$6.3 \times 10^{\square} \qquad 6.03 \times 10^{\square} \qquad 6.103 \times 10^{\square} \qquad 6.31 \times 10^{\square}$$

Order the powers of 10. Arrange the decimals with the same power of 10 in order.

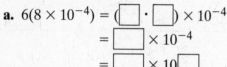

$$\boxed{} \times 10^{\square} \qquad \boxed{} \times 10^{\square} \qquad \boxed{} \times 10^{\square} \qquad \boxed{} \times 10^{\square}$$

Write the original numbers in order.

$$\boxed{} \times 10^{\square} \qquad \boxed{} \qquad \boxed{} \times 10^{\square} \qquad \boxed{} \times 10^{\square}$$

❺ **Multiplying a Number in Scientific Notation** Simplify. Write each answer using scientific notation.

a. $6(8 \times 10^{-4}) = (\boxed{} \cdot \boxed{}) \times 10^{-4}$ **Use the Associative Property of Multiplication.**

$\qquad\qquad = \boxed{} \times 10^{-4}$ **Simplify inside the parentheses.**

$\qquad\qquad = \boxed{} \times 10^{\square}$ **Write the product in scientific notation.**

b. $0.3(1.3 \times 10^3) = (\boxed{} \cdot \boxed{}) \times 10^3$ **Use the Associative Property of Multiplication.**

$\qquad\qquad = \boxed{} \times 10^3$ **Simplify inside the parentheses.**

$\qquad\qquad = \boxed{} \times 10^{\square}$ **Write the product in scientific notation.**

CA Standards Check

4. Order 60.2×10^{-5}, 63×10^4, 0.067×10^3, 61×10^{-2} from least to greatest.

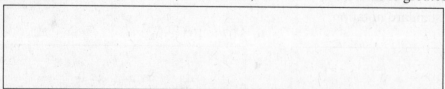

5. Simplify. Write each answer using scientific notation.

    a. $2.5(6 \times 10^3)$ **b.** $0.4(2 \times 10^{-9})$

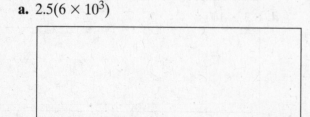

Lesson 7-3

Multiplication Properties of Exponents

Lesson Objectives	California Content Standards
• Multiply powers • Work with scientific notation	2.0, 10.0

Take Note

Multiplying Powers With the Same Base

For every nonzero number a and integers m and n, $a^m \cdot a^n = $ ☐ .

Example $3^5 \cdot 3^4 = 3^{5+4} = 3^9$

Example

① **Multiplying Powers** Rewrite each expression using each base only once.

a. $7^3 \cdot 7^2 = 7^3 \boxed{} 2$

$= \boxed{}$

☐ exponents of powers with the same base.

Simplify the sum of the exponents.

b. $6^8 \cdot 6^{-8} = 6^8 \boxed{}(-8)$

$= \boxed{}$

$= \boxed{}$

☐ exponents of powers with the same base.

Simplify the sum of the exponents.

Use the definition of zero as an exponent.

CA Standards Check

1. Rewrite each expression using each base only once.

a. $5^3 \cdot 5^6$

b. $2^4 \cdot 2^{-3}$

c. $7^{-3} \cdot 7^2 \cdot 7^6$

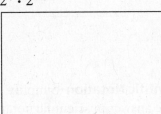

Example

❷ **Multiplying Powers in an Algebraic Expression** Simplify each expression.

a. $4x^6 \cdot 5x^{-4} = (\boxed{} \cdot \boxed{})(x^6 \cdot x^{-4})$ $\boxed{}$ **Property of Multiplication**

$= \boxed{}(x^{\boxed{} + (\boxed{})})$ **Add exponents of powers with the same base.**

$= \boxed{}$ **Simplify.**

b. $2q \cdot 3p^3 \cdot 4q^4 = (2 \cdot \boxed{} \cdot 4)(p^3)(q \cdot \boxed{})$ **Commutative and Associative Properties of Multiplication**

$= \boxed{}(p^3)(\boxed{} \cdot \boxed{})$ **Multiply the coefficients. Write q as $\boxed{}$.**

$= \boxed{}(p^3)(q^{\boxed{}})$ **Add exponents of powers with the same base.**

$= \boxed{}$ **Simplify.**

CA Standards Check

2. Simplify each expression.

a. $n^2 \cdot n^3 \cdot 7n$

b. $2y^3 \cdot 7x^2 \cdot 2y^4$

c. $m^2 \cdot n^{-2} \cdot 7m$

Example

❸ **Multiplying Numbers in Scientific Notation** Simplify $(3 \times 10^{-3})(7 \times 10^{-5})$. Write the answer in scientific notation.

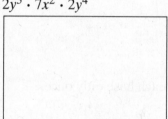

$(3 \times 10^{-3})(7 \times 10^{-5}) = (3 \cdot \boxed{})(10^{\boxed{}} \cdot 10^{\boxed{}})$ **Commutative and Associative Properties of Multiplication**

$= \boxed{} \times 10^{\boxed{}}$ **Simplify.**

$= 2.1 \times 10^{\boxed{}} \cdot 10^{\boxed{}}$ **Write 21 in scientific notation.**

$= 2.1 \times 10^{\boxed{} + \boxed{}}$ **Add exponents of powers with the same base.**

$= 2.1 \times 10^{\boxed{}}$ **Simplify the sum of the exponents.**

Name_____ Class_____ Date _____

CA Standards Check

3. Simplify each expression. Write each answer in scientific notation.

a. $(2.5 \times 10^8)(6 \times 10^3)$

b. $(1.5 \times 10^{-2})(3 \times 10^4)$

c. $(9 \times 10^{-6})(7 \times 10^{-9})$

Example

❹ Application The speed of light is 3×10^8 m/s. If there are 1×10^{-3} km in 1 m, and 3.6×10^3 s in 1 h, find the speed of light in km/h.

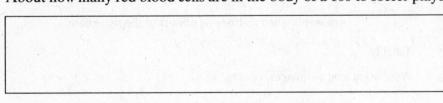

Speed of light $= \dfrac{\text{meters}}{\text{seconds}} \cdot \dfrac{\text{kilometers}}{\text{meters}} \cdot \dfrac{\text{seconds}}{\text{hour}}$ **Use dimensional analysis.**

$= \left(\boxed{} \times 10^{\boxed{}}\right)\frac{m}{s} \cdot \left(\boxed{} \times 10^{\boxed{}}\right)\frac{km}{m} \cdot \left(\boxed{} \times 10^{\boxed{}}\right)\frac{s}{h}$ **Substitute.**

$= \left(\boxed{} \cdot \boxed{} \cdot \boxed{}\right) \times \left(10^{\boxed{}} \cdot 10^{-3} \cdot 10^{\boxed{}}\right)$ **Commutative and Associative Properties of Multiplication**

$= \boxed{} \times \left(10^{\boxed{} + \boxed{} + \boxed{}}\right)$ **Simplify.**

$= 10.8 \times 10^{\boxed{}}$ **Add exponents.**

$= 1.08 \times 10^{\boxed{}} \cdot 10^{\boxed{}}$ **Write 10.8 in scientific notation.**

$= \boxed{} \times 10^{\boxed{}}$ **Add the exponents.**

CA Standards Check

4. A human body contains about 3.2×10^4 microliters of blood for each pound of body weight. Each microliter of blood contains about 5×10^6 red blood cells. About how many red blood cells are in the body of a 160-lb soccer player?

Lesson 7-4

More Multiplication Properties of Exponents

Lesson Objectives	California Content Standards
• Raise a power to a power • Raise a product to a power	2.0, 10.0

Take Note

Raising a Power to a Power

For every nonzero number a and integers m and n, $(a^m)^n = $ ☐ .

Examples $(5^4)^2 = 5^{4 \cdot 2} = 5^8$ $(n^2)^5 = n^{2 \cdot 5} = n^{10}$

Raising a Product to a Power

For every nonzero number a and b and integer n, $(ab)^n = $ ☐ .

Example $(3x)^4 = 3^4 x^4 = 81x^4$

Examples

❶ Simplifying a Power Raised to a Power Simplify $(a^3)^4$.

$(a^3)^4 = a^{3\,\boxed{}\,4}$ ☐ **exponents when raising a power to a power.**

$\quad = a^{\boxed{}}$ **Simplify.**

❷ Simplifying an Expression With Powers Simplify $b^2(b^3)^{-2}$.

$b^2(b^3)^{-2} = b^2 \cdot b^{3\,\boxed{}\,(-2)}$ ☐ **exponents in $(b^3)^{-2}$.**

$\quad = b^2 \cdot b^{\boxed{}}$ **Simplify.**

$\quad = b^{2\,\boxed{}\,(-6)}$ ☐ **exponents when multiplying powers of the same base.**

$\quad = b^{\boxed{}}$ **Simplify.**

$\quad = \boxed{}$ **Write using only positive exponents.**

CA Standards Check

1. Simplify.

  a. $(a^4)^7$ **b.** $(a^{-4})^7$

2. Simplify each expression.

  a. $t^2(t^7)^{-2}$ **b.** $(a^4)^2 \cdot (a^2)^5$

Examples

❸ **Simplifying a Product Raised to a Power** Simplify $(4xy^3)^2(x^3)^{-3}$.

$(4xy^3)^2(x^3)^{-3} = 4^{\square}x^{\square}(y^3)^{\square} \cdot (x^3)^{-3}$ Raise the three factors to the second power.

$\qquad = 4^2 \cdot x^2 \cdot y^{\square} \cdot x^{\boxed{}}$ $\boxed{}$ exponents of a power raised to a power.

$\qquad = 4^2 \cdot x^2 \cdot x^{\boxed{}} \cdot y^{\square}$ Use the Commutative Property of Multiplication.

$\qquad = 4^2 \cdot x^{\boxed{}} \cdot y^6$ Add exponents of powers with the same base.

$\qquad = \boxed{}$ Simplify.

❹ **Application** An object has a mass of 10^2 kg. The expression $10^2 \cdot (3 \times 10^8)^2$ describes the amount of resting energy, in joules, the object contains. Simplify the expression.

$10^2 \cdot (3 \times 10^8)^2 = 10^{\square} \cdot 3^{\square} \cdot (10^8)^{\square}$ Raise each factor within parentheses to the second power.

$\qquad = 10^{\square} \cdot 3^{\square} \cdot 10^{\boxed{}}$ Simplify $(10^8)^2$.

$\qquad = 3^{\square} \cdot 10^{\square} \cdot 10^{\boxed{}}$ Use the Commutative Property of Multiplication.

$\qquad = 3^{\square} \cdot 10^{\square} {}^{+} {}^{\boxed{}}$ Add exponents of powers with the same base.

$\qquad = \boxed{} \times 10^{\boxed{}}$ Simplify. Write in scientific notation.

CA Standards Check

3. Simplify each expression.

a. $(2z)^4$

b. $(4g^5)^{-2}$

c. $(2a^3)^5(3ab^2)^3$

d. $(6mn)^3(5m^{-3})^2$

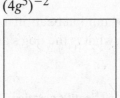 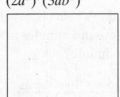 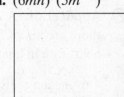

4. The mass of a feather is 10^{-5}. Simplify the expression $(10^{-5})(3 \times 10^8)^2$ to find the amount of resting energy in joules the feather contains.

Lesson 7-5

Division Properties of Exponents

Lesson Objectives	California Content Standards
• Divide powers with the same base • Raise a quotient to a power	2.0, 10.0

Take Note

Dividing Powers With the Same Base

For every nonzero number a and integers m and n, $\dfrac{a^m}{a^n} = \boxed{}$.

Example $\dfrac{3^7}{3^3} = 3^{7-3} = 3^4$

Raising a Quotient to a Power

For every nonzero numbers a and b and integer n, $\left(\dfrac{a}{b}\right)^n = \boxed{}$.

Example $\left(\dfrac{4}{5}\right)^3 = \dfrac{4^3}{5^3} = \dfrac{64}{125}$

Examples

① **Simplifying an Algebraic Expression** Simplify.

$\dfrac{p^3 j^{-4}}{p^{-3} j^6} = p^{3-\left(\boxed{}\right)} j^{-4\,\boxed{}\,6}$ $\boxed{}$ exponents when dividing powers with the same base.

$= p^{\boxed{}} j^{\boxed{}}$ Simplify the exponents.

$= \boxed{}$ Rewrite using positive exponents.

② **Application** A small dog's heart beats about 64 million beats in a year. If there are about 530 thousand minutes in a year, what is the dog's average heart rate in beats per minute?

$\dfrac{64 \text{ million beats}}{530 \text{ thousand min}} = \dfrac{6.4 \times 10^{\boxed{}} \text{beats}}{5.3 \times 10^{\boxed{}} \text{min}}$ Write in scientific notation.

$= \dfrac{6.4}{\boxed{}} \times 10^{7-\boxed{}}$ $\boxed{}$ exponents when dividing powers with the same base.

$= \dfrac{6.4}{\boxed{}} \times 10^{\boxed{}}$ Simplify the exponent.

$\approx 1.21 \times 10^{\boxed{}}$ Divide. Round to the nearest hundredth.

$= \boxed{} \dfrac{\text{beats}}{\text{min}}$ Write in standard notation.

❸ Raising a Quotient to a Power Simplify $\left(\dfrac{3}{y^3}\right)^4$.

$$\left(\dfrac{3}{y^3}\right)^4 = \dfrac{3^{\boxed{}}}{(y^3)^{\boxed{}}}$$ Raise the numerator and the denominator to the $\boxed{}$ power.

$$= \dfrac{3^4}{y^{\boxed{}}}$$ Multiply the exponents in the denominator.

$$= \boxed{}$$ Simplify.

CA Standards Check

1. Simplify each expression.

  a. $\dfrac{b^4}{b^9}$

  b. $\dfrac{a^2 b}{a^4 b^3}$

  c. $\dfrac{m^{-1} n^2}{m^3 n}$

  d. $\dfrac{x^2 y^{-1} z^4}{x y^4 z^{-3}}$

2. Find each quotient. Write each answer in scientific notation.

  a. $\dfrac{2 \times 10^3}{8 \times 10^8}$

  b. $\dfrac{7.5 \times 10^{12}}{2.5 \times 10^{-4}}$

  c. In 2000 the total amount of glass recycled in the United States was 2.7 million tons. The population of the United States in 2000 was 281.4 million people. On average, about how many tons of glass were recycled per person?

3. Simplify each expression.

  a. $\left(\dfrac{3}{x^2}\right)^2$

  b. $\left(\dfrac{x}{y^2}\right)^3$

Example

④ Simplifying an Exponential Expression

a. Simplify $\left(\frac{2}{3}\right)^{-3}$.

$$\left(\frac{2}{3}\right)^{-3} = \left(\boxed{}\right)^{\boxed{}}$$ Rewrite using the reciprocal of $\frac{2}{3}$.

$$= \frac{3^{\boxed{}}}{2^{\boxed{}}}$$ Raise the numerator and denominator to the $\boxed{}$ power.

$$= \boxed{} \text{ or } \boxed{}$$ Simplify.

b. Simplify $\left(-\frac{4b}{c}\right)^{-2}$.

$$\left(-\frac{4b}{c}\right)^{-2} = \left(\boxed{}\right)^{2}$$ Rewrite using the reciprocal of $-\frac{4b}{c}$.

$$= \left(\frac{\boxed{}}{4b}\right)^{2}$$ Write the fraction with a negative numerator.

$$= \frac{(-c)^{\boxed{}}}{(4b)^{\boxed{}}}$$ Raise the numerator and denominator to the $\boxed{}$ power.

$$= \boxed{}$$ Simplify.

CA Standards Check

4. Simplify each expression.

a. $\left(\frac{3}{4}\right)^{-3}$

b. $\left(\frac{-1}{2}\right)^{-5}$

c. $\left(\frac{2r}{s}\right)^{-1}$

d. $\left(\frac{7a}{m}\right)^{-2}$

Lesson 8-1

Lesson Objectives	California Content Standards
• Describe polynomials • Add and subtract polynomials	10.0

Vocabulary

A monomial is _____

_____

The degree of a monomial is _____

_____

A polynomial is _____

_____

In the standard form of a polynomial, _____

_____

The degree of a polynomial is _____

_____

A binomial is _____

A trinomial is _____

Example

① Degree of a Monomial Find the degree of each monomial.

a. 18   Degree: ▢   The degree of a nonzero constant is ▢.

b. $3xy^3$ Degree: ▢   The exponents are ▢ and ▢. Their sum is ▢.

c. $6c$ Degree: ▢ $6c = 6c^1$. The exponent is ▢.

CA Standards Check

1. Find the degree of $9m^4n^2$.

Examples

❷ **Classifying Polynomials** Write each polynomial in standard form. Then name each polynomial based on its degree and the number of its terms.

a. $-2 + 7x$

$7x - \boxed{}$ Place terms in order.

$\boxed{}$ $\boxed{}$

b. $3x^5 - 2 - 2x^5 + 7x$

$3x^5 - \boxed{} + 7x - \boxed{}$ Place terms in order.

$\boxed{} + 7x - 2$ Combine like terms.

$\boxed{}$ degree $\boxed{}$

❸ **Adding Polynomials** Simplify $(6x^2 + 3x + 7) + (2x^2 - 6x - 4)$.

Line up like terms. Then add the coefficients.

$$
\begin{array}{rrrr}
6x^2 & + \quad 3x & + & 7 \\
2x^2 & - \quad 6x & - & 4 \\
\hline
\boxed{} & - \boxed{} & + \boxed{}
\end{array}
$$

❹ **Subtracting Polynomials** Simplify $(2x^3 + 4x^2 - 6) - (5x^3 + 2x - 2)$.

Method 1 Subtract vertically.

Line up like terms. Then add the coefficients.

$$
\begin{array}{rlr}
2x^3 & + \boxed{} & - \quad 6 \\
-(5x^3 & + \boxed{} & - \quad 2) \\
\hline
2x^3 & + \boxed{} & - \quad 6 \\
-5x^3 & \boxed{}\boxed{}\boxed{} & 2 \\
\hline
\boxed{} & + \quad 4x^2 \quad - \quad 2x & - \boxed{}
\end{array}
$$

Line up like terms.

Add the opposite of each term in the polynomial being subtracted.

Method 2 Subtract horizontally.

$(2x^3 + 4x^2 - 6) - (5x^3 + 2x - 2)$

$= 2x^3 + 4x^2 - 6 \boxed{} 5x^3 \boxed{} \boxed{} + 2$ Write the opposite of each term in the polynomial being subtracted.

$= \left(2x^3 - \boxed{}\right) + 4x^2 - 2x + \left(\boxed{} + 2\right)$ Group like terms.

$= \boxed{} + 4x^2 - \boxed{} - \boxed{}$ Simplify.

Name_____ Class_____ Date_____

CA Standards Check

2. Write each polynomial in standard form. Then name each polynomial based on its degree and the number of its terms.

   a. $6x^2 + 7 - 9x^4$

   b. $3y - 4 - y^3$

   c. $8 + 7v - 11v$

3. Simplify each sum.

   a. $(12m^2 + 4) + (8m^2 + 5)$

   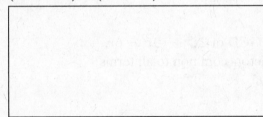

   b. $(t^2 - 6) + (3t^2 + 11)$

   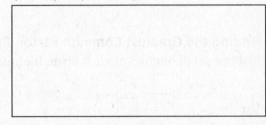

   c. $(9w^3 + 8w^2) + (7w^3 + 4)$

   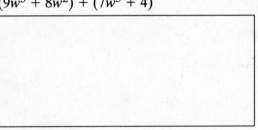

   d. $(2p^3 + 6p^2 + 10p) + (9p^3 + 11p^2 + 3p)$

   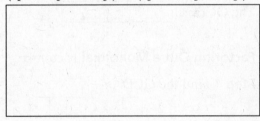

4. Simplify each difference.

   a. $(v^3 + 6v^2 - v) - (9v^3 - 7v^2 + 3v)$

   b. $(30d^3 - 29d^2 - 3d) - (2d^3 + d^2)$

   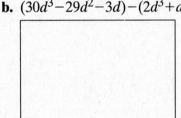

   c. $(4x^2 + 5x + 1) - (6x^2 + x + 8)$

Lesson 8-2

Multiplying and Factoring

Lesson Objectives	California Content Standards
• Multiply a polynomial by a monomial • Factor a monomial from a polynomial	10.0, 11.0

Examples

❶ Multiplying a Monomial and a Trinomial Simplify $-2g^2(3g^3 + 6g - 5)$.

$-2g^2(3g^3 + 6g - 5)$

$= \boxed{}(3g^3) - 2g^2\left(\boxed{}\right) - 2g^2\left(\boxed{}\right)$ Use the Distributive Property.

$= -6g^{2+3} - 12g^{2+\square} + \boxed{}$ Multiply the coefficients and add the exponents of powers with the same base.

$= \boxed{} - \boxed{} + 10g^2$ Simplify.

❷ Finding the Greatest Common Factor Find the GCD of $2x^4 + 10x^2 - 6x$.

List the prime factors of each term. Identify the factors common to all terms.

$2x^4 = 2 \cdot x \cdot \boxed{} \cdot x \cdot \boxed{}$

$10x^2 = 2 \cdot \boxed{} \cdot x \cdot \boxed{}$

$6x = \boxed{} \cdot 3 \cdot x$

The GCD is $\boxed{}$.

❸ Factoring Out a Monomial Factor $4x^3 + 12x^2 - 16x$.

Step 1 Find the GCD.

$4x^3 = 2 \cdot \boxed{} \cdot x \cdot \boxed{} \cdot \boxed{}$

$12x^2 = 2 \cdot 2 \cdot \boxed{} \cdot x \cdot x$

$16x = 2 \cdot \boxed{} \cdot 2 \cdot \boxed{} \cdot x$

The GCD is $\boxed{}$.

Step 2 Factor out the GCD.

$4x^3 + 12x^2 - 16x$

$= 4x\left(\boxed{}\right) + \boxed{}(3x) + 4x(-4)$

$= \boxed{}\left(x^2 + \boxed{} - \boxed{}\right)$

Name_____ Class_____ Date _____

CA Standards Check

1. Simplify each product.

   a. $4b(5b^2 + b + 6)$

   b. $-7h(3h^2 - 8h - 1)$

   c. $2x(x^2 - 6x + 5)$

2. Find the common factor of the terms of each polynomial.

   a. $5v^5 + 10v^3$

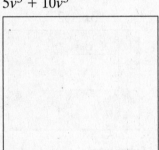

   b. $3t^2 - 18$

   c. $4b^3 - 2b^2 - 6b$

3. Use the common factor to factor each polynomial.

   a. $8x^2 - 12x$

   b. $5d^3 + 10d$

   c. $6m^3 - 12m^2 - 24m$

Lesson 8-3

Multiplying Binomials

Lesson Objectives	California Content Standards
• Multiply binomials using FOIL • Multiply trinomials by binomials	10.0

Examples

❶ Multiplying Using FOIL Simplify $(4x + 2)(3x - 6)$.

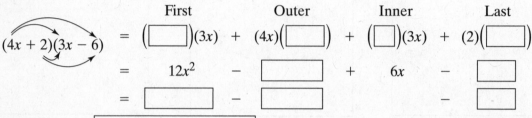

First	Outer	Inner	Last

$$(4x + 2)(3x - 6) = (\boxed{})(3x) + (4x)(\boxed{}) + (\boxed{})(3x) + (2)(\boxed{})$$

$$= 12x^2 - \boxed{} + 6x - \boxed{}$$

$$= \boxed{} - \boxed{} - \boxed{}$$

The product is $\boxed{}$.

❷ Applying Multiplication of Polynomials Find the area of the shaded region. Simplify.

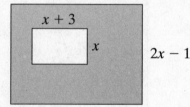

area of outer rectangle = $(3x + 2)(\boxed{})$

area of hole = $x(\boxed{})$

area of shaded region = area of outer rectangle − area of hole

$$= (3x + 2)(\boxed{}) \boxed{} \boxed{}(x + 3) \quad \textbf{Substitute.}$$

$$= \boxed{} - 3x + \boxed{} - 2 - x^2 - \boxed{} \quad \begin{array}{l}\textbf{Use FOIL to simplify } (3x + 2)(2x - 1) \\ \textbf{and the Distributive Property to} \\ \textbf{simplify } x(x + 3).\end{array}$$

$$= 6x^2 - \boxed{} - 3x + \boxed{} - 3x - \boxed{} \quad \textbf{Group like terms.}$$

$$= \boxed{} - \boxed{} - \boxed{} \quad \textbf{Simplify.}$$

CA Standards Check

1. Simplify each product using FOIL.

   a. $(3x + 4)(2x + 5)$ **b.** $(3x - 4)(2x + 5)$

   c. $(3x + 4)(2x - 5)$ **d.** $(3x - 4)(2x - 5)$

Example

❸ Multiplying a Trinomial and a Binomial Simplify the product
$(3x^2 - 2x + 3)(2x + 7)$.

Method 1 Multiply using the vertical method.

$$
\begin{array}{ccccc}
3x^2 & - & 2x & + & 3 \\
 & & 2x & + & 7 \\
\hline
\boxed{} & - 14x & + & \boxed{} & \quad\text{Multiply by } \boxed{}. \\
\boxed{} - 4x^2 & + & \boxed{} & & \quad\text{Multiply by } \boxed{}. \\
\hline
\boxed{} + 17x^2 & - & \boxed{} & + \boxed{} & \quad\text{Add like terms.}
\end{array}
$$

Method 2 Multiply using the horizontal method.

$(2x + 7)(3x^2 - 2x + 3)$

$= \left(\boxed{}\right)(3x^2) - (2x)\left(\boxed{}\right) + \left(\boxed{}\right)(3) + (7)\left(\boxed{}\right) - \left(\boxed{}\right)(2x) + (7)\left(\boxed{}\right)$

$= \quad 6x^3 \quad - \boxed{} \quad + \quad 6x \quad + \boxed{} \quad - \quad 14x \quad + \boxed{}$

$= \boxed{} \quad + \quad 17x^2 \quad - \boxed{} \quad + \quad 21 \quad \textbf{Add like terms.}$

The product is $\boxed{}$.

CA Standards Check

2. Find an expression for the area of each shaded region. Simplify.

a.

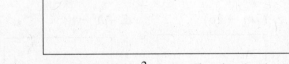
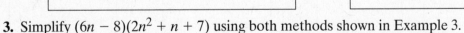

5x + 8

5x

6x + 2

x + 6

b.

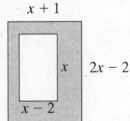

x + 1

x

2x − 2

x − 2

3. Simplify $(6n - 8)(2n^2 + n + 7)$ using both methods shown in Example 3.

Lesson 8-4

Lesson Objectives	California Content Standards
• Find the square of a binomial • Find the difference of squares	10.0

Take Note

The Square of a Binomial

$(a + b)^2 = $ [_____]

$(a - b)^2 = $ [_____]

The square of a binomial is the square of the first term plus twice the product of the two terms plus the square of the last term.

The Difference of Squares

$(a + b)(a - b) = $ [_____]

The product of the sum and difference of the same two terms is the difference of their squares.

Example

❶ Squaring a Binomial

a. Find $(y + 11)^2$.

$(y + 11)^2 = y^2 + $ [____] $(11) + 11^2$ **Square the binomial.**

$= $ [____] $+$ [____] $+$ [____]   **Simplify.**

b. Find $(3w - 6)^2$.

$(3w - 6)^2 = ($ [____] $)^2 - $ [__] $(3w)($ [__] $) + 6^2$ **Square the binomial.**

$= $ [____] $- $ [____] $w + $ [____]   **Simplify.**

CA Standards Check

1. Find each square.

a. $(t + 6)^2$ **b.** $(5y + 1)^2$ **c.** $(7m - 2p)^2$ **d.** $(9c - 8)^2$

  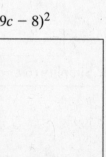

Name_____ Class_____ Date _____

Example

❷ **Application** Among guinea pigs, the black fur gene (*B*) is dominant and the white fur gene (*W*) is recessive. This means that a guinea pig with at least one dominant gene (*BB* or *BW*) will have black fur. A guinea pig with two recessive genes (*WW*) will have white fur.

	B	W
B	BB	BW
W	☐	☐

The Punnett square models the possible combinations that parents who carry both genes can give to their offspring. Since *WW* is $\frac{1}{4}$ of the outcomes, the probability that a guinea pig has white fur is ☐ .

You can model the Punnett square probabilities with the expression $\left(\frac{1}{2}B + \frac{1}{2}W\right)^2$. Show that this product gives the same result as the Punnett square.

$$\left(\tfrac{1}{2}B + \tfrac{1}{2}W\right)^2 = \left(\tfrac{1}{2}B\right)^2 + 2\left(\boxed{}\right)\left(\tfrac{1}{2}W\right) + \left(\boxed{}\right)^2 \quad \textbf{Square the binomial.}$$

$$= \boxed{} + \boxed{} + \tfrac{1}{4}W^2 \quad \textbf{Simplify.}$$

The expressions $\frac{1}{4}B^2$ and $\boxed{}W^2$ show that the probability offspring will have either two dominant genes or two recessive genes is $\boxed{}$. The expression $\frac{1}{2}BW$ shows there is $\boxed{}$ chance that the offspring will inherit both genes. These are the $\boxed{}$ probabilities in the Punnett square.

CA Standards Check

2. When you play a game with two number cubes, you can find probabilities by squaring a binomial. Let *A* represent rolling 1 or 2 and *B* represent rolling 3, 4, 5, or 6. The probability of *A* is $\frac{1}{3}$, and the probability of *B* is $\frac{2}{3}$.

a. Find $\left(\frac{1}{3}A + \frac{2}{3}B\right)^2$.

b. What is the probability that both number cubes you roll show 1 or 2?

c. What is the probability that one number cube shows a 1 or 2 and the other shows 3, 4, 5, or 6?

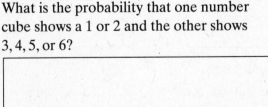

d. What is the probability that both number cubes show 3, 4, 5, or 6?

Examples

❸ **Mental Math**
 a. Find 81^2 using mental math.

$$81^2 = \left(80 + \boxed{}\right)^2$$
$$= 80^2 + \boxed{}\left(\boxed{} \cdot 1\right) + \boxed{}^2 \qquad \text{Square the binomial.}$$
$$= \boxed{} + 160 + \boxed{} = \boxed{} \qquad \text{Simplify.}$$

 b. Find 59^2 using mental math.

$$59^2 = \left(60 - \boxed{}\right)^2$$
$$= \boxed{} - 2\left(\boxed{} \cdot 1\right) + 1^2 \qquad \text{Square the binomial.}$$
$$= \boxed{} - \boxed{} + 1 = \boxed{} \qquad \text{Simplify.}$$

❹ **Finding the Difference of Squares** Find $(p^4 - 8)(p^4 + 8)$.

$$(p^4 - 8)(p^4 + 8) = (p^4)^{\boxed{}} - (\boxed{})^2 \quad \text{Find the difference of squares.}$$
$$= \boxed{} - \boxed{} \qquad \text{Simplify.}$$

❺ **Mental Math** Find $43 \cdot 37$.

$$43 \cdot 37 = \left(40 + \boxed{}\right)\left(40 - \boxed{}\right) \qquad \text{Express each factor using 40 and 3.}$$
$$= \boxed{}^2 - \boxed{} \qquad \text{Find the difference of squares.}$$
$$= \boxed{} - 9 = \boxed{} \qquad \text{Simplify.}$$

CA Standards Check

3. Find each square using mental math.

 a. 31^2 **b.** 29^2 **c.** 98^2 **d.** 203^2

4. Find each product.

 a. $(d + 11)(d - 11)$ **b.** $(c^2 + 8)(c^2 - 8)$ **c.** $(9v^3 + w^4)(9v^3 - w^4)$

5. Find each product.

 a. $18 \cdot 22$ **b.** $19 \cdot 21$ **c.** $59 \cdot 61$ **d.** $87 \cdot 93$

Lesson 8-5

Factoring Trinomials of the Type $x^2 + bx + c$

Lesson Objective	California Content Standards
• Factor trinomials	11.0

Examples

❶ Factoring $x^2 + bx + c$ Factor $x^2 + 8x + 15$.

Find the factors of 15. Identify the pair that has a sum of 8.

$x^2 + 8x + 15 = \left(x + \boxed{}\right)\left(x + \boxed{}\right)$

Check $x^2 + 8x + 15 \stackrel{?}{=} \left(x + \boxed{}\right)(x + \boxed{})$

$= \boxed{} + 5x + 3x + \boxed{}$

$= x^2 + 8x + 15$

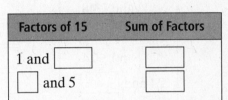

Factors of 15	Sum of Factors
1 and $\boxed{}$	$\boxed{}$
$\boxed{}$ and 5	$\boxed{}$

❷ Factoring $x^2 - bx + c$ Factor $c^2 - 9c + 20$.

Since the middle term is negative, find the negative factors of 20. Identify the pair that has a sum of -9.

$c^2 - 9c + 20 = \left(c - \boxed{}\right)\left(c - \boxed{}\right)$

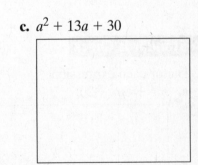

Factors of 20	Sum of Factors
$\boxed{}$ and -20	$\boxed{}$
$\boxed{}$ and -10	$\boxed{}$
$\boxed{}$ and $\boxed{}$	$\boxed{}$

CA Standards Check

1. Factor each expression. Check your answer.

a. $g^2 + 7g + 10$ **b.** $v^2 + 21v + 20$ **c.** $a^2 + 13a + 30$

2. Factor each expression.

a. $k^2 - 10k + 25$ **b.** $x^2 - 11x + 18$ **c.** $q^2 - 15q + 36$

Examples

❸ **Factoring Trinomials With a Negative c**

a. Factor $x^2 + 13x - 48$.

Identify the pair of factors of -48
that has a sum of 13.

Factors of -48	Sum of Factors
☐ and -48	☐
48 and ☐	☐
☐ and -24	☐
24 and ☐	☐
☐ and -16	☐
16 and ☐	☐

$x^2 + 13x - 48 = \left(x + \boxed{}\right)\left(x - \boxed{}\right)$

b. Factor $n^2 - 5n - 24$.

Identify the pair of factors of -24
that has a sum of -5.

Factors of -24	Sum of Factors
☐ and -24	☐
24 and ☐	☐
☐ and -12	☐
12 and ☐	☐
☐ and -8	☐

$n^2 - 5n - 24 = \left(n + \boxed{}\right)\left(n - \boxed{}\right)$

❹ **Factoring Trinomials With Two Variables**

Factor $d^2 + 17dg - 60g^2$.

Find the factors of -60. Identify the pair that has
a sum of 17.

$d^2 + 17dg - 60g^2 = \left(d - \boxed{}g\right)\left(d + \boxed{}g\right)$

Factors of -60	Sum of Factors
☐ and -60	☐
60 and ☐	☐
☐ and -30	☐
30 and ☐	☐
☐ and -20	☐
20 and ☐	☐

CA Standards Check

3. Factor each expression.

a. $m^2 + 8m - 20$

b. $p^2 - 3p - 40$

c. $y^2 - y - 56$

4. a. $x^2 + 11xy + 24y^2$

b. $v^2 + 2vw - 48w^2$

c. $m^2 - 17mn - 60n^2$

Lesson 8-6

Factoring Trinomials
of the Type $ax^2 + bx + c$

Lesson Objective	California Content Standards
• Factor trinomials of the type $ax^2 + bx + c$	11.0

Take Note

FOIL = first, outer, inner, last

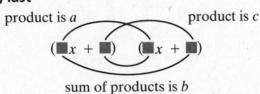

product is a product is c

$(\blacksquare x + \blacksquare)\ (\blacksquare x + \blacksquare)$

sum of products is b

Examples

❶ c Is Positive Factor $20x^2 + 17x + 3$.

$$20x^2 \qquad\qquad + 17x \qquad\qquad + 3$$
$$\boxed{F} \qquad\qquad \boxed{O} \quad\quad \boxed{I} \qquad\qquad \boxed{L}$$

factors of a $\boxed{} \cdot 20$ $1 \cdot 3 + 1 \cdot 20 = \boxed{}$ $1 \cdot 3$ factors of c

$1 \cdot 1 + 3 \cdot 20 = \boxed{}$ $3 \cdot 1$

$2 \cdot \boxed{}$ $2 \cdot \boxed{} + \boxed{} \cdot 10 = \boxed{}$ $1 \cdot 3$

$2 \cdot 1 + 3 \cdot 10 = \boxed{}$ $3 \cdot 1$

$\boxed{} \cdot 5$ $\boxed{} \cdot 3 + 1 \cdot 5 = \boxed{}$ $1 \cdot 3$

$$20x^2 + 17x + 3 = (\boxed{} + 1)(\boxed{} + 3)$$

❷ c Is Negative Factor $3n^2 - 7n - 6$.

$$3n^2 \qquad\qquad -7n \qquad\qquad -6$$

$(1)(3)$ $(1)(-6) + (\boxed{})(3) = \boxed{}$ $(1)(-6)$

$(\boxed{})(1) + (-6)(3) = \boxed{}$ $(-6)(1)$

$(1)(-3) + (\boxed{})(3) = \boxed{}$ $(2)(-3)$

$(1)(\boxed{}) + (-3)(3) = \boxed{}$ $(-3)(2)$

$$3n^2 - 7n - 6 = (\boxed{} - 3)(\boxed{} + 2)$$

❸ **Factoring Out a Monomial First** Factor $18x^2 + 33x - 30$ completely.

$18x^2 + 33x - 30 = \boxed{}\left(6x^2 + \boxed{}x - \boxed{}\right)$ **Factor out the GCD.**

Factor $6x^2 + 11x - 10$.

$$6x^2 \qquad\qquad +11x \qquad\qquad -10$$

$(2)(3)$	$(2)(-10) + (1)\left(\boxed{}\right) = \boxed{}$	$(1)(-10)$
	$\left(\boxed{}\right)(1) + (-10)(3) = \boxed{}$	$(-10)(1)$
	$(2)(-5) + \left(\boxed{}\right)(3) = \boxed{}$	$(2)(-5)$
	$(2)(2) + (-5)(3) = \boxed{}$	$(-5)(2)$
	$(2)\left(\boxed{}\right) + (5)\left(\boxed{}\right) = \boxed{}$	$(5)(-2)$

$6x^2 + 11x - 10 = \left(\boxed{} + 5\right)\left(\boxed{} - 2\right)$

$18x^2 + 33x - 30 = \boxed{}\left(2x + \boxed{}\right)\left(3x - \boxed{}\right)$ **Include the GCD in your final answer.**

CA Standards Check

Factor each expression.

1. a. $2y^2 + 5y + 2$

b. $6n^2 - 23n + 7$

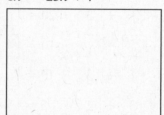

c. $2y^2 - 5y + 2$

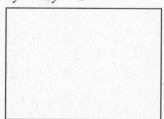

2. a. $5d^2 - 14d - 3$

b. $2n^2 + n - 3$

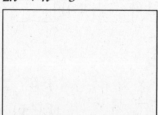

c. $20p^2 - 31p - 9$

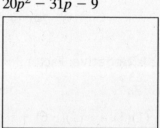

3. a. $2v^2 - 12v + 10$

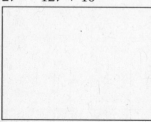

b. $4y^2 + 14y + 6$

c. $18k^2 - 12k - 6$

Daily Notetaking Guide

Lesson 8-7

Lesson Objectives	California Content Standards
• Factor perfect-square trinomials • Factor the difference of squares	11.0

Take Note

Perfect-Square Trinomials

For every real number a and b:

$a^2 + 2ab + b^2 = (a + b)(a + b) =$ [   ]

$a^2 - 2ab + b^2 = (a - b)(a - b) =$ [   ]

Examples

$x^2 + 10x + 25 = (x + 5)(x + 5) = (x + 5)^2$ $\qquad$ $x^2 - 10x + 25 = (x - 5)(x - 5) = (x - 5)^2$

Difference of Two Squares

For every real number a and b:

$a^2 - b^2 =$ [   ]

Examples

$x^2 - 81 = (x + 9)(x - 9)$ $\qquad$ $16x^2 - 49 = (4x + 7)(4x - 7)$

You can factor a perfect-square trinomial into _____

Example

❶ Factoring a Perfect-Square Trinomial With $a = 1$ Factor $m^2 - 6m + 9$.

$m^2 - 6m + 9 = m \cdot m - 6m + 3 \cdot 3$ $\qquad$ Rewrite first and last terms.

$\qquad = m \cdot m - \boxed{}\left(m \cdot \boxed{}\right) + 3 \cdot 3$ $\qquad$ Does the middle term equal 2*ab*? 6*m* = [   ].

$\qquad = \left(m - \boxed{}\right)^2$ $\qquad$ Write the factors as the square of a binomial.

CA Standards Check

1. Factor each expression.

a. $x^2 + 8x + 16$ $\qquad$ **b.** $n^2 + 16n + 64$ $\qquad$ **c.** $n^2 - 16n + 64$

Examples

❷ **Factoring a Perfect-Square Trinomial With $a \neq 1$** The area of a square is $(16h^2 + 40h + 25)$ in.^{2}. Find an expression for the length of a side.

$16h^2 + 40h + 25 = \left(\boxed{}\right)^2 + 40h + \boxed{}^2$ Rewrite $16h^2$ as $\left(\boxed{}\right)^2$ and 25 as $\boxed{}^2$.

Does the middle term equal 2ab?

$\qquad = (4h)^2 + 2\left(\boxed{}\right)(5) + 5^2$ $40h = 2\left(\boxed{}\right)(5)$ ✔

$\qquad = \left(\boxed{} + \boxed{}\right)^2$ Write the factors as the square of a binomial.

The side of the square has a length of $\boxed{}$ in.

❸ **The Difference of Two Squares for $a = 1$** Factor $a^2 - 16$.

$a^2 - 16 = a^2 - \boxed{}^2$ Rewrite 16 as $\boxed{}^2$.

$\qquad = \left(a + \boxed{}\right)\left(a - \boxed{}\right)$ Factor.

Check Use FOIL to multiply.

$\left(a + \boxed{}\right)\left(a - \boxed{}\right)$

$a^2 - \boxed{} + 4a - \boxed{}$

$a^2 - \boxed{}$ ✔

CA Standards Check

2. Factor each expression.

   a. $9g^2 - 12g + 4$

   b. $4t^2 + 36t + 81$

   c. $4t^2 - 36t + 81$

3. Factor each expression. Check your answer.

   a. $x^2 - 36$

   b. $m^2 - 100$

   c. $p^2 - 49$

Examples

❹ **The Difference of Two Squares for $a \neq 1$** Factor $9b^2 - 25$.

$9b^2 - 25 = \left(\boxed{}\right)^2 - \boxed{}^2$ **Rewrite $9b^2$ as $\left(\boxed{}\right)^2$ and 25 as $\boxed{}^2$.**

$= \left(3b + \boxed{}\right)\left(\boxed{} - 5\right)$ **Factor.**

❺ **Factoring Out a Common Factor** Factor $5x^2 - 80$.

$5x^2 - 80 = \boxed{}\left(x^2 - \boxed{}\right)$ **Factor out the common factor of $\boxed{}$.**

$= \boxed{}\left(x + \boxed{}\right)\left(x - \boxed{}\right)$ **Factor ($x^2 - 16$).**

Check Use FOIL to multiply the binomials. Then multiply by the common factor.

$\boxed{}\left(x + \boxed{}\right)\left(x - \boxed{}\right)$

$5\left(x^2 - \boxed{}\right)$

$5x^2 - 80$ ✔

CA Standards Check

4. Factor each expression.

   a. $9v^2 - 4$ **b.** $25x^2 - 64$ **c.** $4w^2 - 49$

5. Factor each expression.

   a. $8y^2 - 50$ **b.** $3c^2 - 75$ **c.** $28k^2 - 7$

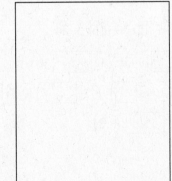
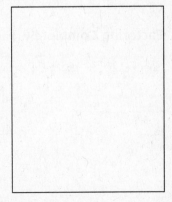

Lesson 8-8

Factoring by Grouping

Lesson Objectives	California Content Standards
• Factor polynomials with four terms • Factor trinomials by grouping	11.0

Take Note

Factoring Polynomials

1. Factor out the greatest common factor (GCD).
2. If the polynomial has two terms or three terms, look for a difference of two squares, a product of two squares, or a pair of binomial factors.
3. If there are four or more terms, group terms and factor to find common binomial factors.
4. As a final check, make sure there are no common factors other than 1.

Factor by grouping is _____

_____

Examples

❶ **Factoring a Four-Term Polynomial** Factor $6x^3 + 3x^2 - 4x - 2$.

$6x^3 + 3x^2 - 4x - 2 = \boxed{}(2x + 1) - 2(\boxed{})$ Factor the GCD from each group of two terms.

$\qquad = (\boxed{})(3x^2 - 2)$ Factor out $(\boxed{})$.

Check $6x^3 + 3x^2 - 4x - 2 \stackrel{?}{=} (\boxed{})(3x^2 - 2)$

$\qquad = 6x^3 - \boxed{} + \boxed{} - 2$ Use FOIL.

$\qquad = 6x^3 + 3x^2 - 4x - 2 ✔$ Write in standard form.

❷ **Factoring Completely** Factor $8t^4 + 12t^3 + 16t + 24$.

$8t^4 + 12t^3 + 16t + 24 = \boxed{}(2\boxed{} + 3t^3 + \boxed{} + 6)$ Factor out the GCD, $\boxed{}$.

$\qquad = 4[\boxed{}(2t + \boxed{}) + 2(\boxed{} + 3)]$ Factor by grouping.

$\qquad = 4(2t + 3)(\boxed{} + 2)$ Factor again.

❸ Application A rectangular box has a volume of $36x^3 + 51x^2 + 18x$. Factor to find the possible expressions for the length, width, and height of the box.

Factor $36x^3 + 51x^2 + 18x$.

Step 1 ☐ $(12x^2 +$ ☐ $+ 6)$ Factor out the GCF, ☐.

Step 2 $12 \cdot 6 =$ ☐   Find the product *ac*.

Step 3 Factors   →   Sum

     $4 \cdot$ ☐ → $4 +$ ☐ $=$ ☐   Find two factors of *ac* that have sum *b*.

     ☐ $\cdot 12$ → ☐ $+ 12 =$ ☐   Use mental math to determine a good place to start.

     $8 \cdot$ ☐ → $8 +$ ☐ $=$ ☐

Step 4 $3x\left(12x^2 + \boxed{} + 9x + \boxed{}\right)$ Rewrite the trinomial.

Step 5 $3x\left[\boxed{}(3x + 2) + \boxed{}(3x + 2)\right]$ Factor by grouping.

     $3x\left(\boxed{} + 3\right)(3x + \boxed{})$ Factor again.

The possible dimensions of the box are ☐ , ☐ , and ☐ .

CA Standards Check

Factor each expression. Check your answer.

1. a. $5t^4 + 20t^3 + 6t + 24$ **b.** $2w^3 + w^2 - 14w - 7$ **2.** $45m^4 - 9m^3 + 30m^2 - 6m$

3. Find expressions for the possible dimensions of each rectangular prism.

a.

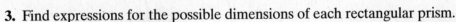

$6g^3 + 20g^2 + 16g$

b.

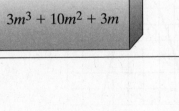

$3m^3 + 10m^2 + 3m$

Lesson 9-1

Exploring Quadratic Graphs

Lesson Objectives	California Content Standards
• Graph quadratic functions of the form $y = ax^2$ • Graph quadratic functions of the form $y = ax^2 + c$	21.0, 23.0

Take Note

Standard Form of a Quadratic Function

A quadratic function is a function that can be written in the form

$y =$ _____ , where $a, b,$ and $c,$ are real numbers and $a \neq 0$. This

form is called the _____ form of a quadratic function.

Examples $\quad y = 5x^2 \qquad\qquad y = x^2 + 7 \qquad\qquad y = x^2 - x - 3$

A parabola is _____

The axis of symmetry is _____

_____

A vertex is _____

The minimum is _____

_____

The maximum is _____

_____

Examples

❶ **Identifying a Vertex** Identify the vertex of each graph. Tell whether it
is a minimum or a maximum.

a.

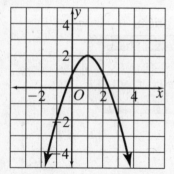

The vertex is [_____] .

It is a [_____] .

b.

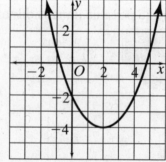

The vertex is [_____] .

It is a [_____] .

Daily Notetaking Guide

2 **Graphing $y = ax^2 + c$** How is the graph of $y = 3x^2 - 2$ different from the graph of $y = 3x^2$? Compare the graphs.

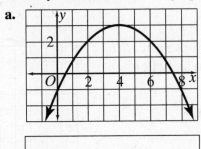

x	$y = 3x^2$	$y = 3x^2 - 2$
2	12	
1		1
0	0	
−1		1
−2	12	

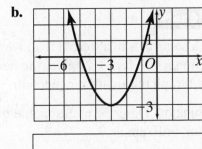

The graph of $y = 3x^2 - 2$ has the same shape as the graph of $y = 3x^2$, but is shifted down ☐ units.

CA Standards Check

1. Identify the vertex of each graph. Tell whether it is a minimum or maximum.

a.

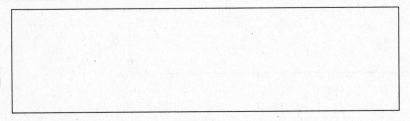

b.

2. a. Graph $y = x^2$ and $y = x^2 - 4$. Compare the graphs.

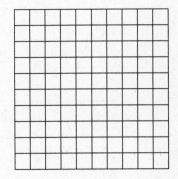

b. **Critical Thinking** Describe what positive and negative values of c do to the position of the vertex.

Example

❸ **Application** A monkey drops an orange from a branch 26 ft above ground. The force of gravity causes the orange to fall toward Earth. The function $h = -16t^2 + 26$ gives the height of the orange, h, in feet after t seconds. Graph this quadratic function.

t	$h = -16t^2 + 26$
0	26
0.25	
0.5	
0.75	
1	
1.25	

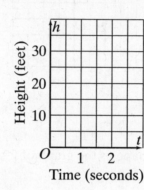

Height h is dependent on time t. Graph t on the x-axis and h on the y-axis. Use nonnegative values for t.

CA Standards Check

3. a. Suppose a squirrel is in a tree 24 ft above the ground. She drops an acorn. The function $h = -16t^2 + 24$ gives the height of the acorn in feet after t seconds. Graph this quadratic function.

   b. Critical Thinking Describe a reasonable domain and range for the function in Example 3.

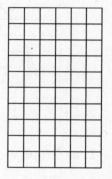

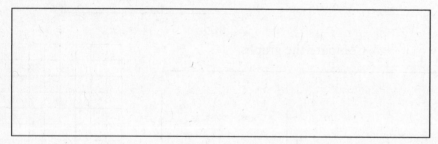

Lesson 9-2

Lesson Objectives	California Content Standards
• Graph quadratic functions of the form $y = ax^2 + bx + c$ • Graph quadratic inequalities	17.0, 21.0, 23.0

Take Note

Graph of a Quadratic Function

The graph of $y = ax^2 + bx + c$, where $a, b,$ and c are real numbers and $a \neq 0$,

has the line $x = \boxed{}$ as its axis of symmetry. The x-coordinate of the vertex

is $\boxed{}$.

Examples

❶ Graphing $y = ax^2 + bx + c$ Graph the function $y = 2x^2 + 4x - 3$. Find the domain and range.

Step 1 Find the axis of symmetry and of the vertex.

$$x = -\frac{b}{2a} = -\frac{\boxed{}}{2(\boxed{})} = \boxed{} \qquad \textbf{Find the equation of the axis of symmetry.}$$

The axis of symmetry is $x = \boxed{}$.

$y = 2x^2 + 4x - 3$

$y = 2(\boxed{})^2 + 4(\boxed{}) - 3$ **To find the y-coordinate of the**

      vertex, substitute $\boxed{}$ **for x.**

$= \boxed{}$

The vertex is $\boxed{}$.

Step 2 Find two other points.
Use the y-intercept.

For $x = 0, y = \boxed{}$, so one point is $\boxed{}$.

Choose a value for x on the same side of the vertex.
Let $x = 1$.

$y = 2(\boxed{})^2 + 4(\boxed{}) - 3$ **Find the y-coordinate for $x = 1$.**

$= \boxed{}$

For $x = 1, y = \boxed{}$, so another point is $\boxed{}$.

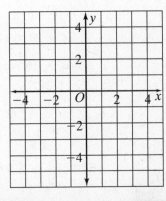

Step 3 Reflect $(0, -3)$ and $(1, 3)$ across the axis of symmetry to get two more points. Then draw the parabola.

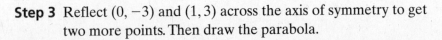

❷ **Graphing Quadratic Inequalities** Graph the quadratic inequality
$y > -x^2 + 6x - 5$.

Graph the boundary curve, $y \boxed{} -x^2 + 6x - 5$.

Use a $\boxed{}$ line because the solution of the inequality

$y > -x^2 + 6x - 5$ does not include the boundary.

Shade $\boxed{}$ the curve.

CA Standards Check

1. Graph $f(x) = x^2 - 6x + 9$. Label the axis of symmetry and the vertex.

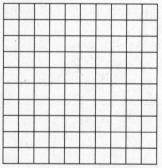

2. Graph each quadratic inequality.

 a. $y \le x^2 + 2x - 5$

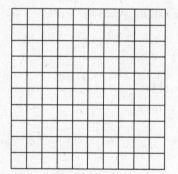

 b. $y > x^2 + x + 1$

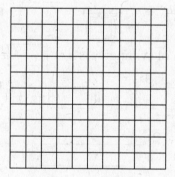

Lesson 9-3

Finding and Estimating Square Roots

Lesson Objectives	California Content Standards
• Find square roots • Estimate and use square roots	2.0, 23.0

Take Note

> **Square Root**
>
> The number a is a square root of b if $a^2 = \boxed{}$.
>
> **Example** $4^2 = \boxed{}$ and $(-4)^2 = \boxed{}$, so 4 and -4 are square roots of $\boxed{}$.

The principal square root is _____

The negative square root of b is $\boxed{}$.

The radicand is _____

Perfect squares are _____

Examples

❶ Simplifying Square Root Expressions Simplify each expression.

a. $\sqrt{25}$ = $\boxed{}$ positive square root

b. $\pm\sqrt{\dfrac{9}{25}}$ = $\pm \boxed{}$ The square roots are $\boxed{}$ and $\boxed{}$.

c. $-\sqrt{64}$ = $\boxed{}$ negative square root

d. $\sqrt{-49}$ = $\boxed{}$ For real numbers, the square root of a negative number is $\boxed{}$.

e. $\pm\sqrt{0}$ = $\boxed{}$ There is only one square root of 0.

❷ Rational and Irrational Square Roots Tell whether each expression is *rational* or *irrational*.

a. $\pm\sqrt{144}$ = $\boxed{}$ $\boxed{}$

b. $\sqrt{\dfrac{1}{5}}$ = $0.44721359\ldots$ $\boxed{}$

c. $-\sqrt{6.25}$ = $\boxed{}$ $\boxed{}$

d. $\sqrt{\dfrac{1}{9}}$ = $0.\overline{3}$ $\boxed{}$

❸ Estimating Square Roots Between what two consecutive integers is $\sqrt{28.34}$?

$\sqrt{\boxed{}} < \sqrt{28.34} < \sqrt{\boxed{}}$ 28.34 is between the two consecutive perfect squares $\boxed{}$ and $\boxed{}$.

$\boxed{} < \sqrt{28.34} < \boxed{}$ The square roots of 25 and 36 are $\boxed{}$ and $\boxed{}$, respectively.

$\sqrt{28.34}$ is between $\boxed{}$ and $\boxed{}$.

❹ Application Suppose a rectangular field has a length y three times its width x. The formula $d = \sqrt{x^2 + y^2}$ gives the length of the diagonal of a rectangle. Find the distance of the diagonal across the field if $x = 8$ ft.

$\sqrt{x^2 + (3x)^2}$ Substitute 3x for $\boxed{}$.

$\sqrt{\boxed{}^2 + \left(3 \cdot \boxed{}\right)^2}$ Substitute $\boxed{}$ for *x*.

$\sqrt{\boxed{} + \boxed{}}$ Simplify.

$\sqrt{\boxed{}}$

$\boxed{}$ Use a calculator. Round to the nearest tenth.

The diagonal is about $\boxed{}$ ft long.

CA Standards Check

1. Simplify each expression.

   a. $\sqrt{49}$ $\boxed{}$ **b.** $\pm\sqrt{36}$ $\boxed{}$ **c.** $-\sqrt{121}$ $\boxed{}$ **d.** $\sqrt{\frac{1}{25}}$ $\boxed{}$

2. Tell whether each expression is rational or irrational.

   a. $\sqrt{8}$ **b.** $\pm\sqrt{225}$ **c.** $-\sqrt{75}$ **d.** $\sqrt{\frac{1}{4}}$

3. Between what two consecutive integers is $-\sqrt{105}$?

4. Using the formula from Example 4, suppose $x = 10$ ft. How long is the diagonal across the field? Round to the nearest tenth of a foot.

Lesson 9-4

Solving Quadratic Equations

Lesson Objectives	California Content Standards
• Solve quadratic equations by graphing • Solve quadratic equations using square roots	21.0, 23.0

Take Note

Standard Form of a Quadratic Equation

A quadratic equation is an equation that can be written in the form [   ]

where a, b, and c are real numbers and $a \neq 0$. This form is called the [   ]

form of a quadratic equation.

Example

❶ **Solving by Graphing** Solve each equation by graphing the related function.

    a. $2x^2 = 0$

    Graph $y = 2x^2$.

    b. $2x^2 + 2 = 0$

    Graph $y = 2x^2 + 2$.

    c. $2x^2 - 2 = 0$

    Graph $y = 2x^2 - 2$.

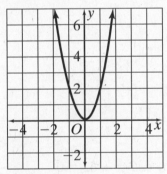 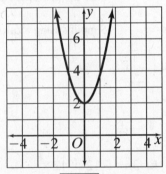 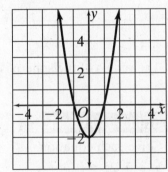

There is one solution,

$x =$ [   ].

There is [   ] solution.

There are two solutions,

$x =$ [   ] and $x =$ [   ].

CA Standards Check

1. Solve each equation by graphing the related function.

    a. $x^2 - 1 = 0$

    b. $2x^2 + 4 = 0$

    c. $x^2 - 16 = -16$

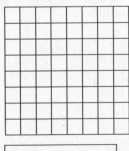 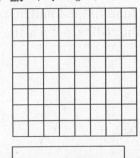 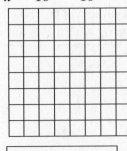

Name_____ Class_____ Date_____

Examples

② Using Square Roots Solve $3x^2 - 75 = 0$.

$3x^2 - 75 + \boxed{} = 0 + \boxed{}$ **Add** $\boxed{}$ **to each side.**

$3x^2 = \boxed{}$

$x^2 = \boxed{}$ **Divide each side by** $\boxed{}$.

$x = \pm\sqrt{\boxed{}}$ **Find the square root of each side.**

$x = \boxed{}$ **Simplify.**

③ Application A museum is planning an exhibit that will contain a large globe. The surface area of the globe will be 315 ft^2. Find the radius of the sphere. Use the equation $S = 4\pi r^2$, where S is the surface area and r is the radius.

$S = 4\pi r^2$

$\boxed{} = 4\pi r^2$ **Substitute** $\boxed{}$ **for S.**

$\dfrac{\boxed{}}{4\pi} = r^2$ **Divide each side by** 4π.

$\sqrt{\dfrac{\boxed{}}{4\pi}} = r$ **Find the principal square root.**

$\boxed{} \approx r$ **Simplify using a calculator.**

The radius of the sphere is about $\boxed{}$ ft.

CA Standards Check

2. Solve each equation.

a. $t^2 - 25 = 0$

b. $3n^2 + 12 = 12$

c. $2g^2 + 32 = 0$
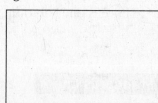

3. A city is planning a circular fountain. The depth of the fountain will be 3 ft and the volume will be 1800 ft.^{3} Find the radius of the fountain using the equation $V = \pi r^2 h$, where V is the volume, r is the radius, and h is the depth.

Page 144 — Algebra 1 Lesson 9-4 — Daily Notetaking Guide

Lesson 9-5

Factoring to Solve Quadratic Equations

Lesson Objective	California Content Standards
• Solve quadratic equations by factoring	14.0, 23.0, 25.1

Take Note

Zero-Product Property
For every real number a and b, if $ab = 0$, then $a = \boxed{}$ or $b = \boxed{}$.
Example If $(x + 3)(x + 2) = 0$, then $x + 3 = 0$ or $x + 2 = 0$.

Examples

❶ Using the Zero-Product Property Solve $(2x + 3)(x - 4) = 0$.
$(2x + 3)(x - 4) = 0$

$\qquad 2x + 3 = 0 \quad \text{or} \quad x - 4 = 0$ **Use the Zero-Product Property.**

$\qquad\qquad 2x = \boxed{}$ **Solve for x.**

$\qquad\qquad x = \boxed{} \quad \text{or} \quad x = \boxed{}$

Check Substitute $\boxed{}$ for x.   Substitute $\boxed{}$ for x.

$\qquad (2x + 3)(x - 4) = 0 \qquad\qquad (2x + 3)(x - 4) = 0$

$\qquad [2(\boxed{}) + 3](\boxed{} - 4) \stackrel{?}{=} 0 \qquad [2(\boxed{}) + 3](\boxed{} - 4) \stackrel{?}{=} 0$

$\qquad\qquad (0)(-5\tfrac{1}{2}) = 0 \checkmark \qquad\qquad\qquad (\boxed{})(0) = 0 \checkmark$

❷ Solving by Factoring Solve $x^2 + x - 42 = 0$.

$\qquad x^2 + x - 42 = 0$

$\left(x + \boxed{}\right)\left(x - \boxed{}\right) = 0$ **Factor $x^2 + x - 42$.**

$\qquad x + \boxed{} = 0 \qquad \text{or} \quad x - \boxed{} = 0$ **Use the Zero-Product Property.**

$\qquad\quad x = \boxed{} \quad \text{or} \qquad x = \boxed{}$ **Solve for x.**

❸ Application The diagram shows a pattern for an open-top box. The total area of the sheet of material used to make the box is 130 in.² The height of the box is 1 in. Therefore, 1 in. × 1 in. squares are cut from each corner. Find the dimensions of the box.

Define Let ☐x = width of a side of the box.

Then the width of the material = $x + 1 + 1$ = [____].

Then the length of the material = $x + 3 + 1 + 1$ = [____].

Relate width × length = area of the sheet

Write $(x + 2)$ $(x + 5)$ = [____]

$x^2 +$ [____] $+ 10 = 130$ **Find the product $\left(x + \boxed{}\right)\left(x + \boxed{}\right)$.**

$x^2 + 7x -$ [____] $= 0$ **Subtract [____] from each side.**

$\left(x - \boxed{}\right)\left(x + \boxed{}\right) = 0$ **Factor $x^2 + 7x -$ [____].**

$x - \boxed{} = 0$ or $x + $ [____] $= 0$ **Use the Zero-Product Property.**

$x = \boxed{}$ or $x =$ [____]   **Solve for x.**

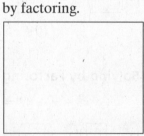

The only reasonable solution is $\boxed{}$. So the dimensions of the box are $\boxed{}$ in. × [____] in. × $\boxed{}$ in.

CA Standards Check

1. Solve each equation.

  a. $(x + 7)(x - 4) = 0$

  b. $(3y - 5)(y - 2) = 0$

2. Solve $x^2 - 8x - 48 = 0$ by factoring.

3. Suppose that a box has a base with a width of x, a length of $x + 1$, and a height of 2 in. It is cut from a rectangular sheet of material with an area of 182 in.² Find the dimensions of the box.

Lesson 9-6

Completing the Square

Lesson Objective	California Content Standards
• Solve quadratic equations by completing the square	14.0, 23.0

Vocabulary

Completing the square is _____

_____

Examples

❶ Finding *n* to Complete the Square Find the value of n such that $x^2 - 16x + n$ is a perfect square trinomial.

The value of b in the expression $x^2 - 16x + n$ is $\boxed{}$.

The term to add to $x^2 - 16x$ is $\boxed{}$.

❷ Solving $x^2 + bx = c$ Solve the equation $x^2 + 5x = 50$.

Step 1 Write the left side of $x^2 + 5x = 50$ as a perfect square.

$$x^2 + 5x = 50$$

$$x^2 + 5x + \left(\boxed{}\right)^2 = 50 + \left(\boxed{}\right)^2 \quad \text{Add } \left(\boxed{}\right)^2, \text{ or } \frac{25}{4}, \text{ to each side.}$$

$$\left(x + \frac{5}{2}\right)^2 = \frac{\boxed{}}{4} + \frac{\boxed{}}{4} \quad \text{Write } x^2 + 5x + \left(\frac{5}{2}\right)^2 \text{ as a square.}$$

$$\left(x + \frac{5}{2}\right)^2 = \frac{\boxed{}}{4} \quad \text{Simplify.}$$

Step 2 Solve the equation.

$$\left(x + \frac{5}{2}\right) = \pm\sqrt{\frac{225}{4}} \quad \text{Find the square root of each side.}$$

$$x + \frac{5}{2} = \pm\frac{\boxed{}}{2} \quad \text{Simplify.}$$

$$x + \frac{5}{2} = \boxed{} \quad \text{or} \quad x + \frac{5}{2} = \boxed{} \quad \text{Write as two equations.}$$

$$x = \boxed{} \quad \text{or} \quad x = \boxed{} \quad \text{Solve for } x.$$

CA Standards Check

1. Find the value of n such that $x^2 + 22x + n$ is a perfect square trinomial.

$\boxed{}$

Example

❸ **Solving $x^2 + bx + c = 0$** Solve $x^2 + 10x - 16 = 0$. Round to the nearest hundredth.

Step 1 Rewrite the equation in the form $x^2 + bx = c$ and complete the square.

$$x^2 + 10x - 16 = 0$$

$$x^2 + 10x = \boxed{}$$ Add $\boxed{}$ to each side of the equation.

$$x^2 + 10x + \boxed{} = 16 + \boxed{}$$ Add $\left(\boxed{}\right)^2$, or $\boxed{}$, to each side of the equation.

$$\left(x + \boxed{}\right)^2 = \boxed{}$$ Write $x^2 + 10x + 25$ as a square.

Step 2 Solve the equation.

$$x + 5 = \pm\sqrt{\boxed{}}$$ Find the square root of each side.

$$x + 5 \approx \pm\boxed{}$$ Approximate $\sqrt{41}$.

$$x + 5 \approx \boxed{} \quad \text{or} \quad x + 5 \approx \boxed{}$$ Write as two equations.

$$x \approx \boxed{} - \boxed{} \quad \text{or} \quad x \approx \boxed{} - \boxed{}$$ Subtract $\boxed{}$ from each side.

$$x \approx \boxed{} \quad \text{or} \quad x \approx \boxed{}$$ Simplify.

CA Standards Check

2. Solve the equation $m^2 - 6m = 247$.

3. Solve each equation. Round to the nearest hundredth.

a. $x^2 + 5x + 3 = 0$ **b.** $x^2 - 14x + 16 = 0$

Name_____ Class_____ Date _____

Example

❹ **Application** Suppose you wish to section off a soccer field as shown in the diagram to run a variety of practice drills. If the area of the field is 6000 yd², what is the value of x?

Define | width | = $x + 10 + 10$ = [＿＿＿].

| length | = $x + x + 10 + 10$ = [＿＿＿].

Relate | Length | × | width | = | area |.

Write ([＿＿＿])([＿＿＿]) = [＿＿＿]

$2x^2 +$ [＿＿＿] + [＿＿＿] = [＿＿＿]

Step 1 Rewrite the equation in the form $x^2 + bx = c$.

$2x^2 +$ [＿＿＿] + [＿＿＿] = [＿＿＿]

$2x^2$ + [＿＿＿] = [＿＿＿] Subtract [＿＿＿] from each side.

x^2 + [＿＿＿] = [＿＿＿] Divide each side by [＿].

Step 2 Complete the square.

$x^2 + 30x +$ [＿＿＿] = $2800 +$ [＿＿＿] Add $\left(\frac{30}{2}\right)^2$, or [＿＿＿], to each side.

$\left(x +\right.$ [＿＿＿] $\left.\right)^2 =$ [＿＿＿] Write $x^2 + 30x +$ [＿＿＿] as a square.

Step 3 Solve the equation.

$(x + 15) = \pm\sqrt{\rule{1.5cm}{0pt}}$ Take the square root of each side.

$x + 15 = \pm$ [＿＿＿] Approximate $\sqrt{3025}$.

$x + 15 =$ [＿＿] or $x + 15 =$ [＿＿] Write as two equations.

$x =$ [＿＿] or $x =$ [＿＿] Use the positive answer for this problem.

The value of x is [＿＿] yd.

CA Content Standards

4. Solve each equation. Round to the nearest hundredth.

   a. $4a^2 + 8a = 24$

   b. $5n^2 - 3n - 15 = 10$

Lesson 9-7

Using the Quadratic Formula

Lesson Objectives	California Content Standards
• Use the quadratic formula when solving quadratic equations • Choose an appropriate method for solving a quadratic equation	19.0, 20.0, 23.0

Take Note

Quadratic Formula

If $ax^2 + bx + c = 0$, a, b, and c are real numbers and $a \neq 0$, then $x =$ 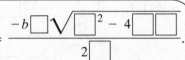.

Example

❶ Using the Quadratic Formula Solve $x^2 + 2 = -3x$ using the quadratic formula.

$x^2 + 3x + 2 = 0$ **Add** ☐ **to each side and write in standard form.**

$x = \boxed{}$ **Use the quadratic formula.**

$x = \dfrac{-\square \pm \sqrt{(\square)^2 - 4(\square)(\square)}}{2(\square)}$ **Substitute** ☐ **for** a, ☐ **for** b, **and** ☐ **for** c.

$x = \dfrac{\square \pm \sqrt{\square}}{\square}$ **Simplify.**

$x = \dfrac{-3 + \square}{2}$ or $x = \dfrac{-3 - \square}{2}$ **Write as two equations.**

$x = \boxed{}$ or $x = \boxed{}$ **Simplify.**

Check   for $x = \boxed{}$ for $x = \boxed{}$

$(\boxed{})^2 + 3(\boxed{}) + 2 \stackrel{?}{=} 0$ $(\boxed{})^2 + 3(\boxed{}) + 2 \stackrel{?}{=} 0$

$1 - 3 + 2 \stackrel{?}{=} 0$ $4 - 6 + 2 \stackrel{?}{=} 0$

$0 = 0 \checkmark$ $0 = 0 \checkmark$

CA Standards Check

1. Use the quadratic formula to solve each equation.

     a. $x^2 - 2x - 8 = 0$ **b.** $x^2 - 4x = 117$

Examples

❷ Application A child throws a ball upward with an initial upward velocity of 15 ft/s from a height of 2 ft. If no one catches the ball, after how many seconds will it land? Use the vertical motion formula $h = -16t^2 + vt + c$, where $h = 0$, v = velocity, c = starting height, and t = time to land. Round to the nearest hundredth of a second.

Step 1 Use the vertical motion formula.

$$h = -16t^2 + vt + c$$
$$0 = -16t^2 + \boxed{}t + \boxed{}$$ Substitute $\boxed{}$ for h, $\boxed{}$ for v, and $\boxed{}$ for c.

Step 2 Use the quadratic formula.

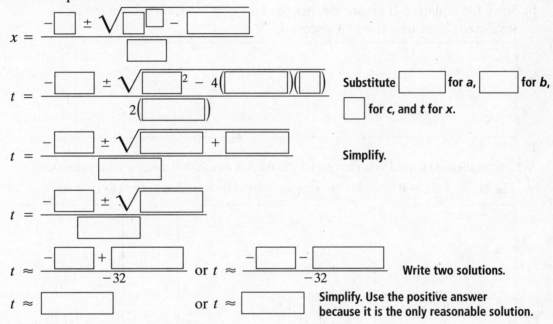

Substitute $\boxed{}$ for a, $\boxed{}$ for b, $\boxed{}$ for c, and t for x.

Simplify.

Write two solutions.

Simplify. Use the positive answer because it is the only reasonable solution.

The ball will land in about $\boxed{}$ seconds.

❸ Choosing an Appropriate Method Which method(s) would you choose to solve each equation? Justify your reasoning.

a. $5x^2 + 8x - 14 = 0$ $\boxed{}$; the equation $\boxed{}$ be factored easily.

b. $25x^2 - 169 = 0$ Square $\boxed{}$; there is no x term.

c. $x^2 - 2x - 3 = 0$ $\boxed{}$; the equation $\boxed{}$ easily factorable.

d. $x^2 - 5x + 3 = 0$ $\boxed{}$, completing the square, or graphing; the x^2 term is 1, but the equation $\boxed{}$ factorable.

Name_____ Class_____ Date _____

CA Standards Check

2. A football player kicks a ball with an initial upward velocity of 38.4 ft/s from a starting height of 3.5 ft.

   a. Substitute the values into the vertical motion formula from Example 2.
Let $h = 0$.

   b. Solve the equation. If no one catches the ball, how long will it be in the air?
Round to the nearest tenth of a second.

3. Which method(s) would you choose to solve each equation? Justify your reasoning.

   a. $13x^2 - 5x + 21 = 0$ **b.** $x^2 - x - 30 = 0$ **c.** $144x^2 = 25$

Lesson 9-8

Using the Discriminant

Lesson Objective	California Content Standards
• Find the number of solutions of a quadratic equation	22.0, 23.0

Take Note

Property of the Discriminant

For real numbers a, b, and c, where $a \neq 0$, the quadratic function is $y = ax + bx + c$, and its related quadratic equation is $ax + bx + c = 0$.

If $b^2 - 4ac > 0$, then
- the graph of the quadratic function intersects the x-axis in [____] points.
- the related quadratic equation has [____] solutions.

If $b^2 - 4ac = 0$, then
- the graph of the quadratic function intersects the x-axis in [____] point.
- the related quadratic equation has [____] solution.

If $b^2 - 4ac < 0$, then
- the graph of the quadratic function intersects the x-axis in [____] points.
- the related quadratic equation has [____] solution.

The discriminant is _____

_____

Example

❶ **Finding the Number of Solutions** Find the number of solutions when $x^2 = -3x - 7$.

$x^2 + 3x + 7 = 0$ **Write in standard form.**

$b^2 - 4ac = []^2 - 4([])([])$ **Evaluate the discriminant. Substitute for a, b, and c.**

$= 9 - []$ **Use the order of operations.**

$= []$ **Simplify.**

Since [____] < 0, the equation has [____] solution.

CA Standards Check

1. Find the number of solutions when $3x^2 - 4x = 7$.

[   ]

Example

② **Application** A football is kicked from a starting height of 3 ft with an initial upward velocity of 40 ft/s. Will the football ever reach a height of 30 ft? Use the vertical motion formula $h = -16t^2 + vt + c$, where $h = 30$, $v =$ velocity, $c =$ starting height, and $t =$ time to land.

$h = -16t^2 + vt + c$ — **Use the vertical motion formula.**

$\boxed{} = -16t^2 + \boxed{}t + 3$ — **Substitute** $\boxed{}$ **for h,** $\boxed{}$ **for v, and** $\boxed{}$ **for c.**

$0 = -16t^2 + 40t - \boxed{}$ — **Write in standard form.**

$b^2 - 4ac = (40)^2 - 4\left(\boxed{}\right)\left(\boxed{}\right)$ — **Evaluate the discriminant.**

$= \boxed{} - 1{,}728$ — **Use the order of operations.**

$= \boxed{}$ — **Simplify.**

The discriminant is $\boxed{}$. The football $\boxed{}$ reach a height of 30 ft.

CA Standards Check

2. A construction worker on the ground tosses an apple to a fellow worker who is 20 ft above the ground. The starting height of the apple is 5 ft with an initial upward velocity of 32 ft/s. Will the apple reach the worker? Use the vertical motion formula.

Lesson 10-1

Lesson Objectives	California Content Standards
• Simplify radicals involving products • Simplify radicals involving quotients	2.0

Take Note

Multiplication Property of Square Roots

For every number $a \geq 0$ and $b \geq 0$, $\sqrt{ab} = \boxed{} \cdot \boxed{}$.

Example $\sqrt{54} = \boxed{} \cdot \boxed{} = \boxed{} \cdot \sqrt{6} = 3\sqrt{6}$

Division Property of Square Roots

For every number $a \geq 0$ and $b > 0$, $\sqrt{\dfrac{a}{b}} = \dfrac{\boxed{}}{\boxed{}}$.

Example $\sqrt{\dfrac{16}{25}} = \dfrac{\boxed{}}{\boxed{}} = \dfrac{4}{5}$

Simplest Radical Form

A radical expression is in simplest radical form when all three statements are true.

• The radicand has no $\boxed{}$.

• The radicand has no $\boxed{}$.

• The $\boxed{}$ has no radical.

A radical expression is _____

Rationalize means _____

_____

_____

Examples

❶ Removing Variable Factors Simplify $\sqrt{28x^7}$.

$\sqrt{28x^7} = \sqrt{\boxed{}^{\boxed{}} \cdot 7x}$ $\boxed{}^{\boxed{}}$ is a perfect square and a factor of $28x^7$.

$= \sqrt{\boxed{}^{\boxed{}}} \cdot \sqrt{7x}$ Use the Multiplication Property of Square Roots.

$= \boxed{}^{\boxed{}} \sqrt{7x}$ Simplify $\sqrt{\boxed{}^{\boxed{}}}$.

❷ Multiplying Two Radicals Simplify each radical expression.

a. $\sqrt{12} \cdot \sqrt{32} = \sqrt{\boxed{} \cdot \boxed{}}$ Use the Multiplication Property of Square Roots.

$= \sqrt{\boxed{}}$ Simplify under the radical.

$= \sqrt{\boxed{} \cdot 6}$ $\boxed{}$ is a perfect square and a factor of 384.

$= \sqrt{\boxed{}} \cdot \sqrt{6}$ Use the Multiplication Property of Square Roots.

$= \boxed{} \sqrt{6}$ Simplify $\sqrt{\boxed{}}$.

b. $7\sqrt{5x} \cdot 3\sqrt{8x} = \boxed{} \sqrt{\boxed{} x^2}$ Multiply the whole numbers and use the Multiplication Property of Square Roots.

$= 21\sqrt{\boxed{}^{\boxed{}} \cdot 10}$ $\boxed{}^{\boxed{}}$ is a perfect square and a factor of $40x^2$.

$= 21\sqrt{\boxed{}^{\boxed{}}} \cdot \sqrt{10}$ Use the Multiplication Property of Square Roots.

$= 21 \cdot \boxed{} \sqrt{10}$ Simplify $\sqrt{\boxed{}^{\boxed{}}}$.

$= \boxed{} \sqrt{10}$ Simplify.

❸ Simplifying Radicals by Dividing Simplify $\sqrt{\dfrac{75x^5}{48x}}$.

$\sqrt{\dfrac{75x^5}{48x}} = \sqrt{\dfrac{\boxed{}^{\boxed{}}}{\boxed{}}}$ Divide the numerator and denominator by $\boxed{}$.

$= \dfrac{\sqrt{\boxed{}^{\boxed{}}}}{\sqrt{\boxed{}}}$ Use the Division Property of Square Roots.

$= \dfrac{\sqrt{\boxed{}} \cdot \sqrt{\boxed{}}}{\sqrt{16}}$ Use the Multiplication Property of Square Roots.

$= \dfrac{\boxed{}^{\boxed{}}}{\boxed{}}$ Simplify $\sqrt{\boxed{}}$, $\sqrt{\boxed{}}$, and $\sqrt{\boxed{}}$.

❹ Rationalizing a Denominator Simplify by rationalizing the denominator.

a. $\dfrac{3}{\sqrt{7}} = \dfrac{3}{\sqrt{7}} \cdot \dfrac{\boxed{}}{\boxed{}}$ **Multiply by** $\dfrac{\boxed{}}{\boxed{}}$ **to make the denominator a perfect square.**

$= \dfrac{\boxed{}}{\boxed{}}$ **Use the Multiplication Property of Square Roots.**

$= \dfrac{3\sqrt{7}}{7}$ **Simplify** $\boxed{}$.

b. $\dfrac{\sqrt{11}}{\sqrt{12x^3}} = \dfrac{\sqrt{11}}{\sqrt{12x^3}} \cdot \dfrac{\boxed{}}{\boxed{}}$ **Multiply by** $\dfrac{\boxed{}}{\boxed{}}$ **to make the denominator a perfect square.**

$= \dfrac{\boxed{}}{\boxed{}}$ **Use the Multiplication Property of Square Roots.**

$= \dfrac{\sqrt{33x}}{6x^2}$ **Simplify** $\boxed{}$.

CA Standards Check

Simplify each radical expression.

1. $-a\sqrt{60a^7}$

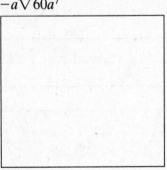

2. a. $\sqrt{13} \cdot \sqrt{52}$

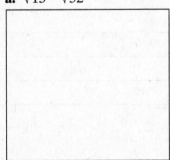

b. $5\sqrt{3c} \cdot \sqrt{6c}$

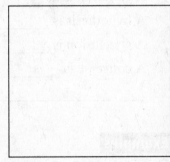

3. $\sqrt{\dfrac{27x^3}{3x}}$

4. a. $\dfrac{3}{\sqrt{3}}$

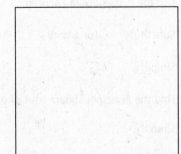

b. $\dfrac{\sqrt{5}}{\sqrt{18t}}$

Lesson 10-2

Lesson Objectives	California Content Standards
• Solve problems using the Pythagorean Theorem • Identify right triangles	2.0, 24.2

Take Note

The Pythagorean Theorem

In any right triangle, the sum of the squares of the lengths of the legs is equal to the square of the length of the hypotenuse.

$$\boxed{}^2 + \boxed{}^2 = \boxed{}^2$$

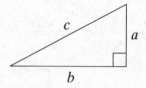

The Converse of the Pythagorean Theorem

If a triangle has sides of lengths a, b, and c, and $a^2 + b^2 = c^2$, then the triangle is a $\boxed{}$ with hypotenuse of length c.

The hypotenuse is _____

_____

The legs are _____

A conditional is _____

A hypothesis is _____

A conclusion is _____

A converse is _____

_____

Examples

❶ **Using the Pythagorean Theorem** What is the length of the hypotenuse of the triangle at the right?

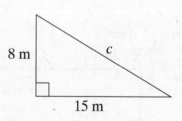

$a^2 + b^2 = c^2$ Use the Pythagorean Theorem.

$\boxed{}^2 + \boxed{}^2 = c^2$ Substitute $\boxed{}$ for a and $\boxed{}$ for b.

$\boxed{} + \boxed{} = c^2$ Simplify.

$\sqrt{\boxed{}} = \sqrt{c^2}$ Find the principal square root of each side.

$\boxed{} = c$ Simplify.

The length of the hypotenuse is 17 m.

❷ Using the Converse of the Pythagorean Theorem Determine whether the given lengths can be sides of a right triangle.

a. 5 in., 5 in., and 7 in.

$\boxed{}^2 + \boxed{}^2 \overset{?}{=} \boxed{}^2$ Determine whether $a^2 + b^2 = c^2$, where c is the longest side.

$\boxed{} + \boxed{} \overset{?}{=} \boxed{}$ Simplify.

$\boxed{} \neq \boxed{}$

This triangle $\boxed{}$ a right triangle.

b. 10 cm, 24 cm, and 26 cm

$\boxed{}^2 + \boxed{}^2 \overset{?}{=} \boxed{}^2$ Determine whether $a^2 + b^2 = c^2$, where c is the longest side.

$\boxed{} + \boxed{} \overset{?}{=} \boxed{}$ Simplify.

$\boxed{} = \boxed{}$

This triangle $\boxed{}$ a right triangle.

❸ Application If two forces pull at right angles to each other, the resultant force is represented as the diagonal of a rectangle, as shown in the diagram. The diagonal forms a right triangle with two of the perpendicular sides of the rectangle.

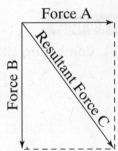

For a 50-lb force and a 120-lb force, the resultant force is 130 lb. Are the forces pulling at right angles to each other?

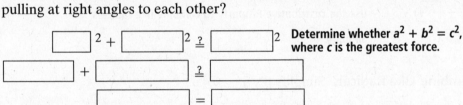

$\boxed{}^2 + \boxed{}^2 \overset{?}{=} \boxed{}^2$ Determine whether $a^2 + b^2 = c^2$, where c is the greatest force.

$\boxed{} + \boxed{} \overset{?}{=} \boxed{}$

$\boxed{} = \boxed{}$

The forces of 50 lb and 120 lb $\boxed{}$ at right angles to each other.

CA Standards Check

1. What is the length of the hypotenuse of a right triangle with legs of lengths 7 cm and 24 cm?

$\boxed{}$

2. A triangle has sides of lengths 10 m, 24 m, and 26 m. Is the triangle a right triangle?

$\boxed{}$

3. Application Consider Example 3. For a 70-lb force and a 60-lb force, the resultant force is 100 lb. Are the forces pulling at right angles to each other?

$\boxed{}$

Lesson 10-3

Operations With Radical Expressions

Lesson Objectives	California Content Standards
• Simplify sums and differences • Simplify products and quotients	2.0, 25.0

Take Note

Like radicals are _____

_____

Unlike radicals are _____

_____

Conjugates are _____

_____

Examples

❶ Combining Like Radicals Simplify $4\sqrt{3} + \sqrt{3}$.

$4\sqrt{3} + \sqrt{3} = \boxed{}\sqrt{3} + \boxed{}\sqrt{3}$ terms contain $\sqrt{\boxed{}}$.

$= (\boxed{} + \boxed{})\sqrt{3}$ Use the Distributive Property to combine like radicals.

$= \boxed{}\sqrt{3}$ Simplify.

❷ Simplifying to Combine Like Radicals Simplify $8\sqrt{5} - \sqrt{45}$.

$8\sqrt{5} - \sqrt{45} = 8\sqrt{5} - \sqrt{\boxed{} \cdot 5}$ $\boxed{}$ is a perfect square and a factor of 45.

$= 8\sqrt{5} - \sqrt{\boxed{}} \cdot \sqrt{5}$ Use the Multiplication Property of Square Roots.

$= \boxed{}\sqrt{5} - \boxed{}\sqrt{5}$ Simplify $\sqrt{\boxed{}}$.

$= (\boxed{} - \boxed{})\sqrt{5}$ Use the Distributive Property to combine like terms.

$= \boxed{}\sqrt{5}$ Simplify.

CA Standards Check

1. Simplify each expression.

a. $-3\sqrt{5} - 4\sqrt{5}$

b. $\sqrt{10} - 5\sqrt{10}$

Examples

❸ Using the Distributive Property Simplify $\sqrt{5}(\sqrt{8} + 9)$.

$\sqrt{5}(\sqrt{8} + 9) = \sqrt{\boxed{}} + \boxed{}\sqrt{5}$ **Use the Distributive Property.**

$= \sqrt{\boxed{}} \cdot \sqrt{\boxed{}} + \boxed{}\sqrt{5}$ **Use the Multiplication Property of Square Roots.**

$= \boxed{}\sqrt{\boxed{}} + \boxed{}\sqrt{5}$ **Simplify.**

❹ Simplifying Using FOIL Simplify $(\sqrt{6} - 3\sqrt{21})(\sqrt{6} + \sqrt{21})$.

$(\sqrt{6} - 3\sqrt{21})(\sqrt{6} + \sqrt{21})$

$= \sqrt{\boxed{}} + \sqrt{\boxed{}} - 3\sqrt{\boxed{}} - 3\sqrt{\boxed{}}$ **Use FOIL.**

$= \boxed{} - \boxed{}\sqrt{126} - 3\left(\boxed{}\right)$ **Combine like radicals and simplify $\sqrt{36}$ and $\sqrt{441}$.**

$= \boxed{} - 2\sqrt{\boxed{} \cdot 14} - \boxed{}$ **$\boxed{}$ is a perfect square factor of 126.**

$= \boxed{} - 2\sqrt{\boxed{}} \cdot \sqrt{\boxed{}} - 63$ **Use the Multiplication Property of Square Roots.**

$= \boxed{} - \boxed{}\sqrt{\boxed{}} - 63$ **Simplify $\sqrt{9}$.**

$= \boxed{} - \boxed{}\sqrt{14}$ **Simplify.**

CA Standards Check

Simplify each expression.

2. a. $3\sqrt{20} + 2\sqrt{5}$

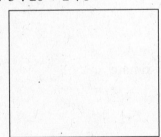

b. $3\sqrt{3} - 2\sqrt{27}$

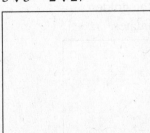

3. a. $\sqrt{5}(2 + \sqrt{10})$

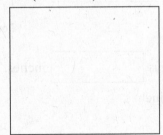

b. $\sqrt{2x}(\sqrt{6x} - 11)$

4. a. $(2\sqrt{6} + 3\sqrt{3})(\sqrt{6} - 5\sqrt{3})$

b. $(\sqrt{7} + 4)^2$

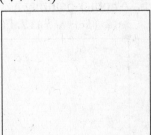

Example

⑤ Application A painting has a length : width ratio approximately equal to the golden ratio $(1 + \sqrt{5}) : 2$. The length of the painting is 51 inches. Find the exact width of the painting in simplest radical form. Then find the approximate width to the nearest inch.

Define $\boxed{51}$ = length of painting

$\boxed{x}$ = width of painting

Relate $(1 + \sqrt{5}) : 2 = $ length : width

Write $\dfrac{(1 + \sqrt{5})}{2} = \dfrac{\boxed{}}{\boxed{}}$

$\boxed{}(1 + \sqrt{5}) = \boxed{}$ **Cross multiply.**

$x\left(\dfrac{1 + \sqrt{5}}{\boxed{}}\right) = \dfrac{102}{\boxed{}}$ **Divide both sides by $(1 + \sqrt{5})$.**

$x = \dfrac{102}{1 + \sqrt{5}} \cdot \dfrac{\boxed{}}{\boxed{}}$ **Multiply the numerator and denominator by the $\boxed{}$ of the denominator.**

$x = \dfrac{102(1 - \sqrt{5})}{\boxed{} - \boxed{}} = \dfrac{102(1 - \sqrt{5})}{\boxed{}}$ **Multiply and simplify the denominator.**

$x = \dfrac{\boxed{}(1 - \sqrt{5})}{\boxed{}}$ **Divide 102 and −4 by the common factor $\boxed{}$.**

$x = \boxed{}$ **Use a calculator.**

$x \approx \boxed{}$ **Round.**

The exact width of the painting is $\boxed{}$ inches. The approximate width of the painting is $\boxed{}$ inches.

CA Standards Check

5. Another painting has a length : width ratio approximately equal to the golden ratio $(1 + \sqrt{5}) : 2$. Find the length of the painting if the width is 34 inches.

Lesson 10-4

Lesson Objectives	**California Content Standards**
• Solve equations containing radicals • Identify extraneous solutions	2.0, 25.2

Take Note

A radical equation is _____

_____

An extraneous solution is _____

_____

Example

1 **Solving by Isolating the Radical** Solve the equation. Check your solution.

$\sqrt{x} - 5 = 4$

$\sqrt{x} = \boxed{}$ Get the radical on the left side of the equation.

$(\sqrt{x})^2 = \boxed{}^2$ Square both sides.

$x = \boxed{}$

Check $\sqrt{x} - 5 = 4$

$\sqrt{\boxed{}} - 5 \overset{?}{=} 4$ Substitute $\boxed{}$ for x.

$\boxed{} - 5 \overset{?}{=} 4$

$4 = 4 \checkmark$

CA Standards Check

1. Solve each equation. Check your solution.

    a. $\sqrt{x} + 7 = 12$ **b.** $\sqrt{a} - 4 = 5$ **c.** $\sqrt{c - 2} = 6$

Name_____ Class_____ Date _____

Examples

❷ **Application** On a roller coaster ride, your speed in a loop depends on the height of the hill you have just come down and the radius of the loop in feet. The equation $v = 8\sqrt{h - 2r}$ gives the velocity v in feet per second of a car at the top of the loop.

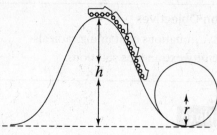

Suppose the loop on a roller coaster ride has a radius of 18 ft. You want the car to have a velocity of 120 ft/s at the top of the loop. How high should the hill be?

Solve $v = 8\sqrt{h - 2r}$ for h when $v = \boxed{}$ and $r = \boxed{}$.

$\boxed{} = 8\sqrt{h - 2\left(\boxed{}\right)}$ **Substitute** $\boxed{}$ **for** *v* **and** $\boxed{}$ **for** *r*.

$\dfrac{120}{\boxed{}} = \dfrac{8\sqrt{h - 2(18)}}{\boxed{}}$ **Divide each side by** $\boxed{}$ **to isolate the radical.**

$\boxed{} = \sqrt{h - \boxed{}}$ **Simplify.**

$\left(\boxed{}\right)^2 = \left(\sqrt{h - \boxed{}}\right)^2$ **Square both sides.**

$\boxed{} = h - 36$

$\boxed{} = h$

The hill should be about $\boxed{}$ ft high.

❸ **Solving With Radical Expressions on Both Sides** Solve $\sqrt{3x - 4} = \sqrt{2x + 3}$.

$\left(\sqrt{3x - 4}\right)^2 = \left(\sqrt{2x + 3}\right)^2$ **Square both sides.**

$3x - 4 = 2x + 3$ **Simplify.**

$3x = 2x + \boxed{}$ **Add** $\boxed{}$ **to each side.**

$\boxed{} = 7$ **Subtract** $\boxed{}$ **from each side.**

Check $\sqrt{3x - 4} = \sqrt{2x + 3}$

$\sqrt{3\left(\boxed{}\right) - 4} \stackrel{?}{=} \sqrt{2\left(\boxed{}\right) + 3}$ **Substitute** $\boxed{}$ **for** *x*.

$\sqrt{\boxed{}} = \sqrt{\boxed{}}$ ✓

The solution is $\boxed{}$.

④ Identifying Extraneous Solutions Solve $x = \sqrt{x + 12}$.

$$(x)^2 = \left(\sqrt{x + 12}\right)^2 \qquad \text{Square both sides.}$$

$$x^2 = x + 12 \qquad \text{Simplify.}$$

$$x^2 - \boxed{} - \boxed{} = 0 \qquad \text{Subtract } x \text{ and 12 from both sides.}$$

$$\left(x - \boxed{}\right)\left(x + \boxed{}\right) = 0 \qquad \text{Solve the quadratic equation by factoring.}$$

$$\left(x - \boxed{}\right) = 0 \text{ or } \left(x + \boxed{}\right) = 0 \qquad \text{Use the Zero-Product Property.}$$

$$x = \boxed{} \text{ or } x = \boxed{} \qquad \text{Solve for } x.$$

Check  $x = \sqrt{x + 12}$

$$\boxed{} \overset{?}{=} \sqrt{\boxed{} + 12} \qquad \boxed{} \overset{?}{=} \sqrt{\boxed{} + 12} \qquad \text{Substitute 4 and } -3 \text{ for } x.$$

$$\boxed{} = \boxed{} \checkmark \qquad \boxed{} \neq 3$$

The solution to the original equation is $\boxed{}$. The value $\boxed{}$ is an extraneous solution.

CA Standards Check

2. Use the formula from Example 2. Find the height of the hill when the velocity at the top of the loop is 35 ft/s, and the radius of the loop is 24 ft.

3. Solve $\sqrt{3t + 4} = \sqrt{5t - 6}$. Check your answer.

4. Critical Thinking In Example 4, how could you determine that -3 was not a solution of $x = \sqrt{x + 12}$ without going through all the steps of the check?

Lesson 10-5

Graphing Square Root Functions

Lesson Objectives	California Content Standards
• Graph square root functions • Translate graphs of square root functions	17.0

Take Note

A square root function is _____

_____

Examples

❶ **Finding Domain and Range** Find the domain and range of each function.

a. $y = \sqrt{x + 5}$

$x + \boxed{} \geq 0$ **Make the radicand greater than or equal to 0.**

$x \geq \boxed{}$

The domain is $\boxed{}$.

The range is $\boxed{}$.

b. $y = \sqrt{4x - 12} - 6$

$4x - 12 \geq \boxed{}$ **Make the radicand greater**

$4x \geq \boxed{}$ **than or equal to $\boxed{}$.**

$x \geq \boxed{}$

The domain is $\boxed{}$.

The range is $\boxed{}$.

❷ **Graphing a Square Root Function** Graph $f(x) = \sqrt{x + 3}$.

$x + 3 \geq \boxed{}$ **Make the radicand $\geq \boxed{}$.**

$x \geq \boxed{}$

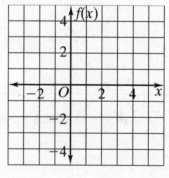

Step 1 Make a table of values.

x	$f(x) = \sqrt{x + 3}$
−3	$\boxed{}$
−2	$\boxed{}$
1	$\boxed{}$
6	$\boxed{}$

Step 2 Plot the points.

Step 3 Join the points to form a $\boxed{}$.

❸ Application The size of a television screen is the length of the screen's diagonal d in inches. The equation $d = \sqrt{2A}$ estimates the length of a diagonal of a television with screen area A. Graph the function.

Domain
$2A \geq 0$

Screen Area (sq. in.)	Length of Diagonal (in.)
$A \geq 0 \rightarrow$ 0	
50	
100	
200	
300	
400	

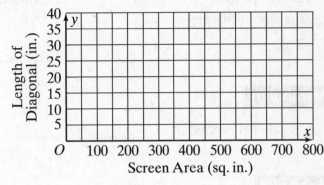

CA Standards Check

1. Find the domain and range of each function.

   a. $y = \sqrt{x - 7}$

   b. $y = \sqrt{3x - 1}$

2. Graph $f(x) = \sqrt{x - 3}$.

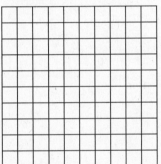

3. **Critical Thinking** What is the area of a television screen with a diagonal length of 45 inches?

Lesson 11-1

Lesson Objective	California Content Standards
• Simplify rational expressions	12.0

Vocabulary

A rational expression is _____

Examples

① Simplifying a Rational Expression Simplify $\dfrac{4x - 20}{x^2 - 9x + 20}$.

$$\frac{4x - 20}{x^2 - 9x + 20} = \frac{\boxed{}(x - 5)}{\left(x - \boxed{}\right)\left(\boxed{} - \boxed{}\right)}$$ Factor the numerator and the denominator.

$$= \frac{4\cancel{(x - 5)}^{\boxed{}}}{(x - 4)\cancel{(x - 5)}^{\boxed{}}}$$ Divide out the common factor $\boxed{}$.

$$= \frac{\boxed{}}{\boxed{}}$$ Simplify.

② Recognizing Opposite Factors Simplify $\dfrac{3x - 27}{81 - x^2}$.

$$\frac{3x - 27}{81 - x^2} = \frac{3\left(\boxed{}\right)}{(9 - x)\left(\boxed{}\right)}$$ Factor the numerator and the denominator.

$$= \frac{3(x - 9)}{-1\left(\boxed{}\right)(9 + x)}$$ Factor $\boxed{}$ from $9 - x$.

$$= \frac{3\cancel{(x - 9)}^{\boxed{}}}{-1\boxed{}\cancel{(x - 9)}(9 + x)}$$ Divide out the common factor $\boxed{}$.

$$= -\frac{\boxed{}}{\boxed{}}$$ Simplify.

❸ Evaluating a Rational Expression The baking time for bread depends, in part, on its size and shape. A good approximation for the baking time, in minutes, of a cylindrical loaf is $\frac{60 \cdot \text{volume}}{\text{surface area}}$, or $\frac{30rh}{r + h}$, where the radius r and the length h of the baked loaf are in inches. Find the baking time for a loaf that is 8 inches long and has a radius of 3 inches. Round your answer to the nearest minute.

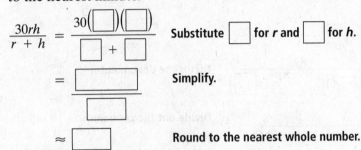

$\frac{30rh}{r + h} = \dfrac{30(\boxed{})(\boxed{})}{\boxed{} + \boxed{}}$ Substitute $\boxed{}$ for r and $\boxed{}$ for h.

$= \boxed{}$ **Simplify.**

$\boxed{}$

$\approx \boxed{}$ **Round to the nearest whole number.**

The baking time is approximately $\boxed{}$ minutes.

CA Standards Check

1. Simplify each expression.

a. $\frac{12c^2}{3c + 6}$

$\boxed{}$

b. $\frac{c^2 - c - 6}{c^2 + 5c + 6}$

$\boxed{}$

2. Simplify each expression.

a. $\frac{x - 4}{4 - x}$

$\boxed{}$

b. $\frac{8 - 4r}{r^2 + 2r - 8}$

$\boxed{}$

3. a. Find the baking time for a loaf that is 4 inches long and has a radius of 3 inches. Round your answer to the nearest minute.

$\boxed{}$

b. Critical Thinking The ratio $\frac{60 \cdot \text{volume}}{\text{surface area}}$ for a cylinder is $\frac{60\pi r^2 h}{2\pi r^2 + 2\pi rh}$. Simplify this expression to show that it is the same as the expression evaluated in Example 3.

$\boxed{}$

Lesson 11-2

Multiplying and Dividing Rational Expressions

Lesson Objectives	California Content Standards
• Multiply rational expressions • Divide rational expressions	2.0, 13.0

Examples

❶ Using Factoring Multiply $\frac{3x+1}{4}$ and $\frac{8x}{9x^2-1}$.

$$\frac{3x+1}{4} \cdot \frac{8x}{9x^2-1} = \frac{3x+1}{4} \cdot \frac{8x}{(3x-1)(\boxed{}+\boxed{})}$$
Factor the denominator.

$$= \frac{\cancel{3x+1}^{\boxed{}}}{\boxed{}4} \cdot \frac{\cancel{8}^{\boxed{}}x}{(3x-1)\cancel{(3x+1)}}$$
Divide out the common factors.

$$= \frac{\boxed{}}{3x-1}$$
Simplify.

❷ Multiplying a Rational Expression by a Polynomial

Multiply $\frac{5x+1}{3x+12}$ and $x^2+7x+12$.

$$\frac{5x+1}{3x+12} \cdot (x^2+7x+12) = \frac{5x+1}{3(\boxed{})} \cdot \frac{(\boxed{})(\boxed{})}{1}$$
Factor.

$$= \frac{5x+1}{3\cancel{(x+4)}} \cdot \frac{(x+3)\cancel{(x+4)}^{\boxed{}}}{1}$$
Divide out the common factor $\boxed{}$.

$$= \frac{(5x+1)(x+3)}{\boxed{}}$$
Leave in factored form.

❸ Dividing Rational Expressions Divide $\frac{x^2+13x+40}{x-7}$ by $\frac{x+8}{x^2-49}$.

$$\frac{x^2+13x+40}{x-7} \div \frac{x+8}{x^2-49}$$

$$= \frac{x^2+13x+40}{x-7} \cdot \frac{\boxed{}}{x+8}$$
Multiply by $\frac{x^2-49}{x+8}$, the $\boxed{}$ of $\frac{x+8}{x^2-49}$.

$$= \frac{(\boxed{})(x+8)}{x-7} \cdot \frac{(\boxed{})(x-7)}{x+8}$$
Factor.

$$= \frac{\boxed{}^{\cancel{(x+8)}}(x+5)}{\cancel{x-7}_{\boxed{}}} \cdot \frac{(x+7)\cancel{(x-7)}^{\boxed{}}}{\cancel{x+8}_{\boxed{}}}$$
Divide out the common factors.

$$= (\boxed{})(\boxed{})$$
Leave in factored form.

❹ Dividing a Rational Expression by a Polynomial

Divide $\dfrac{x^2 + 9x + 14}{11x}$ by $(8x^2 + 16x)$.

$$\dfrac{x^2 + 9x + 14}{11x} \div \dfrac{8x^2 + 16x}{1}$$

$$= \dfrac{x^2 + 9x + 14}{11x} \cdot \dfrac{1}{\boxed{}}$$

Multiply by the $\boxed{}$ of $8x^2 + 16x$.

$$= \dfrac{(x + 7)\left(\boxed{}\right)}{11x} \cdot \dfrac{1}{\boxed{}(x + 2)}$$

Factor.

$$= \dfrac{(x + 7)\cancel{(x + 2)}^{\boxed{}}}{11x} \cdot \dfrac{1}{8x\cancel{(x + 2)}_{\boxed{}}}$$

Divide out the common factor.

$$= \dfrac{\boxed{}}{\boxed{}}$$

Simplify.

CA Standards Check

Multiply.

1. $\dfrac{x - 2}{8x} \cdot \dfrac{-8x - 16}{x^2 - 4}$

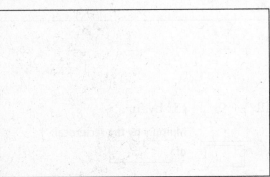

2. $\dfrac{3}{c} \cdot (c^3 - c)$

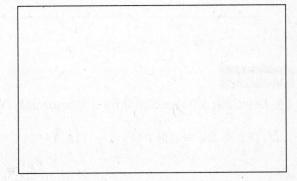

Divide.

3. $\dfrac{a - 2}{ab} \div \dfrac{a - 2}{a}$

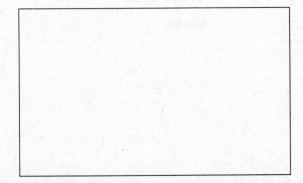

4. $\dfrac{z^2 + 2z - 15}{z^2 + 9z + 20} \div (z - 3)$

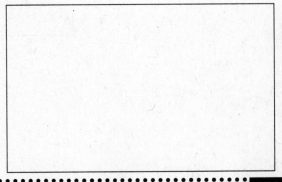

Lesson 11-3

Lesson Objective	California Content Standards
• Divide polynomials	10.0

Take Note

Dividing a Polynomial by a Polynomial

Step 1 Arrange the terms of the dividend and divisor in _____ form.

Step 2 Divide the first term of the dividend by the first term of the divisor. This is the first term of the _____ .

Step 3 Multiply the first term of the quotient by the divisor and place the _____ under the dividend.

Step 4 Subtract this product from the _____ .

Step 5 Bring down the next term.

Repeat Steps 2–5 as necessary until the degree of the remainder is less than the degree of the divisor.

Examples

❶ Dividing a Polynomial by a Monomial Divide $18x^3 + 9x^2 - 15x$ by $3x^2$.

$(18x^3 + 9x^2 - 15x) \div 3x^2 = (18x^3 + 9x^2 - 15x) \cdot \dfrac{1}{\boxed{}}$ **Multiply by the reciprocal of** $\boxed{}$.

$= \dfrac{18x^3}{\boxed{}} + \dfrac{9x^2}{\boxed{}} - \dfrac{15x}{\boxed{}}$ **Use the** $\boxed{}$ **Property.**

$= 6x^1 + \boxed{}x^{\boxed{}} - \dfrac{5}{x}$ **Use the division rules for exponents.**

$= \boxed{}$ **Simplify.**

❷ Dividing a Polynomial by a Binomial Divide $5x^2 + 2x - 3$ by $x + 2$.

Step 1 Begin the long division process.

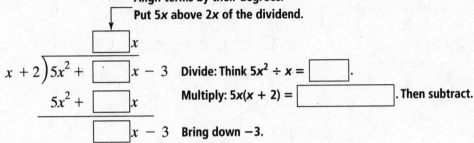

Align terms by their degrees.
Put 5x above 2x of the dividend.

$$\begin{array}{r} \boxed{}\,x \\ x + 2 \overline{)\,5x^2 + \boxed{}\,x - 3} \\ \underline{5x^2 + \boxed{}\,x} \\ \boxed{}\,x - 3 \end{array}$$

Divide: Think $5x^2 \div x = \boxed{}$.

Multiply: $5x(x + 2) = \boxed{}$. Then subtract.

Bring down -3.

Step 2 Repeat the process: Divide, multiply, subtract, bring down.

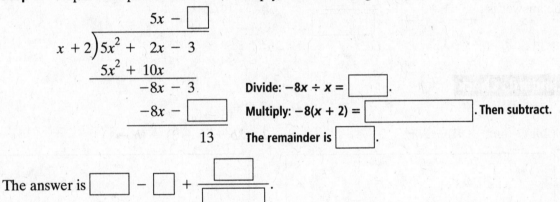

$$\begin{array}{r} 5x - \boxed{} \\ x + 2 \overline{)\,5x^2 + 2x - 3} \\ \underline{5x^2 + 10x} \\ -8x - 3 \\ \underline{-8x - \boxed{}} \\ 13 \end{array}$$

Divide: $-8x \div x = \boxed{}$.

Multiply: $-8(x + 2) = \boxed{}$. Then subtract.

The remainder is $\boxed{}$.

The answer is $\boxed{} - \boxed{} + \dfrac{\boxed{}}{\boxed{}}$.

❸ Dividing Polynomials With a Zero Coefficient The width and area of a rectangle are shown in the figure. What is an expression for the length?

Divide the area by the width to find the length.

$w = 2x + 3$ in.

$A = (6x^3 + 5x^2 + 9)$ in.^{2}

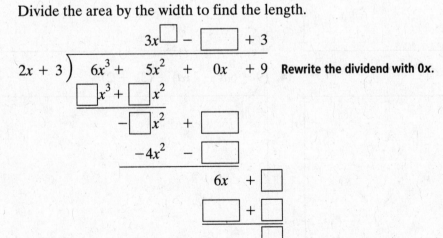

$$\begin{array}{r} 3x^{\boxed{}} - \boxed{} + 3 \\ 2x + 3 \overline{)\,6x^3 + 5x^2 + 0x + 9} \\ \underline{\boxed{}x^3 + \boxed{}x^2} \\ -\boxed{}x^2 + \boxed{} \\ \underline{-4x^2 - \boxed{}} \\ 6x + \boxed{} \\ \underline{\boxed{} + \boxed{}} \\ \boxed{} \end{array}$$

Rewrite the dividend with 0x.

The length of the rectangle is $\left(\boxed{} - \boxed{} + \boxed{} \right)$ in.

❹ Reordering Terms and Dividing Polynomials Divide $-8x - 2 + 6x^2$ by $-1 + x$.

Rewrite $-8x - 2 + 6x^2$ as $6x^2 - 8x - 2$ and $-1 + x$ as $x - 1$. Then divide.

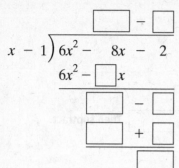

The answer is $\boxed{} - \boxed{} - \dfrac{\boxed{}}{\boxed{}}$.

CA Standards Check

Divide.

1. $(3m^3 - 6m^2 + m) \div 3m^2$

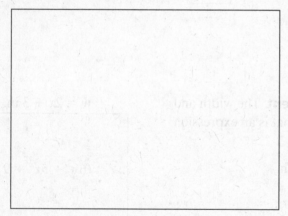

2. $(2b^2 - b - 3) \div (b + 1)$

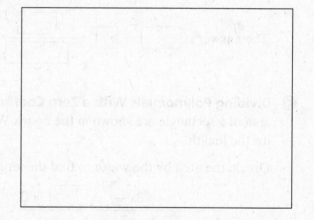

3. $(t^4 + t^2 + t - 3) \div (t - 1)$

4. $(9 - 6a^2 - 11a) \div (3a - 2)$

Lesson 11-4

Adding and Subtracting Rational Expressions

Lesson Objectives	California Content Standards
• Add and subtract rational expressions with like denominators • Add and subtract rational expressions with unlike denominators	13.0

Examples

❶ Subtracting Expressions With Like Denominators

Subtract $\dfrac{3x+5}{3x^2+2x-8}$ from $\dfrac{4x+7}{3x^2+2x-8}$.

$\dfrac{4x+7}{3x^2+2x-8} - \dfrac{3x+5}{3x^2+2x-8} = \dfrac{4x+7 \,\boxed{}\,(3x+5)}{3x^2+2x-8}$ **Subtract the numerators.**

$= \dfrac{4x+7\ -3x-\boxed{}}{3x^2+2x-8}$ **Use the** $\boxed{}$ **Property.**

$= \dfrac{\boxed{}\,\boxed{}}{\left(\boxed{}\right)(x+2)}$ **Simplify the numerator.**
 Factor the denominator.
 Divide out the common factor $\boxed{}$.

$= \dfrac{\boxed{}}{\boxed{}}$ **Simplify.**

❷ Adding Expressions With Monomial Denominators   Add $\dfrac{3}{4x}+\dfrac{1}{8}$.

Step 1 Find the LCD of $\dfrac{3}{4x}$ and $\dfrac{1}{8}$.

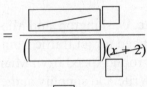

$4x = 2 \cdot 2 \cdot \boxed{}$ **Factor each denominator.**

$8 = 2 \cdot 2 \cdot \boxed{}$

$\text{LCD} = 2 \cdot 2 \cdot 2 \cdot x = \boxed{}$

Step 2   Rewrite using the LCD and add.

$\dfrac{3}{4x}+\dfrac{1}{8} = \dfrac{\boxed{}\cdot 3}{\boxed{}\cdot 4x} + \dfrac{1\cdot\boxed{}}{8\cdot x}$ **Rewrite each fraction using the LCD.**

$= \dfrac{\boxed{}}{8x} + \dfrac{x}{\boxed{}}$ **Simplify numerators and denominators.**

$= \dfrac{\boxed{}}{\boxed{}}$ **Add the numerators.**

❸ Adding Expressions With Polynomial Denominators

Add $\dfrac{7}{x + 4}$ and $\dfrac{3}{x - 5}$.

Step 1 Find the LCD of $x + 4$ and $x - 5$. Since there are no common factors, the LCD is $(x + 4)\left(\boxed{}\right)$.

Step 2 Rewrite using the LCD, and add.

$$\dfrac{7}{x + 4} + \dfrac{3}{x - 5} = \dfrac{7\left(\boxed{}\right)}{(x + 4)(x - 5)} + \dfrac{3\left(\boxed{}\right)}{(x + 4)(x - 5)}$$ Rewrite the fractions using the $\boxed{}$.

$$= \dfrac{7x - \boxed{}}{(x + 4)(x - 5)} + \dfrac{\boxed{} + \boxed{}}{(x + 4)(x - 5)}$$ Simplify each numerator.

$$= \dfrac{7x - 35 + \boxed{} + \boxed{}}{(x + 4)(x - 5)}$$ Add the numerators.

$$= \dfrac{\boxed{} - \boxed{}}{(x + 4)(x - 5)}$$ Simplify the numerator.

❹ Application
The distance between Seattle, Washington, and Miami, Florida, is about 5415 miles. The ground speed for jet traffic from Seattle to Miami can be about 14% faster than the ground speed from Miami to Seattle. Use r for the jet's ground speed. Write and simplify and expression for the round-trip air time.

Miami to Seattle time: $\dfrac{5415}{r}$ time $= \dfrac{\text{distance}}{\text{rate}}$

Seattle to Miami time: $\dfrac{\boxed{}}{\boxed{}\,r}$ time $= \dfrac{\text{distance}}{\text{rate}}$ **14% more than a number is 114% of the number.**

An expression for the total time is $\dfrac{5415}{r} + \dfrac{5415}{1.14r}$.

$$\dfrac{5415}{r} + \dfrac{5415}{1.14r} = \dfrac{6173.1}{\boxed{}\,r} + \dfrac{5415}{1.14r}$$ Rewrite using the LCD $\boxed{}$.

$$= \dfrac{\boxed{}}{1.14r}$$ Add the numerators.

$$= \dfrac{\boxed{}}{r}$$ Simplify.

CA Standards Check

Add or subtract.

1. a. $\dfrac{4}{t-2} - \dfrac{5}{t-2}$

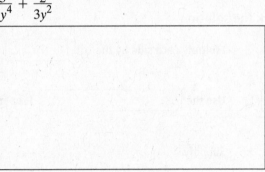

b. $\dfrac{2c+1}{5m+2} - \dfrac{3c-4}{5m+2}$

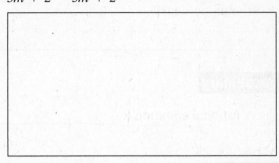

2. a. $\dfrac{3}{7y^4} + \dfrac{2}{3y^2}$

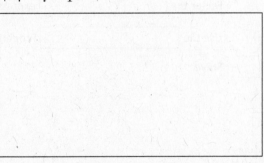

b. $\dfrac{5}{12b} + \dfrac{15}{36b^2}$

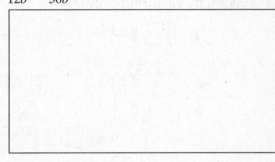

3. a. $\dfrac{5}{t+4} + \dfrac{3}{t-1}$

b. $\dfrac{-2}{a+2} + \dfrac{3a}{2a-1}$

4. The distance between Atlanta, Georgia, and Albuquerque, New Mexico, is about 1270 miles. The ground speed for jet traffic from Atlanta to Albuquerque can be about 12% faster than the ground speed from Albuquerque to Atlanta. Use *r* for a jet's ground speed. Write and simplify an expression for the round-trip air time.

Lesson 11-5

Lesson Objectives	**California Content Standards**
• Solve rational equations • Solve proportions	13.0, 15.0

Vocabulary

A rational equation is _____

Example

❶ Solving by Factoring Solve $\frac{6}{x^2} = \frac{5}{x} - 1$. Check the solution.

$$\boxed{}\left(\frac{6}{x^2}\right) = \boxed{}\left(\frac{5}{x} - 1\right)$$ Multiply each side by the LCD, $\boxed{}$.

$$\frac{\boxed{}}{\boxed{}}\left(\frac{6}{x^2}\right) = \frac{\boxed{}}{\boxed{}}\left(\frac{5}{x}\right) - \boxed{}(1)$$ Use the $\boxed{}$ Property.

$$6 = \boxed{}x - \boxed{}$$ Simplify.

$$x^2 - \boxed{} + \boxed{} = 0$$ Collect terms on one side.

$$\left(\boxed{}\right)\left(\boxed{}\right) = 0$$ Factor the $\boxed{}$ expression.

$$\boxed{} - \boxed{} = 0 \text{ or } \boxed{} - \boxed{} = 0$$ Use the $\boxed{}$ Property.

$$x = \boxed{} \text{ or } \qquad x = \boxed{}$$ Solve.

Check $\dfrac{6}{\boxed{}^2} \overset{?}{=} \dfrac{5}{\boxed{}} - 1$ $\qquad$ $\dfrac{6}{\boxed{}^2} \overset{?}{=} \dfrac{5}{\boxed{}} - 1$

$\dfrac{\boxed{}}{\boxed{}} = \dfrac{\boxed{}}{\boxed{}} \checkmark$ $\qquad$ $\dfrac{\boxed{}}{\boxed{}} = \dfrac{\boxed{}}{\boxed{}} \checkmark$

CA Standards Check

1. Solve each equation. Check your solution.

a. $\dfrac{5}{m} = \dfrac{2}{m^2} + 2$ $\qquad\qquad\qquad$ **b.** $t - 2 = \dfrac{8 - 2t}{t - 1}$

Name_____ Class_____ Date _____

Example

❷ **Work-Rate Problem** Renee can mow the lawn in 20 minutes. Joanne can do the same job in 30 minutes. How long will it take them if they work together?

Define Let n = the time to complete the job if they work together (in minutes).

Person	Work Rate (part of job/min.)	Time Worked (min.)	Part of job done
Renee	$\dfrac{\Box}{\Box}$	n	$\dfrac{\Box}{\Box}$
Joanne	$\dfrac{\Box}{\Box}$	n	$\dfrac{\Box}{\Box}$

Relate Renee's part done + Joanne's part done = complete job

Write $\dfrac{n}{\Box} \quad + \quad \dfrac{n}{\Box} \quad = \quad 1$

$\Box\left(\dfrac{n}{\Box} + \dfrac{n}{\Box}\right) = \Box$ (1) **Multiply each side by the LCD,** $\Box$.

$3n + 2n = \Box$ **Use the** $\Box$ **Property.**

$\Box = \Box$ **Simplify.**

$\Box = \Box$ **Simplify.**

It will take them $\Box$ minutes to mow the lawn together.

CA Standards Check

2. Peggy can pick a bushel of apples in 45 min. Peter can pick a bushel of apples in 75 min. How long will it take them to pick a bushel if they work together?

Example

❸ **Checking to Find an Extraneous Solution** Solve $\dfrac{x+3}{x-1} = \dfrac{4}{x-1}$.

$(x+3)\left(\boxed{} - \boxed{}\right) = \boxed{}(x-1)$ **Write cross products.**

$\boxed{} - x + \boxed{} - 3 = 4x - \boxed{}$ **Use the** $\boxed{}$ **Property.**

$x^2 + \boxed{} - \boxed{} = 4x - \boxed{}$ **Combine** $\boxed{}$ **terms.**

$x^2 - \boxed{} + \boxed{} = \boxed{}$ **Subtract** $\boxed{}$ **from each side.**

$\left(x - \boxed{}\right)\left(x - \boxed{}\right) = 0$ **Factor.**

$\boxed{} - \boxed{} = 0$ **Use the Zero-Product Property.**

$\boxed{} = \boxed{}$ **Simplify.**

Check 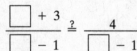 $\dfrac{\boxed{} + 3}{\boxed{} - 1} \overset{?}{=} \dfrac{4}{\boxed{} - 1}$

 $\dfrac{\boxed{}}{\boxed{}} = \dfrac{\boxed{}}{\boxed{}}$ **Undefined! There is no division by** $\boxed{}$**.**

The equation has no solution because $\boxed{}$ makes the denominator equal $\boxed{}$.

CA Standards Check

3. Solve each equation. Check your solution.

   a. $\dfrac{3}{a} = \dfrac{5}{a-2}$

   b. $\dfrac{n}{5} = \dfrac{4}{n+1}$

   c. $\dfrac{2}{c^2} = \dfrac{2}{c^2+1}$

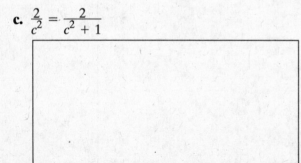

   d. $\dfrac{w^2}{w-1} = \dfrac{1}{w-1}$

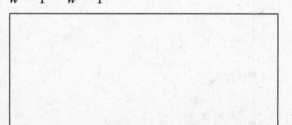

A Note to the Student:

This section of your workbook contains a series of pages that support your mathematics understandings for each chapter and lesson presented in your student edition.

- Practice pages provide additional practice for every lesson.

- Guided Problem Solving pages lead you through a step-by-step solution to an application problem in each lesson.

- Vocabulary pages contain a variety of activities to increase your reading and math understanding, ranging from graphic organizers to vocabulary review puzzles.

Practice 1-1

Write an algebraic expression for each phrase.

1. 7 increased by x

2. p multiplied by 3

3. 10 decreased by m

4. n less than 7

5. the product of 2 and q

6. 3 more than m

Write a phrase for each algebraic expression.

7. $\frac{8}{a}$ **8.** $s - 10$ **9.** $x + 13$ **10.** $ab + 2$

Define a variable and write an algebraic expression for each phrase.

11. the difference of 8 and a number

12. the sum of 4 and a number

13. the product of 2 and a number

14. 3 increased by a number

15. 10 plus the quotient of a number and 15

16. 12 less than a number

Define a variable and write an algebraic equation to model each situation.

17. What is the total cost of buying several shirts at $24.95 each?

18. The number of gal of water used to water trees is 30 times the number of trees.

19. What is the amount of money in a bank containing only dimes?

20. What is the number of marbles left in a 48-marble bag after some marbles have been given away?

21. The total cost equals the price of the tickets multiplied by eight people.

22. What is the cost of buying several pairs of pants at $32.95 per pair?

Define variables and write an equation to model the relationship in each table.

23.

Number of Tickets	Total Cost
2	$7
4	$14
6	$21

24.

Number of Hours	Distance Traveled
1	55 mi
3	165 mi
5	275 mi

25.

Number of Hours	Total Pay
8	$40
12	$60
16	$80

26.

Total Cost	Change From $10
$10.00	$0
$9.00	$1.00
$7.50	$2.50

27.

Number of Days	Length
1	0.45 in.
4	1.80 in.
8	3.60 in.

28.

Miles Traveled	Miles Remaining
0	500
125	375
350	150

1-1 • Guided Problem Solving

GPS **Exercise 42**

Which equation best describes the relationship between the amount of money a in a bag of quarters and the number of quarters q?

A. $a = 0.25q$ **B.** $a = 0.25 + q$ **C.** $q = 0.25a$ **D.** $q = 0.25 + q$

Read and Understand

1. What two quantities are related? _____

Plan and Solve

2. How much money is 1 quarter worth? _____

3. How much money are 2 quarters worth? _____

4. Explain how you would determine the amount of money 5 quarters are worth.

   _____

5. How would you express the amount of money q quarters are worth? _____

6. Write an equation that describes the relationship between the amount of money a in a bag of quarters and the number of quarters q. _____

Look Back and Check

7. Check the reasonableness of your answer by explaining why the other answer choices do not make sense.

   _____

Solve Another Problem

8. Mark has a pocket full of nickels. Which equation best describes the relationship between the amount of money a in his pocket and the number of nickels n?

   A. $a = n + 0.05$ **B.** $a = 0.05n$ **C.** $n = 0.05 + a$ **D.** $n = 0.05a$

Name _____ Class _____ Date _____

Practice 1-2

Exponents and Order of Operations

Simplify each expression.

1. $4 + 6(8)$

2. $\dfrac{4(8 - 2)}{3 + 9}$

3. $4 \times 3^2 + 2$

4. $40 \div 5(2)$

5. $2.7 + 3.6 \times 4.5$

6. $3[4(8 - 2) + 5]$

7. $4 + 3(15 - 2^3)$

8. $17 - [(3 + 2) \times 2]$

9. $6 \times (3 + 2) \div 15$

Evaluate each expression.

10. $\dfrac{a + 2b}{5}$ for $a = 1$ and $b = 2$

11. $\dfrac{5m + n}{5}$ for $m = 6$ and $n = 15$

12. $x + 3y^2$ for $x = 3.4$ and $y = 3$

13. $7a - 4(b + 2)$ for $a = 5$ and $b = 2$

Simplify each expression.

14. $\dfrac{100 - 15}{9 + 8}$

15. $\dfrac{2(3 + 4)}{7}$

16. $\dfrac{3(4 + 12)}{2(7 - 3)}$

17. $14 + 3 \times 4$

18. $8 + 3(4 + 3)$

19. $3 + 4[13 - 2(6 - 3)]$

20. $8(5 + 30 \div 5)$

21. $(3.4)(2.7) + 5$

22. $50 \div 2 + 15 \times 4$

23. $7(9 - 5)$

24. $2(3^2) - 3(2)$

25. $4 + 8 \div 2 + 6 \times 3$

26. $(7 + 8) \div (4 - 1)$

27. $5[2(8 + 5) - 15]$

28. $(6 + 8) \times (8 - 4)$

29. $12\left(\dfrac{6 + 30}{9 - 3}\right)$

30. $14 + 6 \times 2^3 - 8 \div 2^2$

31. $\dfrac{7(14) - 3(6)}{2}$

32. $14 \div [3(8 - 2) - 11]$

33. $3\left(\dfrac{9 + 13}{6}\right)$

34. $\dfrac{4(8 - 3)}{3 + 2}$

35. $5 + 4^2 \times 8 - 2^3 \div 2^2$

36. $4^2 + 5^2(8 - 3)$

37. $5(3^2 + 2) - 2(6^2 - 5^2)$

Evaluate each expression for $a = 2$ and $b = 6$.

38. $2(7a - b)$

39. $(a^3 + b^2) \div a$

40. $3b \div (2a - 1) + b$

41. $\dfrac{5a + 2}{b}$

42. $\dfrac{3(b - 2)}{4(a + 1)}$

43. $9b + a^4 \div 8$

Use the expression $r + 0.12m$ to calculate the cost of renting a car. The basic rate is r. The number of miles driven is m.

44. The basic rate is $15.95. The car is driven 150 mi.

45. The basic rate is $32.50. The car is driven 257 mi.

Evaluate each expression for $s = 3$ and $t = 9$.

46. $8(4s - t)$

47. $(2t - 3s) \div 4$

48. $t^2 - s^4$

49. $s(3t + 6)$

50. $\dfrac{5s^2}{t}$

51. $\dfrac{2t^2}{s^3}$

1-2 • Guided Problem Solving

GPS Exercise 62

a. The formula for the volume of a cylinder is $V = \pi r^2 h$. What is the volume of the cylinder at the right? Round your answer to the nearest hundredth of a cubic inch.

b. **Critical Thinking** About how many cubic inches does an ounce of juice fill? Round your answer to the nearest tenth of a cubic inch.

c. The formula for the surface area of a cylinder is $SA = 2\pi r(r + h)$. What is the surface area of the cylinder? Round your answer to the nearest hundredth of a square inch.

Read and Understand

1. What are the two formulas that you will need to use? _____

2. What information is given in the picture? _____

Plan and Solve

3. What is the value you will use for r? _____

4. What is the value you will use for h? _____

5. What is the decimal approximation for π? _____

6. What is the volume of the cylinder? _____

7. What is the surface area of the cylinder? _____

8. About how many cubic inches does an ounce of juice fill? _____

Look Back and Check

9. Round your volume to the nearest cubic inch. Check the reasonableness of your answer by dividing your volume by 2. Your answer should be close to 12, which is the number of ounces of juice in the cylinder.

Solve Another Problem

10. What is the volume of a cylinder if the radius is 2.0 inches and the height is 2.5 inches?

_____

Practice 1-3

Name the set(s) of numbers to which each number belongs.

1. -0.002

2. $12\frac{1}{2}$

3. 8

4. 5π

5. $\sqrt{7}$

6. -22

7. -3.4

8. $\sqrt{36}$

Is each statement *true* or *false*? If the statement is false, give a counterexample.

9. Every whole number is an integer.

10. Every integer is a whole number.

11. Every rational number is a real number.

12. Every multiple of 7 is odd.

Use <, =, or > to compare.

13. $-10.98 \ \blacksquare \ -10.99$

14. $-\frac{1}{3} \ \blacksquare \ -0.3$

15. $-\frac{11}{5} \ \blacksquare \ -\frac{4}{5}$

16. $-\frac{1}{2} \ \blacksquare \ -\frac{5}{10}$

17. $-\frac{3}{8} \ \blacksquare \ -\frac{7}{16}$

18. $\frac{3}{4} \ \blacksquare \ \frac{13}{16}$

Order the numbers in each group from least to greatest.

19. $-\frac{8}{9}, -\frac{7}{8}, -\frac{22}{25}$

20. $-3\frac{4}{9}, -3.45, -3\frac{12}{25}$

21. $-\frac{1}{4}, -\frac{1}{5}, -\frac{1}{3}$

22. $-1.7, -1\frac{3}{4}, -1\frac{7}{9}$

23. $-\frac{3}{4}, -\frac{7}{8}, -\frac{2}{3}$

24. $2\frac{3}{4}, 2\frac{5}{8}, 2.7$

Determine which set of numbers is most reasonable for each situation.

25. the number of dolphins in the ocean

26. the height of a basketball player

27. the number of pets you have

28. the circumference of a compact disk

Find each absolute value.

29. $\left|\frac{3}{10}\right|$

30. $|-327|$

31. $|-3.46|$

32. $\left|-\frac{1}{2}\right|$

33. Name the sets(s) of numbers to which each number in the table belongs. Choose among: whole numbers, integers, rational numbers, irrational numbers, and real numbers.

Type of Account	Principal	Rate	Time (years)	Interest
Checking	$154.23	0.0375	$\frac{30}{365}$	$.48
Savings	$8000	0.055	$3\frac{1}{2}$	$1540

1-3 • Guided Problem Solving

GPS Exercise 64

If the distance between each tick mark is one unit and *R* and *T* are opposites, what is the value of *Q*?

A. 7   **B.** 0   **C.** −3   **D.** −7

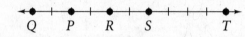
$$Q \qquad P \quad R \quad S \qquad\qquad T$$

Read and Understand

1. Give an example of two numbers that are opposites. _____

Plan and Solve

2. On the number line above, mark the location of the number 0.

3. On the number line above, label the points *R* and *T* with their values.

4. What is the value of *Q*? _____

Look Back and Check

5. Check that your answer is correct by labeling all the remaining points on the number line.

Solve Another Problem

6. Use the number line. If *P* and *T* are opposites, what is the value of *R*?

    A. 0   **B.** 2   **C.** −2   **D.** −6

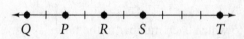
$$Q \qquad P \quad R \quad S \qquad\qquad T$$

Practice 1-4

Write the expression modeled by each number line. Then find the sum.

1.

2.

3.

4.

Simplify each expression.

5. $6 + (-4)$

6. $-2 + (-13)$

7. $-18 + 4$

8. $15 + (-32)$

9. $-27 + (-14)$

10. $8 + (-3)$

11. $-12.2 + 31.9$

12. $-2.3 + (-13.9)$

13. $19.8 + (-27.4)$

14. $\frac{1}{4} + \left(-\frac{3}{4}\right)$

15. $\frac{2}{3} + \left(-\frac{1}{3}\right)$

16. $-\frac{7}{12} + \frac{1}{6}$

17. $2\frac{2}{3} + (-1)$

18. $-3\frac{3}{4} + 1\frac{1}{2}$

19. $2\frac{1}{3} + \left(-4\frac{2}{3}\right)$

20. $-6.3 + 8.2$

21. $-3.82 + 2.83$

22. $-7.8 + 9$

23. The temperature at 5:00 A.M. is $-38°$F. The temperature rises 20° by 11:00 A.M. Use addition to find the temperature at 11:00 A.M.

24. A football team has possession of the ball on their own 15-yd line. The next two plays result in a loss of 7 yd and a gain of 3 yd, respectively. Use addition to find the position of the ball after the two plays.

25. Suppose your opening checking account balance is $124.53. You write a check for $57.49 and make a deposit of $103.49. Use addition to find your new balance.

26. During an emergency exercise, a submarine dives 37 ft, rises 16 ft, and then dives 18 ft. Use addition to find the net change in the submarine's position after the second dive.

Evaluate each expression for $m = 2.5$.

27. $-m + 1.6$

28. $-3.2 + m$

29. $-2.5 + (-m)$

30. $-m + (-4.1)$

31. $5.7 + m$

32. $m + (-1.9)$

Simplify.

33. $-3 + (-6) + 14$

34. $4 + (-8) + (-14)$

35. $2.7 + (-3.2) + 1.5$

36. $-2.5 + (-1.2) + (-2.3)$

37. $\frac{1}{2} + \left(-\frac{1}{3}\right) + \frac{1}{4}$

38. $-\frac{2}{3} + \left(-\frac{1}{3}\right) + \left(-1\frac{1}{3}\right)$

39. A hiker starts at an elevation of 542 feet. Define a variable and write an expression to find her elevation after it changes. Then evaluate your expression for each change.
   a. an increase of 125 feet
   b. a decrease of 31 feet
   c. a decrease of 89 feet
   d. an increase of 62 feet

1-4 • Guided Problem Solving

GPS **Exercise 65**

Suppose you overdrew your bank account. You have a balance of −$34. You then deposit checks for $17 and $49. At the same time the bank charges you a $25 fee for overdrawing your account. What is your balance?

Read and Understand

1. What is the problem asking you to do? _____
   _____

2. What is the rule for adding two numbers with different signs? _____
   _____
   _____

Plan and Solve

3. Write and evaluate an expression for the sum of the two deposits. _____

4. How do you express "a charge of $25" as an integral? _____

5. Write and evaluate an expression for the sum of the two deposits and the bank fee. _____
   _____

6. Write and evaluate an expression for the sum of the two deposits, the bank fee, and the starting balance. _____

7. What is your balance? _____

Look Back and Check

8. Check your answer by adding the changes to your account in a different order. Add the starting balance to the first deposit, then add the second deposit, and lastly, add the bank fee.
   _____

Solve Another Problem

9. Now you deposit a check for $142, withdraw $20 in cash, and write a check for $16. What is your balance? _____

Practice 1-5

Simplify.

1. $13 - 6$

2. $19 - 35$

3. $-4 - 8$

4. $-14 - (-6)$

5. $18 - (-25)$

6. $-32 - 17$

7. $-6.8 - 14.6$

8. $-9.3 - (-23.9)$

9. $-8.2 - 0.8$

10. $18.3 - (-8.1)$

11. $-3 - (-15)$

12. $6.4 - 17$

13. $\frac{3}{4} - 1\frac{1}{4}$

14. $-\frac{1}{3} - \frac{2}{3}$

15. $-\frac{1}{4} - \left(-\frac{3}{4}\right)$

16. $|-11| - |-29|$

17. $|-4 - 8|$

18. $|9.8| - |-15.7|$

19. $|-8 - (-32)|$

20. $|3.7 - (-6.8)|$

21. $2.83 - 3.82$

Evaluate each expression for $c = -3$ and $d = -6$.

22. $c - d$

23. $-c - d$

24. $-c - (-d)$

25. $|c + d|$

26. $-c + d$

27. $3c - 2d$

Simplify.

28. $8 - (-4) - (-5)$

29. $6 - 10 - 4$

30. $10 - 14 - 15$

31. $-6 - 3 - (-2)$

32. $-5 + 7 - 9$

33. $-2 - 2 - 4$

Evaluate each expression for $p = -1.5$, $q = -3$, and $r = 2$.

34. $p + q - r$

35. $-q - r + p$

36. $|-r|$

37. $|p| - |r| + |q|$

38. $3r + |p|$

39. $|q - r| + q$

40. The temperature in the evening was 68°F. The following morning, the temperature was 39°F. What is the difference between the two temperatures?

41. What is the difference in altitude between Mt. Everest, which is about 29,028 ft above sea level, and Death Valley, which is about 282 ft below sea level?

42. Suppose the balance in your checking account was $234.15 when you wrote a check for $439.87. (This is known as overdrawing your account.) Describe the account's new balance.

43. After three plays in which a football team lost 7 yd, gained 3 yd, and lost 1 yd, respectively, the ball was placed on the team's own 30-yd line. Where was the ball before the three plays?

1-5 • Guided Problem Solving

GPS Exercise 55

Use the data in the table at the right.

a. Find the change in participation for tennis at each school level.

b. Find the change in participation for soccer at each school level.

c. **Writing** Suppose you invest in sporting goods. In which of the two sports would you invest? Explain.

City-Wide Participation in Sports Activities (thousands)

2000	Sport	Elementary	High School	College
	Basketball	5.5	8.2	4.9
	Tennis	1.4	3.2	3.9
	Soccer	4.2	3.8	1.3
	Volleyball	1.6	5.2	5.1

2005	Sport	Elementary	High School	College
	Basketball	6.8	7.9	4.9
	Tennis	1.0	1.8	1.7
	Soccer	5.6	4.1	1.3
	Volleyball	1.8	4.9	2.9

Read and Understand

1. What information is given in the tables?

_____

_____

2. To find the change in participation, you need to _____

_____

Plan and Solve

3. Find the change in participation for tennis at each school level.

Elementary _____

High School _____

College _____

4. Find the change in participation for soccer at each school level.

Elementary _____

High School _____

College _____

5. Suppose you invest in sporting goods. In which of the two sports would you invest? Explain.

_____

Look Back and Check

6. Check your answers by estimating the total partcipation in each sport. Then find the change in total particpation from 2000 to 2005. _____

_____

Solve Another Problem

7. Find the change in participation for basketball and volleyball at each school level. In which of the two sports would you invest? _____

_____

Practice 1-6

Multiplying and Dividing Real Numbers

Simplify each expression.

1. $(-2)(8)$

2. $(-6)(-9)$

3. $(-3)^4$

4. -2^5

5. $(6)(-8)$

6. $(-14)^2$

7. $2(-4)(-6)$

8. $-30 \div (-5)$

9. $\frac{-52}{-13}$

10. $(-8)(5)(-3)$

11. -7^2

12. -3^5

13. $\frac{-68}{17}$

14. $\frac{(-4)(-13)}{-26}$

15. $\frac{225}{(-3)(-5)}$

Evaluate each expression.

16. x^3 for $x = -5$

17. $s^2t \div 10$ for $s = -2$ and $t = 10$

18. $-2m + 4n^2$ for $m = -6$ and $n = -5$

19. $\frac{v}{w}$ for $v = \frac{2}{5}$ and $w = -\frac{1}{2}$

20. $-cd^2$ for $c = 2$ and $d = -4$

21. $(x + 4)^2$ for $x = -11$

22. $\left(\frac{a}{b}\right)^2 + b^3$ for $a = 24$ and $b = -6$

23. $4p^2 + 7q^3$ for $p = -3$ and $q = -2$

24. $(e + f)^4$ for $e = -3$ and $f = 7$

25. $5f^2 - z^2$ for $f = -1$ and $z = -4$

Simplify each expression.

26. $2^4 - 3^2 + 5^2$

27. $(-8)^2 - 4^3$

28. $32 \div (-7 + 5)^3$

29. $\frac{3}{4} \div \left(-\frac{3}{7}\right)$

30. $18 + 4^2 \div (-8)$

31. $26 \div [4 - (-9)]$

32. $4^3 - (2 - 5)^3$

33. $-(-4)^3$

34. $(-8)(-5)(-3)$

35. $(-3)^2 - 4^2$

36. $\frac{-45}{-15}$

37. $(-2)^6$

38. $\frac{-90}{6}$

39. $\frac{-15}{(7 - 4)}$

40. $\frac{195}{-13}$

Evaluate each expression.

41. $(a + b)^2$ for $a = 6$ and $b = -8$

42. $d^3 \div e$ for $d = -6$ and $e = -3$

43. $(m + 5n)^3$ for $m = 2$ and $n = -1$

44. $j^5 - 5k$ for $j = -4$ and $k = -1$

45. $xy + z$ for $x = -4, y = 3$, and $z = -3$

46. $4s \div (-3t)$ for $s = -6$ and $t = -2$

47. $\frac{r^3}{s}$ for $r = -6$ and $s = -2$

48. $\frac{-h^5}{-4}$ for $h = 4$

1-6 • Guided Problem Solving

GPS **Exercise 82**

As riders plunge down the hill of a roller coaster, you can approximate the height h, in feet, above the ground of their roller-coaster car. Use the function $h = 155 - 16t^2$, where t is the number of seconds since the start of the descent.

155 ft

a. How far is a rider from the bottom of the hill after 1 second? 2 seconds?

b. **Critical Thinking** Does it take more than or less than 4 seconds to reach the bottom? Explain.

Read and Understand

1. What do each of the variables in the function represent?

   _____

2. What are the units that would be used for values of h and t? _____

Plan and Solve

3. How far is the rider from the bottom of the hill after 1 second? _____

4. How far is the rider from the bottom of the hill after 2 seconds? _____

5. What value would you use for h if the roller coaster car were at the bottom of the hill? _____

6. Does it take more than or less than 4 seconds to reach the bottom? Explain. _____

   _____

Look Back and Check

7. Explain how you use order of operations when using the roller coaster function.

   _____

Solve Another Problem

8. For a different roller coaster, the height h, in feet, above the ground of the roller-coaster car is approximated by the function $h = 200 - 16t^2$. How far is a rider from the bottom of the hill on this roller coaster after 2 seconds?

Practice 1-7

The Distributive Property

Simplify each expression.

1. $2(x + 6)$ **2.** $-5(8 - b)$ **3.** $4(-x + 7)$

4. $(5c - 7)(-3)$ **5.** $-2.5(3a + 5)$ **6.** $-(3k - 12)$

7. $-\frac{3}{4}(12 - 16d)$ **8.** $\frac{2}{3}(6h - 1)$ **9.** $(-3.2x + 2.1)(-6)$

10. $3.5(3x - 8)$ **11.** $4(x + 7)$ **12.** $-2.5(2a - 4)$

13. $\frac{2}{3}(12 - 15d)$ **14.** $-2(k - 11)$ **15.** $-\frac{1}{3}(6h + 15)$

16. $(2c - 8)(-4)$ **17.** $-(4 - 2b)$ **18.** $2(3x - 9)$

19. $4(2r + 8)$ **20.** $-5(b - 5)$ **21.** $3(f + 2)$

22. $6h + 5(h - 5)$ **23.** $-5d + 3(2d - 7)$ **24.** $7 + 2(4x - 3)$

25. $2(3h + 2) - 4h$ **26.** $2(4 + y)$ **27.** $\frac{1}{2}(2n - 4) - 2n$

28. $-w + 4(w + 3)$ **29.** $0.4(3d - 5)$ **30.** $-4d + 2(3 + d)$

31. $2x + \frac{3}{4}(4x + 16)$ **32.** $2(3a + 2)$ **33.** $5(t - 3) - 2t$

34. $5(b + 4) - 6b$ **35.** $\frac{2}{5}(5k + 35) - 8$ **36.** $0.4(2s + 4)$

37. $\frac{2}{3}(9b - 27)$ **38.** $\frac{1}{2}(12n - 8)$ **39.** $0.5(2x - 4)$

40. $2(a - 4) + 15$ **41.** $13 + 2(5c - 2)$ **42.** $7 + 2(\frac{1}{5}a - 3)$

43. $5(3x + 12)$ **44.** $2(m + 1)$ **45.** $4(2a + 2) - 17$

46. $-4x + 3(2x - 5)$ **47.** $3(t - 12)$ **48.** $-6 - 3(2k + 4)$

Write an expression for each phrase.

49. 5 times the quantity x plus 6

50. twice the quantity y minus 8

51. the product of -15 and the quantity x minus 5

52. 32 divided by the quantity y plus 12

53. -8 times the quantity 4 decreased by w

54. the quantity x plus 9, times the quantity 7 minus x

1-7 • Guided Problem Solving

GPS **Exercise 80**

Suppose you buy 4 cans of tomatoes at $1.02 each, 3 cans of tuna for $.99 each, and 3 boxes of pasta at $.52 each. Write an expression to model this situation. Then use the Distributive Property to find the total cost.

Read and Understand

1. What is the Distributive Property? _____

2. What type of information is given to you in the problem? _____

Plan and Solve

3. Write an expression that shows how to determine the total amount spent on tomatoes. _____

4. Write an expression that shows how to determine the total amount spent on tuna. _____

5. Write an expression that shows how to determine the total amount spent on pasta. _____

6. Write an expression that models the total amount of money you will spend. _____

7. Use the Distributive Property to find the total cost. _____

Look Back and Check

8. Check the reasonableness of your answer by rounding the cost of each item and estimating the total cost. _____

_____

Solve Another Problem

9. In order to paint your bedroom, you buy 2 gallons of paint that cost $10.50 each, 3 paint brushes that cost $2.99 each, and 2 paint rollers that cost $1.25 each. Write an expression to model this situation. Then use the Distributive Property to find the total cost.

_____

_____

Practice 1-8

Properties of Numbers

Name the property that each equation illustrates.

1. $83 + 6 = 6 + 83$

2. $8 + x = x + 8$

3. $1 \cdot 4y = 4y$

4. $15x + 15y = 15(x + y)$

5. $(8 \cdot 7) \cdot 6 = 8 \cdot (7 \cdot 6)$

6. $\frac{2}{3}\left(\frac{3}{2}\right) = 1$

7. $3(a + 2b) = 3a + 6b$

8. $7x + 2y = 2y + 7x$

9. $7 + (8 + 15) = (7 + 8) + 15$

10. $x + (-x) = 0$

11. $x + y = y + x$

12. $6 \cdot (x \cdot y) = (6 \cdot x) \cdot y$

13. $16 + 0 = 16$

14. $3w + 5y = 5y + 3w$

15. $7(3 + 4y) = 21 + 28y$

16. $0 = 30 \cdot 0$

17. $4a + (5b + 6c) = (4a + 5b) + 6c$

18. $ab + c = ba + c$

19. $wr = rw$

20. $20(a + b) = 20(b + a)$

Give a reason to justify each step.

21. a. $4c + 3(2 + c) = 4c + 6 + 3c$
 b. $ = 4c + 3c + 6$
 c. $ = (4c + 3c) + 6$
 d. $ = (4 + 3)c + 6$
 e. $ = 7c + 6$

22. a. $8w - 4(7 - w) = 8w - 28 + 4w$
 b. $ = 8w + (-28) + 4w$
 c. $ = 8w + 4w + (-28)$
 d. $ = (8 + 4)w + (-28)$
 e. $ = 12w + (-28)$
 f. $ = 12w - 28$

23. a. $5(x + y) + 2(x + y) = 5x + 5y + 2x + 2y$
 b. $ = 5x + 2x + 5y + 2y$
 c. $ = (5 + 2)x + (5 + 2)y$
 d. $ = 7x + 7y$

Use mental math to simplify each expression.

24. $48 + 27 + 2 + 3$

25. $10 \cdot 72 \cdot 5 \cdot 2$

26. $10 \cdot 8 \cdot 3 \cdot 10$

27. $8\frac{1}{2} + 4\frac{1}{3} + 2\frac{1}{2} + 2\frac{2}{3}$

28. Henry bought an apple for $0.75, some apricots for $1.50, some cherries for $3.25, and three bananas for $1.50. Find the total cost of the fruit.

29. Suppose you buy some camping supplies. You purchase waterproof matches for $3.95, a compass for $18.25, flashlight batteries for $3.75, and a map for $2.05. Find the total cost of the supplies.

30. You go to the video store and rent some DVDs for $8.50 and a video game for $3.69. While there, you buy a box of popcorn for $2.31 and a candy bar for $1.50. Find the total cost of the items.

Algebra 1 Lesson 1-8

197

1-8 • Guided Problem Solving

GPS **Exercise 30**

Suppose you are buying soccer equipment: a pair of cleats for $31.50, a
soccer ball for $14.97, and shin guards for $6.50. Use mental math to find
the total cost.

Read and Understand

1. What is the problem asking you to do? _____

2. What two properties of real numbers will
   help you solve this problem using mental math? _____   _____

Plan and Solve

3. Explain what the Commutative Property of Addition states. _____

   _____

4. Explain what the Associative Property of Addition states. _____

   _____

5. How can you use the Commutative Property to rewrite the expression $31.50 + 14.97 + 6.50$ in
   order to be able to use mental math? _____

6. How will you use the Associative Property to find the total cost? _____

   _____

7. What is your total cost? _____

Look Back and Check

8. Check the reasonableness of your answer by rounding the cost of each item and estimating the
   total cost. _____

   _____

Solve Another Problem

9. Suppose you are buying new clothes for school: a pair of pants for $24.50, a shirt for $13.99, and
   a pair of shoes for $12.50. Use mental math to find the total cost. _____

   _____

1A: Graphic Organizer

For use before Lesson 1-1

Study Skill Always write down your assignments. Do not rely on your memory to recall all assignments from all your classes.

Write your answers.

1. What is the chapter title? _____

2. Find the Table of Contents page for this chapter at the front of the book.
   Name four topics you will study in this chapter.

   _____   _____

   _____   _____

3. Complete the graphic organizer as you work through the chapter.
   1. Write the title of the chapter in the center oval.
   2. When you begin a lesson, write the name of the lesson in a rectangle.
   3. When you complete that lesson, write a skill or key concept from that lesson in the outer oval linked to that rectangle.
   Continue with steps 2 and 3 clockwise around the graphic organizer.

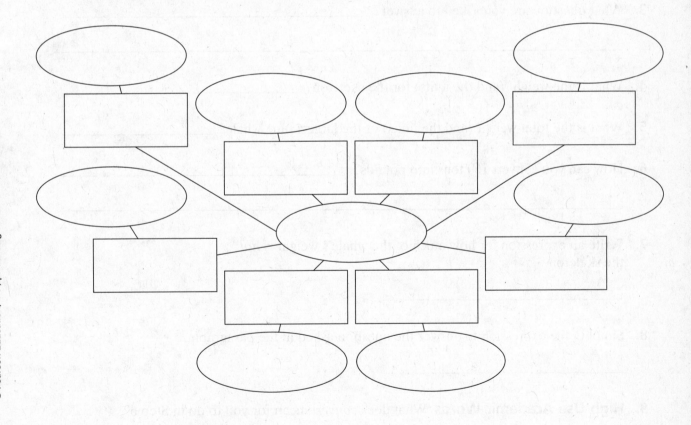

1B: Reading Comprehension

Study Skill When you read a paragraph, it is a good idea to read it twice: once to get an overview, then again to find the essential information.

Read the passage below and answer the following questions.

> The blue whale is the largest animal on earth. A blue whale is about 100 million times larger than the krill, one of the smallest creatures it eats. The skeleton of a blue whale can weigh about 50,000 pounds. The heart of a blue whale can be the size of a small car. The largest recorded blue whale weighed 160 tons. About how much of that weight was *not* the skeleton?

1. What is the subject of this paragraph? _____

2. What are the numbers 50,000 and 160 in the paragraph referring to?

   _____

3. What question are you asked to answer? _____

   _____

4. What is the weight (and the units) for the skeleton? _____

5. What is the total weight (and the units) of the largest blue whale? _____

6. How can you convert 160 tons into pounds? _____

   _____

7. Write an expression for how much of the whale's weight is *not* the skeleton.

   _____

8. Simplify the expression to answer the question asked in the paragraph.

   _____

9. **High-Use Academic Words** What does *convert* mean for you to do in Step 6?

   a. measure   **b.** change

1C: Reading/Writing Math Symbols

For use after Lesson 1-2

Study Skill When you take notes in class, keep up with what is being said by using abbreviations. Use abbreviations that you will be able to understand when you review your notes.

Mathematics is a language made up of symbols that represent words and amounts. For example, the mathematical expression 5 × 2 symbolizes five times two.

Explain the meaning of each mathematical expression using words.

1. $3 \cdot 7$ _____

_____

2. $5n$ _____

_____

3. $3 \div 4$ _____

_____

4. $\dfrac{7}{12}$ _____

_____

5. 2^x _____

_____

6. $6(7)$ _____

_____

Write each phrase with math symbols.

7. 7 minus 3 _____

8. p divided by 2 _____

9. 4 divided by x _____

10. y equals 9 _____

1D: Visual Vocabulary Practice

For use after Lesson 1-6

Study Skill The Glossary contains the key vocabulary for this course, as well as illustrated examples.

Concept List

absolute value	Multiplication Property of −1	reciprocal
inequality	opposites	variable
Multiplication Property of Zero	power	whole numbers

Write the concept that best describes each exercise.
Choose from the concept list above.

1. m	**2.** 5^3	**3.** $\frac{3}{5}$ and $\frac{5}{3}$
_____	_____	_____
4. -12 and 12	**5.** For every real number n, $n \cdot 0 = 0$	**6.** $\lvert -52 \rvert$
_____	_____	_____
7. $-4 < 10$	**8.** $0, 1, 2, 3, \ldots$	**9.** For every real number n, $-1 \cdot n = -n$ and $n \cdot -1 = -n$
_____	_____	_____

1E: Vocabulary Check

Study Skill Strengthen your vocabulary. Use these pages and add cues and summaries by applying the Cornell Notetaking style.

Write the definition for each word at the right. To check your work, fold the paper back along the dotted line to see the correct answers.

_____

_____

_____

_____   Algebraic Expression

_____

_____

_____   Equation

_____

_____

_____   Natural Numbers

_____

_____

_____   Integers

_____

_____

_____   Absolute Value

_____

_____

Vocabulary and Study Skills

1E: Vocabulary Check (continued)

For use after Lesson 1-3

Write the vocabulary word for each definition. To check your work,
fold the paper forward along the dotted line to see the correct answers.

A mathematical phrase
that can include numbers,
variables, and operation
symbols.

_____

A mathematical sentence
that uses an equal sign.

_____

The counting numbers.

_____

Whole numbers and their
opposites.

_____

The distance that a
number is from zero on a
number line.

_____

1F: Vocabulary Review

For use with Chapter Review

Study Skill Many words in English have more than one meaning. Often a word has one meaning in ordinary conversation, and a different specific meaning or exact definition when it is used in math or science or grammar. You can often figure out which meaning to use by looking at the sentence that contains the word. To help you decide what a word means, consider the surroundings, or context, in which you see the word.

Read the mathematical definition in the left column and the sentence in the right column. In the blank in the middle, write the one word from the list below that fits both the definition and the sentence.

base	like	identity	constant
power	real	whole	term

Definition		**Sentence**
1. a term that has no variable	_____	That noise is _____. It just never seems to stop.
2. a number that is multiplied repeatedly	_____	Put this statue on its _____ so it will not fall over.
3. the kind of terms that have exactly the same variable factors	_____	I really _____ that kind of food. It is my favorite.
4. The set of numbers made up of the rational numbers and the irrational numbers.	_____	The recording was so _____ it sounded like a live concert.
5. the base and exponent of an expression of the form a^n	_____	Turn off the _____ before you try to repair those wires.
6. The property of addition that states $a + 0 = a$.	_____	He stole the _____ of another person to open a credit card account.
7. a number, a variable, or the product of a number and one or more variables	_____	He will come home from college at the end of the _____.
8. The set of numbers $0, 1, 2, 3, \ldots$	_____	Lauren ate a _____ bagel for breakfast today.

Practice 2-1

Solve each equation. Check your answer.

1. $5a + 2 = 7$

2. $2x + 3 = 7$

3. $3b + 6 = 12$

4. $9 = 5 + 4t$

5. $4a + 1 = 13$

6. $-t + 2 = 12$

Define a variable and write an equation to model each situation. Then solve.

7. You want to buy a bouquet of yellow roses and baby's breath for $16. The baby's breath costs $3.50 per bunch, and the roses cost $2.50 each. You want one bunch of baby's breath and some roses for your bouquet. How many roses can you buy?

8. Suppose you walk at the rate of 210 ft/min. You need to walk 10,000 ft. How many more minutes will it take you to finish if you have already walked 550 ft?

9. Suppose you have shelled 6.5 lb of pecans, and you can shell pecans at a rate of 1.5 lb per hour. How many more hours will it take you to shell a total of 11 lb of pecans?

10. To mail a first class letter, the U.S. Postal Service charges $.34 for the first ounce and $.21 for each additional ounce. It costs $1.18 to mail your letter. How many ounces does your letter weigh?

11. Suppose you want to buy one pair of pants and several pairs of socks. The pants cost $24.95, and the socks are $5.95 per pair. How many pairs of socks can you buy if you have $50.00 to spend?

Solve each equation. Check your solution.

12. $5.8n + 3.7 = 29.8$

13. $67 = -3y + 16$

14. $-d + 7 = 3$

15. $\frac{m}{9} + 7 = 3$

16. $6.78 + 5.2x = -36.9$

17. $5z + 9 = -21$

18. $3x - 7 = 35$

19. $36.9 = 3.7b - 14.9$

20. $4s - 13 = 51$

21. $9f + 16 = 70$

22. $11.6 + 3a = -16.9$

23. $-9 = -\frac{h}{12} + 5$

24. $-c + 2 = 5$

25. $-67 = -8n + 5$

26. $22 = 7 - 3a$

27. $\frac{k}{3} - 19 = -26$

28. $-21 = \frac{n}{3} + 2$

29. $3x + 5.7 = 15$

30. $\frac{a}{5} - 2 = -13$

31. $2x + 23 = 49$

32. $\frac{x}{2} + 8 = -3$

Justify each step.

33. $\qquad 24 - x = -16$

a. $24 - x - 24 = -16 - 24$

b. $\qquad -x = -40$

c. $\qquad -1(-x) = -1(-40)$

d. $\qquad x = 40$

34. $\qquad \frac{x}{7} + 4 = 15$

a. $\frac{x}{7} + 4 - 4 = 15 - 4$

b. $\qquad \frac{x}{7} = 11$

c. $\qquad 7(\frac{x}{7}) = 7(11)$

d. $\qquad x = 77$

35. $\qquad -8 = 2x - 5$

a. $-8 + 5 = 2x - 5 + 5$

b. $\qquad -3 = 2x$

c. $\qquad -\frac{3}{2} = \frac{2x}{2}$

d. $\qquad -\frac{3}{2} = x$

2-1 • Guided Problem Solving

 Exercise 44

One health insurance policy pays people for claims by multiplying the claim amount by 0.8 and then subtracting $500. Define a variable and write an equation for this situation. Then find the claim amount for an insurance payment of $4650.

Read and Understand

1. Describe in words how the insurance company
   determines how to pay people for their insurance claims. _____

2. What two quantities will be related by the equation? _____

Plan and Solve

3. Define your two variables.

   _____   _____

4. Write an equation that describes the insurance
   payment as a function of the claim amount. _____

5. For which variable will you substitute the value $4650? _____

6. Substitute $4650 in your equation and solve for the claim amount. _____

Look Back and Check

7. Multiplying by 0.8 is equivalent to finding 80% of a number. Check
   the reasonableness of your answer by finding 80% of your claim
   amount. Your answer should be $500 more than $4650.

Solve Another Problem

8. What would the insurance payment be for a claim of $3000? _____

Practice 2-2

Solving Multi-Step Equations

Solve each equation. Check your answer.

1. $2n + 3n + 7 = -41$ **2.** $2x - 5x + 6.3 = -14.4$ **3.** $2z + 9.75 - 7z = -5.15$

4. $3h - 5h + 11 = 17$ **5.** $2t + 8 - t = -3$ **6.** $6a - 2a = -36$

7. $3c - 8c + 7 = -18$ **8.** $7g + 14 - 5g = -8$ **9.** $2b - 6 + 3b = 14$

10. $2(a - 4) + 15 = 13$ **11.** $7 + 2(a - 3) = -9$ **12.** $13 + 2(5c - 2) = 29$

13. $5(3x + 12) = -15$ **14.** $4(2a + 2) - 17 = 15$ **15.** $2(m + 1) = 16$

16. $-4x + 3(2x - 5) = 31$ **17.** $-6 - 3(2k + 4) = 18$ **18.** $3(t - 12) = 27$

19. $-w + 4(w + 3) = -12$ **20.** $4 = 0.4(3d - 5)$ **21.** $-4d + 2(3 + d) = -14$

22. $2x + \frac{3}{4}(4x + 16) = 7$ **23.** $2(3a + 2) = -8$ **24.** $5(t - 3) - 2t = -30$

25. $5(b + 4) - 6b = -24$ **26.** $\frac{2}{5}(5k + 35) - 8 = 12$ **27.** $0.4(2s + 4) = 4.8$

28. $\frac{2}{3}(9b - 27) = 36$ **29.** $\frac{1}{2}(12n - 8) = 26$ **30.** $0.5(2x - 4) = -17$

31. $18 = \frac{c + 5}{2}$ **32.** $\frac{2}{9}s = -6$ **33.** $\frac{1}{3}x = \frac{1}{2}$

34. $\frac{2}{3}g + \frac{1}{2}g = 14$ **35.** $\frac{3x + 7}{2} = 8$ **36.** $\frac{2x - 6}{4} = -7$

37. $\frac{2}{3}k + \frac{1}{4}k = 22$ **38.** $-\frac{4}{7}h = -28$ **39.** $-8 = \frac{4}{5}k$

40. $\frac{3}{4} - \frac{1}{3}z = \frac{1}{4}$ **41.** $-9 = \frac{3}{4}m$ **42.** $\frac{5}{6}c - \frac{2}{3}c = \frac{1}{3}$

43. $\frac{4}{5} = -\frac{4}{7}g$ **44.** $\frac{9x + 6 - 4x}{2} = 8$ **45.** $-\frac{1}{6}d = -4$

Write an equation to model each situation. Solve your equation.

46. The attendance at a baseball game was 400 people. Student tickets cost $2 and adult tickets cost $3. Total ticket sales were $1050. How many tickets of each type were sold?

47. The perimeter of a pool table is 30 ft. The table is twice as long as it is wide. What is the length of the pool table?

48. Lopez spent $\frac{1}{3}$ of his vacation money for travel and $\frac{2}{5}$ of his vacation money for lodging. He spent $1100 for travel and lodging. What is the total amount of money he spent on his vacation?

49. Victoria weighs $\frac{5}{7}$ as much as Mario. Victoria weighs 125 lb. How much does Mario weigh?

50. Denise's cell phone plan is $29.95 per month plus $.10 per minute for each minute over 300 minutes of call time. Denise's cell phone bill is $99.95. For how many minutes was she billed?

2-2 • Guided Problem Solving

 Exercise 60

Jane's cell phone plan is $40 per month plus $.15 per minute for each minute over 200 minutes of call time. If Jane's cell phone bill is $58.00, for how many extra calling minutes was she billed?

Read and Understand

1. Explain how the amount of Jane's phone bill is determined? _____

2. What is the problem asking you to determine? _____

Plan and Solve

3. What would Jane's phone bill be if she talked for exactly 200 minutes? _____

4. What would Jane's phone bill be if she talked for 10 extra minutes? _____

5. Write an equation to model this situation. _____

6. Use your equation to determine how many extra calling minutes Jane was billed for if her phone bill was $58.00. _____

Look Back and Check

7. Is this a reasonable plan? How many minutes do you talk on the telephone each month? Is it reasonable to allow 200 minutes before charging extra? _____

_____

Solve Another Problem

8. Janet's cable company charges her a basic fee of $59. For each premium channel, she is charged an extra $12. How many premium channels does she have if her total bill is $107 each month?

_____

Practice 2-3

Equations With Variables on Both Sides

• •

Solve each equation. Check your answer. If appropriate, write *identity* or *no solution*.

1. $7 - 2n = n - 14$

2. $2(4 - 2r) = -2(r + 5)$

3. $3d + 8 = 2d - 7$

4. $6t = 3(t + 4) - t$

5. $8z - 7 = 3z - 7 + 5z$

6. $7x - 8 = 3x + 12$

7. $3(n - 1) = 5n + 3 - 2n$

8. $2(6 - 4d) = 25 - 9d$

9. $4s - 12 = -5s + 51$

10. $8(2f - 3) = 4(4f - 8)$

11. $6k - 25 = 7 - 2k$

12. $3v - 9 = 7 + 2v - v$

13. $4(b - 1) = -4 + 4b$

14. $\frac{1}{4}x + \frac{1}{2} = \frac{1}{4}x - \frac{1}{2}$

15. $6 - 4d = 16 - 9d$

16. $\frac{2}{3}a - \frac{3}{4} = \frac{3}{4}a$

17. $2s - 12 + 2s = 4s - 12$

18. $3.6y = 5.4 + 3.3y$

19. $4.3v - 6 = 8 + 2.3v$

20. $4b - 1 = -4 + 4b + 3$

21. $\frac{2}{3}(6x + 3) = 4x + 2$

22. $6y + 9 = 3(2y + 3)$

23. $4g + 7 = 5g - 1 - g$

24. $2(n + 2) = 5n - 5$

25. $6 - 3d = 5(2 - d)$

26. $6.1h = 9.3 - 3.2h$

27. $-4.4s - 2 = -5.5s - 4.2$

28. $3(2f + 4) = 2(3f - 6)$

29. $\frac{3}{4}t - \frac{5}{6} = \frac{2}{3}t$

30. $3v + 8 = 8 + 2v + v$

31. $\frac{1}{2}d - \frac{3}{4} = \frac{3}{5}d$

32. $5(r + 3) = 2r + 6$

33. $8 - 3(p - 4) = 2p$

Write and solve an equation for each situation. Check your solution.

34. Hans needs to rent a moving truck. Suppose Company A charges a rate of $40 per day and Company B charges a $60 fee plus $20 per day. For what number of days is the cost the same?

35. Suppose a video store charges nonmembers $4 to rent each video. A store membership costs $21 and members pay only $2.50 to rent each video. For what number of videos is the cost the same?

36. Suppose your club is selling candles to raise money. It costs $100 to rent a booth from which to sell the candles. If the candles cost your club $1 each and are sold for $5 each, how many candles must be sold to equal your expenses?

Find the value of *x*.

37.
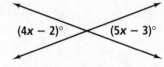
$(4x - 2)°$ $(5x - 3)°$

38.
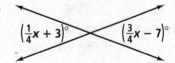
$\left(\frac{1}{4}x + 3\right)°$ $\left(\frac{3}{4}x - 7\right)°$

39.
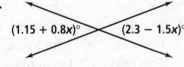
$(1.15 + 0.8x)°$ $(2.3 - 1.5x)°$

2-3 • Guided Problem Solving

GPS **Exercise 39**

Don set up a table to solve
$5(x - 3) = 4 - 3(x + 1)$.

a. Does Don's table show a solution to the equation?

b. Between which two values of x is the solution to the equation? How do you know?

c. For what values of x is $4 - 3(x + 1)$ less than $5(x - 3)$?

	A	B	C
1	x	$5(x - 3)$	$4 - 3(x + 1)$
2	−5	−40	16
3	−3	−30	10
4	−1	−20	4
5	1	−10	−2
6	3	0	−8

Read and Understand

1. Describe what the values in each column represent. _____

_____

2. What is Don trying to use the table for? _____

Plan and Solve

3. Explain what a solution to an equation is. _____

_____

4. Does Don's table show a solution to the equation? _____

5. Between what two values of x is the solution to the equation? _____

   How do you know? _____

6. For what values of x is $4 - 3(x + 1)$ less than $5(x - 3)$? _____

Look Back and Check

7. Check the reasonableness of your answer by substituting a value between 1 and 3 into your equation to see if the sides are approximately equal to each other.

Solve Another Problem

8. Describe how Don could set up a table to solve $2(x + 5) - 2 = 4(x - 7)$.

Practice 2-4

Ratio and Proportion

Find each unit rate.

1. $60 for 8 h

2. $\dfrac{\$3}{4\,lb}$

3. $\dfrac{861\text{ mi}}{41\text{ gal}}$

4. $\dfrac{850\text{ cal}}{1.25\text{ h}}$

5. An 8-ounce bottle of lotion costs $4.50. What is the cost per ounce?

6. A pound of coffee costs $14.99. What is the cost per ounce?

Which pairs of ratios could form a proportion? Justify your answer.

7. $\dfrac{10}{24}, \dfrac{7}{18}$

8. $\dfrac{6}{9}, \dfrac{10}{15}$

9. $\dfrac{3}{4}, \dfrac{18}{24}$

10. $\dfrac{16}{2}, \dfrac{8}{1}$

11. $-\dfrac{4.8}{4}, -\dfrac{6.4}{5}$

Solve each proportion.

12. $\dfrac{g}{5} = \dfrac{6}{10}$

13. $\dfrac{z}{4} = \dfrac{7}{8}$

14. $\dfrac{13.2}{6} = \dfrac{m}{12}$

15. $-\dfrac{m}{5} = -\dfrac{2}{5}$

16. $\dfrac{5.5}{11} = \dfrac{x}{5}$

17. $-\dfrac{2}{3} = -\dfrac{10}{t}$

18. $\dfrac{4}{6} = \dfrac{x}{24}$

19. $\dfrac{s}{3} = \dfrac{7}{10}$

20. $\dfrac{4}{9} = \dfrac{10}{r}$

21. $\dfrac{x}{4.8} = \dfrac{6}{3.2}$

22. $\dfrac{5}{4} = \dfrac{c}{12}$

23. $-\dfrac{32}{h} = -\dfrac{1}{3}$

24. $\dfrac{2}{6} = \dfrac{p}{9}$

25. $\dfrac{f}{6} = \dfrac{3}{4}$

26. $\dfrac{15}{a} = \dfrac{3}{8}$

27. $\dfrac{3}{4} = \dfrac{k}{24}$

28. $\dfrac{a}{6} = \dfrac{3}{9}$

29. $\dfrac{4}{5} = \dfrac{k}{9}$

30. $\dfrac{3}{y} = \dfrac{5}{8}$

31. $\dfrac{t}{7} = \dfrac{9}{21}$

32. $\dfrac{2}{9} = \dfrac{10}{x}$

33. $\dfrac{x}{15} = \dfrac{3}{4}$

34. $\dfrac{18}{11} = \dfrac{49.5}{x}$

35. $\dfrac{2}{1.2} = \dfrac{5}{x}$

36. $-\dfrac{x-1}{4} = \dfrac{2}{3}$

37. $\dfrac{3}{6} = \dfrac{x-3}{8}$

38. $\dfrac{2x-2}{14} = \dfrac{2x-4}{6}$

39. $\dfrac{x+2}{x-2} = \dfrac{4}{8}$

40. $\dfrac{x+2}{6} = \dfrac{x-1}{12}$

41. $-\dfrac{x+8}{10} = -\dfrac{x-3}{2}$

42. You are riding your bicycle. It takes you 28 min to go 8 mi. If you continue traveling at the same rate, how long will it take you to go 15 mi?

43. Suppose you traveled 84 mi in 1.5 h. Moving at the same speed, how many mi would you cover in $3\frac{1}{4}$ h?

44. A canary's heart beats 130 times in 12 s. Use a proportion to find how many times its heart beats in 50 s.

45. Your car averages 18 mi per gal on the highway. If gas costs $1.85 per gal, how much does it cost in dollars per mi to drive your car on the highway?

2-4 • Guided Problem Solving

GPS Exercise 56

Bonnie and Tim do some yardwork for their neighbor. The ratio comparing the amount of time each one works is 7 : 4. The neighbor pays them $88. If Bonnie worked more, how much should each of them receive?

Read and Understand

1. What does the ratio 7 : 4 describe? _____

2. If an equation were used to solve this problem, what would x represent? _____

Plan and Solve

3. Write a verbal model for this problem. _____

4. Let b represent the amount of money Bonnie earns. Write an expression that represents how much money Tim will make. _____

5. Write an equation to model this situation. _____

6. Solve the equation to find b. _____

7. How much money did each person receive? _____

Look Back and Check

8. Check the amount each person earned to make sure Bonnie made more money than Tim. Why is this reasonable?

Solve Another Problem

9. If 2 tons of rock costs $15.50, then how many tons of rock can you buy for $45?

_____

Practice 2-5

Write and solve an equation for each situation.

1. A passenger train's speed is 60 mi/h, and a freight train's speed is 40 mi/h. The passenger train travels the same distance in 1.5 h less time than the freight train. How long does each train take to make the trip?

2. Lois rode her bike to visit a friend. She traveled at 10 mi/h. While she was there, it began to rain. Her friend drove her home in a car traveling at 25 mi/h. Lois took 1.5 h longer to go to her friend's than to return home. How many hours did it take Lois to ride to her friend's house?

3. May rides her bike the same distance that Leah walks. May rides her bike 10 km/h faster than Leah walks. If it takes May 1 h and Leah 3 h to travel that distance, how fast does each travel?

4. The length of a rectangle is 4 in. greater than the width. The perimeter of the rectangle is 24 in. Find the dimensions of the rectangle.

5. The length of a rectangle is twice the width. The perimeter is 48 in. Find the dimensions of the rectangle.

6. At 10:00 A.M., a car leaves a house at a rate of 60 mi/h. At the same time, another car leaves the same house at a rate of 50 mi/h in the opposite direction. At what time will the cars be 330 miles apart?

7. Marla begins walking at 3 mi/h toward the library. Her friend meets her at the halfway point and drives her the rest of the way to the library. The distance to the library is 4 miles. How many hours did Marla walk?

8. Fred begins walking toward John's house at 3 mi/h. John leaves his house at the same time and walks toward Fred's house on the same path at a rate of 2 mi/h. How long will it be before they meet if the distance between the houses is 4 miles?

9. A train leaves the station at 6:00 P.M. traveling west at 80 mi/h. On a parallel track, a second train leaves the station 3 hours later traveling west at 100 mi/h. At what time will the second train catch up with the first?

10. It takes 1 hour longer to fly to St. Paul at 200 mi/h than it does to return at 250 mi/h. How far away is St. Paul?

11. Find three consecutive integers whose sum is 126.

12. The sum of four consecutive odd integers is 216. Find the four integers.

13. A rectangular picture frame is to be 8 in. longer than it is wide. Dennis uses 84 in. of oak to frame the picture. What is the width of the frame?

14. Each of two congruent sides of an isosceles triangle is 8 in. less than twice the base. The perimeter of the triangle is 74 in. What is the length of the base?

2-5 • Guided Problem Solving

GPS **Exercise 21**

At 12:00 P.M. a truck leaves Centerville traveling 45 mi/h. One hour later a train leaves Centerville traveling 60 mi/h. They arrive in Smithfield at the same time.

Time	Truck 45t	Train 60(t − 1)
1 P.M.	45 mi	0 mi
2 P.M.	90 mi	60 mi
3 P.M.	135 mi	120 mi
4 P.M.	180 mi	180 mi
5 P.M.	225 mi	240 mi

a. Use the table to find when the train and truck arrive in Smithfield.

b. **Critical Thinking** What piece of information can you get from the table that you would NOT get by solving the equation $45t = 60(t − 1)$?

Read and Understand

1. What information are you given in the problem? _____

2. What is the problem asking you to figure out? _____

Plan and Solve

3. Explain how you can use the table to determine when the train and truck arrive in Smithfield. _____

4. At what time did the train and truck arrive in Smithfield? _____

5. What information would you have if you solved the equation for *t*? _____

6. What piece of information can you get from the table that you would *not* get by solving the equation? _____

Look Back and Check

7. The truck traveled for 4 hours, and the train traveled for 3 hours. Check the reasonableness of your answer by evaluating the appropriate expressions for each time to see if the distances are equal.

Solve Another Problem

8. A delivery van drives due east toward its destination at 55 mph. Another van drives due west at 60 mph. After 3 hours they are 345 miles apart. How far did each van travel?

_____

Practice 2-6

Write and solve an equation for each situation.

1. A store sells mixtures of almonds and cashews for $6.50 per pound. Peanuts sell for $2.95 per pound and cashews sell for $7.95 per pound. How many pounds of each should be used to make 80 pounds of this mixture?

2. A solution is 30% chlorine and another solution is 60% chlorine. How many liters of each solution should you use to make 120 liters of a solution that is 40% chlorine?

3. A 30-lb mixture of dried cranberries and blueberries costs $8.98 per pound. The mixture contains 12 pounds of dried cranberries that cost $4.99 per pound. What is the cost per pound of the dried blueberries?

4. The manager of a tea shop mixes two types of teas to make a specialty blend. Alone, the teas sell for $3.99 and $8.99 per ounce. How many ounces of each type of tea should be used to make 32 ounces of a mixture that sells for $5.99 per ounce?

5. A chemist needs a saline solution that is 20% sodium chloride but only has solutions that are 15% and 40% sodium chloride. If the chemist measures 150 mL of the 15% solution, how many milliliters of the 40% solution should she add to make a 20% solution?

6. A beverage company plans to make a fruit juice blend using grape juice and cranberry juice that sells for $3.80 per gallon. If grape juice costs $2.99 per gallon and cranberry juice costs $4.99 per gallon, how much grape juice will be needed to make 50 gallons of the fruit juice blend?

7. A chemistry student mixes together 12 mL of a 10% chlorine solution, 5 mL of a 80% chlorine solution and 20 mL of a 45% solution. About what percent chlorine is the final solution?

8. A boat owner mixes together oil and gasoline to make 40 gallons of fuel for his boat. The mixture must be 2% oil and 98% gasoline. Oil costs $64 per gallon and gasoline costs $2.50 per gallon. If the total cost for the fuel was $149.20, how much oil did he buy?

9. Mr. Hackney wants to winterize his motor home and needs a 40% antifreeze solution. How much pure antifreeze must he add to 10 liters of 20% antifreeze to make a 40% antifreeze solution?

2-6 • Guided Problem Solving

GPS Exercise 9

A 20-lb mixture of banana chips and dried apricots costs $6.89 per pound.
The mixture contains 6 pounds of banana chips that cost $1.99 per pound.
What is the cost per pound of the dried apricots?

Read and Understand

1. What information are you given in the problem? _____

   _____

2. How can you use the given information to find out the number of pounds of apricots the mixture contains? _____

   _____

Plan and Solve

3. Define a variable for the cost of the apricots. Then write an expression that represents the cost of the apricots. _____

4. Write a verbal sentence that represents the situation. _____

   _____

5. Write an expression that represents the situation and solve for the variable. _____

   _____

6. What does the variable represent? _____

Look Back and Check

7. The banana chips cost $1.99 per pound and the drided apricots cost $8.99 per pound. Check the reasonableness of your answer by evaluating the appropriate expressions for each cost to see if the costs are equal. _____

   _____

Solve Another Problem

8. A snack company wants to sell a mixture of dried cherries and dried pineapple for $7.99 per pound. Dried cherries sell for $9.99 per pound and dried pineapple sells for $4.99 per pound. How many pounds of each should be used to make 80 pounds of this mixture? _____

   _____

2A: Graphic Organizer

For use before Lesson 2-1

Study Skill Keep notes as you work through each chapter to help you organize your thinking and to make it easier to review the material when you complete the chapter.

Write your answers.

1. What is the chapter title? _____

2. Find the Table of Contents page for this chapter at the front of the book. Name four topics you will study in this chapter.

   _____   _____

   _____   _____

3. Complete the graphic organizer as you work through the chapter.
   1. Write the title of the chapter in the center oval.
   2. When you begin a lesson, write the name of the lesson in a rectangle.
   3. When you complete that lesson, write a skill or key concept from that lesson in the outer oval linked to that rectangle.

   Continue with steps 2 and 3 clockwise around the graphic organizer.

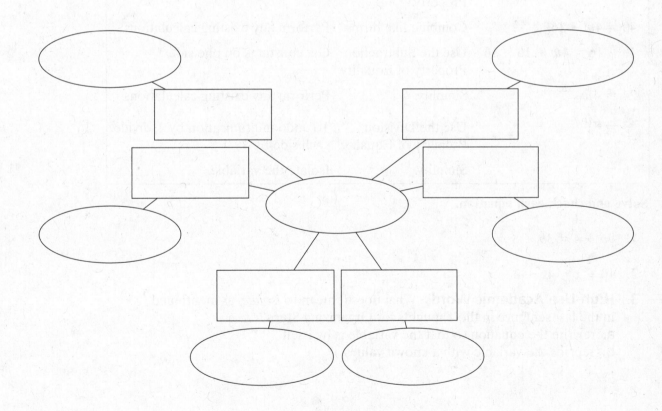

2B: Reading Comprehension

Study Skill Some math problems have many steps and can be confusing. Sometimes, if you hurry through a problem, you leave out important steps. Think carefully about what the next step to solving a problem might be.

The equations and justification statements given below are the correct ones to find the dimensions of a rectangle with the given properties:
1. The length of a rectangle is 8 cm more than its width.
2. The perimeter of the rectangle is 40 cm.

Steps	Justifications	Thoughts for Organizing Steps
Let w = width.		The length is described in terms of the width. So defined a variable for the width first.
Then $w + 8$ = the length.		
$P = 2l + 2w$		Use the perimeter formula.
$40 = 2(w + 8) + 2v$	Substitute 40 for P and $w + 8$ for l.	Replace variables with any known values.
$40 = 2w + 16 + 2w$	Use the Distributive Property.	Perform any existing calculations.
$40 = 4w + 16$	Combine like terms.	Perform any existing calculations.
$40 - 16 = 4w + 16 - 16$	Use the Subtraction Property of Equality.	Get constants on one side.
$24 = 4w$	Simplify.	Perform any existing calculations.
$\dfrac{24}{4} = \dfrac{4w}{4}$	Use the Division Property of Equality.	To undo multiplication by 4, divide each side by 4.
$6 = w$	Simplify.	Isolate the variable.

Solve and check each equation.

1. $9b + 4 = 3b - 8$

2. $10 - x = 4x + 2 - x$

3. High-Use Academic Words What does it mean to *isolate*, as mentioned in the last sentence in the Thoughts for Organizing Steps?
a. rewrite the equation so that the variable is by itself
b. replace the variable with a known value

2C: Reading/Writing Math Symbols

For use after Lesson 2-4

Study Skill There are many symbols that are abbreviations for longer words. Using these symbols when taking notes helps you keep up with the person giving the notes. Learn these symbols for quicker note taking.

Write what each abbreviated math symbol means.

1. ¢/oz _____

2. mi/h _____

3. ft/min _____

4. km/h _____

5. ft/mi _____

6. $/yr _____

7. $/lb _____

8. ft/wk _____

9. gal/wk _____

10. mi/gal _____

11. lb/in.^{2} _____

12. ft/s^2 _____

13. m/s^2 _____

14. $/oz _____

Write each phrase in symbol form.

15. miles per gallon _____

16. dollars per pound _____

17. kilometers per hour _____

18. feet per minute _____

2D: Visual Vocabulary Practice
High-Use Academic Words

Study Skills If a word is not in the Glossary, use a dictionary to find its meaning.

Concept List

approximate	compare	convert
define	describe	evaluate
explain	identify	model

Write the concept that best describes each exercise. Choose from the concept list above.

1. Let n = number of CDs. _____	**2.** $a = -5$ $3 \cdot a + 4 = 3 \cdot (-5) + 4$ $\qquad = -15 + 4$ $\qquad = -11$ _____	**3.** $\pi \approx \frac{22}{7}$ _____
4. x-coordinate $\downarrow$ $(-2, 4)$ $\uparrow$ y-coordinate _____	**5.** $2 + (-5)$ 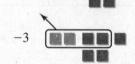 -3 $2 + (-5) = -3$ _____	**6.** The graph is a function because there is exactly one range value for each domain value. _____
7. $-6 < 5$ _____	**8.** To plot $(-2, 3)$, move 2 units to the left of the origin. Then move 3 units up. _____	**9.** $10 \text{ gal} \cdot \dfrac{4 \text{ qt}}{1 \text{ gal}} = 40 \text{ qt}$ _____

2E: Vocabulary Check

Study Skill Strengthen your vocabulary. Use these pages and add cues and summaries by applying the Cornell Notetaking style.

Write the definition for each word at the right. To check your work, fold the paper back along the dotted line to see the correct answers.

_____

_____

_____

_____

_____

_____

_____

_____

_____

_____

_____

_____

Identity

Rate

Unit Analysis

Proportion

Cross Products

Vocabulary and Study Skills

2E: Vocabulary Check (continued)

For use after Lesson 2-5

Write the vocabulary word for each definition. To check your work,
fold the paper forward along the dotted line to see the correct answers.

An equation that is
true for every value of
the variable.

_____

A ratio where the two
quantities being compared
are measured in different
units.

_____

The process of selecting
conversion factors to
produce appropriate units.

_____

An equation that states
that two ratios are equal.

_____

In a proportion, $\frac{a}{b} = \frac{c}{d}$,
the products ad and bc.
These products are equal.

_____

2F: Vocabulary Review Puzzle

For use with Chapter Review

Study Skill When you complete a puzzle such as a word search, read the list of words carefully and completely. As you identify each word in the word search, circle it and then cross off the word from the list. Pay special attention to the spelling of each word.

Complete the word search.

identity	rate	solution	ratio
unit analysis	means	cross products	equivalent
proportion	equation	unit rate	extremes
uniform motion	solve	inverse	consecutive

```
S  S  A  E  T  E  U  E  Q  U  A  T  O  I  N
P  A  L  N  R  V  Q  N  U  N  I  T  R  N  E
R  L  S  O  L  U  T  U  I  S  T  I  A  V  E
O  V  R  E  T  I  O  E  I  T  O  S  T  E  S
P  E  Q  U  A  T  I  O  N  V  R  L  E  R  U
O  R  M  R  M  E  A  N  S  T  A  A  V  S  E
R  A  T  E  X  T  R  E  M  E  S  L  T  E  T
T  T  I  D  E  N  T  I  T  Y  Y  S  E  E  I
I  I  C  O  N  S  I  C  U  T  I  V  E  N  O
O  O  E  S  O  L  U  T  I  O  N  Q  E  E  T
N  U  N  I  F  O  R  M  M  O  T  I  O  N  A
M  C  R  O  S  S  P  R  O  D  U  C  T  S  I
E  C  O  N  S  E  C  U  T  I  V  E  R  A  C
F  E  U  N  I  T  A  N  A  L  Y  S  I  S  V
E  P  E  O  A  N  I  E  T  E  N  N  N  N  P
```

Practice 3-1

Is each number a solution of the given inequality?

1. $x \leq -8$ **a.** -10 **b.** 6 **c.** -8

2. $-1 > x$ **a.** 0 **b.** -3 **c.** -6

3. $w < \frac{18}{7}$ **a.** 5 **b.** -2 **c.** $3\frac{1}{2}$

4. $0.65 \geq y$ **a.** 0.43 **b.** -0.65 **c.** 0.56

5. $2y + 1 > -5$ **a.** -4 **b.** -2 **c.** 4

6. $7x - 14 \leq 6x - 16$ **a.** 0 **b.** -4 **c.** 2

7. $n(n - 6) \geq -4$ **a.** 3 **b.** -2 **c.** 5

Write an inequality for each graph.

8.

9.

10.

11.

Graph each inequality.

12. $x > 6$ **13.** $y \leq -10$ **14.** $8 \geq b$

15. $-4 < w$ **16.** $x < -7$ **17.** $x \geq 12$

Define a variable and write an inequality to model each situation.

18. The temperature in a refrigerated truck must be kept at or below 38°F. _____

19. The maximum weight on an elevator is 2000 pounds. _____

20. A least 20 students were sick with the flu. _____

21. The maximum occupancy in an auditorium is 250 people. _____

22. The maximum speed on the highway is 55 mi/h. _____

23. A student must have at least 450 out of 500 points to earn an A. _____

24. The circumference of an official major league baseball is at least 9.00 inches. _____

Match each inequality with its graph.

25. $6 < x$ **26.** $-6 \geq x$ **27.** $4 > x$ **28.** $x \leq -4$

A.

B.

C.

D.

3-1 • Guided Problem Solving

GPS Exercise 65

Your travel agent is making plans
for you to go from Chicago to
New Orleans. A direct flight costs too
much. Option A consists of flights from
Chicago to Dallas to New Orleans.
Option B consists of flights from
Chicago to Orlando to New Orleans.
Write an inequality comparing the
mileage of these two options.

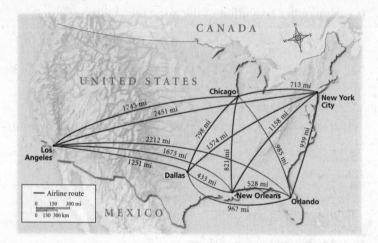

Read and Understand

1. Describe option A. _____

2. Describe option B. _____

3. The problem asks you to write an inequality for what? _____

Plan and Solve

4. What is the mileage between each of the cities in option A?

   Chicago to Dallas _____   Dallas to New Orleans _____

5. What is the total mileage for option A? _____

6. What is the mileage between each of the cities in option B?

   Chicago to Orlando _____   Orlando to New Orleans _____

7. What is the total mileage for option B? _____

8. Write an inequality comparing the mileage for option A and option B. _____

Look Back and Check

9. Write a sentence to describe the relationship between the mileage for option A and option B.
   Check that this sentence matches your inequality written above.

   _____

Solve Another Problem

10. An office supply store sells a pack of pencils for $.99, a notebook for $1.29,
    and scissors for $1.39. A discount store sells the same pack of pencils
    for $1.09, the notebook for $1.25, and the scissors for $1.19. Write an
    inequality comparing the total cost of school supplies at each store. _____

Practice 3-2

Solving Inequalities Using Addition and Subtraction

Solve each inequality. Check your solution.

1. $n - 7 \geq 2$

2. $10 + y > 12$

3. $3.2 < r + 4.7$

4. $7 + b > 13$

5. $n + \frac{3}{4} > \frac{1}{2}$

6. $-\frac{5}{7} \geq c + \frac{2}{7}$

7. $g + 4.6 < 5.9$

8. $0 > d - 2.7$

9. $f + 4 \geq 14$

10. $x + 1 \leq -3$

11. $d - 13 \leq -8$

12. $m - 7 \geq -8$

13. $12 + v < 19$

14. $-4 \leq t + 9$

15. $6 < y - 3$

16. $a + 15 > 19$

17. $8 + d < 9$

18. $s + 3 \leq 3$

19. $9 + h \leq 5$

20. $7.6 \geq t - 2.4$

Write and solve an inequality that models each situation.

21. It will take at least 360 points for Kiko's team to win the math contest. The scores for Kiko's teammates were 94, 82, and 87, but one of Kiko's teammates lost 2 of those points for an incomplete answer. How many points must Kiko earn for her team to win the contest?

22. This season, Nora has 125 at-bats in softball. By the end of the season she wants to have at least 140 at-bats. How many more at-bats does Nora need to reach her goal?

23. The average wind speed increased 19 mi/h from 8 A.M. to noon. The average wind speed decreased 5 mi/h from noon to 4 P.M. At 4 P.M., the average wind speed was at least 32 mi/h. What is the minimum value of the average wind speed at 8 A.M.?

24. Suppose it takes no more than 25 min for you to get to school. If you have traveled for 13.5 min already, how much longer, at most, might you take to get to school?

25. Joan has started a physical fitness program. One of her goals is to be able to run at least 5 mi without stopping. She can now run 3.5 mi without stopping. How many more miles must she run non-stop to achieve her goal?

26. Suppose you can get a higher interest rate on your savings if you maintain a balance of at least $1000 in your savings account. The balance in your savings account is now $1058. You deposit $44.50 into your account. What is the greatest amount that you can withdraw and still get the higher interest rate?

Solve each inequality. Graph and check your solution.

27. $\frac{3}{4} + z \geq -\frac{3}{4}$

28. $12 + d + 3 \leq 10$

29. $v - \frac{3}{4} > 1\frac{1}{4}$

30. $8 + m > 4$

31. $2 + f > -3$

32. $-27 \geq w - 24$

33. $b + \frac{1}{2} > \frac{3}{4}$

34. $12 + t < 4 - 15$

35. $-14 > -16 + u$

36. $-7 \leq -11 + z$

37. $38 \geq 33 + b$

38. $k - 27 < -29$

39. $a + 8 \leq 10$

40. $b + 6 > 17$

41. $13 < 8 + k - 6$

42. $j + 1.3 > 2.8$

3-2 • Guided Problem Solving

GPS **Exercise 60**

Suppose your sister wants to qualify for a regional gymnastics competition.
At today's competition she must score at least 57.0 points. She scored 13.8
on the vault, 14.9 on the balance beam, and 13.2 on the uneven parallel bars.
The event that remains is the floor exercise.

a. Write and solve an inequality that models the information.
b. Explain what the solution means in terms of the original situation.
c. Write three scores your sister could make that would allow her to
qualify for the regional gymnastics competition.

Read and Understand

1. How many points must your sister score at today's competition? _____

2. How many points did
she score on the vault? _____ balance beam? _____ uneven parallel bars? _____

Plan and Solve

3. How many total points has your sister scored at the competition so far? _____

4. Write an inequality that models the information. _____

5. What is the solution to the inequality? _____

6. Explain what the solution means in terms of the original situation. _____

_____

7. Write three scores that your sister could make that would
allow her to qualify for the regional gymnastics competition. _____

Look Back and Check

8. Check each of your scores by adding 41.9 to each one. Your answers should all be at least 57.0.

_____

Solve Another Problem

9. Samuel's mother has set a limit of 8 hours per week of Internet use. On Monday Samuel used
the Internet for 0.75 hour, on Tuesday for 1.5 hours, and on Wednesday for 0.5 hour. Write and
solve an inequality in order to determine the maximum amount of Internet time Samuel has for
the remaining days of the week.

_____

Practice 3-3

Solving Inequalities Using Multiplication and Division

Solve each inequality. Graph and check your solution.

1. $\frac{15}{8} \le \frac{5}{2}s$

2. $60 \le 12b$

3. $-\frac{4}{5}r < 8$

4. $\frac{5}{2} < \frac{n}{8}$

5. $-9n \ge -36$

6. $\frac{n}{7} \ge -6$

7. $-7c < 28$

8. $16d > -64$

9. $-\frac{t}{3} < -5$

10. $54 < -6k$

11. $\frac{w}{7} > 0$

12. $2.6v > 6.5$

13. $-4 < -\frac{2}{5}m$

14. $17 < \frac{p}{2}$

15. $0.9 \le -1.8v$

16. $-5 \le -\frac{x}{9}$

17. $-1 \ge \frac{d}{7}$

18. $-3x \ge 21$

19. $\frac{c}{12} < \frac{3}{4}$

20. $\frac{a}{4} \le -1$

Write and solve an inequality that models each situation.

21. Suppose you and a friend are working for a nursery planting trees. Together you can plant 8 trees per hour. What is the greatest number of hours that you and your friend would need to plant at most 40 trees?

22. Suppose the physics club is going on a field trip. Members will be riding in vans that will hold 7 people each including the driver. At least 28 people will be going on the field trip. What is the least number of vans needed to make the trip?

23. You need to buy stamps to mail some letters. The stamps cost $.34 each. What is the maximum number of stamps that you can buy with $3.84?

24. The Garcias are putting a brick border along one edge of their flower garden. The flower garden is no more than 31 ft long. If each brick is 6 in. long, what is the greatest number of bricks needed?

25. Janet needs to travel 275 mi for a conference. She needs to be at the conference in no more than 5.5 h. What is the slowest average speed that she can drive and still arrive at the conference on time?

Solve each inequality. Graph and check your solution.

26. $\frac{1}{4}h < 4.9$

27. $\frac{7}{3}x < 21$

28. $-\frac{1}{9}a > 9$

29. $\frac{b}{6} \le 2.5$

30. $-\frac{3}{5}q > 15$

31. $84 \le 21b$

32. $\frac{c}{12} > -\frac{5}{6}$

33. $80.6 \le -6.5b$

34. $-\frac{1}{9}p > \frac{1}{3}$

35. $-9z > 45$

36. $\frac{1}{7}y \le 6$

37. $-\frac{5}{7} > -\frac{k}{14}$

38. $6.8 > \frac{y}{5}$

39. $75 \le 15b$

40. $39 < -13k$

41. $2d < 8.8$

42. $8.5v > 61.2$

43. $-11n \ge -55$

44. $\frac{1}{4}y < 17$

45. $92 < -23k$

Algebra 1 Lesson 3-3 **231**

3-3 • Guided Problem Solving

GPS **Exercise 76**

A friend calls you and asks you to meet at a location 3 miles from your
home in 20 minutes. You set off on your bicycle after the telephone call.
Write and solve an inequality to find the average rate in miles per minute
you could ride to be at your meeting place within 20 minutes.

Read and Understand

1. How far away is the meeting location? _____

2. How much time do you have to get there? _____

3. What unit should be used to represent rate? _____

Plan and Solve

4. Let r represent your rate. Write and solve an inequality to find the average
   rate you could ride to be at your meeting place *within* 20 minutes.

   _____

5. Express your minimum rate as miles/hour. _____

Look Back and Check

6. Give one rate in mi/min that would allow you to meet your friend
   within 20 minutes. Check your answer by multiplying your rate by 20.
   Your answer is the distance you will travel at that rate in 20 minutes.
   Is your answer more than 3 miles?

Solve Another Problem

7. The student council is planning the next school dance. The total expenses
   for the dance will be $2500 and they expect 200 students to attend. Write
   and solve an inequality to find the minimum ticket price per student that
   should be charged in order to cover expenses.

   _____

Practice 3-4

Solving Multi-Step Inequalities

Solve each inequality. Check your solution.

1. $2z + 7 < z + 10$

2. $4(k - 1) > 4$

3. $1.5 + 2.1y < 1.1y + 4.5$

4. $h + 2(3h + 4) \geq 1$

5. $r + 4 > 13 - 2r$

6. $6u - 18 - 4u < 22$

7. $2(3 + 3g) \geq 2g + 14$

8. $2h - 13 < -3$

9. $-4p + 28 > 8$

10. $8m - 8 \geq 12 + 4m$

11. $5 + 6a > -1$

12. $\frac{1}{2}(2t + 8) \geq 4 + 6t$

13. $-5x + 12 < -18$

14. $2(3f + 2) > 4f + 12$

15. $13t - 8t > -45$

16. $2(c - 4) \leq 10 - c$

17. $\frac{1}{2}t - \frac{1}{3}t > -1$

18. $3.4 + 1.6v < 5.9 - 0.9v$

Write and solve an inequality that models each situation.

19. Ernest works in the shipping department loading shipping crates with boxes. Each empty crate weighs 150 lb. How many boxes, each weighing 35 lb, can Ernest put in the crate if the total weight is to be no more than 850 lb?

20. Beatriz is in charge of setting up a banquet hall. She has five tables that will seat six people each. If no more than 62 people will attend, how many tables seating four people each will she need?

21. Suppose it costs $5 to enter a carnival. Each ride costs $1.25. You have $15 to spend at the carnival. What is the greatest number of rides that you can go on?

22. The cost to rent a car is $19.50 plus $.25 per mile. If you have $44 to rent a car, what is the greatest number of miles that you can drive?

23. The student council is sponsoring a concert as a fund raiser. Tickets are $3 for students and $5 for adults. The student council wants to raise at least $1000. If 200 students attend, how many adults must attend?

Solve each inequality. Check your solution.

24. $-18 < 2(12 - 3b)$

25. $5n + 3 - 4n < -5 - 3n$

26. $36 > 4(2d + 10)$

27. $2(5t - 25) + 5t < -80$

28. $3j + 2 - 2j < -10$

29. $\frac{2}{5}(5x - 15) \geq 4$

30. $7(2z + 3) > 35$

31. $2(3b - 2) < 4b + 8$

32. $\frac{1}{2}y + \frac{1}{4}y \geq -6$

33. $8(3f - 6) < -24$

34. $\frac{3}{4}k < \frac{3}{4} - \frac{1}{4}k$

35. $3(4g - 6) \geq 6(g + 2)$

36. $\frac{1}{2}(2g + 4) > -7$

37. $4(1.25y + 4.2) < 16.8$

38. $38 + 7t > -3(t + 4)$

39. $4(2d + 1) > 28$

40. $4(n - 3) < 2 - 3n$

41. $\frac{3}{4}d - \frac{1}{2} \leq 2\frac{1}{2}$

3-4 • Guided Problem Solving

GPS **Exercise 42**

The sophomore class is planning a picnic. The cost of a permit to use a city park is $250. To pay for the permit, there is a fee of $.75 for each sophomore and $1.25 for each guest who is not a sophomore. Two hundred sophomores plan to attend. Write and solve an inequality to find out how many guests must attend for the sophomores to pay for the permit.

Read and Understand

1. What is the cost of a permit? _____

2. How many sophomores are expected to attend? _____

3. What is the cost for each guest that attends? _____

Plan and Solve

4. How much money will the class earn from sophomores? _____

5. Write and solve an inequality to find out how many
   guests must attend for the sophomores to pay for the permit. _____

Look Back and Check

6. Use your original inequality to check if the sophomores
   would be able to pay for the permit if 90 guests attended. _____

Solve Another Problem

7. Mark and Anthony are going to a movie tonight. They know that each
   ticket will cost $9. Together they have $30 to spend on tickets and a
   large popcorn for each of them. Write and solve an inequality to
   determine how much the popcorn can cost in order for Mark and
   Anthony to have enough money.

   _____

Practice 3-5

Solve each compound inequality. Graph your solution.

1. $-5 < s + 5 < 5$

2. $1 < 3x + 4 < 10$

3. $k - 3 > 1$ or $k - 3 < -1$

4. $b - 2 > 18$ or $3b < 54$

5. $-4d > 8$ and $2d > -6$

6. $-4 < t + 2 < 4$

7. $-3 < 3 + s < 7$

8. $3j \geq 6$ or $3j \leq -6$

9. $-1 < \frac{1}{2}x < 1$

10. $g + 2 > -1$ or $g - 6 < -9$

11. $-6 < 9 + 3y < 6$

12. $3f > 15$ or $2f < -4$

13. $d - 3 > 4$ or $d - 3 < -4$

14. $1 > 2h + 3 > -1$

15. $7 + 2a > 9$ or $-4a > 8$

16. $2z > 2.1$ or $3z < -5.85$

17. $c - 1 \geq 2$ or $c - 1 \leq -2$

18. $h + 2.8 < 1.8$ or $h + 2.8 > 4.8$

Write and solve a compound inequality that represents each situation. Graph your solution.

19. The crowd that heard the President speak was estimated to be 10,000 people. The actual crowd could be 750 people more or less than this. What are the possible values for the actual crowd size?

20. Susie has designed an exercise program for herself. One part of the program requires her to walk between 25 and 30 miles each week. She plans to walk the same distance each day five days a week. What is the range of miles that she should walk each day?

21. A box of cereal must weigh more than 629.4 g and less than 630.6 g to pass inspection. The box in which the cereal is packaged weighs 5.5 g. What are the possible weights for the cereal?

22. Carmen works in a sporting goods store. Her goal is to sell between $500 and $600 worth of sporting equipment every week. So far this week, she has sold $395 worth of equipment. During the rest of the week, what dollar amount must Carmen sell in order to reach her goal?

Solve each compound inequality. Graph your solution.

23. $2n - 1 \geq 1$ or $2n - 1 \leq -1$

24. $2k - 3 > 3$ or $2k - 3 < -3$

25. $-1 < h - 2 < 1$

26. $2.2 + p > 1$ and $1.5p < -0.3$

27. $9 < x + 2 < 11$

28. $5m + 8 < 23$ or $6m > 48$

29. $-3 \leq \frac{3}{2}x + 6 \leq 3$

30. $7 > 5 - x > 6$

31. $\frac{1}{2}x + 1 > 1$ or $\frac{1}{2}x + 1 < -1$

32. $-2 \leq s - 4 \leq 2$

33. $w - 3 > 4$ or $w - 3 < -4$

34. $6 > 4x - 2 > -6$

35. $t + 5 < 2$ or $3t + 1 > 10$

36. $2g > 12$ and $3g < 24$

37. $6x - 3 \geq 3$ or $6x - 3 \leq -3$

38. $2y - 3 > -1$ or $5 - y > 4$

3-5 • Guided Problem Solving

•••

GPS **Exercise 42**

The graph below shows the average monthly high and low temperatures for Detroit, Michigan, and Charlotte, North Carolina. Write a compound inequality for Charlotte's average temperature in June.

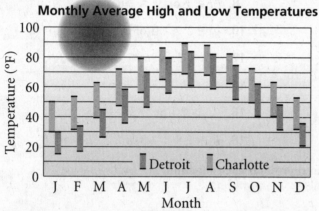

Monthly Average High and Low Temperatures

SOURCE: Statistical Abstract of the United States

Read and Understand
••••••••••••••••••••••••

1. What is the high temperature in June for Charlotte? _____

2. What is the low temperature in June for Charlotte? _____

Plan and Solve
•••••••••••••••••

3. Will this compound inequality be formed by the word *and* or the word *or*? _____

   Explain. _____

   _____

4. Write a compound inequality for Charlotte's average temperature in June. _____

Look Back and Check
•••••••••••••••••••••••••

5. Explain why your inequality makes sense. _____

   _____

Solve Another Problem

6. Write a compound inequality for Detroit's average temperature
   in the winter months of December, January, February, and March. _____

Practice 3-6

Absolute Value Equations and Inequalities

Solve each inequality. Graph your solution.

1. $|d| > 2$ **2.** $|h| > 6$ **3.** $|2k| > 8$ **4.** $|s + 4| > 2$

5. $|3c - 6| \geq 3$ **6.** $|2n + 3| \leq 5$ **7.** $|3.5z| > |7|$ **8.** $\left|\frac{2}{3}x\right| \leq 4$

9. $9 > |6 + 3t|$ **10.** $|j| - 2 \geq 6$ **11.** $5 > |v + 2| + 3$ **12.** $|4y + 11| < 7$

13. $|2n - 1| \geq 1$ **14.** $\left|\frac{1}{2}x + 1\right| > 1$ **15.** $-2|h - 2| > -2$ **16.** $3|2x| \leq 12$

17. $3|s - 4| + 21 \leq 27$ **18.** $-6|w - 3| < -24$ **19.** $-\frac{1}{2}|6x - 3| \leq -\frac{3}{2}$ **20.** $-2|3j| - 8 \leq -20$

Solve each equation. If there is no solution, write *no solution*.

21. $|a| = 9.5$ **22.** $|b| = -2$ **23.** $|d| - 25 = -13$ **24.** $|6z| + 3 = 21$

25. $|3c| - 45 = -18$ **26.** $-2 = -\dfrac{|z|}{7}$ **27.** $|x| = -0.8$ **28.** $-4|7 + d| = -44$

Write and solve an absolute value inequality that represents each situation.

29. The average number of cucumber seeds in a package is 25. The number of seeds in the package can vary by three. Find the range of acceptable numbers of seeds in each package.

30. The mean distance of the earth from the sun is 93 million miles. The distance varies by 1.6 million miles. Find the range of distances of the earth from the sun.

31. Leona was in a golf tournament last week. All four of her rounds of golf were within 2 strokes of par. If par was 72, find the range of scores that Leona could have shot for each round of the golf tournament.

32. Victor's goal is to earn $75 per week at his after-school job. Last month he was within $6.50 of his goal. Find the range of amounts that Victor might have earned last month.

33. Members of the track team can run 400 m in an average time of 58.2 s. The fastest and slowest times vary from the average by 6.4 s. Find the range of times for the track team.

34. The ideal length of a particular metal rod is 25.5 cm. The measured length may vary from the ideal length by at most 0.025 cm. Find the range of acceptable lengths for the rod.

35. When measured on a particular scale, the weight of an object may vary from its actual weight by at most 0.4 lb. If the reading on the scale is 125.2 lb, find the range of actual weights of the object.

36. One poll reported that the approval rating of the job performance of the President of the United States was 63%. The poll was said to be accurate to within 3.8%. What is the range of actual approval ratings?

3-6 • Guided Problem Solving

GPS Exercise 56

In a poll for the upcoming mayoral election, 42% of likely voters said they planned to vote for Lucy Jones. This poll has a margin of error of ±3 percentage points. Use the inequality $|v - 42| \leq 3$ to find the least and greatest percent of voters v likely to vote for Lucy Jones according to this poll.

Read and Understand

1. What percentage of voters said they planned to vote for Lucy Jones?
   _____

2. What is the margin of error for this poll? _____

Plan and Solve

3. Write an inequality to determine the greatest percent of voters. _____

4. Solve the inequality in Step 3. _____

5. What is the greatest percent of voters? _____

6. Write an inequality to determine the least percent of voters. _____

7. Solve the inequality in Step 6. _____

8. What is the least percent of voters? _____

Look Back and Check

9. Show that your answers fall within the margin of error for this poll. _____
   _____

Solve Another Problem

10. On average a household of 4 people uses 242 gallons of water each day.
    A 30-gallon change from the previous months could indicate a problem.
    More than a 30-gallon increase in water use could indicate a leak in a pipe.
    More than a 30-gallon decrease in water use could indicate a faulty water
    meter. Solve the inequality $|g - 242| \leq 30$ to determine the upper and
    lower limits of normal water usage.

    upper limit: _____

    lower limit: _____

3A: Graphic Organizer

For use before Lesson 3-1

Study Skill Before you start your new chapter, read the major headings and summaries. This will give you a good overview of the chapter.

Write your answers.

1. What is the chapter title? _____

2. Find the Table of Contents page for this chapter at the front of the book. Name four topics you will study in this chapter.

   _____   _____

   _____   _____

3. Complete the graphic organizer as you work through the chapter.
   1. Write the title of the chapter in the center oval.
   2. When you begin a lesson, write the name of the lesson in a rectangle.
   3. When you complete that lesson, write a skill or key concept from that lesson in the outer oval linked to that rectangle.

   Continue with steps 2 and 3 clockwise around the graphic organizer.

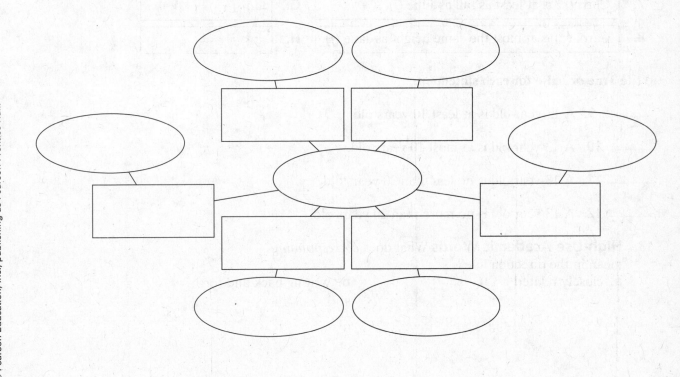

3B: Reading Comprehension

For use after Lesson 3-4

Study Skill When reading a word problem, it is sometimes difficult to determine which inequality sign should be used.

For Exercises 1–8, match each expression in Column A with its corresponding inequality symbol or expression in Column B by drawing a line between them.

	Column A		Column B
1.	is less than	**A.**	$\geq$
2.	is greater than	**B.**	$\leq$
3.	is less than or equal to	**C.**	$>$
4.	is greater than or equal to	**D.**	$<$
5.	Connie (c) is not as tall as Jose (j).	**E.**	$c \geq j$
6.	Cory (c) is older than Janishia (j).	**F.**	$c \leq j$
7.	Chris (c) is at least as tall as Julie (j).	**G.**	$c > j$
8.	Carol (c) is at most the same height as Jane (j).	**H.**	$c < j$

Write True or False for each statement.

_____ **9.** A 13-year-old is at least 10 years old.

_____ **10.** A 13-year-old is at most 10 years old.

_____ **11.** A 13-year-old is no less than 20 years old.

_____ **12.** A 13-year-old is no more than 20 years old.

13. High-Use Academic Words What does *corresponding* mean in the direction line?
  a. closely related   **b.** writing back and forth

3C: Reading/Writing Math Symbols   For use after Lesson 3-2

Study Skill Keep your homework in a special notebook or section in a loose-leaf binder. This way you will always be able to find it quickly.

Write how to read each symbol.

1. <   _____

2. >   _____

3. ≤   _____

4. ≥   _____

5. =   _____

Write how to read each expression.

6. $8 > 4$ _____

7. $12 < 25$ _____

8. $3x \leq 15$ _____

9. $4x + 2 \geq 12$ _____

10. $12x = 36$ _____

Write each phrase in symbols.

11. 8 is less than 12   _____

12. 17 is greater than 2   _____

13. $12x$ is more than 36   _____

14. $15x$ minus 8 is less than 32   _____

15. $10x$ plus 4 is greater than or equal to 15   _____

16. $3x$ take away 12 is less than or equal to 21   _____

17. $32x$ equals $4x$ more than 12   _____

3D: Visual Vocabulary Practice

For use after Lesson 3-6

Study Skills When a math exercise is difficult, try to determine what makes it difficult. Is it a word that you don't understand? Are the numbers difficult to use?

Concept List

absolute value	absolute value inequality	Addition Property of Inequality
compound inequality	graph of a compound inequality	graph of an inequality
equivalent inequalities	identity	inequality

Write the concept that best describes each exercise.
Choose from the concept list above.

1. $\quad |-10|$	**2.** $\quad$ 3 4 5 6 7	**3.** $\quad -2 < x < 10$
4. $2m - 6 \geq 2(m - 3)$	**5.** $\quad x - 5 > 2$ $\quad\quad x > 7$	**6.** $\quad p \leq -12$
7. $\quad$ If $a < b,$ then $a + c < b + c.$	**8.** $\quad$ -4 -3 -2 -1 0 1	**9.** $\quad |-6r + 7| > 12$

3E: Vocabulary Check

Study Skill Strengthen your vocabulary. Use these pages and add cues and summaries by applying the Cornell Notetaking style.

Write the definition for each word at the right. To check your work, fold the paper back along the dotted line to see the correct answers.

_____

_____

_____

Inequality

_____

_____

Solution of an inequality

_____

_____

_____

Variable

_____

_____

Identity

_____

_____

Evaluate an expression

_____

_____

3E: Vocabulary Check (continued) For use after Lesson 3-3

Write the vocabulary word for each definition. To check your work,
fold the paper forward along the dotted line to see the correct answers.

A mathematical sentence
that compares the values
of two expressions using a
less-than or greater-than
symbol.

_____

The value or values of a
variable in an inequality
that makes the inequality
true.

_____

A symbol, usually a letter,
that represents one or
more numbers.

_____

An equation that is true
for every value.

_____

Substitute a given number
for each variable, and then
simplify.

_____

3F: Vocabulary Review Puzzle

For use with Chapter Review

Study Skill You will encounter many new terms as you read a mathematics textbook. Read aloud or recite the new terms as you read them. This will help you remember and recall rules, definitions, and formulas for future use.

Unscramble the UPPERCASE letters to form a math word or phrase that completes each sentence.

1. The multiplicative inverse of a number is always its RLREIPACCO.

2. An XENNPTEO shows repeated multiplication.

3. LOHWE SURBEMN are the nonnegative integers.

4. A EVBALRAI is a symbol, usually a letter, that represents one or more numbers.

5. The numerical factor when a term has a variable is a CINCEFFITOE.

6. A coordinate plane is divided by its axes into four TANQAUSRD.

7. An TEITINYD is an equation that is true for every value.

8. COOPDUNM EUNIISAQELTI are joined by *and* or *or*.

Practice 4-1

Graphing on the Coordinate Plane

Name the coordinates of each point in the graph at the right.

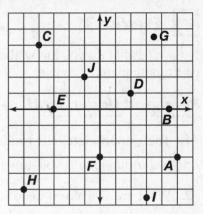

1. A **2.** B

3. C **4.** D

5. E **6.** F

7. G **8.** H

9. I **10.** J

Graph the points on the same coordinate plane.

11. $(5, -2)$ **12.** $\left(-2\frac{1}{2}, 1\right)$

13. $\left(-2, -3\frac{1}{2}\right)$ **14.** $(0, 5)$

In which quadrant or on which axis would you find each point?

15. $(15, 0)$ **16.** $(-17, 8)$

17. $(3, 20)$ **18.** $(0, -24)$

19. $(30, -30)$ **20.** $\left(-19\frac{1}{2}, -7\frac{1}{2}\right)$

4-1 • Guided Problem Solving

GPS **Exercise 31**

If $xy = 0$, what do you know about the location of point (x, y) on the coordinate plane? Explain.

Read and Understand

1. The x-coordinate tells you how far to move _____ or _____ from the origin. The y-coordinate tells you how far to move _____ or _____ from the origin.

2. What are you asked to do? _____

Plan and Solve

3. What do you know about the value of x or the value of y if $xy = 0$? _____

4. Fill in the table below with values of x and y, and the corresponding ordered pair (x, y).

x	y	xy	(x, y)
2	0	0	
0	5	0	
	0	0	
0		0	

5. Plot the ordered pairs found in Step 4 on the coordinate plane.

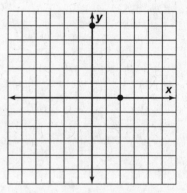

6. Explain what you know about the location of point (x, y) on the coordinate plane when $xy = 0$.

_____

Look Back and Check

7. Choose several points on the coordinate plane and check to see if your answer holds true.

_____

Solve Another Problem

8. If $\frac{x}{y} = 0$, what do you know about the location of point (x, y) on the coordinate plane? Explain.

_____

Name_____ Class_____ Date_____

Practice 4-2

Find the domain and range of each relation. Is each relation a function?

1.

x	y
6	3
9	−7
6	−2
−1	−5

2.

x	y
−30	−30
20	20
−10	−10
0	0

3.

x	y
100	7
50	7
−50	0
25	0

4.

x	y
8	2
8	4
8	−5
8	−2

Find the domain and range of each relation. Use a mapping diagram to determine whether each relation is a function.

5. $\{(4, 2), (9, 11), (4, -5), (10, -1)\}$

6. $\{(7, 0), (-3, -2), (6, -5), (-4, 0)\}$

7. $\{(-3, -7), (-1, -3), (0, -1), (2, 3), (4, 7)\}$

8. $\{(-5, -4), (-4, 2), (0, 2), (1, 3), (2, 4)\}$

Find the domain and range of each relation. Use the vertical-line test to determine whether each relation is a function.

9. $\{(14, 18), (18, 14), (22, 12), (12, 22)\}$

10. $\{(-5, -1), (-5, -2), (-5, 3)\}$

11. $\left\{(-4, -3), (-2, -2), (0, -1), \left(1, -\dfrac{1}{2}\right)\right\}$

12. $\{(0, 0), (1, 1), (4, 2), (1, -1)\}$

13.

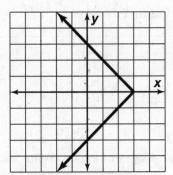

14.

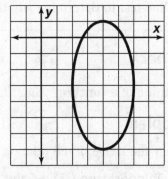

15.

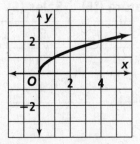

16.

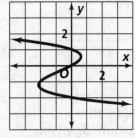

4-2 • Guided Problem Solving

GPS **Exercise 17**

a. Find the domain and range of the relation between grams of fat and number of calories.

Calories Per Serving of Some Common Foods

Food	Grams of Fat	Number of Calories	Food	Grams of Fat	Number of Calories
Whole Milk	8	150	Eggs	6	80
Chicken	4	90	Ham	19	245
Corn	1	70	Broccoli	1	45
Ground Beef	10	185	Cheese	9	115

b. Make a graph of the relation.

c. Is the relation a function? Explain.

Read and Understand

1. What does x represent? What does y represent? _____

2. What are you asked to do? _____

Plan and Solve

3. Use the data in the table to list the ordered pairs. _____

4. What is the domain and range? _____

5. Using the ordered pairs, graph the points of the relation.

6. Use the vertical-line test to determine whether the relation is a function. Explain.

_____

Look Back and Check

7. What is the definition of a function? _____

Solve Another Problem

8. **a.** Find the domain and range of the relation between temperature and sales of an ice cream shop.

Day	Temperature (°F)	Sales ($)	Day	Temperature (°F)	Sales ($)
Monday	72	250	Thursday	75	275
Tuesday	85	300	Friday	80	300
Wednesday	78	240	Saturday	88	490

b. Make a graph of the relation.

c. Is the relation a function? Explain.

Practice 4-3

Find the range of each function for the given domain.

1. $f(x) = -3x + 1; \{-2, -1, 0\}$

2. $f(x) = x^2 + x - 2; \{-2, 0, 1\}$

3. $h(x) = -x^2; \{-3, -1, 1\}$

4. $g(x) = -\frac{1}{2}|x| + 1; \{-2, -1, 1\}$

Model each rule with a table of values and a graph.

5. $f(x) = x + 1$

6. $f(x) = 2x$

7. $y = 3x - 2$

8. $f(x) = \frac{3}{2}x - 2$

9. $y = \frac{1}{2}x$

10. $f(x) = -\frac{2}{3}x + 1$

11. $g(x) = x^2 + 1$

12. $h(x) = -x^2 + 2$

13. $y = x - 3$

14. Suppose a van gets 22 mi/gal. The distance traveled $D(g)$ is a function of the gallons of gas used.

   a. Use the rule $D(g) = 22g$ to make a table of values and then a graph.

   b. How far did the van travel if it used 10.5 gallons of gas?

   c. Should the points of the graph be connected by a line? Explain.

Graph each function. Then find the domain and range.

15. $y = 4x + 2$

16. $f(x) = |-2x|$

17. $f(x) = -3x + 7$

18. $y = -|x| - 1$

19. $g(x) = 8 - \frac{3}{4}x$

20. $h(x) = \frac{2}{3}x - 7$

21. $f(x) = -\frac{2}{3}x + 6$

22. $y = x^2 - 2x + 1$

23. $f(x) = -\frac{1}{2}x + 3$

24. $y = -x^2 + 1$

25. $y = 9 - x^2$

26. $y = 2x^2 + x - 2$

Find the domain of each relation. Determine whether each relation is a function.

27. $y = 2x - 10$

28. $x = y^2 - 2$

29. $y = \frac{2x}{x + 1}$

30. $y = x^2 + 5$

31. $x = -3|y|$

32. $y = -\frac{2}{x}$

Algebra 1 Lesson 4-3

4-3 • Guided Problem Solving

GPS Exercise 46

a. Make a table for the perimeters of the rectangles
formed by each set of darkened tiles.

b. The perimeter $P(t)$ is a function of the number of
tiles t. Write a rule for the data in your table and graph
the function.

| | Fig. 1 | Fig. 2 | Fig. 3 | Fig. 4 |

Read and Understand

1. How many darkened tiles are there in each figure? _____

2. What are you asked to find? _____

Plan and Solve

3. Counting each darkened tile as a 1-by-1 square, find the perimeter of each block of tiles.
Enter the answers in the table.

Number of tiles (t)	1	2	3	4
Perimeter (P)				

4. Find two numbers *a* and *b* that allow you
to write a rule for the data in the form $P(t) = at + b$. _____

5. Graph the function found in Step 4.

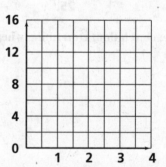

Look Back and Check

6. Draw a block of five tiles in a row, and verify that the
function from Step 4 correctly predicts the perimeter. _____

Solve Another Problem

7. Write a function rule based on the following table. _____

x	1	2	3	4
y	4	1	−2	−5

Guided Problem Solving

Practice 4-4

Write a function rule for each table.

1.

x	f(x)
0	3
2	5
4	7
6	9

2.

x	f(x)
0	0
1	3
3	9
5	15

3.

x	f(x)
5	0
10	5
15	10
20	15

4. a. Write a function rule to calculate the cost of buying bananas at $.39 a pound.

   b. How much would it cost to buy 3.5 pounds of bananas?

5. To rent a cabin, a resort charges $50 plus $10 per person.

   a. Write a function rule to calculate the total cost of renting the cabin.

   b. Use your rule to find the total cost for six people to stay in the cabin.

Write a function rule for each table.

6.

x	f(x)
−4	−2
−2	−1
6	3
8	4

7.

x	f(x)
−3	9
0	0
1	1
5	25

8.

x	f(x)
0	20
2	18
4	16
8	12

9. Pens are shipped to the office supply store in boxes of 12 each.

   a. Write a function rule to calculate the total number of pens when you know the number of boxes.

   b. Calculate the total number of pens in 16 boxes.

10. a. Write a function rule to determine the change you would get from a $20 bill when purchasing items that cost $1.25 each.

   b. Calculate the change when five of these items are purchased.

   c. Can you purchase 17 of these items with a $20 bill?

11. You invest $209 to buy shirts and then sell them for $9.50 each.

   a. Write a function rule to determine your profit.

   b. Use your rule to find your profit after selling 24 shirts.

   c. How many shirts do you need to sell to get back your investment?

4-4 • Guided Problem Solving

GPS **Exercise 23**

Use the table at the right.

a. Identify the dependent and independent variables.
b. Write a function rule that models the data in the table.
c. How many gallons of water would you use for 7 loads of laundry?
d. **Critical Thinking** In one month, you used 442 gallons of water for laundry. How many loads did you wash?

Water Used for Laundry	
1 load	34 gallons
2 loads	68 gallons
3 loads	102 gallons
4 loads	136 gallons

Read and Understand

1. What are the dependent and independent variables? _____

2. After you have identified the dependent and
   independent variables, what else are you asked to do? _____

Plan and Solve

3. Subtract 34 from 68, then subtract 68 from 102, and then subtract
   102 from 136. The answer should be the same each time. What is it? _____

4. Complete the sentence: "Each load of laundry requires _____."

5. Use the answer to Step 4 to write a function rule. _____

6. Use the function found in Step 5 to find the number
   of gallons of water required for 7 loads of laundry. _____

7. Set the function found in Step 5 equal to 442 gallons, then
   solve the resulting equation to find the number of loads. _____

Look Back and Check

8. No loads of laundry should require zero gallons of water.
   Check that the function you wrote supports this conclusion. _____

Solve Another Problem

9. A motorcycle on the freeway gets 45 miles per gallon. Write
   a rule that describes miles covered as a function of gallons used. _____

Practice 4-5

Is each equation a direct variation? If it is, find the constant of variation.

1. $y = 5x$ **2.** $8x + 2y = 0$ **3.** $y = \frac{3}{4}x - 7$ **4.** $y = 2x + 5$

5. $3x - y = 0$ **6.** $y = \frac{3}{5}x$ **7.** $-3x + 2y = 0$ **8.** $-5x + 2y = 9$

9. $8x + 4y = 12$ **10.** $6x - 3y = 0$ **11.** $x - 3y = 6$ **12.** $9x + 5y = 0$

Write an equation of the direct variation that includes the given point.

13. $(3, 2)$ **14.** $(-2, 8)$ **15.** $(16, 12)$ **16.** $(6, -16)$

17. $(9, 15)$ **18.** $(10, 15)$ **19.** $(-4, 3)$ **20.** $(1, 8)$

21. $(-30, -6)$ **22.** $(7, -1)$ **23.** $(-1, -5)$ **24.** $(9, 3)$

For the data in each table, tell whether y varies directly with x. If it does, write an equation for the direct variation.

25.

x	y
4	8
7	14
10	20

26.

x	y
-3	-2
3	2
9	6

27.

x	y
4	3
5	4.5
11	13.5

28.

x	y
-2	-2.8
3	4.2
8	11.2

29. Charles's Law states that at constant pressure, the volume of a fixed amount of gas varies directly with its temperature measured in kelvins. A gas has a volume of 250 mL at 300 K.

   a. Write an equation for the relationship between volume and temperature.

   b. What is the volume if the temperature increases to 420 K?

30. Your percent grade varies directly with the number of correct answers. You got a grade of 80 when you had 20 correct answers.

   a. Write an equation for the relationship between percent grade and number of correct answers.

   b. What would your percent grade be with 24 correct answers?

31. The amount of simple interest earned in a savings account varies directly with the amount of money in the savings account. You have $1000 in your savings account and earn $50 in simple interest. How much interest would you earn if you had $1500 in your savings account?

4-5 • Guided Problem Solving

GPS Exercise 45

The amount of blood in a person's body varies directly with body weight. A person who weighs 160 lb has about 5 qt of blood.

  a. Find the constant of variation.
  b. Write an equation relating quarts of blood to weight.
  c. Estimate the number of quarts of blood in your body.

Read and Understand

1. What is another way of saying "y varies directly with x"? _____

2. What are you being asked to do? _____

Plan and Solve

3. What is the general form of a direct variation? _____

4. When $x = 160$, $y = 5$. Use this information to find k, the constant of variation. _____

5. Use the answer to Step 4 to write an equation relating quarts of blood to weight in pounds. _____

6. Use the equation found in Step 5 to estimate the volume of blood in your own body. _____

Look Back and Check

7. If blood volume varies directly with body weight, and a 160-lb person has 5 quarts of blood, then a person twice as big ought to have twice as much blood. Verify that your equation supports this conclusion. _____

Solve Another Problem

8. "A pint is a pound the whole world round." That's not exactly true, but it's pretty close for a liquid such as water or blood. Since 1 quart = 2 pints, a quart of blood weighs about 2 pounds. Write an equation relating *pounds* of blood to pounds of overall body weight. What fraction of your body weight consists of blood? _____

Practice 4-6

Suppose *y* varies inversely with *x*. Write an equation for the inverse variation.

1. $x = 9$ when $y = 6$

2. $x = 3.6$ when $y = 5$

3. $x = \frac{3}{4}$ when $y = \frac{2}{9}$

4. $x = 7$ when $y = 13$

5. $x = 8$ when $y = 9$

6. $x = 4.9$ when $y = 0.8$

7. $x = 11$ when $y = 44$

8. $y = 8$ when $x = 9.5$

9. $y = 12$ when $x = \frac{5}{6}$

Each pair of points is on the graph of an inverse variation. Find the missing value.

10. $(5, 8)$ and $(4, m)$

11. $(16, 5)$ and $(10, h)$

12. $(14, 8)$ and $(c, 7)$

13. $(3, 18)$ and $(a, 27)$

14. $(4, 28)$ and $(3, p)$

15. $(100, 25)$ and $(4, a)$

16. $(x, 7)$ and $(2, 14)$

17. $\left(\frac{2}{5}, \frac{3}{2}\right)$ and $\left(k, \frac{5}{2}\right)$

18. $(16, 3)$ and $(g, 24)$

19. $(2.4, 19.8)$ and $(h, 13.2)$

20. $(12.4, 6.6)$ and $(f, 8.8)$

21. $(3.2, k)$ and $(9.2, 0.8)$

22. $(18, 24)$ and $(72, v)$

23. $(17, 0.9)$ and $(5.1, x)$

24. $\left(\frac{3}{4}, y\right)$ and $\left(\frac{2}{3}, 18\right)$

Explain whether each situation represents a direct variation or an inverse variation.

25. The cost of a \$50 birthday gift is split among some friends.

26. You purchase some peaches at \$1.29/lb.

Do the data in each table represent a direct variation, or an inverse variation? Write an equation to model the data in each table.

27.

x	2	7	10
y	35	10	7

28.

x	3	6	24
y	16	8	2

29.

x	5	6	8
y	55	66	88

30.

x	2	8	16
y	9	36	72

31.

x	2	3	9
y	18	12	4

32.

x	2	6	10
y	4.2	12.6	21

33.

x	2	5	12
y	12.8	32	76.8

34.

x	1.2	1.5	2.4
y	5	4	2.5

35.

x	6	9	36
y	3	2	0.5

36. The volume *V* of a gas in a closed container varies inversely with the pressure *p*, in atmospheres, that is applied to that gas.

   a. If $V = 20$ m^3 when $p = 1$ atm, find *V* when $p = 4$ atm.

   b. If $V = 24$ m^3 when $p = 3$ atm, find *p* when $V = 36$ m^3.

   c. If $V = 48$ m^3 when $p = 2$ atm, find *V* when $p = 5$ atm.

37. The time *t* to travel a fixed distance varies inversely with the rate *r* of travel.

   a. If $t = 3$ h and $r = 25$ mi/h, find *t* when $r = 50$ mi/h.

   b. If $t = 120$ s and $r = 40$ ft/s, find *r* when $t = 25$ s.

4-6 • Guided Problem Solving

GPS **Exercise 45**

a. Suppose you want to earn $80. How long will it take you if you are paid $5/h; $8/h; $10/h; $20/h?

b. What are the two variable quantities in part (a)?

c. Write an equation to represent this situation.

Read and Understand

1. What are you asked to find?

_____

Plan and Solve

2. How are the quantities "pay," "hours worked," and "hourly rate of pay" related?

_____

3. Use division to fill in the table with the number of hours needed to earn $80 for each pay rate.

Rate of Pay	$5/hr	$8/hr	$10/hr	$20/hr
Hours Worked				

4. Of the three quantities in Step 2, which one is given as a fixed quantity in this problem? At what value is it fixed? _____

5. What are the variable quantities in the problem? _____

6. Use your answer to Step 2 to write an equation relating the fixed and variable quantities in this problem. _____

Look Back and Check

7. Use the table to confirm that you have written the correct equation.

Solve Another Problem

8. A shopper has $200 to spend and plans to spend all the money to buy a single type of item. Write an equation relating the price of each item and the number of items being purchased to the total amount being spent, which is $200. _____

Practice 4-7

Use inductive reasoning to describe each pattern. Then find the next two numbers in each pattern.

1. $10, 16, 22, 28, \ldots$

2. $9, 6, 3, 0, \ldots$

3. $-12, -17, -22, -27, \ldots$

4. $-11, -8, -5, -2, \ldots$

5. $80, 40, 20, 10, \ldots$

6. $3, 9, 27, 81, \ldots$

7. $9, 10.5, 12, 13.5, \ldots$

8. $1, -1.5, -4, -6.5, \ldots$

9. $2, 10, 50, 250, \ldots$

10. $256, 64, 16, 4, \ldots$

11. $-3, -0.6, 1.8, 4.2, \ldots$

12. $6.2, 4.5, 2.8, 1.1, \ldots$

Look at the pattern of sums below. Write a function rule that gives the sum of the first n numbers in each pattern, where n is a natural number. Then predict the sum for $n = 10$.

13. $-1 = -1 = 1(2 \cdot 1 - 3)$
$-1 + 3 = 2 = 2(2 \cdot 2 - 3)$
$-1 + 3 + 7 = 9 = 3(2 \cdot 3 - 3)$
$-1 + 3 + 7 + 11 = 20 = 4(2 \cdot 4 - 3)$

14. $\frac{1}{4} = \frac{1}{4} = -\frac{1}{4}(1 - 2^1)$

$\frac{1}{4} + \frac{2}{4} = \frac{3}{4} = -\frac{1}{4}(1 - 2^2)$

$\frac{1}{4} + \frac{2}{4} + \frac{4}{4} = \frac{7}{4} = -\frac{1}{4}(1 - 2^3)$

$\frac{1}{4} + \frac{2}{4} + \frac{4}{4} + \frac{8}{4} = \frac{15}{4} = -\frac{1}{4}(1 - 2^4)$

Explain whether each situation represents inductive reasoning or deductive reasoning.

15. Sandra only has one $20 bill when she enters a grocery store. Each container of laundry detergent costs $8.50. She concludes that she can buy at most two containers.

16. When the alarm rings in the morning, David gets up and takes a shower. David's mom hears the bell ring one morning and concludes that David will be getting up and taking a shower.

17. A meteorologist uses a graph showing the relative humidity versus the amount of rainfall. Based on the points, she concludes that the greater the rainfall, the higher the humidity.

18. The length of a garden is 20 feet and the width is 30 feet. You conclude that the area of the garden is 600 square feet.

Find the next two numbers in each pattern.

19. $1, 10, 100, 1000, \ldots$

20. $3, 18, 33, 48, \ldots$

21. $1, -4, -9, -14, \ldots$

22. $\frac{1}{2}, -\frac{1}{2}, -\frac{3}{2}, -\frac{5}{2}, \ldots$

23. $2.7, 4, 5.3, 6.6, \ldots$

24. $9.8, 0.7, -8.4, -17.5, \ldots$

25. $729, 243, 81, 27, \ldots$

26. $3, 12, 48, 192, \ldots$

4-7 • Guided Problem Solving

GPS **Exercise 35**

The first five rows of Pascal's Triangle are at the right.

a. Predict the numbers in the sixth row.
b. Find the sum of the numbers in each of the first five rows. Predict the sum of the numbers in the sixth row.

```
        1
      1   1
    1   2   1
  1   3   3   1
1   4   6   4   1
```

Read and Understand

1. What are you asked to do? _____

Plan and Solve

2. Except for the 1's, every number in a row is based on two other nearby numbers. What is the relationship? _____

3. Predict the numbers in the sixth row. _____

4. What is the sum of the numbers in each of the first five rows? _____

5. What is the pattern of numbers in your answer to Step 4?

_____

6. Based on the pattern in Step 5, what should be the sum for row six? _____

Look Back and Check

7. Check your answer to Step 6 by adding up the numbers predicted in Step 3.

_____

Solve Another Problem

8. The first five rows of another triangle of numbers are at the right. Predict the numbers in the sixth row.

```
        1
      1   1
    1   3   1
  1   5   5   1
1   7  13   7   1
```

4A: Graphic Organizer

For use before Lesson 4-1

Study Skill Develop a method of note taking, including punctuation and abbreviations. Take your notes in a large notebook. A large notebook will allow you to jot down information without running out of paper or space.

Write your answers.

1. What is the chapter title? _____

2. Find the Table of Contents page for this chapter at the front of the book. Name four topics you will study in this chapter.

    _____   _____

    _____   _____

3. Complete the graphic organizer as you work through the chapter.
   1. Write the title of the chapter in the center oval.
   2. When you begin a lesson, write the name of the lesson in a rectangle.
   3. When you complete that lesson, write a skill or key concept from that lesson in the outer oval linked to that rectangle.
   Continue with steps 2 and 3 clockwise around the graphic organizer.

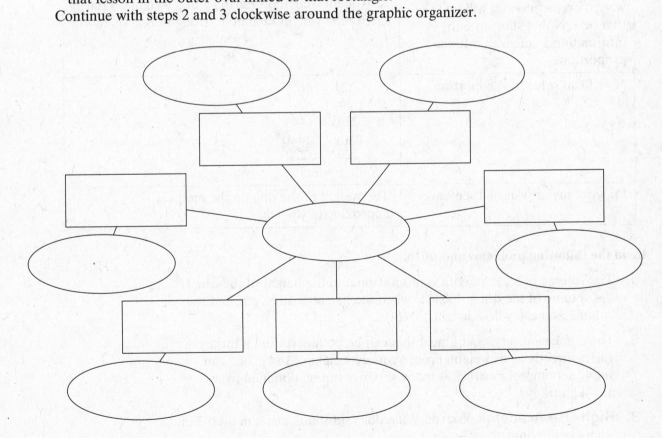

4B: Reading Comprehension

Study Skill After reading a section, try and recall the information. Ask yourself questions. If you cannot remember enough information re-read parts you forgot.

Read the problem and follow along with Carlita as she solves the problem.

> The weight of an object on Earth is directly proportional to the weight of the same object on the moon. A 220-lb astronaut would weigh 36 lb on the moon. How much would a 40-lb dog weigh on the moon?

What Carlita Thinks	What Carlita Writes
I read the problem and write down the important information.	220 lb astronaut = 36 lb on moon 40 lb dog = ?
Where should I start? It says the object is directly proportional, so I set up a proportion.	$\dfrac{\text{astronaut weight on Earth}}{\text{astronaut weight on moon}} = \dfrac{\text{dog weight on Earth}}{\text{dog weight on moon}}$
Since I am looking for the dog weight on the moon, I will let that be x. Now I substitute the information I am given into the proportions.	$\dfrac{\text{astronaut weight on Earth}}{\text{astronaut weight on moon}} = \dfrac{\text{dog weight on Earth}}{\text{dog weight on moon}}$ $\dfrac{220}{36} = \dfrac{40}{x}$
Now I can solve the proportion.	$\dfrac{220}{36} = \dfrac{40}{x}$ $220x = 1440$ $\dfrac{220x}{220} = \dfrac{1440}{220}$ $x \approx 6.5$
I'll write my answer in a sentence.	The weight of the dog on the moon is approximately 6.5 lb.

Read the following problems and solve.

1. The volume of a can of corn is proportional to the height of the can. If the volume of the can is 300 cm^3 when the height is 10.62 cm, find the volume of a can with a height 15.92 cm.

2. The number of servings of meat that can be obtained from a turkey varies directly as its weight. From a turkey weighing 16 kg, one can get 42 servings of meat. How many servings can be obtained from a 10-kg turkey?

3. **High-Use Academic Words** What does *substitute* mean in Step 3 of what Carlita thinks?
   a. replace a description with its numerical value
   b. guess a value for x and see if it makes the proportion true

4C: Reading/Writing Math Symbols

For use after Lesson 4-2

Study Skill When you take notes, it helps if you learn to use abbreviations and symbols that represent words. You should also use math symbols whenever possible.

For Exercises 1–8, match the symbolic expression in Column A with its written expression in Column B by drawing a line between them.

Column A

1. $k - 14 < 12$

2. $12 + y$

3. $|-4|$

4. $15x = 12 + x$

5. km/h

6. $/gal

7. $12x$

8. $21 - w$

Column B

A. 15 times x equals 12 more than x

B. twelve times x

C. kilometers per hour

D. a number take away 14 is less than 12

E. twelve plus y

F. 21 decreased by w

G. dollars per gallon

H. absolute value of negative four

For Exercises 9–16, match the symbolic expression in Column C with its written expression in Column D by drawing a line between them.

Column C

9. $12 \geq 12x$

10. 25%

11. $12 < x$

12. $/lb

13. mi/gal

14. $\frac{1}{4}x$

15. $5x \leq 25$

16. $4 \div w$

Column D

A. miles per gallon

B. dollars per pound

C. 12 is greater than or equal to twelve times x

D. twenty-five percent

E. 5 times a number x is less than or equal to 25

F. 12 is less than a number x

G. 4 divided into w parts

H. one-fourth of x

4D: Visual Vocabulary Practice

For use after Lesson 4-7

Study Skill When you come across something you don't understand, view it as an opportunity to increase your brain power.

Concept List

conjecture	constant of variation for inverse variation	coordinate plane
direct variation	domain	function notation
inverse variation	range	relation

Write the concept that best describes each exercise. Choose from the concept list above.

1. 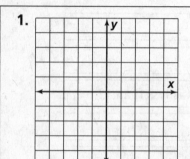 _____	**2.** The pattern is "divide the previous term by 5." _____	**3.** $\{(-2, 1), (3, 0), (5, -9)\}$ _____
4. $y = \dfrac{9}{x}$ _____	**5.** Given: $\{(-2, 1), (3, 0), (5, -9)\}$ What is: $\{-9, 0, 1\}$ _____	**6.** $k = xy$ for an ordered pair (x, y) _____
7. Given: $\{(-2, 1), (3, 0), (5, -9)\}$ What is: $\{-2, 3, 5\}$ _____	**8.** $f(x) = 3x - 11$ _____	**9.** $y = 14x$ _____

4E: Vocabulary Check

Study Skill Strengthen your vocabulary. Use these pages and add cues and summaries by applying the Cornell Notetaking style.

Write the definition for each word at the right. To check your work, fold the paper back along the dotted line to see the correct answers.

_____   Relation

_____

_____

_____   Vertical-line test

_____

_____   Function notation

_____

_____   Inductive Reasoning

_____

_____

_____   Direct variation

_____

_____

4E: Vocabulary Check (continued)

Write the vocabulary word for each definition. To check your work,
fold the paper forward along the dotted line to see the correct answers.

A set of ordered pairs.

_____

If any vertical line passes
through more than one
point of the graph, then for
some value of *x* there is
more than one value of *y*.

_____

Using *f(x)* to indicate the
outputs of a function.

_____

Making conclusions
based on patterns you
observe.

_____

A function of the form
$y = kx$, where $k \neq 0$.

_____

4F: Vocabulary Review Puzzle

For use with Chapter Review

Study Skill When you read, your eyes make small stops along a line of words. Good readers make fewer stops when they read. The more stops you make when you read, the harder it is for you to comprehend what you've read. Try to concentrate and free yourself of distractions as you read.

Complete the crossword puzzle.

ACROSS	DOWN
3. type of reasoning where conclusions are based on given facts	**1.** set of second coordinates in a collection of ordered pairs
5. a comparison of two numbers by division	**2.** has two parts, a base and an exponent
6. the motion of an object that moves at a constant rate	**4.** a term that has no variable
9. a conclusion you reach by inductive reasoning	**7.** a relation that assigns exactly one value in the range to each value in the domain
11. multiplicative inverse	**8.** an equation that is true for every value of the variable
13. a type of variation in the form $y = kx$	**10.** substitute a given value for each variable in an algebraic expression
14. the variable corresponding to the output of a function	**12.** an equation involving two or more variables
15. set of numbers made up of rational numbers and irrational numbers	

Practice 5-1

Rate of Change and Slope

The rate of change is constant in each table and graph. Find the rate of change. Explain what the rate of change means for each situation.

1.

Number of Baskets	Points Scored
1	3
2	6
3	9
4	12
5	15

2.

Miles Traveled	Fuel used (gallons)
80	4
120	6
160	8
200	10
240	12

3.

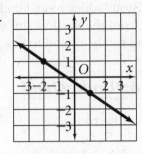

4.

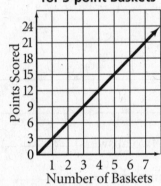

Points Scored for 3-point Baskets

5.

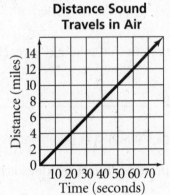

Distance Sound Travels in Air

6.

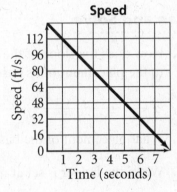

Speed

Find the slope of each line.

7.

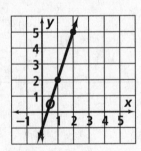

8.

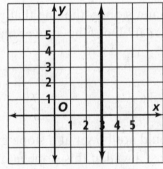

9.

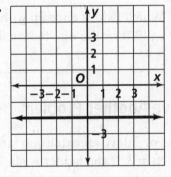

Find the slope of the line that passes through each pair of points.

10. $(-2, 5), (3, -4)$

11. $(2, 4), (6, 4)$

12. $(-2, -5), (4, 5)$

13. $(-3, -2), (4, -2)$

14. $(4, -2), (4, 9)$

15. $(5, 2), (5, -4)$

Through the given point, draw the line with the given slope.

16. $P(3, -2)$

slope 3

17. $K(0, 4)$

slope -1

18. $M(-2, 3)$

slope $-\dfrac{5}{3}$

5-1 • Guided Problem Solving

GPS Exercise 42

An extension ladder has a label that says, "Do not place base of ladder less than 5 ft from the vertical surface." What is the greatest slope possible if the ladder can safely extend to reach a height of 12 ft? Of 18 ft?

Read and Understand

1. How close to the vertical surface can the base of the ladder be placed? _____

2. How high can the ladder safely reach? (Two answers) _____

3. What are you asked to find? _____

Plan and Solve

4. How does the slope of the ladder relate to the height it reaches and to the placement of its base?

_____

_____

5. What placement of the base makes the slope as great as possible? _____

6. When the ladder is set at maximum slope, how high does it reach? (Two answers) _____

7. When the ladder is set at maximum slope, what is the slope? (Two answers) _____

Look Back and Check

8. Which ladder ends up with the greater slope—the one that reaches to 12 ft or the one that reaches to 18 ft? Does the answer make sense?

_____

Solve Another Problem

9. For safety, an extension ladder should not be set at a slope greater than 3. If the ladder is placed against a wall at this slope and reaches a height of 12 ft, how far is the base from the wall?

_____

Practice 5-2

Find the slope and *y*-intercept of each equation.

1. $y = x + 2$ **2.** $y + 3 = -\frac{1}{3}x$ **3.** $y = 2x - 1$ **4.** $y - \frac{3}{5}x = -1$

5. $y = \frac{1}{2}x - 4$ **6.** $y - 2x = -3$ **7.** $y = \frac{2}{5}x + 3$ **8.** $y + \frac{1}{3}x = -2$

9. $y = -x - 2$ **10.** $y - 6 = -2x$ **11.** $y = -5x - 2$ **12.** $y + x = 0$

Write an equation of a line with the given slope and *y*-intercept.

13. $m = 4, b = 8$ **14.** $m = -2, b = -6$ **15.** $m = \frac{4}{3}, b = 0$

16. $m = -\frac{9}{5}, b = -7$ **17.** $m = -6, b = 1$ **18.** $m = \frac{3}{7}, b = -1$

19. $m = -\frac{1}{5}, b = -3$ **20.** $m = 9, b = 4$ **21.** $m = -8, b = 11$

Write the slope-intercept form of the equation for each line.

22.

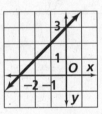

23.

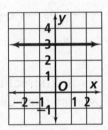

24.

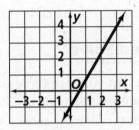

Determine whether the ordered pair lies on the graph of the given equation.

25. $(2, -7); y = -3x - 1$ **26.** $(-8, -2); y = 5x + 2$ **27.** $(0, 5); 3y = -x + 15$

28. $(-7, -6); -6x + 5y = 12$ **29.** $(1, -5); x - 3y = -8$ **30.** $(2, -2); 2y = 3x - 10$

Use the slope and *y*-intercept to graph each equation.

31. $y = \frac{2}{3}x + 3$ **32.** $y = \frac{1}{5}x - 2$ **33.** $y = 4x - 3$

34. $y = -\frac{1}{2}x - 4$ **35.** $y = -0.5x + 5$ **36.** $y = \frac{3}{4}x + 7$

37. A television production company charges a basic fee of $4000 and then $2000 per hour when filming a commercial.

    a. Write an equation in slope-intercept form relating the basic fee and per-hour charge.

    b. Graph your equation.

    c. Use your graph to find the production costs if 4 hours of filming were needed.

5-2 • Guided Problem Solving

Exercise 63

a. A candle begins burning at time $t = 0$. Its original height is 12 in. After 30 min the height of the candle is 8 in. Draw a graph showing the change in the height of the candle.

b. Write an equation that relates the height of the candle to the time it has been burning.

c. How many minutes after the candle has been lit will it burn out?

Read and Understand

1. What is the candle's starting height at time $t = 0$? _____

2. What is the candle's height at time $t = 30$ min? _____

3. What are you asked to do? _____

Plan and Solve

4. Plot two points to represent the candle heights at different times. Graph the changing candle height by drawing a ray from the first point through the second one.

5. What is the y-intercept of the graph? _____

6. What is the slope of the graph? _____

7. Use the y-intercept and the slope to write the slope-intercept form of the equation relating candle height h to time t. _____

8. Use the equation from Step 7 to find t when the candle height h equals zero. _____

Look Back and Check

9. Check that the time it takes the candle to burn down its full length of 12 in. is three times the time it takes to burn down a third of that distance, namely 4 in. _____

Solve Another Problem

10. A stalk of bamboo is 30 cm tall when measured one day (call this $t = 0$) and is 42 cm tall 24 hours later. Write an equation that relates height in cm to time in hours. Then predict the time when the bamboo reaches a height of 90 cm.

_____

Practice 5-3

Find the x- and y-intercepts of each equation.

1. $x + y = 3$ **2.** $x + 3y = -3$ **3.** $-2x + 3y = 6$ **4.** $5x - 4y = -20$

5. $3x + y = 12$ **6.** $7x + 3y = 21$ **7.** $y = -2.5$ **8.** $2x - 3y = 4$

Match each equation with its graph.

9. $3x + 4y = 12$ **10.** $-3x + 4y = 12$ **11.** $3x - 4y = 12$

A. 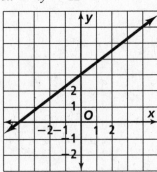   **B.** 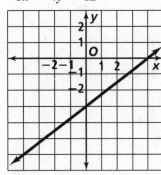   **C.**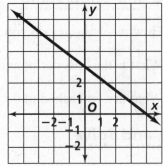

Graph each equation using x- and y-intercepts.

12. $3x + y = 3$ **13.** $-3x + 5y = 15$ **14.** $2x + y = 3$ **15.** $8x - 3y = 24$

16. $3x - 5y = 15$ **17.** $x + 4y = 4$ **18.** $x = -3.5$ **19.** $y = 6$

For each equation, tell whether its graph is a horizontal or a vertical line.

20. $x = -2$ **21.** $y = 4$ **22.** $y = -1.5$ **23.** $x = 2\frac{1}{2}$

Write each equation in standard form using integers.

24. $y = 4x - 11$ **25.** $y = 2x - 6$ **26.** $y = -2x - 3$ **27.** $y = 5x - 32$

28. $y = \frac{2}{3}x - \frac{25}{3}$ **29.** $y = 43 - 4x$ **30.** $y = -\frac{4}{5}x + \frac{6}{5}$ **31.** $y = -\frac{x}{5}$

32. The drama club sells 200 lb of fruit to raise money. The fruit is sold in 5-lb bags and 10-lb bags.

   a. Write an equation to find the number of each type of bag that the club should sell.

   b. Graph your equation.

   c. Use your graph to find two different combinations of types of bags.

33. The student council is sponsoring a carnival to raise money. Tickets cost $5 for adults and $3 for students. The student council wants to raise $450.

   a. Write an equation to find the number of each type of ticket they should sell.

   b. Graph your equation.

   c. Use your graph to find two different combinations of tickets sold.

Practice

5-3 • Guided Problem Solving

GPS **Exercise 48**

You are sent to the store to buy sliced meat for a party. You are told to get roast beef and turkey, and you are given $30. Roast beef is $4.29/lb and turkey is $3.99/lb. Write an equation in standard form to relate the pounds of each kind of meat you could buy at the store with $30.

Read and Understand

1. How much money do you have to spend? _____

2. What is the cost per pound for roast beef? For turkey? _____

3. What are you asked to do? _____

Plan and Solve

4. What will the variables x and y represent in this situation? _____

5. Write an expression for how much money is spent on roast beef, and another expression for how much money is spent on turkey. _____

6. Write an expression for how much money is spent altogether. _____

7. Write an equation which says that the total amount spent equals the amount you have to spend. _____

Look Back and Check

8. Suppose you bought all beef and no turkey. How much beef would you bring back to the party? Does this seem like a reasonable real-world amount? _____

_____

Solve Another Problem

9. A street vendor who sells hot dogs and sodas makes $0.75 of profit on every soda but loses $0.10 on every hot dog. Using x for sodas and y for hot dogs, write an equation in standard form to describe a morning on which the vendor made a profit of exactly $81.

_____

Guided Problem Solving

Practice 5-4

Point-Slope Form and Writing Linear Equations

Write an equation in point-slope form for the line through the given points or through the given point with the given slope.

1. $(5, 7), (6, 8)$ **2.** $(-2, 3); m = -1$ **3.** $(1, 2), (3, 8)$ **4.** $(-2, 3); m = 4$

5. $(4, 7); m = \frac{3}{2}$ **6.** $(6, -2); m = -\frac{4}{3}$ **7.** $(0, 5), (-3, 2)$ **8.** $(8, 11), (6, 16)$

9. $(4, 2), (-4, -2)$ **10.** $(15, 16), (13, 10)$ **11.** $(0, -7); m = -4$ **12.** $(-3, 4), (1, 6)$

13. $(1, 2); m$ undefined **14.** $(-6, 7); m = -\frac{1}{2}$ **15.** $(21, -2), (27, 2)$ **16.** $(7, 5); m = 0$

Write the equation of the line through the given points in slope-intercept form. Then rewrite the equation in standard form using integers.

17. $(8, -2), (14, 1)$ **18.** $(4, 8), (2, 12)$ **19.** $(-5, 13), (-10, 9)$ **20.** $(6, 2), (-1, 7)$

21. $(5, -3), (-2, 0)$ **22.** $(0, 7), (-5, 12)$ **23.** $(-6, 2), \left(\frac{5}{3}, \frac{3}{2}\right)$ **24.** $(100, 90), (80, 120)$

25. $(-3, 6), (3, -6)$ **26.** $(11, 7), (9, 3)$ **27.** $(2, 7), \left(\frac{5}{2}, 3\right)$ **28.** $(-9, 8), \left(-\frac{5}{3}, 2\right)$

Is the relationship shown by the data linear? If so, model the data with an equation.

29.

x	y
2	3
3	7
4	11
5	15

30.

x	y
-3	4
-1	6
1	7
3	10

31.

x	y
-4	12
-1	8
5	-4
10	-8

32.

x	y
-2	5
3	-5
7	-13
11	-21

Write an equation for each line in point-slope form.

33.
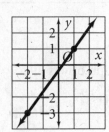

34.
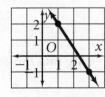

35.
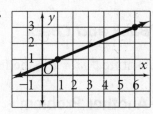

5-4 • Guided Problem Solving

GPS **Exercise 55**

Worldwide carbon monoxide emissions are decreasing about 2.6 million
metric tons each year. In 1991, carbon monoxide emissions were 79 million
metric tons. Use a linear equation to model the relationship between carbon
monoxide emissions and time. Let $x = 91$ correspond to 1991.

Read and Understand

1. What is the annual rate of decrease of worldwide carbon monoxide emissions?

   _____

2. What was the total of worldwide carbon monoxide emissions in 1991? _____

3. What are you being asked to do? _____

Plan and Solve

4. Write the information about worldwide emissions
   in 1991 as an ordered pair representing a data point. _____

5. How does the rate of emissions describe the graph of the relation
   between time and emissions? What form of linear equation is
   easiest to write, given the information in the problem?

   _____

6. Write the appropriate linear equation. _____

7. Convert the equation to slope-intercept form. _____

Look Back and Check

8. Substitute 91 for x in the final equation and verify that the corresponding value of y is 79.

Solve Another Problem

9. An accountant at a manufacturing company assumes that
   a particular piece of company-owned machinery declines
   in value by $1800 per year. When the machine is 3 years old,
   it is valued at $21,600. Use a linear equation to model the
   relation between the machine's age and its accounting value. _____

Practice 5-5

Parallel and Perpendicular Lines

Find the slope of a line parallel to the graph of each equation.

1. $y = 4x + 2$ **2.** $y = \frac{2}{7}x + 1$ **3.** $y = -9x - 13$ **4.** $y = -\frac{1}{2}x + 1$

5. $6x + 2y = 4$ **6.** $y - 3 = 0$ **7.** $-5x + 5y = 4$ **8.** $9x - 5y = 4$

9. $-x + 3y = 6$ **10.** $6x - 7y = 10$ **11.** $x = -4$ **12.** $-3x - 5y = 6$

Write an equation for the line that is perpendicular to the given line and that passes through the given point.

13. $(6, 4); y = 3x - 2$ **14.** $(-5, 5); y = -5x + 9$ **15.** $(-1, -4); y = \frac{1}{6}x + 1$

16. $(1, 1); y = -\frac{1}{4}x + 7$ **17.** $(12, -6); y = 4x + 1$ **18.** $(0, -3); y = -\frac{4}{3}x - 7$

19. 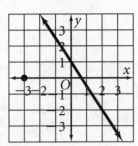   **20.** 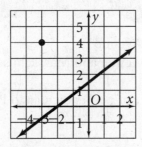   **21.**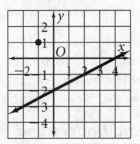

Write an equation for the line that is parallel to the given line and that passes through the given point.

22. $(3, 4); y = 2x - 7$ **23.** $(1, 3); y = -4x + 5$ **24.** $(4, -1); y = x - 3$

25. $(4, 0); y = \frac{3}{2}x + 9$ **26.** $(-8, -4); y = -\frac{3}{4}x + 5$ **27.** $(9, -7); -7x - 3y = 3$

28. 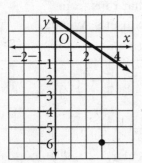   **29.** 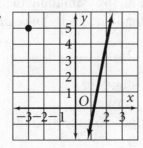   **30.**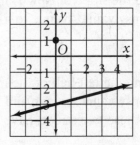

Tell whether the lines for each pair of equations are *parallel*, *perpendicular*, or *neither*.

31. $y = 3x - 8$
   $3x - y = -1$

32. $3x + 2y = -5$
   $y = \frac{2}{3}x + 6$

33. $y = -\frac{5}{2}x + 11$
   $-5x + 2y = 20$

34. $9x + 3y = 6$
   $3x + 9y = 6$

35. $y = -4$
   $y = 4$

36. $x = 10$
   $y = -2$

5-5 • Guided Problem Solving

GPS Exercises 47–49

Use the map below to answer the questions that follow.

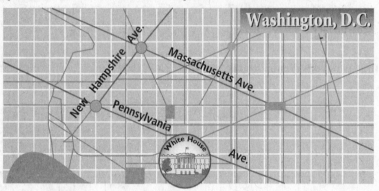

a. What is the slope of New Hampshire Avenue?

b. Show that the parts of Pennsylvania Avenue and Massachusetts Avenue near New Hampshire Avenue are parallel.

c. Show that New Hampshire Avenue is not perpendicular to Pennsylvania Avenue.

Read and Understand

1. Find New Hampshire Avenue, Pennsylvania Avenue, and Massachusetts Avenue on the map. What is the white grid for? _____

Plan and Solve

2. Find the slope of New Hampshire Avenue by examining the segment that runs from Pennsylvania Avenue to a little more than one grid square past Massachusetts Avenue.

_____

3. Using the left half of the map, find the slopes of Pennsylvania Avenue and Massachusetts Avenue. Do these two streets have the same slope? Are they parallel? _____

4. For New Hampshire Avenue and Pennsylvania Avenue to be perpendicular, their slopes must be negative reciprocals of each other. Are they? _____

Look Back and Check

5. On the left half of the map, draw a line with a slope of 2 through Pennsylvania Avenue and Massachusetts Avenue, and verify by inspection that the line is perpendicular to those two streets and not parallel to New Hampshire Avenue.

Solve Another Problem

6. What slope would a street have to have to be perpendicular to New Hampshire Avenue? Draw a line on the map to verify your result. _____

5A: Graphic Organizer

For use before Lesson 5-1

Study Skill When taking notes, do not try and write down everything that the teacher is saying. Spend more time listening and write down the main points and examples. If you are writing as fast as you can, you cannot be listening as well.

Write your answers.

1. What is the chapter title? _____

2. Find the Table of Contents page for this chapter at the front of the book. Name four topics you will study in this chapter.

   _____   _____

   _____   _____

3. Complete the graphic organizer as you work through the chapter.
   1. Write the title of the chapter in the center oval.
   2. When you begin a lesson, write the name of the lesson in a rectangle.
   3. When you complete that lesson, write a skill or key concept from that lesson in the outer oval linked to that rectangle.
   Continue with steps 2 and 3 clockwise around the graphic organizer.

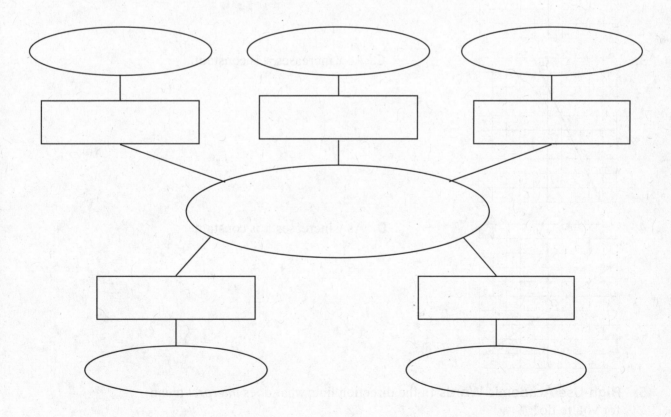

5B: Reading Comprehension

For use after Lesson 5-2

Study Skill Reading and interpreting diagrams, graphs, and charts is an important skill in algebra and in everyday life. When you read diagrams, graphs, and charts, pay close attention to the details they contain.

Interpret each graph. Then match the graph to the sentence that describes the relationship shown.

1.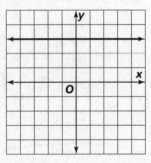

A. As x increases, y increases.

2.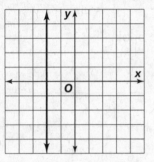

B. As x increases, y decreases.

3.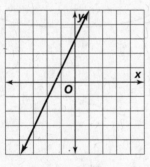

C. As x increases, y is constant.

4.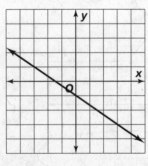

D. As y increases, x is constant.

5. High-Use Academic Words In the direction line, what does *interpret* mean for you to do?

    a. identify the slope and *y*-intercept   **b.** understand what is being conveyed

5C: Reading/Writing Math Symbols

For use after Lesson 5-5

Study Skill Many times you need to refer to concepts taught in previous lessons. Use the Table of Contents or Index to locate these concepts.

Write what each of the symbols, variables, or equations represents. The first one is done for you.

1. $(x, 0)$ _____ x-intercept _____

2. $|x|$ _____

3. $\geq$ _____

4. $y = mx + b$ _____

5. $<$ _____

6. $Ax + By = C$ _____

7. $=$ _____

8. m, in $y = mx + b$ _____

9. b, in $y = mx + b$ _____

10. $-x$ _____

11. $(0, y)$ _____

12. $\times$ _____

Algebra 1 Chapter 5   **281**

5D: Visual Vocabulary Practice
High-Use Academic Words

For use after Lesson 5-5

Study Skills Use Venn diagrams to understand the relationship between words whose meanings overlap, such as *square*, *rectangle*, and *quadrilateral* or *real number*, *integer*, and *counting number*.

Concept List

analyze	common	equivalent
graph	order	pattern
property	rule	table

Write the concept that best describes each exercise. Choose from the concept list above.

1. To solve an inequality in the form $|A| < b$, where A is a variable expression and $b > 0$, solve $-b < A < b$. _____	**2.** $y = -\frac{3}{2}$ and $4y = -6$ _____	**3.** <table><tr><td>x</td><td>y</td></tr><tr><td>1</td><td>12</td></tr><tr><td>2</td><td>13</td></tr><tr><td>3</td><td>14</td></tr><tr><td>4</td><td>15</td></tr></table> _____
4. $-8, 16, -32, 64, \ldots$ _____	**5.** 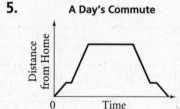 A Day's Commute _____	**6.** $-5, -2, 0, \frac{1}{2}, 7$ _____
7. The difference between terms in the sequence $17, 13, 9, 5, \ldots$ _____	**8.** $-4 \cdot 3 = 3 \cdot -4$ _____	**9.** Jorge found his average speed after taking 2 hours to walk 4 miles to be 0.5 miles per hour. _____

5E: Vocabulary Check

Study Skill Strengthen your vocabulary. Use these pages and add cues and summaries by applying the Cornell Notetaking style.

Write the definition for each word at the right. To check your work, fold the paper back along the dotted line to see the correct answers.

_____

_____

Rate of change

_____

_____

Slope

_____

_____

Linear equation

_____

_____

Parent function

_____

_____

Slope-intercept form

_____

_____

5E: Vocabulary Check (continued)

Write the vocabulary word for each definition. To check your work, fold the paper forward along the dotted line to see the correct answers.

Change in the dependent
variable divided by
change in the independent
variable.

_____

The rate of change
of a line on a graph.

_____

An equation whose
graph is a line.

_____

The simplest equation
of a function.

_____

$y = mx + b$.

_____

5F: Vocabulary Review

Study Skill Always read direction lines before doing any exercises. What you think you are supposed to do may be different from what the directions call for.

Circle the word that best completes the sentence.

1. (*Parallel lines*, *Perpendicular lines*) are lines in the same plane that never intersect.

2. The point where a line crosses the y-axis is known as the (*x-intercept*, *y-intercept*).

3. The linear equation $y = mx + b$ is in (*slope-intercept*, *point-slope*) form.

4. The (*slope*, *equation*) of a line is its rate of vertical change over horizontal change.

5. The (*domain*, *range*) of a relation is the set of second coordinates in the ordered pairs.

6. A(n) (*rational*, *irrational*) number is any number that can be written as $\frac{a}{b}$, where a and b are integers and $b \neq 0$.

7. A (*constant*, *coefficient*) is a numerical factor of a term.

8. A(n) (*exponent*, *variable*) is a symbol, usually a letter, that represents one or more numbers.

9. The (*absolute value*, *reciprocal*) of a number is its multiplicative inverse.

10. The equation $3 + 4 = 4 + 3$ illustrates the (*Identity Property of Addition*, *Commutative Property of Addition*).

11. The equation $\frac{1}{3} = \frac{3}{9}$ is an example of a (*ratio*, *proportion*).

12. The function $y = 5x$ is a (*direct*, *indirect*) variation.

Vocabulary and Study Skills

Practice 6-1

Solving Systems by Graphing

Solve by graphing. Check your solution.

1. $y = 3x - 1$
$y = -2x + 4$

2. $y = x - 1$
$y = -x + 7$

3. $y = 4x + 7$
$y = -3x$

4. $y = x - 3$
$y = \frac{1}{7}x + 3$

5. $y = -x - 3$
$y = -2x - 8$

6. $y = x$
$y = 3x + 2$

7. $y = 4x - 3$
$y = -3x - 3$

8. $y = \frac{5}{3}x - 4$
$y = 2x - 6$

9. $y = 3x + 2$
$2x + y = -8$

10. $x + y = 2$
$y = -2x - 1$

11. $2x - y = 3$
$y = x + 4$

12. $x - y = 1$
$y = \frac{3}{4}x + 1$

13. $y = x$
$x = 2y + 2$

14. $3x - y = 9$
$y = x + 1$

15. $2x + y = 0$
$y = 2x - 4$

16. $y = 2x - 6$
$x + y = 9$

17. $y = -x$
$y = 3x + 12$

18. $y = 4x$
$y = -3x$

19. $y = x$
$2x + y = \frac{3}{2}$

20. $3x + y = 6$
$2x - y = \frac{3}{2}$

21. $x + 4y = -\frac{1}{2}$
$-2x - 3y = 1$

22. $x - y = -\frac{3}{2}$
$-2x + 5y = -4.5$

23. $y = 2x - 20$
$y = -x + 34$

24. $x + y = -10$
$2x + 3y = -30$

25. $x + 2y = 2$
$3x + 4y = 22$

26. $x = -2y - 3.5$
$-5x + 3y = -15$

Graph each system. Tell whether the system has *no solution* or *infinitely many solutions*.

27. $y = \frac{3}{4}x + 2$
$\frac{3}{4}x - y = 4$

28. $y = -3x - 4$
$3x + y = -4$

29. $y = -x + 2$
$3x + 3y = 12$

30. $x = y + 4$
$y = x + 4$

31. $3x - 6y = 12$
$2x - 4y = 8$

32. $4x + y = 6$
$y = -4x - 1$

Without graphing, decide whether each system has *one solution, no solution,* or *infinitely many solutions*. Explain.

33. $y = \frac{5}{6}x + 12$
$y = \frac{4}{3}x - 6$

34. $2x + y = 6$
$3y = -6x + 9$

35. $y = \frac{2}{3}x + 4$
$2x - 3y = 3$

36. $y = -x - 3$
$-y = x + 3$

6-1 • Guided Problem Solving

GPS **Exercise 25**

Jim and Tony are on opposing teams in a soccer match. They are running after the same ball. Jim's path is the line $y = 3x$. Tony's path is the line $y = -2x + 100$. Solve by graphing to find the coordinates of the ball.

Read and Understand

1. What is the equation for Jim's path to the ball? _____

2. What is the equation for Tony's path to the ball? _____

3. What are you asked to find? _____

Plan and Solve

4. Find the slope and y-intercept for $y = 3x$. _____

5. Find the slope and y-intercept for $y = -2x + 100$. _____

6. Graph the two equations on the same set of axes.

100 m

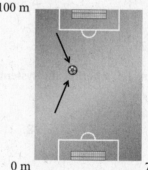

0 m   73 m

7. What are the coordinates of the point where the two lines cross? _____

Look Back and Check

8. Does it makes sense that the paths of two opposing players would cross at the ball? Would it make sense for two players on the same team?

_____

Solve Another Problem

9. Suppose Tony's path were instead given by $y = -x + 40$. Where would you locate the ball?

_____

Practice 6-2

Graph each system to estimate the solution. Then use substitution to find the exact solution of the system.

1. $y = x$
$y = -x + 2$

2. $y = x + 4$
$y = 3x$

3. $y = 3x - 10$
$y = 2x - 5$

4. $x = -2y + 1$
$x = y - 5$

5. $y = 5x + 5$
$y = 15x - 1$

6. $y = x - 3$
$y = -3x + 25$

Solve each system using substitution. Write *no solution* or *infinitely many solutions* where appropriate.

7. $y = x - 7$
$2x + y = 8$

8. $y = 3x - 6$
$-3x + y = -6$

9. $x + 2y = 200$
$x = y + 50$

10. $3x + y = 10$
$y = -3x + 4$

11. $y = 2x + 7$
$y = 5x + 4$

12. $3x - 2y = 0$
$x + y = -5$

13. $4x + 2y = 8$
$y = -2x + 4$

14. $6x - 3y = 6$
$y = 2x + 5$

15. $2x + 4y = -6$
$x - 3y = 7$

16. $5x - 3y = -4$
$x + y = -4$

17. $y = -\frac{2}{3}x + 4$
$2x + 3y = -6$

18. $2x + 3y = 8$
$\frac{3}{2}y = 4 - x$

19. $3x - y = 4$
$2x + y = 16$

20. $x + y = 0$
$x = y + 4$

21. $5x + 2y = 6$
$y = -\frac{5}{2}x + 1$

22. $2x + 5y = -6$
$4x + y = -12$

23. $4x + 3y = -3$
$2x + y = -1$

24. $y = -\frac{2}{3}x + 1$
$4x + 6y = 6$

25. $5x - 6y = 19$
$4x + 3y = 10$

26. $2x + y = 6.6$
$5x - 2y = 0.3$

27. $2x - 4y = 3.8$
$3x - y = 17.7$

28. $3x + 4y = 8$
$4.5x + 6y = 12$

29. $3x - 4y = -5$
$x = y + 2$

30. $y = \frac{1}{3}x + 10$
$x = 3y + 6$

31. $2x + 5y = 62$
$3x - y = 23.3$

32. $-5x + y = 6$
$2x - 3y = 60$

33. $x = \frac{3}{4}y - 6$
$y = \frac{4}{3}x + 8$

34. $5x + 6y = -76$
$x + 2y = -44$

35. $3x - 2y = 10$
$y = \frac{3}{2}x - 1$

36. $-3x + 2y = -6$
$-2x + y = 6$

37. At an ice cream parlor, ice cream cones cost $1.10 and sundaes cost $2.35. One day, the receipts for a total of 172 cones and sundaes were $294.20. How many cones were sold?

38. You purchase 8 gal of paint and 3 brushes for $152.50. The next day, you purchase 6 gal of paint and 2 brushes for $113.00. How much does each gallon of paint and each brush cost?

Algebra 1 Lesson 6-2

6-2 • Guided Problem Solving

GPS **Exercise 23**

Suppose you are thinking about buying one of two cars. Car A will cost
$17,655. You can expect to pay an average of $1230 per year for fuel,
maintenance, and repairs. Car B will cost about $15,900. Fuel, maintenance,
and repairs for it will average about $1425 per year. After how many years
are the total costs for the cars the same?

Read and Understand

1. What are the costs involved in owning car A? _____

2. What are the costs involved in owning car B? _____

3. What are you asked to find? _____

Plan and Solve

4. Write an equation for car A that describes total cost as a function of time. _____

5. Write another equation that does the same for car B. _____

6. Why will solving the two equations as a system give the answer to the problem?

_____

7. To solve the system of two equations, does
it make more sense to replace c with an
expression containing t, or vice versa? Explain. _____

8. Make the appropriate replacement, then solve for the remaining variable. _____

9. Use your answer to Step 8 to give the solution to the problem as stated. _____

Look Back and Check

10. Explain why it makes sense that the total costs
would be the same after several years of ownership. _____

Solve Another Problem

11. Suppose car C costs $16,815 to buy and $1350 per year to operate.
At what time are the total costs the same as for car A? At what time
are they the same as for car B?

_____

Practice 6-3

Solving Systems Using Elimination

Solve by elimination. Show your work.

1. $x + 2y = 7$
$3x - 2y = -3$

2. $3x + y = 20$
$x + y = 12$

3. $5x + 7y = 77$
$5x + 3y = 53$

4. $2x + 5y = -1$
$x + 2y = 0$

5. $3x + 6y = 6$
$2x - 3y = 4$

6. $2x + y = 3$
$-2x + y = 1$

7. $9x - 3y = 24$
$7x - 3y = 20$

8. $2x + 7y = 5$
$2x + 3y = 9$

9. $x + y = 30$
$x - y = 6$

10. $4x - y = 6$
$3x + 2y = 21$

11. $x + 2y = 9$
$3x + 2y = 7$

12. $3x + 5y = 10$
$x - 5y = -10$

13. $2x - 3y = -11$
$3x + 2y = 29$

14. $8x - 9y = 19$
$4x + y = -7$

15. $2x + 6y = 0$
$-2x - 5y = 0$

16. $-2x + 3y = -9$
$x + 3y = 3$

17. $4x - 3y = 11$
$3x - 5y = -11$

18. $3x + 7y = 48$
$5x - 7y = -32$

19. $-2x + 3y = 25$
$-2x + 6y = 58$

20. $3x + 8y = 81$
$5x - 6y = -39$

21. $8x + 13y = 179$
$2x - 13y = -69$

22. $-x + 8y = -32$
$3x - y = 27$

23. $2x + 7y = -7$
$5x + 7y = 14$

24. $x + 6y = 48$
$-x + y = 8$

25. $6x + 3y = 0$
$-3x + 3y = 9$

26. $7x + 3y = 25$
$-2x - y = -8$

27. $3x - 8y = 32$
$-x + 8y = -16$

28. $4x - 7y = -15$
$-4x - 3y = -15$

29. $5x + 7y = -1$
$4x - 2y = 22$

30. $6x - 3y = 69$
$7x - 3y = 76$

31. $x + 8y = 28$
$-3x + 5y = 3$

32. $8x - 6y = -122$
$-4x + 6y = 94$

33. $2x + 9y = 36$
$2x - y = 16$

34. $-6x + 12y = 120$
$5x - 6y = -48$

35. $-x + 3y = 5$
$-x - 3y = 1$

36. $10x - 4y = 6$
$10x + 3y = 13$

37. $6x + 3y = 27$
$-4x + 7y = 27$

38. $6x - 8y = 40$
$5x + 8y = 48$

39. $3x + y = 27$
$-3x + 4y = -42$

40. $2x + 8y = -42$
$-x + 8y = -63$

41. $5x + 9y = 112$
$3x - 2y = 8$

42. $-3x + 2y = 0$
$-3x + 5y = 9$

43. $8x - 2y = 58$
$6x - 2y = 40$

44. $7x - 9y = -57$
$-7x + 10y = 68$

45. $9x + 3y = 2$
$-9x - y = 0$

46. Shopping at Savers Mart, Lisa buys her children four shirts and three pairs of pants for $85.50. She returns the next day and buys three shirts and five pairs of pants for $115.00. What is the price of each shirt and each pair of pants?

47. Grandma's Bakery sells single-crust apple pies for $6.99 and double-crust cherry pies for $10.99. The total number of pies sold on a busy Friday was 36. If the amount collected for all the pies that day was $331.64, how many of each type were sold?

6-3 • Guided Problem Solving

GPS **Exercise 30**

  a. A company sells brass and steel machine parts. One shipment contains
  3 brass and 10 steel parts and costs $48. A second shipment contains
  7 brass and 4 steel parts and costs $54. Find the cost of each type of
  machine part.

  b. How much would a shipment containing 10 brass and 13 steel
  machine parts cost?

Read and Understand

  1. What kind of information are you given about each of the two shipments?

  _____

  2. What are you asked to find? _____

Plan and Solve

  3. Write an equation relating the known cost of the first shipment to the
  unknown cost of each type of part. Use b for brass and s for steel. _____

  4. Write another equation that does the same for the second shipment. _____

  5. What will be the first step in solving the pair of equations by the elimination method?

  _____

  6. Eliminate the variable s to obtain an equation in b only. _____

  7. Solve the equation from Step 6 for b, then substitute the value for b back into one of the original
  equations and find the value for s. Interpret the results.

  _____

  _____

  8. Use the cost of each part to predict the cost of a shipment containing 10 brass and 13 steel parts.

  _____

Look Back and Check

  9. Does it seem right that one type of part costs significantly more than the other? Explain.

  _____

Solve Another Problem

  10. You have $10,000 to divide between two investments. One investment will yield a profit of 3%,
  while the other will yield 5%. How much would you put into each investment for a profit of $445?

  _____

Practice 6-4

Use a system of linear equations to solve each problem.

1. Your teacher is giving you a test worth 100 points containing 40 questions. There are two-point and four-point questions on the test. How many of each type of question are on the test?

2. Suppose you are starting an office-cleaning service. You have spent $315 on equipment. To clean an office, you use $4 worth of supplies. You charge $25 per office. How many offices must you clean to break even?

3. The math club and the science club had fundraisers to buy supplies for a hospice. The math club spent $135 buying six cases of juice and one case of bottled water. The science club spent $110 buying four cases of juice and two cases of bottled water. How much did a case of juice cost? How much did a case of bottled water cost?

4. On a canoe trip, Rita paddled upstream (against the current) at an average speed of 2 mi/h relative to the riverbank. On the return trip downstream (with the current), her average speed was 3 mi/h. Find Rita's paddling speed in still water and the speed of the river's current.

5. Kay spends 250 min/wk exercising. Her ratio of time spent on aerobics to time spent on weight training is 3 to 2. How many minutes per week does she spend on aerobics? How many minutes per week does she spend on weight training?

6. Suppose you invest $1500 in equipment to put pictures on T-shirts. You buy each T-shirt for $3. After you have placed the picture on a shirt, you sell it for $20. How many T-shirts must you sell to break even?

7. A light plane flew from its home base to an airport 255 miles away. With a head wind, the trip took 1.7 hours. The return trip with a tail wind took 1.5 hours. Find the average airspeed of the plane and the average windspeed.

8. Suppose you bought supplies for a party. Three rolls of streamers and 15 party hats cost $30. Later, you bought 2 rolls of streamers and 4 party hats for $11. How much did each roll of streamers cost? How much did each party hat cost?

9. A new parking lot has spaces for 450 cars. The ratio of spaces for full-sized cars to compact cars is 11 to 4. How many spaces are for full-sized cars? How many spaces are for compact cars?

10. While on vacation, Kevin went for a swim in a nearby lake. Swimming against the current, it took him 8 minutes to swim 200 meters. Swimming back to shore with the current took half as long. Find Kevin's average swimming speed and the speed of the lake's current.

6-4 • Guided Problem Solving

GPS **Exercise 22**

Suppose you are trying to decide whether to buy ski equipment. Typically, it costs you $60 a day to rent ski equipment and buy a lift ticket. You can buy ski equipment for about $400. A lift ticket alone costs $35 for one day.

a. Find the break-even point.
b. **Critical Thinking** If you expect to ski five days a year, should you buy the ski equipment? Explain.

Read and Understand

1. What are your total costs if you buy the equipment? If you don't? _____

2. What are you asked to find out? _____

Plan and Solve

3. Write an equation relating your total cost to the number of days you ski, assuming you buy the equipment. _____

4. Write another equation relating costs to days, assuming you don't buy the equipment.

_____

5. Which method of solving the system is best? Explain why. _____

6. Solve the system to find the break-even point. Interpret the answer. _____

7. If you expect to ski five days a year, does it make sense to buy the ski equipment? Give your

reasons. _____

_____

Look Back and Check

8. Does the break-even point seem realistic? _____

_____

Solve Another Problem

9. Suppose you cannot afford the new equipment but have an opportunity to buy used equipment for $275. If the used equipment can be expected to last two seasons, what should you do?

_____

Guided Problem Solving

Practice 6-5

Linear Inequalities

Graph each linear inequality.

1. $y \geq -4$

2. $x + y < -2$

3. $y < x$

4. $x > 2$

5. $4x + y > -6$

6. $-3x + y \leq -3$

7. $x + 4y \leq 8$

8. $y > 2x + 6$

9. $y > -x + 2$

10. $2x + 3y < -9$

11. $y \leq \frac{3}{7}x + 2$

12. $4x + 2y < -8$

13. $y \leq \frac{3}{4}x + 1$

14. $x - y > 4$

15. $y \geq -\frac{2}{5}x - 2$

16. Suppose your class is raising money for the Red Cross. You make $5 on each basket of fruit and $3 on each box of cheese that you sell. How many items of each type must you sell to raise more than $150?

    a. Write a linear inequality that describes the situation.

    b. Graph the inequality.

    c. Write two possible solutions to the problem.

17. Suppose you intend to spend no more than $60 buying books. Hardback books cost $12 and paperbacks cost $5. How many books of each type can you buy?

    a. Write a linear inequality that describes the situation.

    b. Graph the inequality.

    c. Write two possible solutions to the problem.

18. Suppose that for your exercise program, you either walk 5 mi/d or ride your bicycle 10 mi/d. How many days will it take you to cover a distance of at least 150 mi?

    a. Write a linear inequality that describes the situation.

    b. Graph the inequality.

    c. Write two possible solutions to the problem.

Write each linear inequality in slope-intercept form. Then graph the inequality.

19. $6x - 4y > -16$

20. $y \geq -\frac{1}{4}x - 3$

21. $-5x + 4y < -24$

22. $y < -5x + 6$

23. $6x - 4y < -12$

24. $y \geq -\frac{9}{5}x + 7$

25. $y > \frac{5}{7}x - 3$

26. $y < -5x + 9$

27. $-7x + 3y < -18$

28. $y \geq \frac{6}{5}x - 8$

29. $-12x + 8y < 56$

30. $16x + 6y > 36$

6-5 • Guided Problem Solving

GPS **Exercise 37**

Suppose you work at a local radio station. You are in charge of a
$180 budget for new tapes and CDs. Record companies will give you
21 promotional (free) CDs. You can buy tapes for $8 and CDs for $12.

Let x = the number of CDs you buy.
Let y = the number of tapes you buy.

a. Write an inequality that shows
the number of tapes and CDs
you can buy.

b. Graph the inequality.

c. Is $(8, 9)$ a solution of the inequality? Explain
what the solution means.

d. If you buy only tapes and you buy as many as
possible, how many new recordings will the station get?

Read and Understand

1. How much do tapes cost? _____

2. How much do CDs cost? _____

3. How much do you have to spend? _____

4. How many CDs can you get for free? _____

Plan and Solve

5. Write an inequality which says that the amount spent on tapes and
CDs has to be less than or equal to $180, using x for CDs and y for tapes. _____

6. Graph the inequality.

7. Does the point $(8, 9)$ lie inside the solution region? If yes, what does does that mean?

_____

_____

_____

8. Assuming you buy only tapes (which are cheaper), how many can
you buy? Consult the graph. Then add the free CDs to find the
maximum number of recordings you can obtain on your budget. _____

Look Back and Check

9. How many recordings could you obtain if you bought only CDs? Does it make sense that the
answer is less than for Step 8?

Solve Another Problem

10. How many tapes and CDs should you buy to end up with twice as many CDs as tapes (including
the free CDs), while having as little money left over as possible? _____

Practice 6-6

Solve each system of inequalities by graphing. Show your work.

1. $y < 6$
$\quad y > 3$

2. $x < 7$
$\quad y > 2$

3. $x < 2$
$\quad x > 5$

4. $\quad x + y > -2$
$\quad -x + y < 1$

5. $x + y < 2$
$\quad x + y > 5$

6. $y < -5x + 6$
$\quad y > 2x - 1$

7. $y < 2x - 3$
$\quad -2x + y > 5$

8. $-x + 3y < 12$
$\quad y \geq -x + 4$

9. $y \leq -\frac{1}{2}x + 3$
$\quad y \geq -\frac{5}{3}x + 2$

10. $y \geq \frac{3}{4}x + 1$
$\quad y \geq -\frac{2}{3}x - 1$

11. $\quad 6x + 4y > 12$
$\quad -3x + 4y > 12$

12. $\quad 3x + y < 6$
$\quad -2x + y < 6$

13. $-4x + 2y < -2$
$\quad -2x + y > 3$

14. $-5x + y > -2$
$\quad 4x + y < 1$

15. $y < \frac{9}{5}x - 8$
$\quad -9x + 5y > 25$

16. $5x + 4y < 1$
$\quad 8y \geq -10x + 24$

17. $\quad 6x + 8y < 32$
$\quad -4x + 6y < 24$

18. $x + 7y < 14$
$\quad x - 6y > -12$

19. In basketball you score 2 points for a field goal and 1 point for a free throw. Suppose that you have scored at least 3 points in every game this season, and have a season high score of 15 points in one game. How many field goals and free throws could you have made in any one game?

   a. Write a system of two inequalities that describes this situation.

   b. Graph the system to show all possible solutions.

   c. Write one possible solution to the problem.

20. Suppose you need to use at least $1.00 worth of stamps to mail a package. You have as many $.03 stamps as you need but only four $.32 stamps. How many of each stamp can you use?

   a. Write a system of two inequalities that describes this situation.

   b. Graph the system to show all possible solutions.

   c. Write one possible solution to the problem.

21. A grandmother wants to spend at least $40 but no more than $60 on school clothes for her grandson. T-shirts sell for $10 and pants sell for $20. How many T-shirts and pants could she buy?

   a. Write a system of two inequalities that describes this situation.

   b. Graph the system to show all possible solutions.

   c. Write two possible solutions to the problem.

6-6 • Guided Problem Solving

GPS **Exercise 35**

a. A clothing store has a going-out-of-business sale. They are selling pants for $10.99 and shirts for $4.99. You can spend as much as $45 and want to buy at least one pair of pants. Write and graph a system of inequalities that describes this situation.

b. Suppose you need to buy at least three pairs of pants. From your graph, find all the ordered pairs that are possible solutions.

Read and Understand

1. What is the cost of a pair of pants, and of two shirts, and how much can you spend?

   _____

2. What other restrictions are there on how many pants and shirts you buy?

   _____

3. What are you asked to do? _____

Plan and Solve

4. Write an inequality which says that the amount spent on pants and shirts has to be less than or equal to $45, using x for pants and y for shirts. Write another inequality stating that you buy at least 1 pair of pants. _____

5. Graph the system of inequalities.

6. List all the ordered pair solutions where x is greater than or equal to 3.

   _____

Look Back and Check

7. Suppose you were to buy just pants, as many as you could. How many would you buy? Is this one of the solutions found in Step 6? _____

Solve Another Problem

8. Suppose that instead of having to buy some minimum number of pants, you had to buy at least 6 shirts. List all the ordered pair solutions. _____

6A: Graphic Organizer

For use before Lesson 6-1

Study Skill When taking notes, write as clearly as possible.
Use abbreviations of your own invention when possible.
The amount of time needed to recopy messy notes would
be better spent rereading and thinking about them.

Write your answers.

1. What is the chapter title? _____

2. Find the Table of Contents page for this chapter at the front of the book.
   Name four topics you will study in this chapter.

   _____   _____

   _____   _____

3. Complete the graphic organizer as you work through the chapter.
   1. Write the title of the chapter in the center oval.
   2. When you begin a lesson, write the name of the lesson in a
      rectangle.
   3. When you complete that lesson, write a skill or key concept from
      that lesson in the outer oval linked to that rectangle.
   Continue with steps 2 and 3 clockwise around the graphic organizer.

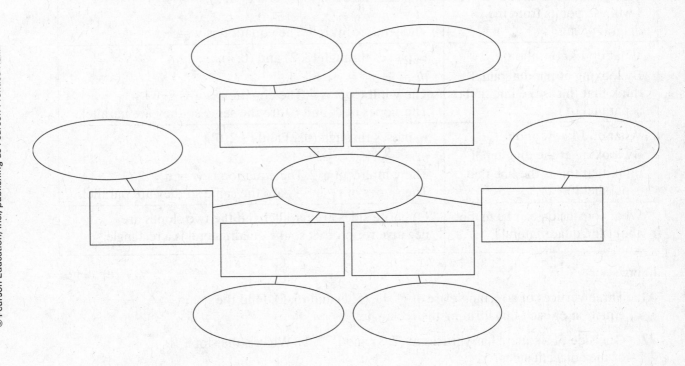

6B: Reading Comprehension

For use after Lesson 6-5

Study Skill Reading a math textbook requires being able to extract information from a graph, figure, diagram, or picture. Take time to look for relationships between lines, points, etc.

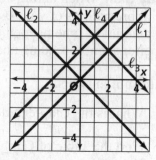

Follow the thought process that Matthew thinks and writes.

In the graph, a quadrilateral is formed by four intersecting lines denoted ℓ_1, ℓ_2, ℓ_3, and ℓ_4. Find the equation of each line. Use this information to draw a conclusion about the quadrilateral.

What Matthew Thinks	What Matthew Writes
I have to find the equations of four lines. What information appears to be true about the lines?	There appear to be two pairs of parallel lines. If that is true, there will only be two slopes. The shape also appears to be a rectangle. If that is true, the two slopes will be negative reciprocals of each other since the lines are perpendicular.
What do I know about ℓ_1? I must look at the diagram to find points that the line passes through.	ℓ_1 passes through $(0, 0)$ and $(2, 2)$. $m = \frac{2-0}{2-0} = 1$ The y-intercept is 0. The equation of ℓ_1 is $y = x$.
What do I know about ℓ_2? I will use points from the diagram again.	ℓ_2 passes through $(0, 0)$ and $(-1, 1)$. $m = \frac{1-0}{-1-0} = -1$ The y-intercept is 0. The equation is $y = -x$.
What do I know about ℓ_3? By looking at the diagram, I think that this is the line that is parallel to ℓ_2.	ℓ_3 passes through $(2, 2)$ and $(0, 4)$. $m = \frac{4-2}{0-2} = \frac{2}{-2} = -1$ The y-intercept is 4. The equation is $y = -x + 4$. The slopes of ℓ_2 and ℓ_3 are the same so they are parallel.
What do I know about ℓ_4? By looking at the diagram, I think that this is the line that is parallel to ℓ_1.	ℓ_4 passes through $(0, 2)$ and $(-2, 0)$. $m = \frac{0-2}{-2-0} = \frac{-2}{-2} = 1$ The y-intercept is 2. The equation is $y = x + 2$. The slopes of ℓ_1 and ℓ_4 are the same so they are parallel.
What conclusion can be made about the quadrilateral?	Opposite sides are parallel and the two slopes are negative reciprocals, so the quadrilateral is a rectangle.

Exercises

1. Three vertices of a rectangle are at $(1, 1)$, $(5, 1)$ and $(5, 5)$. Find the equation of each line forming the rectangle.

2. One side of a square has vertices at $(2, 3)$ and $(-2, 1)$. What is the slope of the adjacent sides?

3. **High-Use Academic Words** In the direction box at the top of the page, what does *draw a conclusion* mean for you to do?
   a. identify special characteristics
   b. identify general characteristics

6C: Reading/Writing Math Symbols

For use after Lesson 6-2

Study Skill Many graphs look very similar. You must look for details in the graphs and their equations, and decide what those details symbolize.

Look at each inequality, and then choose its correct graph.

1. $y \geq 3$

A. 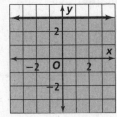 **B.** 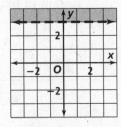 **C.**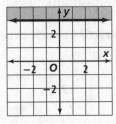

2. $x < 2$

A. 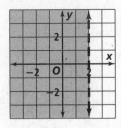 **B.** 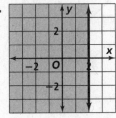 **C.**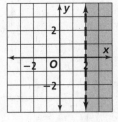

3. $y \leq x + 2$

A. 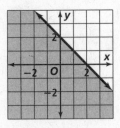 **B.** 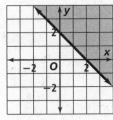 **C.**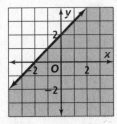

4. $y > 2x + 5$

A. 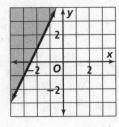 **B.** 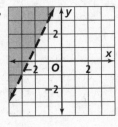 **C.**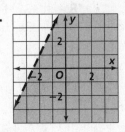

6D: Visual Vocabulary Practice

For use after Lesson 6-6

Study Skill Making sense of mathematical symbols is like reading a foreign language that uses different letters.

Concept List

elimination method	infinitely many solutions	solution of a system of equations
no solution	linear inequality	solution of a system of linear inequalities
solutions of an inequality	substitution method	system of linear inequalities

Write the concept that best describes each exercise.
Choose from the concept list above.

1. $y = 4 - 3x$ $x + 2y = -1$ $x + 2(4 - 3x) = -1$ _____	**2.** 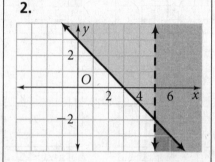 _____	**3.** $y > 9x + 8$ _____
4. 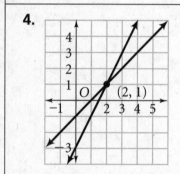 _____	**5.** $5x + 9y = 11$ $-5x + 3y = -5$ $12y = 6$ _____	**6.** $4x - y = 10$ $8x - 2y = 20$ _____
7. $y \geq 3x - 1$ $6x + y < 5$ _____	**8.** $3x + 5y = 10$ $3x + 5y = -2$ _____	**9.** 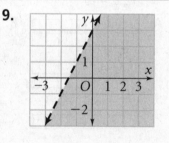 _____

6E: Vocabulary Check

Study Skill Strengthen your vocabulary. Use these pages and add cues and summaries by applying the Cornell Notetaking style.

Write the definition for each word at the right. To check your work, fold the paper back along the dotted line to see the correct answers.

_____

_____

_____

_____

System of linear equations

_____

_____

Solution of a system

_____

_____

No solution

_____

_____

_____

Substitution method

_____

_____

Elimination method

_____

_____

6E: Vocabulary Check (continued) For use after Lesson 6-4

Write the vocabulary word for each definition. To check your work,
fold the paper forward along the dotted line to see the correct answers.

Two or more linear
equations together.

_____

Any ordered pair in a
system that makes *all* the
equations true.

_____

A system of equations
whose graphs do not
intersect.

_____

Solving a system by
replacing one variable
with an equivalent
expression containing the
other variable.

_____

Using the Addition and
Subtraction Properties of
Equality to solve a system.

_____

6F: Vocabulary Review

For use with Chapter Review

Study Skill To be successful in math you need to understand meanings of words. Learn one term at a time, moving on to the next when you are confident of your knowledge of the first.

For Exercises 1–7 match each term in Column A with its definition in Column B by drawing a line between them.

Column A		Column B
1. system of linear equations	**A.**	a comparison of two numbers by division
2. solutions of an inequality	**B.**	two or more linear equations using the same variables
3. constant	**C.**	a term that has no variable
4. linear inequality	**D.**	lines in the same plane that never intersect
5. parallel lines	**E.**	a statement representing a region of the coordinate plane
6. variable	**F.**	a symbol that represents one or more numbers
7. ratio	**G.**	the coordinates of the points that make the inequality true

For Exercises 8–14 match each term in Column C with its definition in Column D by drawing a line between them.

Column C		Column D
	A.	any ordered pair that makes all of the equations in the system true
8. counterexample	**B.**	multiplicative inverse
9. substitution method	**C.**	a method of solving systems of equations by replacing one variable with an equivalent expression
10. power		
11. solution of the system	**D.**	a number pattern
12. sequence	**E.**	has 2 parts, a base and an exponent
13. reciprocal	**F.**	the rate of vertical change to horizontal change of a line
14. slope	**G.**	any example that proves a statement false

Practice 7-1

Simplify each expression.

1. 16^0

2. 4^{-2}

3. 3^{-3}

4. 8^{-4}

5. $\dfrac{1}{2^{-5}}$

6. $\dfrac{4}{4^{-3}}$

7. $\dfrac{3}{6^{-1}}$

8. $\dfrac{2^{-1}}{2^{-5}}$

9. $3 \cdot 8^0$

10. $16 \cdot 2^{-2}$

11. 12^{-1}

12. -7^{-2}

13. $16 \cdot 4^0$

14. 9^0

15. $\dfrac{32^{-1}}{8^{-1}}$

16. $\dfrac{9}{2^{-1}}$

17. $\dfrac{8^{-2}}{4^0}$

18. $\dfrac{9^{-1}}{3^{-2}}$

19. $5(-6)^0$

20. $(3.7)^0$

21. $(-9)^{-2}$

22. $(-4.9)^0$

23. $-6 \cdot 3^{-4}$

24. $\dfrac{7^{-2}}{4^{-1}}$

Evaluate each expression for $a = -2$ and $b = 6$.

25. b^{-2}

26. a^{-3}

27. $(-a)^{-4}$

28. $-b^{-3}$

29. $4a^{-3}$

30. $2b^{-2}$

31. $(3a)^{-2}$

32. $(-b)^{-2}$

33. $2a^{-1}b^{-2}$

34. $-4a^{-2}b^{-3}$

35. $3^{-2}a^{-2}b^{-1}$

36. $(3ab)^{-2}$

Simplify each expression.

37. x^{-8}

38. xy^{-3}

39. $a^{-5}b$

40. m^2n^{-9}

41. $\dfrac{1}{x^{-7}}$

42. $\dfrac{3}{a^{-4}}$

43. $\dfrac{5}{d^{-3}}$

44. $\dfrac{6}{r^{-5}s^{-1}}$

45. $3x^{-6}y^{-5}$

46. $8a^{-3}b^2c^{-2}$

47. $15s^{-9}t^{-1}$

48. $-7p^{-5}q^{-3}r^2$

49. $\dfrac{d^{-4}}{e^{-7}}$

50. $\dfrac{3m^{-4}}{n^{-8}}$

51. $\dfrac{6m^{-8}n}{p^{-1}}$

52. $\dfrac{a^{-2}b^{-1}}{cd^{-3}}$

Write each number as a power of 10 using negative exponents.

53. $\dfrac{1}{10,000}$

54. $\dfrac{1}{1,000,000}$

55. $\dfrac{1}{10,000,000}$

56. $\dfrac{1}{1,000,000,000}$

Write each expression as a decimal.

57. 10^{-5}

58. 10^{-8}

59. $4 \cdot 10^{-1}$

60. $6 \cdot 10^{-4}$

Evaluate each expression for $m = 4, n = 5,$ and $p = -2$.

61. m^p

62. n^m

63. p^p

64. n^p

65. $m^p n$

66. m^{-n}

67. p^{-n}

68. mn^p

69. p^{-m}

70. $\dfrac{m}{n^p}$

71. $\dfrac{1}{n^{-m}}$

72. $-n^{-m}$

7-1 • Guided Problem Solving

GPS **Exercise 81**

Suppose you are the only person in your class who knows a certain story. After a minute you tell a classmate. Every minute after that, every student who knows the story tells another student (sometimes the person being told will have heard it already). In a class of 30 students, the expression $\frac{30}{1 + 29 \cdot 2^{-t}}$ predicts the approximate number of people who will have heard the story after t minutes. About how many students will have heard your story after 2 min? After 5 min? After 10 min?

Read and Understand

1. What are you asked to do? _____

Plan and Solve

2. Rewrite the expression using a positive exponent. _____

3. Use the expression to predict the approximate number of students who have heard the story after 2 minutes. _____

4. Repeat step 3 with each of the values given for t. Record your results in the table below.

Time (min)	Number of Students
2	
5	
10	

Look Back and Check

5. How many people have heard the story after 0 minutes? In the expression you wrote in Step 3, substitute 0 for t. Why should your answer be 1? Is it? _____

Solve Another Problem

6. Suppose there are 40 people in your class. Use the expression $\frac{40}{1 + 39 \cdot 2^{-t}}$ to predict the approximate number of people who will have heard your story after t minutes. About how many students will have heard your story after 2 min? After 6 min? After 9 min?

_____

_____

Name _____ Class _____ Date _____

Practice 7-2

Write each number in standard notation.

1. 7×10^4 **2.** 3×10^{-2} **3.** 2.6×10^5 **4.** 7.1×10^{-4}

5. 5.71×10^{-5} **6.** 4.155×10^7 **7.** 3.0107×10^2 **8.** 9.407×10^{-5}

9. 31.3×10^6 **10.** 83.7×10^{-4} **11.** 0.018×10^{-1} **12.** 0.016×10^5

13. 8.0023×10^{-3} **14.** 6.902×10^8 **15.** 1005×10^2 **16.** 0.095×10^{-1}

Write each number in scientific notation.

17. 51,000,000   **18.** 975,000,000,000   **19.** 0.00000012   **20.** 0.000005008

21. 1560 billion   **22.** 0.5 million   **23.** 2 thousandths   **24.** 1095 millionths

25. 194×10^3 **26.** 154×10^{-3} **27.** 0.05×10^6 **28.** 0.031×10^{-4}

29. 790 thousand   **30.** 25 hundredths   **31.** 0.000000000159   **32.** 5,000,900,000,000

Order the numbers in each list from least to greatest.

33. $7 \times 10^{-7}, 6 \times 10^{-8}, 5 \times 10^{-6}, 4 \times 10^{-10}$

34. $5.01 \times 10^{-4}, 4.8 \times 10^{-3}, 5.2 \times 10^{-2}, 5.6 \times 10^{-2}$

35. $62,040, 6.2 \times 10^2, 6.207 \times 10^3, 6.34 \times 10^{-1}$

36. $10^{-3}, 5 \times 10^{-3}, 8 \times 10^{-2}, 4 \times 10^{-1}$

Simplify. Write each answer using scientific notation.

37. $4(3 \times 10^5)$ **38.** $5(7 \times 10^{-2})$ **39.** $8(9 \times 10^9)$

40. $7(9 \times 10^6)$ **41.** $3(1.2 \times 10^{-4})$ **42.** $2(6.1 \times 10^{-8})$

43. $3(1.2 \times 10^{-4})$ **44.** $3(4.3 \times 10^{-4})$ **45.** $3(3.2 \times 10^{-2})$

Complete the table.

	Units of Area in Square Feet		
	Unit	Standard Form	Scientific Notation
46.	1 in.^{2}		6.9444×10^{-3}
47.	1 link^2	0.4356	
48.	1 rod^2	272.25	
49.	1 mi^2		2.78×10^7
50.	1 cm^2	0.001076	
51.	1 hectare		1.08×10^7

Practice   Algebra 1 Lesson 7-2   **309**

All rights reserved. © Pearson Education, Inc., publishing as Pearson Prentice Hall.

7-2 • Guided Problem Solving

GPS Exercise 43

A computer can perform 4.66×10^8 instructions per second. How many instructions is that per minute? Per hour? Use scientific notation.

Read and Understand

1. How many instructions can the computer perform in one second? _____

2. What are you asked to do? _____

Plan and Solve

3. What conversion factor do you multiply by to convert instructions per second into instructions per minute? _____

4. Perform the multiplication to find the number of instructions per minute. Do not yet worry about proper scientific notation form. _____

5. Now put the answer from Step 4 in proper scientific notation form by moving the decimal point and adjusting the exponent on the 10. _____

6. Repeat Steps 3 through 5 for the conversion from instructions per minute to instructions per hour. _____

Look Back and Check

7. You should be able to get the answer to Step 6 by converting directly from instructions per second to instructions per hour. Verify that this works. _____

Solve Another Problem

8. Light travels at a speed of 3×10^8 meters per second. Use the number of seconds in a minute, the number of minutes in an hour, the number of hours in a day, and the number of days in a year to write the speed of light in meters per year. Then convert to kilometers per year. Use scientific notation.

_____

Practice 7-3

Multiplication Properties of Exponents

• •

Simplify each expression.

1. $(3d^{-4})(5d^8)$ **2.** $(-8m^4)(4m^8)$ **3.** $n^{-6} \cdot n^{-9}$

4. $a^3 \cdot a$ **5.** $3^8 \cdot 3^5$ **6.** $(3p^{-15})(6p^{11})$

7. $p^7 \cdot q^5 \cdot p^6$ **8.** $(-1.5a^5b^2)(6a)$ **9.** $(-2d^3e^3)(6d^4e^6)$

10. $\dfrac{1}{b^{-7} \cdot b^5}$ **11.** $p^5 \cdot q^2 \cdot p^4$ **12.** $\dfrac{1}{n^7 \cdot n^{-5}}$

13. $(8d^4)(4d^7)$ **14.** $x^{-9} \cdot x^3 \cdot x^2$ **15.** $2^3 \cdot 2^2$

16. $r^7 \cdot s^4 \cdot s \cdot r^3$ **17.** $b^7 \cdot b^{13}$ **18.** $(7p^4)(5p^9)$

19. $2^8 \cdot 2^{-9} \cdot 2^3$ **20.** $(6r^4s^3)(9rs^2)$ **21.** $4^3 \cdot 4^2$

22. $m^{12} \cdot m^{-14}$ **23.** $s^7 \cdot t^4 \cdot t^8$ **24.** $(-3xy^6)(3.2x^5y)$

25. $5^{-7} \cdot 5^9$ **26.** $\dfrac{1}{h^7 \cdot h^3}$ **27.** $\dfrac{1}{t^{-5} \cdot t^{-3}}$

28. $f^5 \cdot f^2 \cdot f^0$ **29.** $r^6 \cdot r^{-13}$ **30.** $5^{-6} \cdot 5^4$

Simplify each expression. Write each answer in scientific notation.

31. $(7 \times 10^7)(5 \times 10^{-5})$ **32.** $(3 \times 10^8)(3 \times 10^4)$ **33.** $(9.5 \times 10^{-4})(2 \times 10^{-5})$

34. $(4 \times 10^9)(4.1 \times 10^8)$ **35.** $(7.2 \times 10^{-7})(2 \times 10^{-5})$ **36.** $(5 \times 10^7)(4 \times 10^3)$

37. $(6 \times 10^{-6})(5.2 \times 10^4)$ **38.** $(4 \times 10^6)(9 \times 10^8)$ **39.** $(6.1 \times 10^9)(8 \times 10^{14})$

40. $(2.1 \times 10^{-4})(4 \times 10^{-7})$ **41.** $(1.6 \times 10^5)(3 \times 10^{11})$ **42.** $(9 \times 10^{12})(0.3 \times 10^{-18})$

43. $(4 \times 10^9)(11 \times 10^3)$ **44.** $(5 \times 10^{13})(9 \times 10^{-9})$ **45.** $(7 \times 10^6)(4 \times 10^9)$

46. $(6 \times 10^{-8})(12 \times 10^{-7})$ **47.** $(6 \times 10^{15})(3.2 \times 10^2)$ **48.** $(5 \times 10^8)(2.6 \times 10^{-16})$

49. In 1990, the St. Louis metropolitan area had an average of 82×10^{-6} g/m^3 of pollutants in the air. How many grams of pollutants were there in 2×10^3 m^3 of air?

50. Light travels approximately 5.87×10^{12} mi in one year. This distance is called a light-year. Suppose a star is 2×10^4 light-years away. How many miles away is that star?

51. The weight of 1 m^3 of air is approximately 1.3×10^3 g. Suppose that the volume of air inside of a building is 3×10^6 m^3. How much does the air inside the building weigh?

52. Light travels 1.18×10^{10} in. in 1 second. How far will light travel in 1 nanosecond or 1×10^{-9} s?

• •

7-3 • Guided Problem Solving

GPS **Exercise 56**

Medicine Medical X-rays, with a wavelength of about 10^{-10} meter, can penetrate your skin.

a. Ultraviolet rays, which cause sunburn by penetrating only the top layers of skin, have a wavelength about 1000 times the wavelength of an X-ray. Find the wavelength of ultraviolet rays.

b. **Critical Thinking** The wavelengths of visible light are between 4×10^{-7} meters and 7.5×10^{-7} meters. Are these wavelengths longer or shorter than those of ultraviolet rays? Explain.

Read and Understand

1. What is given as the wavelength of medical X-rays? _____

2. What is the conversion factor relating the wavelengths of medical X-rays and ultraviolet rays?

_____

3. What are you asked to do? _____

_____

Plan and Solve

4. Multiply the wavelength of medical X-rays by the appropriate conversion factor to find the approximate wavelength of ultraviolet rays. _____

5. Compare the wavelengths of ultraviolet rays to the wavelengths for visible light. Which is longer? Explain. _____

Look Back and Check

6. If ultraviolet rays can burn the skin more than visible light rays can, what would you expect for X-rays, given how all the wavelengths compare? Explain. Does your conclusion fit with what you know to be true?

_____

_____

Solve Another Problem

7. Infrared rays have wavelengths in the neighborhood of 10^{-5} meter. Is this longer or shorter than X-rays? Than ultraviolet rays? Than visible light?

_____

Practice 7-4

More Multiplication Properties of Exponents

Simplify each expression.

1. $(4a^5)^3$ 2. $(2^{-3})^4$ 3. $(m^{-3}n^4)^{-4}$

4. $(x^5)^2$ 5. $2^5 \cdot (2^4)^2$ 6. $(4x^4)^3(2xy^3)^2$

7. $x^4 \cdot (x^4)^3$ 8. $(x^5y^3)^3(xy^5)^2$ 9. $(5^2)^2$

10. $(a^4)^{-5} \cdot a^{13}$ 11. $(3f^4g^{-3})^3(f^2g^{-2})^{-1}$ 12. $x^3 \cdot (x^3)^5$

13. $(d^2)^{-4}$ 14. $(a^3b^4)^{-2}(a^{-3}b^{-5})^{-4}$ 15. $(x^2y)^4$

16. $(12b^{-2})^2$ 17. $(m^{-5})^{-3}$ 18. $(x^{-4})^5(x^3y^2)^5$

19. $(y^6)^{-3} \cdot y^{21}$ 20. $n^6 \cdot (n^{-2})^5$ 21. $(m^5)^{-3}(m^4n^5)^4$

22. $(a^3)^6$ 23. $b^{-9} \cdot (b^2)^4$ 24. $(4^{-1}s^3)^{-2}$

25. $(5a^3b^5)^4$ 26. $(b^{-3})^6$ 27. $(y^6)^3$

28. $a^{-4} \cdot (a^4b^3)^2$ 29. $(x^4y)^3$ 30. $d^3 \cdot (d^2)^5$

Simplify. Write each answer in scientific notation.

31. $10^{-9} \cdot (2 \times 10^2)^2$ 32. $(3 \times 10^{-6})^3$ 33. $10^4 \cdot (4 \times 10^6)^3$

34. $(9 \times 10^7)^2$ 35. $10^{-3} \cdot (2 \times 10^3)^5$ 36. $(7 \times 10^5)^3$

37. $(5 \times 10^5)^4$ 38. $(2 \times 10^{-3})^3$ 39. $(5 \times 10^2)^{-3}$

40. $(3 \times 10^5)^4$ 41. $(4 \times 10^8)^{-3}$ 42. $(1 \times 10^{-5})^{-5}$

43. $10^5 \cdot (8 \times 10^7)^3$ 44. $(10^2)^3(6 \times 10^{-3})^3$ 45. $10^7 \cdot (2 \times 10^2)^4$

46. The kinetic energy, in joules, of a moving object is found by using the formula $E = \frac{1}{2}mv^2$, where m is the mass and v is the speed of the object. The mass of a car is 1.59×10^3 kg. The car is traveling at 2.7×10^1 m/s. What is the kinetic energy of the car?

47. The moon is shaped somewhat like a sphere. The surface area of the moon is found by using the formula $S = 12.56r^2$. What is the surface area of the moon if the radius is 1.08×10^3 mi?

48. Because of a record corn harvest, excess corn is stored on the ground in a pile. The pile is shaped like a cone. The height of the pile is 25 ft, and the radius of the pile is 1.2×10^2 ft. Use the formula $V = \frac{1}{3}\pi r^2 h$ to find the volume.

49. Suppose the distance in feet that an object travels in t seconds is given by the formula $d = 64t^2$. How far would the object travel after 1.5×10^3 seconds?

7-4 • Guided Problem Solving

GPS **Exercise 51**

a. Write an expression for the surface area of each cube.
b. How many times greater than the surface area of the small cube is the surface area of the large cube?
c. Write an expression for the volume of each cube.
d. How many times greater than the volume of the small cube is the volume of the large cube?

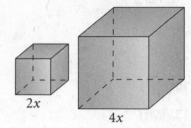

2x

4x

Read and Understand

1. What are you asked to do? _____

Plan and Solve

2. How many faces (sides) does a cube have? _____

3. For a cube whose edges have length x, what expression represents the area of each face?

   _____

4. Write an expression for the surface area of a cube with edges of length x. Then write an expression for the surface area of each cube pictured above. _____

5. Use division to find the ratio of the large cube's surface area to the small cube's surface area.

   _____

6. Write an expression for the volume of a cube with edges of length x. _____

7. Write an expression for the volume of each cube pictured above. _____

8. Use division to find the ratio of the large cube's volume to the small cube's volume. _____

Look Back and Check

9. If the side length x of a cube is doubled, by what factor should the quantity x^2 increase? What about the quantity x^3? Check that your answer agrees with your earlier findings. _____

Solve Another Problem

10. Suppose the larger cube had a side length of $6x$ instead of $4x$. Write expressions for its surface area and volume, and compare those to the surface area and volume of the small cube.

    _____

Practice 7-5

Simplify each expression.

1. $\dfrac{c^{15}}{c^9}$

2. $\left(\dfrac{x^3 y^{-2}}{z^{-5}}\right)^{-4}$

3. $\dfrac{x^7 y^9 z^3}{x^4 y^7 z^8}$

4. $\left(\dfrac{a^2}{b^3}\right)^5$

5. $\dfrac{3^7}{3^4}$

6. $\left(\dfrac{a^3}{b^2}\right)^4$

7. $\left(\dfrac{2}{3}\right)^{-2}$

8. $\left(\dfrac{p^{-3} q^{-2}}{q^{-3} r^5}\right)^4$

9. $\dfrac{a^6 b^{-5}}{a^{-2} b^7}$

10. $\dfrac{7^{-4}}{7^{-7}}$

11. $\dfrac{a^7 b^6}{a^5 b}$

12. $\left(\dfrac{a^2 b^{-4}}{b^2}\right)^5$

13. $\left(-\dfrac{3}{2^3}\right)^{-2}$

14. $\dfrac{z^7}{z^{-3}}$

15. $\left(\dfrac{5 a^0 b^4}{c^{-3}}\right)^2$

16. $\dfrac{x^4 y^{-8} z^{-2}}{x^{-1} y^6 z^{-10}}$

17. $\dfrac{m^6}{m^{10}}$

18. $\left(\dfrac{2^3 m^4 n^{-1}}{p^2}\right)^0$

19. $\left(\dfrac{s^{-4}}{t^{-1}}\right)^{-2}$

20. $\left(\dfrac{2 a^3 b^{-2}}{c^3}\right)^5$

21. $\left(\dfrac{x^{-3} y}{xz^{-4}}\right)^{-2}$

22. $\dfrac{h^{-13}}{h^{-8}}$

23. $\dfrac{4^6}{4^8}$

24. $\left(\dfrac{1}{3}\right)^3$

25. $\dfrac{x^5 y^3}{x^2 y^9}$

26. $\left(\dfrac{m^{-3} n^4}{n^{-2}}\right)^4$

27. $\dfrac{4^{-1}}{4^2}$

28. $\left(\dfrac{a^8 b^6}{a^{11}}\right)^5$

29. $\dfrac{n^9}{n^{15}}$

30. $\left(\dfrac{r^3 s^{-1}}{r^2 s^6}\right)^{-1}$

31. $\dfrac{n^{-8}}{n^4}$

32. $\dfrac{m^8 n^3}{m^{10} n^5}$

Simplify each quotient. Write each answer in scientific notation.

33. $\dfrac{3.54 \times 10^{-9}}{6.15 \times 10^{-5}}$

34. $\dfrac{9.35 \times 10^{-3}}{3.71 \times 10^{-5}}$

35. $\dfrac{495 \text{ billion}}{23.9 \text{ million}}$

36. $\dfrac{8 \times 10^9}{4 \times 10^5}$

37. $\dfrac{9.5 \times 10^9}{5 \times 10^{12}}$

38. $\dfrac{6.4 \times 10^9}{8 \times 10^7}$

39. $\dfrac{298 \text{ billion}}{49 \text{ million}}$

40. $\dfrac{1.8 \times 10^{-8}}{0.9 \times 10^3}$

41. $\dfrac{3.6 \times 10^6}{9 \times 10^{-3}}$

42. $\dfrac{8.19 \times 10^7}{4.76 \times 10^{-2}}$

43. $\dfrac{65 \text{ million}}{19.5 \text{ billion}}$

44. $\dfrac{4.9 \times 10^{12}}{7 \times 10^3}$

45. $\dfrac{36.2 \text{ trillion}}{98.5 \text{ billion}}$

46. $\dfrac{3.9 \times 10^3}{1.3 \times 10^8}$

47. $\dfrac{5.6 \times 10^{-5}}{8 \times 10^{-7}}$

48. $\dfrac{40 \text{ million}}{985 \text{ million}}$

49. The half-life of uranium-238 is 4.5×10^9 years. The half-life of uranium-234 is 2.5×10^5 years. How many times greater is the half-life of uranium-238 than that of uranium-234?

7-5 • Guided Problem Solving

GPS **Exercise 50**

In 2003, there were 158.7 million wireless telephone subscribers. These subscribers made about 23.7 billion calls and used about 80.5 billion minutes per month.

  a. Write each number in scientific notation.

  b. What was the average number of minutes used by each subscriber per month? Round to the nearest whole number.

  c. What was the average length of a phone call? Round to the nearest tenth.

Read and Understand

1. How many subscribers had wireless telephones in the year 2003? _____

2. How many calls were made and how many minutes were used by these subscribers?

    _____

3. What are you being asked to find? _____

Plan and Solve

4. What are 1 million and 1 billion written as powers of 10? _____

5. Write 158.7 million subscribers, 23.7 billion calls, and 80.5 billion minutes using the powers of 10 from Step 4, then convert to scientific notation. _____

    _____

6. Use division to find the average number of minutes used by each subscriber to the nearest whole number. _____

7. Use division to find the average length of a call per subscriber to the nearest whole number.

    _____

Look Back and Check

8. The ratio of your answers in Steps 6 and 7 should equal the ratio of total minutes to total length of calls. What is that ratio? _____

Solve Another Problem

9. In 2000, Los Angeles County, with an area of 4061 square miles, was home to 6.1 million motor vehicles. Write each number in scientific notation and find the average number of vehicles per square mile to the nearest whole number. _____

Guided Problem Solving

7A: Graphic Organizer

For use before Lesson 7-1

Study Skill When taking notes, write down everything written on the chalkboard or overhead. What you write down may be a clue as to what might be on an exam or test.

Write your answers.

1. What is the chapter title? _____

2. Find the Table of Contents page for this chapter at the front of the book. Name four topics you will study in this chapter.

_____   _____

_____   _____

3. Complete the graphic organizer as you work through the chapter.
   1. Write the title of the chapter in the center oval.
   2. When you begin a lesson, write the name of the lesson in a rectangle.
   3. When you complete that lesson, write a skill or key concept from that lesson in the outer oval linked to that rectangle.

   Continue with steps 2 and 3 clockwise around the graphic organizer.

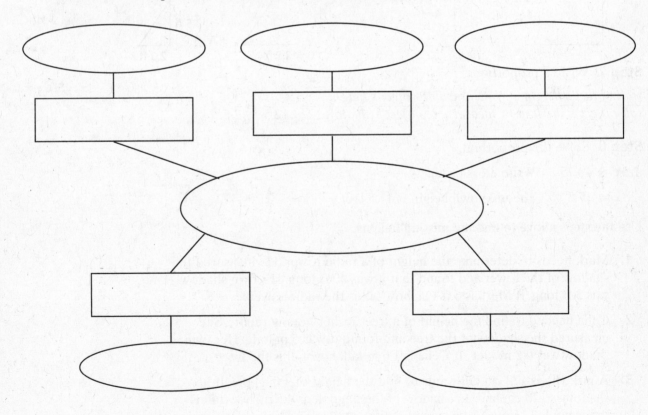

7B: Reading Comprehension

Study Skill You often need to follow written directions. Read carefully and slowly, and do not skip steps.

The following procedure can be used to measure the height of tall objects.

Step 1. Draw a vertical line to represent the tall object.

Step 2. Draw a horizontal line to represent the object's shadow.

Step 3. Draw a vertical line to represent the height of something you can measure, such as your height or the height of a mailbox.

Step 4. Draw a horizontal line to represent the shadow of the measurable object.

Step 5. Connect endpoints of the segments to make two similar triangles.

Step 6. Measure the second object and the two shadows, and label each corresponding part of the drawing. Make sure the measurements are in the same unit. Label the missing height x.

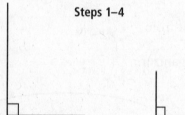

Steps 1–4

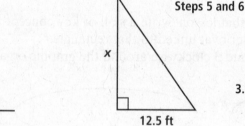

Steps 5 and 6

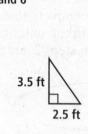

x

12.5 ft

3.5 ft

2.5 ft

Step 7 Write a proportion.

$$\frac{tall\ object's\ height}{tall\ object's\ shadow} = \frac{measurable\ object's\ height}{measurable\ object's\ shadow} \Rightarrow \frac{x}{12.5} = \frac{3.5}{2.5}$$

Step 8 Solve the proportion.

$2.5x = 43.75$ Write cross products.

$x = 17.5$ The unknown height is 17.5 feet.

Use the steps above to find the missing heights.

1. Mark needs to determine the height of a radio tower. He measured the shadow of the tower and found that it was 40 ft long. His own shadow was 3 ft long. If Mark is 6 ft tall, how tall is the radio tower?

2. Celia needed to find the height of a tree for her botany report. She measured the shadow of the tree and found it was 5 m long. Her own shadow was 0.8 m long. If Celia is 1.6 m tall, how tall is the tree?

3. A girl who is 172 cm tall wants to find the height of a flagpole. If her shadow is 120 cm and the shadow of the flagpole is 4.5 m, how tall is the flagpole? (*Hint:* Make sure all units are the same before calculating.)

4. **High-Use Academic Words** In Step 6, what does *measure* mean for you to do?
   a. use a tool to find the weight of an object
   b. use a tool to find the distance from one point to another

7C: Reading/Writing Math Symbols

For use after Lesson 7-2

Study Skill After completing your homework, take a break. Then come back and check your homework. You will sometimes discover mistakes that you missed before.

Write how you would read each of the following expressions. The first one has been done for you.

Expression	Read as:
1. $2x^3y^4$	2 times x cubed, y to the fourth power
2. 4^{-3}	_____
3. x^2	_____
4. xy	_____
5. $(x^2)^3$	_____
6. $\frac{x}{y}$	_____
7. $5x \cdot y^4$	_____
8. $x^5 + x^7$	_____
9. $\sqrt{x^2y}$	_____
10. $8x^2 - 3y$	_____
11. $\frac{x^2}{x^8}$	_____
12. $4x^{11}$	_____

7D: Visual Vocabulary Practice

For use after Lesson 7-5

Study Skill A rational number can be written as a decimal, a fraction, in factored form, or in scientific notation. Use the context of the situation to choose the form.

Concept List

algebraic expression	integers	power
base	number pattern	proportion
exponent	order of operations	scientific notation

Write the concept that best describes each exercise.
Choose from the concept list above.

1. $\dfrac{3}{7} = \dfrac{9}{21}$	**2.** $\begin{aligned} 3^{7-5} + 4 &= 3^2 + 4 \\ &= 9 + 4 \\ &= 13 \end{aligned}$	**3.** The number 4 in the expression 4^5
4. 7.36×10^8	**5.** $2, 4, 8, 16, \ldots$	**6.** $\ldots, -2, -1, 0, 1, 2, \ldots$
7. The number 2 in the expression 7^2	**8.** $3x - 5^x$	**9.** An expression like 5^x

7E: Vocabulary Check

Study Skill Strengthen your vocabulary. Use these pages and add cues and summaries by applying the Cornell Notetaking style.

Write the definition for each word at the right. To check your work, fold the paper back along the dotted line to see the correct answers.

_____

_____

_____

Equivalent equations

_____

_____

Exponent

_____

_____

Base

_____

_____

Power

_____

_____

Scientific notation

_____

_____

7E: Vocabulary Check (continued)

For use after Lesson 7-3

Write the vocabulary word for each definition. To check your work,
fold the paper forward along the dotted line to see the correct answers.

Equations that have the
same solution.

_____

A number that shows
repeated multiplication.

_____

A number that is
multiplied repeatedly.

_____

The base and the exponent
of an expression of the
form a^x.

_____

A number expressed in
the form $a \times 10^n$, where
n is an integer and
$1 \le a < 10$.

_____

7F: Vocabulary Review

Study Skill Always read direction lines carefully before doing any exercises.

Circle the word that best completes the sentence.

1. A number in (*standard form*, *scientific notation*) is written as a product of two factors in the form $a \times 10^n$, where n is an integer and $1 \le a < 10$.

2. Each number in a sequence is called a (*term*, *constant*).

3. When you make conclusions based on patterns you observe, you are using (*inductive*, *deductive*) reasoning.

4. The (*Substitution*, *Elimination*) method is a way of solving systems of equations by replacing one variable with an equivalent expression.

5. A system of linear equations has (*no solution*, *many solutions*) when the graphs of the equations are parallel lines.

6. In the function $f(x) = -3x + 10$, as the values of the domain increase, the values of the range (*increase*, *decrease*).

7. An equation in the form $xy = k$ is a(n) (*direct*, *inverse*) variation.

8. The *y*-intercept is the *y*-coordinate of the point where a line crosses the (*x-axis*, *y-axis*).

9. Lines in the same plane that intersect to form a 90° angle are said to be (*perpendicular*, *parallel*).

10. The (*standard*, *point-slope*) form of a linear equation is $Ax + By = C$, where A, B, and C are real numbers, and A and B are not both zero.

11. The set of integers is closed for (*multiplication*, *division*).

12. $-2, 4, \frac{1}{2}, \frac{3}{4}, -8$, and 6 are examples of (*real numbers*, *integers*).

Practice 8-1

Write each polynomial in standard form. Then name each polynomial based on its degree and number of terms.

1. $4y^3 - 4y^2 + 3 - y$

2. $x^2 + x^4 - 6$

3. $x + 2$

4. $2m^2 - 7m^3 + 3m$

5. $4 - x + 2x^2$

6. $7x^3 + 2x^2$

7. $n^2 - 5n$

8. $6 + 7x^2$

9. $3a^2 + a^3 - 4a + 3$

10. $5 + 3x$

11. $7 - 8a^2 + 6a$

12. $5x + 4 - x^2$

13. $2 + 4x^2 - x^3$

14. $4x^3 - 2x^2$

15. $y^2 - 7 - 3y$

16. $x - 6x^2 - 3$

17. $v^3 - v + 2v^2$

18. $8d + 3d^2$

Simplify. Write each answer in standard form.

19. $(3x^2 - 5x) - (x^2 + 4x + 3)$

20. $(2x^3 - 4x^2 + 3) + (x^3 - 3x^2 + 1)$

21. $(3y^3 - 11y + 3) - (5y^3 + y^2 + 2)$

22. $(3x^2 + 2x^3) - (3x^2 + 7x - 1)$

23. $(2a^3 + 3a^2 + 7a) + (a^3 + a^2 - 2a)$

24. $(8y^3 - y + 7) - (6y^3 + 3y - 3)$

25. $(x^2 - 6) + (5x^2 + x - 3)$

26. $(5n^2 - 7) - (2n^2 + n - 3)$

27. $(5n^3 + 2n^2 + 2) - (n^3 + 3n^2 - 2)$

28. $(3y^2 - 7y + 3) - (5y + 3 - 4y^2)$

29. $(2x^2 + 9x - 17) + (x^2 - 6x - 3)$

30. $(3 - x^3 - 5x^2) + (x + 2x^3 - 3)$

31. $(3x + x^2 - x^3) - (x^3 + 2x^2 + 5x)$

32. $(d^2 + 8 - 5d) - (5d^2 + d - 2d^3 + 3)$

33. $(3x^3 + 7x^2) + (x^2 - 2x^3)$

34. $(6c^2 + 5c - 3) - (3c^2 + 8c)$

35. $(3y^2 - 5y - 7) + (y^2 - 6y + 7)$

36. $(3c^2 - 8c + 4) - (7 + c^2 - 8c)$

37. $(4x^2 + 13x + 9) + (12x^2 + x + 6)$

38. $(2x - 13x^2 + 3) - (2x^2 + 8x)$

39. $(7x - 4x^2 + 11) + (7x^2 + 5)$

40. $(4x + 7x^3 - 9x^2) + (3 - 2x^2 - 5x)$

41. $(y^3 + y^2 - 2) + (y - 6y^2)$

42. $(x^2 - 8x - 3) - (x^3 + 8x^2 - 8)$

43. $(3x^2 - 2x + 9) - (x^2 - x + 7)$

44. $(2x^2 - 6x + 3) - (2x + 4x^2 + 2)$

45. $(2x^2 - 2x^3 - 7) + (9x^2 + 2 + x)$

46. $(3a^2 + a^3 - 1) + (2a^2 + 3a + 1)$

47. $(2x^2 + 3 - x) - (2 + 2x^2 - 5x)$

48. $(n^4 - 2n - 1) + (5n - n^4 + 5)$

49. $(x^3 + 3x) - (x^2 + 6 - 4x)$

50. $(7s^2 + 4s + 2) + (3s + 2 - s^2)$

51. $(6x^2 - 3x + 9) - (x^2 + 3x - 5)$

52. $(3x^3 - x^2 + 4) + (2x^3 - 3x + 9)$

53. $(y^3 + 3y - 1) - (y^3 + 3y + 5)$

54. $(3 + 5x^3 + 2x) - (x + 2x^2 + 4x^3)$

55. $(x^2 + 15x + 13) + (3x^2 - 15x + 7)$

56. $(7 - 8x^2) + (x^3 - x + 5)$

57. $(2x + 3) - (x - 4) + (x + 2)$

58. $(x^2 + 4) - (x - 4) + (x^2 - 2x)$

8-1 • Guided Problem Solving

GPS **Exercise 39**

Find an expression for the perimeter of the figure.

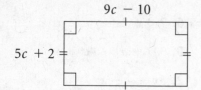

Read and Understand

1. Describe how to determine the perimeter of a rectangle. _____
_____

2. What do the single and double marks drawn on the sides of the figure mean? _____
_____

Plan and Solve

3. What additional information do you need to know before
you can determine the perimeter of the rectangle above? _____

4. Label the lengths of the two missing sides of the rectangle above.

5. Write an expression for the perimeter of the rectangle. _____

Look Back and Check

6. Check the reasonableness of your answer by substituting a number for c.
Substitute the number in the expressions for each side of the rectangle.
Add the numbers and determine the perimeter. Substitute the same number
in the expression you wrote for the perimeter and simplify. The answers should
be the same.

Solve Another Problem

7. Find an expression for the perimeter of the rectangle above
if the length is $7x - 2$ and the width is $5x + 1$.

_____

Practice 8-2

Simplify each product.

1. $4(a - 3)$

2. $-5(x - 2)$

3. $-3x^2(x^2 + 3x)$

4. $4x^3(x - 3)$

5. $-5x^2(x^2 + 2x + 1)$

6. $3x(x^2 - 5x - 3)$

7. $-x^2(-2x^2 + 3x - 2)$

8. $4d^2(d^2 - 3d - 7)$

9. $5m^3(m + 6)$

10. $a^2(2a + 4)$

11. $4(x^2 - 3) + x(x + 1)$

12. $4x(5x - 6)$

Find the GCD of the terms of each polynomial.

13. $8x - 4$

14. $15x + 45x^2$

15. $x^2 + 3x$

16. $4c^3 - 8c^2 + 8$

17. $12x - 36$

18. $12n^3 + 4n^2$

19. $14x^3 + 7x^2$

20. $8x^3 - 12x$

21. $9 - 27x^3$

22. $25x^3 - 15x^2$

23. $11x^2 - 33x$

24. $4n^4 + 6n^3 - 8n^2$

25. $8d^3 + 4d^2 + 12d$

26. $6x^2 + 12x - 21$

27. $8g^2 + 16g - 8$

Factor each polynomial.

28. $8x + 10$

29. $12n^3 - 8n$

30. $14d - 2$

31. $6h^2 - 8h$

32. $3z^4 - 15z^3 - 9z^2$

33. $3y^3 - 8y^2 - 9y$

34. $x^3 - 5x^2$

35. $8x^3 - 12x^2 + 4x$

36. $7x^3 + 21x^4$

37. $6a^3 - 12a^2 + 14a$

38. $6x^4 + 12x^2$

39. $3n^4 - 6n^2 + 9n$

40. $2w^3 + 6w^2 - 4w$

41. $12c^3 - 30c^2$

42. $2x^2 + 8x - 14$

43. $4x^3 + 12x^2 + 16x$

44. $16m^3 - 8m^2 + 12m$

45. $4a^3 - 20a^2 - 8a$

46. $18c^4 - 9c^2 + 7c$

47. $6y^4 + 9y^3 - 27y^2$

48. $6c^2 - 3c$

49. A circular pond will be placed on a square piece of land. The length of a side of the square is $2x$. The radius of the pond is x. The part of the square not covered by the pond will be planted with flowers. What is the area of the region that will be planted with flowers? Write your answer in factored form.

50. A square poster of length $3x$ is to have a square painting centered on it. The length of the painting is $2x$. The area of the poster not covered by the painting will be painted black. What is the area of the poster that will be painted black?

51. The formula for the surface area of a sphere is $A = 4\pi r^2$. A square sticker of side x is placed on a ball of radius $3x$. What is the surface area of the sphere not covered by the sticker? Write your answer in factored form.

8-2 • Guided Problem Solving

GPS **Exercise 33**

Suppose you are building a model of the square castle shown
on the right. The moat of the model castle is made of blue paper.

a. Find the area of the moat using the diagram with the photo.
b. Write your answer in factored form.

Read and Understand

1. What shape is the moat? _____

2. What is the formula for finding the area of a circle? _____

3. What does the white square in the middle of the blue circle represent? _____

Plan and Solve

4. Suppose the entire circle were shaded blue.
   Write an expression for the area of the entire blue circle. _____

5. Write an expression that represents the area of the castle. _____

6. Write an expression that represents the area of the moat only. _____

7. Write your answer in factored form. _____

Look Back and Check

8. Of the three different areas determined above (complete circle,
   castle, moat), which should have the largest area? Check the
   reasonableness of your answer by determining each area if $x = 5$.

   _____

Solve Another Problem

9. Determine the area of the moat if the castle is rectangular, with a
   width of $2x$ and a length of $3x$.

   _____

Name _____ Class _____ Date _____

Practice 8-3

Multiplying Binomials

Simplify each product. Write in standard form.

1. $(x + 3)(2x - 5)$ **2.** $(x^2 + x - 1)(x + 1)$ **3.** $(3w + 4)(2w - 1)$

4. $(x + 5)(x + 4)$ **5.** $(2b - 1)(b^2 - 3b + 4)$ **6.** $(a - 11)(a + 5)$

7. $(2g - 3)(2g^2 + g - 4)$ **8.** $(3s - 4)(s - 5)$ **9.** $(4x + 3)(x - 7)$

10. $(x + 6)(x^2 - 4x + 3)$ **11.** $(5x - 3)(4x + 2)$ **12.** $(3y + 7)(4y + 5)$

13. $(3x + 7)(x + 5)$ **14.** $(5x - 2)(x + 3)$ **15.** $(3m^2 - 7m + 8)(m - 2)$

16. $(a - 6)(a + 8)$ **17.** $(x + 2)(2x^2 - 3x + 2)$ **18.** $(a^2 + a + 1)(a - 1)$

19. $(x - 2)(x^2 + 4x + 4)$ **20.** $(2r + 1)(3r - 1)$ **21.** $(k + 4)(3k - 4)$

22. $(2n - 3)(n^2 - 2n + 5)$ **23.** $(p - 4)(2p + 3)$ **24.** $(3x + 1)(4x^2 - 2x + 1)$

25. $(2x^2 - 5x + 2)(4x - 3)$ **26.** $(x + 7)(x + 5)$ **27.** $(6x - 11)(x + 2)$

28. $(2x + 1)(4x + 3)$ **29.** $(3x + 4)(3x - 4)$ **30.** $(6x - 5)(3x + 1)$

31. $(n - 7)(n + 4)$ **32.** $(3x - 1)(2x + 1)$ **33.** $(d + 9)(d - 11)$

34. $(2x^2 + 5x - 3)(2x + 1)$ **35.** $(b + 8)(2b - 5)$ **36.** $(2x - 5)(x + 4)$

37. $(3x + 5)(5x - 7)$ **38.** $(x - 5)(2x^2 - 7x - 2)$ **39.** $(2x^2 - 9x + 11)(2x + 1)$

40. $(2x^2 + 5x - 4)(2x + 7)$ **41.** $(x^2 + 6x + 11)(3x + 5)$ **42.** $(5x + 7)(7x + 3)$

43. $(4x - 7)(2x - 5)$ **44.** $(x - 9)(3x + 5)$ **45.** $(2x - 1)(x^2 - 7x + 1)$

46. The width of a rectangular painting is 3 in. more than twice the height. A frame that is 2.5 in. wide goes around the painting.

    a. Write an expression for the combined area of the painting and frame.

    b. Use the expression to find the combined area when the height of the painting is 12 in.

    c. Use the expression to find the combined area when the height of the painting is 15 in.

47. The Robertsons put a rectangular pool with a stone walkway around it in their backyard. The total length of the pool and walkway is 3 times the total width. The walkway is 2 ft wide all around.

    a. Write an expression for the area of the pool.

    b. Find the area of the pool when the total width is 10 ft.

    c. Find the area of the pool when the total width is 9 ft.

48. The Cutting Edge frame shop makes a mat by cutting out the inside of a rectangular board. Use the diagram to find the length and width of the original board if the area of the mat is 184 in.^{2}.

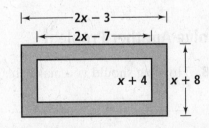

8-3 • Guided Problem Solving

GPS **Exercise 39**

You are planning a rectangular garden. Its length is twice its width x. You want a walkway 2 ft wide around the garden.

  a. Write an expression for the area of the garden and walk.

  b. Write an expression for the area of the walk only.

  c. You have enough gravel to cover 76 ft^2 and want to use it all on the walk. How big should you make the garden?

Read and Understand

  1. Draw a picture of the garden and its walk. Shade in the walk only.

  2. Label the dimensions of the garden.

  3. Label the dimensions of the outside of the walkway.

Plan and Solve

  4. Write an expression for the area of the garden and walk. _____

  5. Write an expression for the area of the walk only. _____

  6. You have enough gravel to cover 76 ft^2 and want to use it all on the walk. How big should you make the garden? _____

Look Back and Check

  7. Check if your answer is reasonable by subtracting the area of the garden from the area of the garden and walk and verifying that this amount is less than or equal to 76 ft^2.

Solve Another Problem

  8. How big should you make the garden if you now have 100 ft^2 of gravel?

Guided Problem Solving

Name_____ Class_____ Date_____

Practice 8-4

Find each product.

1. $(w - 2)^2$ **2.** $(y + 4)^2$

3. $(4w + 2)^2$ **4.** $(w - 9)^2$

5. $(3x + 7)^2$ **6.** $(3x - 7)^2$

7. $(2x - 9)^2$ **8.** $(x - 12)^2$

9. $(6x + 1)^2$ **10.** $(4x - 7)^2$

11. $(x + 8)(x - 8)$ **12.** $(x - 11)(x + 11)$

13. $(x - 12)(x + 12)$ **14.** $(y + w)(y - w)$

15. $(2x + 1)(2x - 1)$ **16.** $(5x - 2)(5x + 2)$

17. $(6x + 1)(6x - 1)$ **18.** $(2x - 4)(2x + 4)$

19. $(x^2 + y^2)^2$ **20.** $(2x^2 + y^2)^2$

21. $(a^2 - b^2)^2$ **22.** $(y^2 - 4w^2)^2$

23. $(3 - 6x^2)^2$ **24.** $(4a - 3y)^2$

25. $(3y + 2a)(3y - 2a)$ **26.** $(x^2 + 2y)(x^2 - 2y)$

27. $(3x^2 + 4w^2)(3x^2 - 4w^2)$ **28.** $(4x + 3w^2)(4x - 3w^2)$

29. $(2a + 7b)(2a - 7b)$ **30.** $(5a^2 - 6x)(5a^2 + 6x)$

31. 18^2 **32.** $(64)^2$

33. $(29)(31)$ **34.** $(97)(103)$

35. $(19)(42)$ **36.** $(95)(205)$

Find the area.

37.
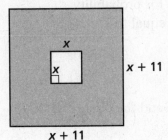
$2x + 1$
$2x + 1$

38.
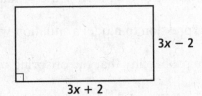
$3x - 2$
$3x + 2$

Find an expression for the area of each shaded region. Write your answers in standard form.

39.

x
x
$x + 11$
$x + 11$

40.
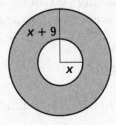
$x + 9$
x

8-4 • Guided Problem Solving

GPS **Exercise 40**

The coat color of shorthorn cattle is determined by two genes, Red R and White W.

RR produces red, WW produces white, and RW produces a third type of coat color called roan.

a. Model the Punnett square with the square of a binomial.
b. If both parents have RW, what is the probability the offspring will also be RW?
c. Write an expression to model a situation where one parent is RW while the other is RR.
d. What is the probability that the offspring of the parents in part (c) will have a white coat?

	R	W
R	RR	RW
W	RW	WW

Read and Understand

1. Describe the information given in the Punnett square. _____
_____

2. Explain how to determine the probability that an event will occur. _____
_____

3. What does the notation RW mean? _____

Plan and Solve

4. Model the Punnett square with the square of a binomial. _____

5. If both parents have RW, what is the probability the offspring will also be RW? _____

6. Write an expression to model a situation where one parent is RW and the other is RR. _____

7. What is the probability that the offspring of the parents in Step 6 will have a white coat? _____

Look Back and Check

8. Check that the probability you found in Step 7 is a possible value for probability. That is, check that it is greater than or equal to 0 and less than or equal to 1.

Solve Another Problem

9. Write an expression to model a situation where one parent is RW and the other is WW.
_____

Practice 8-5

Factoring Trinomials of the Type $x^2 + bx + c$

Factor each expression.

1. $x^2 + 8x + 16$ **2.** $d^2 + 8d + 7$ **3.** $y^2 + 6y + 8$

4. $b^2 - 2b - 3$ **5.** $s^2 - 4s - 5$ **6.** $x^2 + 12x + 32$

7. $x^2 - 9x + 20$ **8.** $x^2 - 5x + 6$ **9.** $a^2 + 3a + 2$

10. $p^2 - 8p + 7$ **11.** $d^2 + 6d + 5$ **12.** $n^2 + n - 6$

13. $x^2 + 5x - 14$ **14.** $b^2 + 9b + 14$ **15.** $x^2 + 14x + 45$

16. $a^2 + 7a + 12$ **17.** $x^2 + 13x + 22$ **18.** $x^2 + 3x - 4$

19. $x^2 - 8x + 12$ **20.** $x^2 + 7x - 18$ **21.** $n^2 - 7n + 10$

22. $s^2 - 5s - 14$ **23.** $x^2 - 9x + 8$ **24.** $x^2 - 2x - 24$

25. $x^2 - 6x - 27$ **26.** $x^2 - 16x - 36$ **27.** $x^2 + 7x + 10$

28. $x^2 - 3x - 28$ **29.** $m^2 - 4m - 21$ **30.** $x^2 - 2x - 15$

31. $x^2 - 5x - 24$ **32.** $b^2 - 4b - 60$ **33.** $x^2 - 3x - 18$

34. $m^2 + 7m + 10$ **35.** $n^2 - n - 72$ **36.** $k^2 - 6k + 5$

37. $x^2 + 9x + 20$ **38.** $x^2 - 10x + 9$ **39.** $x^2 - 8x + 16$

40. $d^2 - 4d + 3$ **41.** $b^2 - 26b + 48$ **42.** $n^2 - 15n + 26$

43. $n^2 - n - 6$ **44.** $z^2 - 14z + 49$ **45.** $x^2 + 7x + 12$

46. $x^2 - 18x + 17$ **47.** $x^2 + 16x + 28$ **48.** $t^2 - 6t - 27$

49. $b^2 + 4b - 12$ **50.** $d^2 + 11d + 18$ **51.** $x^2 + x - 20$

52. $x^2 - 13x + 42$ **53.** $x^2 + x - 6$ **54.** $x^2 + 4x - 21$

55. $a^2 + 2a - 35$ **56.** $h^2 + 7h - 18$ **57.** $x^2 + 3x - 10$

58. $p^2 - 12p - 28$ **59.** $y^2 + 6y - 55$ **60.** $b^2 + 3b - 4$

61. $x^2 + 2x - 63$ **62.** $x^2 - 2x - 8$ **63.** $x^2 - 11x - 60$

64. $r^2 + 2r - 35$ **65.** $c^2 - 3c - 10$ **66.** $x^2 + 8x + 15$

67. $x^2 - 8x + 15$ **68.** $n^2 - 23n + 60$ **69.** $c^2 + 3c - 10$

70. $x^2 - 9x + 14$ **71.** $x^2 - 10x + 24$ **72.** $x^2 + 6x - 27$

73. $y^2 - 16y + 64$ **74.** $n^2 + 10n + 25$ **75.** $r^2 - 14r - 51$

76. $x^2 + 3x - 40$ **77.** $x^2 - x - 42$ **78.** $n^2 - 2n - 63$

79. $a^2 + 7a + 6$ **80.** $x^2 - 14x + 48$ **81.** $x^2 - 11x + 28$

82. $n^2 + 16n - 36$ **83.** $n^2 - 4n - 21$ **84.** $y^2 + 16y - 17$

8-5 • Guided Problem Solving

GPS Exercise 55

Write the standard form for the polynomial modeled below. Then factor.

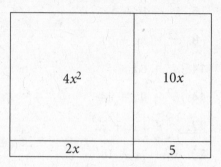

Read and Understand

1. Explain what the standard form of a polynomial is. _____

_____

2. Describe how you can write a polynomial from a rectangle model. _____

_____

Plan and Solve

3. Write the standard form of the polynomial by adding the area of each rectangle. _____

4. Factor the standard form of the polynomial you wrote in Step 3. _____

Look Back and Check

5. Check the reasonableness of your answer in Steps 3 and 4 by substituting a number in each expression. Why should the result be the same for each expression?

Solve Another Problem

6. Write the standard form for the polynomial modeled below. Then factor.

$9x^2$	$3x$
$6x$	2

_____

Practice 8-6

Factoring Trinomials of the Type $ax^2 + bx + c$

Factor each expression.

1. $2x^2 + 3x + 1$ **2.** $2x^2 + 5x + 3$ **3.** $2n^2 + n - 6$

4. $3x^2 - x - 4$ **5.** $2y^2 - 9y - 5$ **6.** $5x^2 - 2x - 7$

7. $7n^2 + 9n + 2$ **8.** $3c^2 - 17c - 6$ **9.** $3x^2 + 8x + 4$

10. $6x^2 - 7x - 10$ **11.** $3x^2 - 10x + 8$ **12.** $3y^2 - 16y - 12$

13. $5x^2 + 2x - 3$ **14.** $3x^2 + 7x + 2$ **15.** $7x^2 - 10x + 3$

16. $3x^2 + 8x + 5$ **17.** $2x^2 + 9x + 4$ **18.** $5x^2 - 7x + 2$

19. $5x^2 - 22x + 8$ **20.** $4x^2 + 17x - 15$ **21.** $5x^2 - 33x - 14$

22. $3x^2 - 2x - 8$ **23.** $3y^2 + 7y - 6$ **24.** $2x^2 + 13x - 24$

25. $4y^2 - 11y - 3$ **26.** $2y^2 + 9y + 7$ **27.** $5y^2 - 3y - 2$

28. $7y^2 + 19y + 10$ **29.** $7x^2 - 30x + 8$ **30.** $3x^2 + 17x + 10$

31. $2x^2 + 5x - 3$ **32.** $2x^2 - 5x + 3$ **33.** $3x^2 + 10x + 3$

34. $2x^2 - x - 21$ **35.** $5x^2 - 11x + 2$ **36.** $4x^2 + 4x - 15$

37. $6x^2 - 19x + 15$ **38.** $2x^2 - x - 15$ **39.** $3x^2 - 7x - 6$

40. $2x^2 - 5x - 12$ **41.** $6x^2 - 7x - 5$ **42.** $4x^2 + 7x + 3$

43. $12y^2 - 7y + 1$ **44.** $6y^2 - 5y + 1$ **45.** $6x^2 - 11x + 4$

46. $12x^2 + 19x + 5$ **47.** $7y^2 + 47y - 14$ **48.** $11x^2 - 54x - 5$

49. $15x^2 - 19x + 6$ **50.** $8x^2 - 30x + 25$ **51.** $14y^2 + 15y - 9$

52. $22x^2 + 51x - 10$ **53.** $14x^2 - 41x + 15$ **54.** $8y^2 + 17y + 9$

55. $8x^2 + 65x + 8$ **56.** $20x^2 + 37x + 15$ **57.** $24y^2 + 41y + 12$

58. $18x^2 - 27x + 4$ **59.** $10x^2 + 3x - 4$ **60.** $10y^2 - 29y + 10$

8-6 • Guided Problem Solving

GPS **Exercise 31**

a. Write each area as a product of two binomials.

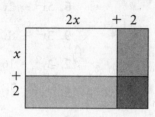
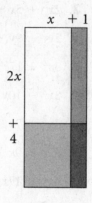

b. Are the products equal?

c. **Critical Thinking** Explain how the two products you found in part (a) can equal the same trinomial.

Read and Understand

1. What does the word *product* mean? _____

2. What are binomials? _____

Plan and Solve

3. Write each area as a product of two binomials. _____

4. Are the products equal? _____

5. Explain how the two products you found in Step 3 can equal the same trinomial.

_____

_____

Look Back and Check

6. Check the reasonableness of your answer by factoring each product completely to show that they are the same.

Solve Another Problem

7. Show that these two products are equal: $(3x - 1)(2x + 2)$ and $(6x - 2)(x + 1)$.

_____

Practice 8-7

Factoring Special Cases

Factor each expression.

1. $x^2 - 9$

2. $4m^2 - 1$

3. $a^2 + 2a + 1$

4. $4x^2 + 12x + 9$

5. $x^2 - 22x + 121$

6. $n^2 - 4$

7. $9x^2 - 4$

8. $16c^2 - 49$

9. $9x^2 - 30x + 25$

10. $4x^2 - 20x + 25$

11. $2a^2 - 18$

12. $x^2 - 24x + 144$

13. $3n^2 - 3$

14. $9h^2 + 60h + 100$

15. $9d^2 - 49$

16. $81a^2 - 400$

17. $r^2 - 36$

18. $3a^2 - 48$

19. $b^2 + 4b + 4$

20. $10x^2 - 90$

21. $25x^2 - 64$

22. $12w^2 - 27$

23. $g^3 - 25g$

24. $x^2 + 6x + 9$

25. $a^2 - 25$

26. $36s^2 - 225$

27. $4b^2 + 44b + 121$

28. $x^2 - 16x + 64$

29. $x^2 - 2x + 1$

30. $d^2 - 49$

31. $x^3 - 36x$

32. $9y^2 - 289$

33. $x^2 - 30x + 225$

34. $100a^2 - 9$

35. $2x^2 + 4x + 2$

36. $5n^3 - 20n$

37. $9n^2 + 12n + 4$

38. $d^2 - 169$

39. $4a^2 - 81$

40. $x^2 - 121$

41. $5x^2 + 40x + 80$

42. $16n^2 + 56n + 49$

43. $3n^2 - 30n + 75$

44. $a^2 + 26a + 169$

45. $25x^2 - 144$

46. $9d^2 - 64$

47. $n^2 - 28n + 196$

48. $49a^2 - 14a + 1$

49. $y^2 + 8y + 16$

50. $y^2 - 400$

51. $x^2 - 10x + 25$

52. $4x^2 - 60x + 225$

53. $3x^2 - 363$

54. $y^2 - 81$

55. $a^2 - 100$

56. $256a^2 - 1$

57. $n^2 + 34n + 289$

58. $2d^3 - 50d$

59. $y^2 + 22y + 121$

60. $144x^2 - 25$

61. $4x^2 - 169$

62. $x^2 - 12x + 36$

63. $64r^2 + 80r + 25$

64. $50m^3 - 32m$

65. $b^2 - 225$

66. $x^2 - 18x + 81$

67. $b^2 - 64$

68. $16x^2 - 72x + 81$

69. $b^2 - 256$

70. $x^2 + 24x + 144$

71. $225x^2 - 16$

72. $2x^3 + 40x^2 + 200x$

73. $4r^2 - 25$

74. $16x^2 + 8x + 1$

75. $b^2 - 14b + 49$

76. $x^2 + 30x + 225$

77. $m^2 - 28m + 196$

78. $9r^2 - 256$

79. $b^2 + 20b + 100$

80. $m^2 - 16$

81. $4x^2 - 32x + 64$

82. $x^2 - 196$

83. $8x^3 - 32x$

84. $25x^2 - 30x + 9$

85. $8m^2 - 16m + 8$

86. $9x^2 - 400$

87. $m^2 - 144$

8-7 • Guided Problem Solving

Exercise 54

a. Write an expression in terms of n and m for the area of the top of the block that was drilled at the right. Use 3.14 for π. Factor your expression.

b. Find the area of the top of the block if $n = 10$ in. and $m = 3$ in.

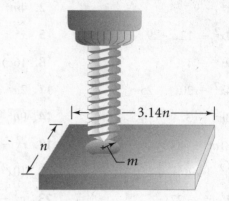

Read and Understand

1. Describe the information given to you in the picture. _____

   _____

2. What is the formula used to find the area of a rectangle? _____

3. What is the formula used to find the area of a circle? _____

Plan and Solve

4. Write an expression for the area of the rectangular block. _____

5. Write an expression for the area of the circular hole drilled into the block. _____

6. Write an expression for the area of the top of the block that was drilled. _____

7. Factor your expression from Step 6. _____

8. Find the area of the top of the block if $n = 10$ and $m = 3$. _____

Look Back and Check

9. In Steps 6 and 7 you wrote two different expressions for the area of the block. Check your answer in Step 8 by substituting the values into the expression that you did not use.

Solve Another Problem

10. What is the area of the top of the block if $n = 15$ and $m = 6$?

    _____

Guided Problem Solving

Practice 8-8

Factoring by Grouping

Factor each expression.

1. $x(a + 2) - 2(a + 2)$ **2.** $3(x + y) + a(x + y)$ **3.** $m(x - 3) + k(x - 3)$

4. $a(y + 1) - b(y + 1)$ **5.** $x^2 + 3x + 2xy + 6y$ **6.** $y^2 - 5wy + 4y - 20w$

7. $xy + 4y - 2x - 8$ **8.** $ab + 7b - 3a - 21$ **9.** $ax + bx + ay + by$

10. $ax + bx - ay - by$ **11.** $2x^2 - 6xy + 5x - 15y$ **12.** $3x^2 - 6xy + 2x - 4y$

13. $2ax + 6xc + ba + 3bc$ **14.** $x^2y - 3x^2 - 2y + 6$ **15.** $6 + 2y + 3x^2 + x^2y$

16. $2x^2 - 3x + 1$ **17.** $2x^2 - 7x + 3$ **18.** $6x^2 + 7x + 2$

19. $4x^2 + 8x + 3$ **20.** $6x^2 - 7x + 2$ **21.** $4x^2 - 9x + 2$

22. $2x^2 - 3x - 2$ **23.** $12x^2 - x - 1$ **24.** $6x^2 + 19x + 3$

25. $12y^2 - 5y - 2$ **26.** $10y^2 + 21y - 10$ **27.** $5y^2 + 13y + 6$

28. $16y^2 + 10y + 1$ **29.** $16x^2 - 14x + 3$ **30.** $16x^2 + 16x + 3$

31. $10x^2 - 3x - 1$ **32.** $9x^2 + 25x - 6$ **33.** $14x^2 + 15x - 9$

34. $2x^3 + 8x^2 + x + 4$ **35.** $8x^4 + 6x - 28x^3 - 21$ **36.** $5x^3 - x^2 + 15x - 3$

37. $x^3 + 3x^2 + 4x + 12$ **38.** $6x^3 + 3x^2 + 2x + 1$ **39.** $3x^3 + 9x^2 + 2x + 6$

40. $9x^3 - 12x^2 + 3x - 4$ **41.** $10x^3 - 25x^2 + 4x - 10$ **42.** $4x^3 - 20x^2 + 3x - 15$

Find expressions for the possible dimensions of each rectangular prism.

43. The volume of the prism is given.   **44.** The volume of the prism is given.

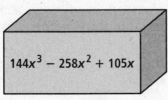

$144x^3 - 258x^2 + 105x$

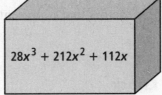

$28x^3 + 212x^2 + 112x$

8-8 • Guided Problem Solving

GPS **Exercise 39**

The polynomial shown at the right represents the volume of the rectangular prism. Factor the polynomial to find possible expressions for the length, width, and height of the prism.

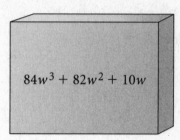

$84w^3 + 82w^2 + 10w$

Read and Understand

1. What is the formula for finding the volume of a rectangular prism? _____

   _____

2. What is the first type of factoring that you should look for? _____

   _____

Plan and Solve

3. What is the common factor for the expression $84w^3 + 82w^2 + 10w$? _____

4. What polynomial is left after factoring out the common factor? _____

5. Factor the polynomial you wrote in Step 5. _____

6. What are the three factors that represent the length, width, and height of the prism?

   _____

Look Back and Check

7. Multiply the three factors you wrote for Step 7. How can you tell if these are the correct factors?

   _____

   _____

Solve Another Problem

8. What are the possible expressions for the length, width, and height of a rectangular prism that has a volume of $18m^3 + 33m^2 + 9m$?

   _____

Guided Problem Solving

Name_____ Class_____ Date_____

8A: Graphic Organizer

For use before Lesson 8-1

Study Skill To remember the math concepts, you can study with a friend. Quiz each other on the details of the algebra rules and procedures. Use your notes to help you determine possible test questions. Reviewing right before bedtime will help you retain the material you study.

Write your answers.

1. What is the chapter title? _____

2. Find the Table of Contents page for this chapter at the front of the book. Name four topics you will study in this chapter.

_____   _____

_____   _____

3. Complete the graphic organizer as you work through the chapter.
   1. Write the title of the chapter in the center oval.
   2. When you begin a lesson, write the name of the lesson in a rectangle.
   3. When you complete that lesson, write a skill or key concept from that lesson in the outer oval linked to that rectangle.
   Continue with steps 2 and 3 clockwise around the graphic organizer.

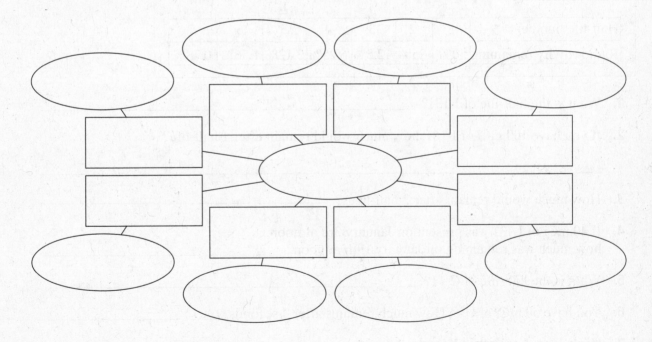

8B: Reading Comprehension

Study Skill Many reading passages contain a great amount of information. It is essential to recognize which information is necessary for a particular question. You can designate corresponding information by circling, underlining, or boxing that information.

Read the passage below and answer the following questions.

Radioactive material is here today and gone tomorrow. Radioisotopes disintegrate into stable isotopes of different elements at a decreasing rate, but never quite reach zero. Radioactive material is measured in curies (Ci) and 1 Ci = 3.7×10^{10} atoms. A mathematical formula known as the radioactive decay law can measure the rate of radioactive decay and the quantity of material present at any given time. From this formula we obtain a quantity known as half-life. Half-life is the amount of time required for a quantity of radioactive material to be reduced to one-half its original quantity.

Each radioisotope has a unique half-life. For example I-131 has a half-life of 8 days, C-11 has a half-life of 20 minutes, and H-6 has a half-life of 0.8 seconds.

Although this can sound quite difficult, it does not have to be. The following chart can help you calculate the amount of radioactive material that has decayed.

Half-life number	1	2	3	4	5	6	7
Radioactivity remaining	50%	25%	12.5%	6.25%	3.12%	1.56%	0.78%

1. What is the half-life of I-131? _____

2. If you have 100 mCi of I-131, how much would remain after 1 half-life?

   _____

3. How much would remain after 2 half-lives? _____

4. If 40 mCi of I-131 was present on January 3rd at noon, how much was remaining on January 19th at noon? _____

5. What is the half-life of C-11? _____

6. You have 50 mCi of H-6. How much remains after 4 seconds? _____

7. **High-Use Academic Words** What does *unique* mean in the second paragraph of the passage?

   a. unpredictable   **b.** its own

8C: Reading/Writing Math Symbols

For use after Lesson 8-7

Study Skill Make mental pictures from what you read. This will help you remember it.

In equations and inequalities, *x* and *y* represent coordinates of points, *b* represents the *y*-intercept, and *m* represents the slope. Inequality symbols mean to shade on one side of a boundary line. Match each equation or inequality to the graph that best represents it.

1. $y < b$

2. $x = k$

3. $y = mx + b; m < 0$

4. $y \geq mx + b$

5. $y < mx + b; b \neq 0$

6. $y = mx; m > 0$

A.

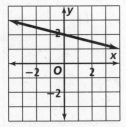

B.

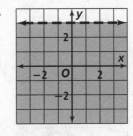

C.

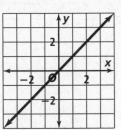

D.

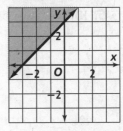

E.

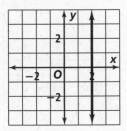

F.

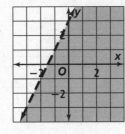

8D: Visual Vocabulary Practice

For use after Lesson 8-8

Study Skill Mathematics is like learning a foreign language. You have to know the vocabulary before you can speak the language correctly.

Concept List

binomial	difference of two squares	Distributive Property
factor by grouping	factor out a monomial	monomial
perfect square trinomial	square of a binomial	trinomial

Write the concept that best describes each exercise. Choose from the concept list above.

1. $(x + 5)^2$	**2.** $3m^2n^5$	**3.** $6x^2 + 12y + 7x + 14$ $= 6x(x + 2) + 7(x + 2)$ $= (6x + 7)(x + 2)$
4. $x^2 - 49$	**5.** $10v^3 - 5v = 5v(2v^2 - 1)$	**6.** $x^2 - 12x + 36$
7. $9x + 15$	**8.** $-5xy^2 + 2xy + 11x^2y$	**9.** $6xy^2(2x - 7)$ $= 12x^2y - 2xy$

8E: Vocabulary Check

Study Skill Strengthen your vocabulary. Use these pages and add cues and summaries by applying the Cornell Notetaking style.

Write the definition for each word at the right. To check your work, fold the paper back along the dotted line to see the correct answers.

_____

_____

_____

Degree of a monomial

_____

_____

Polynomial

_____

_____

Standard form of a polynomial

_____

_____

_____

Degree of a polynomial

_____

_____

Greatest common divisor

_____

_____

8E: Vocabulary Check (continued)   For use after Lesson 8-3

**Write the vocabulary word for each definition. To check your work, fold
the paper forward along the dotted line to see the correct answers.**

The sum of the exponents
of its variables.

_____

A monomial or the sum
or difference of two or
more monomials.

_____

The form of a polynomial
in which the degree of the
terms decreases from
left to right.

_____

The degree of the term
with the greatest exponent
for a polynomial in one
variable.

_____

The greatest factor that
divides evenly into each
term of the expression.

_____

8F: Vocabulary Review Puzzle

For use with Chapter Review

Study Skill When you complete a puzzle such as a word search, remember to read the list of words carefully and completely. As you identify each word in the word search, circle it and then cross off the word from the list. Pay special attention to the spelling of each word.

Complete the word search.

binomial	property	translation
factor	inequality	solution
monomial	deductive	distributive
standard form	absolute value	variable
polynomial	identity	consecutive
trinomial	reciprocal	degree
systems	elimination	substitution

```
S  R  C  O  N  S  E  C  U  T  I  V  E  D  D
N  L  V  S  W  F  G  S  P  E  V  U  I  S  M
W  P  O  L  Y  N  O  M  I  A  L  S  Y  Y  O
M  R  O  F  D  R  A  D  N  A  T  S  N  N  N
N  O  I  T  U  L  O  S  V  R  T  E  W  O  O
M  P  D  E  G  R  E  E  I  E  V  Y  I  I  M
B  E  Y  R  H  Z  T  B  M  I  V  T  N  T  I
I  R  J  H  Y  U  U  S  T  D  A  T  E  A  A
N  T  L  D  L  T  A  C  Y  N  L  J  Q  L  L
O  Y  N  O  I  T  U  T  I  T  S  B  U  S  F
M  V  S  V  O  D  A  M  P  H  R  F  A  N  A
I  B  E  R  E  C  I  P  R  O  C  A  L  A  C
A  W  I  D  J  L  L  A  I  M  O  N  I  R  T
L  Z  I  D  E  N  T  I  T  Y  G  M  T  T  O
E  L  B  A  I  R  A  V  M  F  E  D  Y  M  R
```

Practice 9-1

Identify the vertex of each graph. Tell whether it is a minimum or a maximum.

1. $y = -3x^2$

2. $y = -7x^2$

3. $f(x) = 0.5x^2$

4. $f(x) = 5x^2$

5. $y = -4x^2$

6. $f(x) = \frac{3}{2}x^2$

Order each group of quadratic functions from widest to narrowest graph.

7. $y = x^2, y = 5x^2, y = 3x^2$

8. $y = -8x^2, y = \frac{1}{2}x^2, y = -x^2$

9. $f(x) = 5x^2, f(x) = -4x^2, f(x) = 2x^2$

10. $y = -\frac{1}{2}x^2, y = \frac{1}{3}x^2, y = -3x^2$

Match each graph with its function.

A. $f(x) = 3x^2 + 5$

B. $f(x) = -3x^2 - 5$

C. $f(x) = 3x^2 - 5x$

11.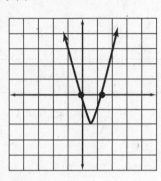

12.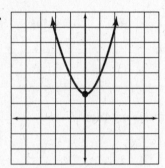

13.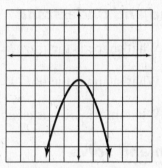

Graph each function.

14. $y = 4x^2$

15. $y = -3x^2$

16. $y = -x^2 - 4$

17. $f(x) = 2x^2 - 2$

18. $y = 2x^2 + 3$

19. $y = \frac{1}{2}x^2 + 2$

20. $y = \frac{1}{2}x^2 - 3$

21. $f(x) = \frac{1}{3}x^2 + 5$

22. $y = \frac{1}{3}x^2 - 4$

23. $f(x) = 2.5x^2 + 3$

24. $y = 2.5x^2 + 5$

25. $f(x) = 5x^2 + 8$

26. $y = 5x^2 - 8$

27. $y = -3.5x^2 - 4$

28. $f(x) = 3x^2 - 2$

29. The price of a stock on the NYSE is modeled by the function
$y = 0.005x^2 + 10$, where x is the number of months the stock has been available.

a. Graph the function.

b. What x-values make sense for the domain? Explain why.

c. What y-values make sense for the range? Explain why.

30. You are designing a poster. The poster is 24 in. wide by 36 in. high. On the poster, you want to place a square photograph and some printing. If each side of the photograph is x in., the function $y = 864 - x^2$ gives the area of the poster available for printing.

a. Graph the function.

b. What x-values make sense for the domain? Explain why.

c. What y-values make sense for the range? Explain why.

9-1 • Guided Problem Solving

GPS **Exercise 39**

Suppose that a pizza must fit into a box with a base that is 12 in. long and 12 in. wide. You can use the quadratic function $A = \pi r^2$ to find the area of a pizza in terms of its radius.

   a. What values of r make sense for the function?
   b. What values of A make sense for the function?
   c. Graph the function. Round values of A to the nearest tenth.

Read and Understand

   1. What shape is the pizza? _____

   2. What shape is the box? _____

   3. What information is given to you in the problem? _____

Plan and Solve

   4. What values of r make sense for the function? _____

   5. What values of A make sense for the function? _____

   6. Graph the function. Round values of A to the nearest tenth.

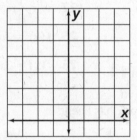

Look Back and Check

   7. The equation $A = \pi r^2$ is a quadratic function. What shape is the graph of a quadratic function? Verify the reasonableness of your graph by verifying that it is the shape you would expect.

_____

Solve Another Problem

   8. If the size of the box is changed so the base is now 10 in. long and 10 in. wide, what values of r and A would make sense? _____

Guided Problem Solving

Practice 9-2

Find the equation of the axis of symmetry and the coordinates of the vertex of the graph of each function. Find the domain and range

1. $y = x^2 - 10x + 2$

2. $y = x^2 + 12x - 9$

3. $y = -x^2 + 2x + 1$

4. $f(x) = 3x^2 + 18x + 9$

5. $y = 3x^2 + 3$

6. $f(x) = 16x - 4x^2$

7. $y = 0.5x^2 + 4x - 2$

8. $y = -4x^2 + 24x + 6$

9. $y = -1.5x^2 + 6x$

Match each graph with its function.

A. $y = -x^2 - 3x$

B. $y = x^2 - 3x$

C. $y = x^2 + 3x$

D. $y = -x^2 + 3$

E. $y = x^2 - 3$

F. $y = -x^2 + 3x$

10.

11.

12.

13.

14.

15.

Graph each function. Label the axis of symmetry and the vertex.

16. $y = x^2 - 6x + 4$

17. $f(x) = x^2 + 4x - 1$

18. $y = x^2 + 10x + 14$

19. $y = x^2 + 2x + 1$

20. $y = -x^2 - 4x + 4$

21. $f(x) = -4x^2 + 24x + 13$

22. $f(x) = -2x^2 - 8x + 5$

23. $y = 4x^2 - 16x + 10$

24. $y = -x^2 + 6x + 5$

25. $y = 4x^2 + 8x$

26. $f(x) = -3x^2 + 6$

27. $y = 6x^2 + 48x + 98$

Graph each quadratic inequality.

28. $y > x^2 + 1$

29. $y \geq x^2 - 4$

30. $f(x) < -x^2 + 1$

31. $f(x) > x^2 + 6x + 3$

32. $y < x^2 - 4x + 4$

33. $y < -x^2 + 2x - 3$

34. $y \geq -2x^2 - 8x - 5$

35. $f(x) \leq -3x^2 + 6x + 1$

36. $y \geq 2x^2 - 4x - 3$

37. You and a friend are hiking in the mountains. You want to climb to a ledge that is 20 ft above you. The height of the grappling hook you throw is given by the function $h = -16t^2 - 32t + 5$. What is the maximum height of the grappling hook? Can you throw it high enough to reach the ledge?

38. The total profit made by an engineering firm is given by the function $p = x^2 - 25x + 5000$. Find the minimum profit made by the company.

39. You are trying to dunk a basketball. You need to jump 2.5 ft in the air to dunk the ball. The height that your feet are above the ground is given by the function $h = -16t^2 + 12t$. What is the maximum height your feet will be above the ground? Will you be able to dunk the basketball?

9-2 • Guided Problem Solving

•••

GPS **Exercise 41**

An archway over a road is cut out of rock. Its shape is modeled by the quadratic function $y = -0.1x^2 + 12$ for $y \geq 0$.

   a. Write an inequality that describes the opening of the archway.

   b. Graph the inequality.

   c. Critical Thinking Can a camper 6 ft wide and 7 ft high fit under the arch without crossing the median line? Explain.

Read and Understand

•••••••••••••••••••••••••••••••

   1. Make a rough sketch of what the archway should look like.

   2. What information do you know about the archway? _____

Plan and Solve

•••••••••••••••••••

   3. Write an inequality that describes the opening of the archway. _____

   4. Graph the inequality.

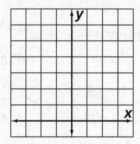

   5. On your graph above, show where the camper would be located.

   6. Can a camper 6 ft wide and 7 ft high fit under the arch without crossing the median line? Explain. _____

_____

Look Back and Check

•••••••••••••••••••••••••••••

   7. Check the reasonableness of your inequality graph. Pick a point in the shaded region and check to see that it makes the inequality true.

Solve Another Problem

   8. The road passing through the archway is being converted to a one-way road so a trailer with an extra-wide load can pass through it. If the trailer's load is 12 feet wide and 10 feet high, can the trailer fit under the arch?

Practice 9-3

Finding and Estimating Square Roots

Tell whether each expression is *rational* or *irrational*.

1. $-\sqrt{64}$

2. $\sqrt{1600}$

3. $\pm\sqrt{160}$

4. $\sqrt{144}$

5. $\sqrt{125}$

6. $-\sqrt{340}$

7. $\sqrt{1.96}$

8. $-\sqrt{0.09}$

Between what two consecutive integers is each square root?

9. $\sqrt{20}$

10. $\sqrt{73}$

11. $-\sqrt{38}$

12. $\sqrt{130}$

13. $\sqrt{149.3}$

14. $-\sqrt{8.7}$

15. $\sqrt{213.8}$

16. $-\sqrt{320.7}$

17. $\sqrt{113.9}$

18. $-\sqrt{840.6}$

19. $-\sqrt{1348.9}$

20. $\sqrt{928.2}$

Find the square root(s) of each number.

21. 49

22. 2.25

23. $\frac{1}{16}$

24. 400

25. 6.25

26. $\frac{36}{25}$

27. 196

28. 2.56

Simplify each expression.

29. $\sqrt{0.25}$

30. $\pm\sqrt{\frac{9}{100}}$

31. $\sqrt{576}$

32. $\pm\sqrt{\frac{121}{36}}$

33. $\sqrt{1600}$

34. $-\sqrt{0.04}$

35. $\sqrt{2500}$

36. $\sqrt{4.41}$

Find the value of each expression. If necessary, round to the nearest hundredth.

37. $\sqrt{49}$

38. $\sqrt{196}$

39. $-\sqrt{\frac{9}{25}}$

40. $\sqrt{1.44}$

41. $-\sqrt{1225}$

42. $-\sqrt{173.2}$

43. $\sqrt{1123.7}$

44. $\sqrt{216.9}$

Solve the following problems. Round to the nearest tenth if necessary.

45. You are to put a metal brace inside a square shipping container. The formula $d = \sqrt{2x^2}$ gives the length of the metal brace, where x is the length of the side of the container. Find the length of the brace for each container side length.

    a. $x = 3$ ft

    b. $x = 4.5$ ft

    c. $x = 5$ ft

    d. $x = 8$ ft

46. You are designing a cone-shaped storage container. Use the formula $r = \sqrt{\frac{3V}{\pi h}}$ to find the radius of the storage container. Find the radius when $V = 10,000$ ft^3 and $h = 10$ ft.

9-3 • Guided Problem Solving

GPS Exercise 48

If you drop an object, the time t in seconds that it takes to fall d feet is given

by the formula $t = \sqrt{\dfrac{d}{16}}$.

   a. Find the time it takes an object to fall 400 ft.

   b. Find the time it takes an object to fall 1600 ft.

   c. **Critical Thinking** In part (b), the object falls four times as far as in part (a). Does it take four times as long to fall? Explain.

Read and Understand

   1. What information is given in the problem? _____

   2. Explain what each variable represents. _____

Plan and Solve

   3. Find the time it takes an object to fall 400 ft. _____

   4. Find the time it takes an object to fall 1600 ft. _____

   5. Does it take four times as long for an object to fall four times as far? _____

Look Back and Check

   6. Explain why it is reasonable that the time does not increase at the same rate as the distance.

   _____

   _____

Solve Another Problem

   7. Find the time it takes an object to fall 800 ft. _____

Practice 9-4

Solving Quadratic Equations

Solve each equation by graphing the related function. If the equation has no solution, write *no solution*.

1. $x^2 = 16$ 2. $x^2 - 144 = 0$ 3. $3x^2 - 27 = 0$
4. $x^2 + 16 = 0$ 5. $x^2 = 25$ 6. $x^2 = 49$

Solve each equation by finding square roots. If the equation has no solution, write *no solution*. If necessary, round to the nearest tenth.

7. $x^2 + 8 = -10$ 8. $3x^2 = 300$ 9. $2x^2 - 6 = 26$
10. $x^2 = 80$ 11. $81x^2 - 10 = 15$ 12. $2x^2 = 90$
13. $x^2 = 300$ 14. $4x^2 + 9 = 41$ 15. $2x^2 + 8 = 4$
16. $x^2 + 8 = 72$ 17. $4x^2 + 6 = 7$ 18. $x^2 = 121$
19. $5x^2 + 20 = 30$ 20. $x^2 + 6 = 17$ 21. $3x^2 + 1 = 54$
22. $2x^2 - 7 = 74$ 23. $x^2 + 1 = 0$ 24. $4x^2 - 8 = -20$
25. $9x^2 = 1$ 26. $x^2 + 4 = 4$ 27. $3x^2 = 1875$
28. $x^2 = 9$ 29. $5x^2 - 980 = 0$ 30. $x^2 - 10 = 100$
31. $4x^2 - 2 = 1$ 32. $3x^2 - 75 = 0$ 33. $x^2 + 25 = 0$
34. $2x^2 - 10 = -4$ 35. $4x^2 + 3 = 3$ 36. $4x^2 - 8 = 32$
37. $7x^2 + 8 = 15$ 38. $x^2 + 1 = 26$ 39. $6x^2 = -3$
40. $x^2 - 400 = 0$ 41. $7x^2 - 8 = 20$ 42. $2x^2 - 1400 = 0$
43. $5x^2 + 25 = 90$ 44. $x^2 + 4x^2 = 20$ 45. $5x^2 - 18 = -23$
46. $3x^2 - x^2 = 10$ 47. $2x^2 + 6 - x^2 = 9$ 48. $x^2 - 225 = 0$
49. $-3 + 4x^2 = 2$ 50. $7x^2 - 1008 = 0$ 51. $6x^2 - 6 = 12$

Solve each problem. If necessary, round to the nearest tenth.

52. You want to build a fence around a square garden that covers 506.25 ft². How many feet of fence will you need to complete the job?

53. The formula $A = 6s^2$ will calculate the surface area of a cube. Suppose you have a cube that has a surface area of 216 in.². What is the length of each side?

54. You drop a pencil out of a window that is 20 ft above the ground. Use the formula $V^2 = 64s$, where V is the speed and s is the distance fallen, to calculate the speed the pencil is traveling when it hits the ground.

55. Suppose you are going to construct a circular fish pond in your garden. You want the pond to cover an area of 300 ft². What is the radius of the pond?

56. During the construction of a skyscraper, a bolt fell from 400 ft. What was the speed of the bolt when it hit the ground? Use $V^2 = 64s$.

All rights reserved.

© Pearson Education, Inc., publishing as Pearson Prentice Hall.

Practice *Algebra 1 Lesson 9-4* **355**

9-4 • Guided Problem Solving

GPS **Exercise 26**

Find dimensions for the square picture at the right that would make the area of the picture equal to 75% of the total area enclosed by the square frame. Round to the nearest tenth of an inch.

12 in.

x

Read and Understand

1. What information is given to you in the problem? _____

2. What additional information is given to you in the picture? _____

_____

Plan and Solve

3. Write an expression for the area of the picture only. _____

4. Write an expression for the total area enclosed by the frame. _____

5. What is 75% of the total area enclosed by the frame? _____

6. Write and solve an equation to find the dimensions of the square picture that would make the area of the picture equal to 75% of the total area enclosed by the square frame. _____

Look Back and Check

7. Use the dimensions you found in Step 6 to check if the area of the picture is 75% of the total area enclosed by the square frame. Explain why it is not exactly 75%.

_____

Solve Another Problem

8. What would the dimensions of the square picture be that would make the area of the picture equal to 60% of the total area enclosed by the square frame?

_____

Practice 9-5

Factoring to Solve Quadratic Equations

Use the Zero-Product Property to solve each equation.

1. $(x + 5)(x - 3) = 0$ **2.** $(x - 2)(x + 9) = 0$ **3.** $(b - 12)(b + 12) = 0$

4. $(2n + 3)(n - 4) = 0$ **5.** $(x + 7)(4x - 5) = 0$ **6.** $(2x + 7)(2x - 7) = 0$

7. $(3x - 7)(2x + 1) = 0$ **8.** $(8y - 3)(4y + 1) = 0$ **9.** $(5x + 6)(4x + 5) = 0$

Solve by factoring.

10. $x^2 + 5x + 6 = 0$ **11.** $b^2 - 7b - 18 = 0$ **12.** $r^2 - 4 = 0$

13. $x^2 + 8x - 20 = 0$ **14.** $y^2 + 14y + 13 = 0$ **15.** $s^2 - 3s - 10 = 0$

16. $x^2 + 7x = 8$ **17.** $x^2 = 25$ **18.** $h^2 + 10h = -21$

19. $2t^2 + 8t - 64 = 0$ **20.** $3a^2 - 36a + 81 = 0$ **21.** $5x^2 - 45 = 0$

22. $2a^2 - a - 21 = 0$ **23.** $3n^2 - 11n + 10 = 0$ **24.** $2x^2 - 7x - 9 = 0$

25. $2n^2 - 5n = 12$ **26.** $3m^2 - 5m = -2$ **27.** $5s^2 - 17s = -6$

28. $6m^2 = 13m + 28$ **29.** $4a^2 - 4a = 15$ **30.** $4r^2 = r + 3$

31. Suppose you are building a storage box of volume 4368 in.^{3}. The length of the box will be 24 in. The height of the box will be 1 in. more than its width. Find the height and width of the box.

32. A banner is in the shape of a right triangle of area 63 in.^{2}. The height of the banner is 4 in. less than twice the width of the banner. Find the height and width of the banner.

33. A rectangular poster has an area of 190 in.^{2}. The height of the poster is 1 in. less than twice its width. Find the dimensions of the poster.

34. A diver is standing on a platform 24 ft above the pool. He jumps from the platform with an initial upward velocity of 8 ft/s. Use the formula $h = -16t^2 + vt + s$, where h is his height above the water, t is the time, v is his starting upward velocity, and s is his starting height. How long will it take for him to hit the water?

Solve each equation.

35. $(x - 9)(x + 8) = 0$ **36.** $x^2 - 9x - 10 = 0$ **37.** $(c - 21)(c + 21) = 0$

38. $(x - 12)(5x - 13) = 0$ **39.** $2a^2 - 21a - 65 = 0$ **40.** $x^2 + 6x - 91 = 0$

41. $a^2 + 6a - 72 = 0$ **42.** $4x^2 + 8x - 21 = 0$ **43.** $20d^2 - 82d + 80 = 0$

44. $3n^2 + 12n - 288 = 0$ **45.** $2s^2 - 13s - 24 = 0$ **46.** $x^2 + 5x = 150$

47. $3c^2 + 8c = 3$ **48.** $30a^2 + 121a - 21 = 0$ **49.** $c^2 - 81 = 0$

50. $x^2 + 306 = -35x$ **51.** $x^2 = 121$ **52.** $x^2 - 21x + 108 = 0$

Algebra 1 Lesson 9-5   **357**

9-5 • Guided Problem Solving

GPS **Exercise 33**

Suppose you throw a baseball into the air with an initial upward velocity of 29 ft/s and an initial height of 6 ft. The formula $h = -16t^2 + 29t + 6$ gives the ball's height h in feet at time t in seconds.

a. The ball's height h is 0 when it is on the ground. Find the number of seconds that pass before the ball lands by solving $0 = -16t^2 + 29t + 6$.

b. Graph the related function for the equation in part (a). Use your graph to estimate the maximum height of the ball.

Read and Understand

1. What information about the baseball is given to you in the problem? _____

   _____

2. Explain what each variable in the formula represents. _____

   _____

Plan and Solve

3. What method will you use to solve the quadratic equation $0 = -16t^2 + 29t + 6$? _____

   _____

4. Solve the equation $0 = -16t^2 + 29t + 6$ to find the number of
   seconds that pass before the ball lands. _____

5. What is the related function for the equation $0 = -16t^2 + 29t + 6$? _____

6. Graph the related function from Step 5 and use your graph to estimate the maximum height of the ball.

Look Back and Check

7. What is the time when the ball reaches the maximum height? Substitute that value for t in the equation to see if your height estimate is reasonable.

   _____

Solve Another Problem

8. The formula $h = -16t^2 + 45t + 9$ also gives the ball's height h in feet at time t in seconds. How many seconds pass before the ball lands on the ground?

   _____

Practice 9-6

Find the value of n such that each expression is a perfect square trinomial.

1. $x^2 - 14x + n$

2. $x^2 - \frac{2}{9}x + n$

3. $x^2 - \frac{4}{9}x + n$

4. $x^2 - \frac{2}{6}x + n$

Solve each equation by completing the square. If necessary, round to the nearest hundredth.

5. $x^2 - 4x = 5$

6. $x^2 - x - 2 = 0$

7. $x^2 - 6x = 10$

8. $x^2 + 4x + 4 = 0$

9. $x^2 - 3x = 18$

10. $x^2 - 8x - 4 = 0$

11. $x^2 - 6x = 0$

12. $x^2 - 6x = 8$

13. $x^2 - 7x = 0$

14. $x^2 + 4x - 12 = 0$

15. $x^2 + 11x + 10 = 0$

16. $x^2 + 2x = 15$

17. $x^2 - 8x = 9$

18. $x^2 + 5x = -6$

19. $x^2 - 2x = 120$

20. $x^2 - 22x = -105$

21. $2x^2 = 3x + 9$

22. $2x^2 + 8x - 10 = 0$

23. $2x^2 - 3x - 2 = 0$

24. $2x^2 + 12x - 32 = 0$

25. $3x^2 + 17x - 6 = 0$

26. $2x^2 - x - 28 = 0$

27. $3x^2 - 4x + 1 = 0$

28. $2x^2 - 5x - 3 = 0$

29. $6x^2 - 2x = 28$

30. $2x^2 - 16x = -30$

31. $4x^2 = -2x + 12$

32. $9x^2 + 6x = 3$

33. $10x^2 + 3x = 4$

34. $12x^2 - 29x + 15 = 0$

What term do you need to add to each side to complete the square?

35. $x^2 + 4x = 10$

36. $2x^2 + 4x = 8$

37. $3x^2 + 9x = 6$

38. $2x^2 + 5x = 7$

39. $5b^2 + 7b = 10$

40. $3y^2 + 8y = 4$

9-6 • Guided Problem Solving

GPS **Exercise 35**

Suppose you want to enclose a rectangular garden plot against a house using fencing on three sides, as shown. Assume you have 50 ft of fencing material and want to create a garden with an area of 150 ft².

a. Let w = the width. Write an expression for the length of the plot.
b. Write and solve an equation for the area of the plot. Round to the nearest tenth of a foot.
c. What dimensions should the garden have?
d. **Critical Thinking** Find the area of the garden by using the dimensions you found in part (b). Does the area equal 150 ft²? Explain.

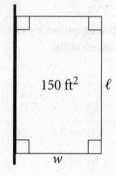

Read and Understand

1. What information is given to you in the problem? _____
_____

2. How many sides of the garden must be fenced in? _____

Plan and Solve

3. Write an expression for the length of the plot. _____

4. Write and solve an equation for the area of the plot. Round to the nearest foot.
_____
_____

5. What dimensions should the garden have? _____

Look Back and Check

6. Find the area of the garden by using the dimensions you found in part (b). Does the area equal 150 ft²? Explain. _____
_____

Solve Another Problem

7. Suppose you decide to move your garden away from the house, so you now have to use 50 ft of fencing for four sides. The length of the garden must be twice as long as the width. If the area is now 139 ft², what dimensions should the garden have?
_____
_____

Practice 9-7

Using the Quadratic Formula

Use the quadratic formula to solve each equation. If the equation has no solutions, write *no solution*. If necessary, round to the nearest hundredth.

1. $x^2 + 8x + 5 = 0$

2. $x^2 - 36 = 0$

3. $d^2 - 4d - 96 = 0$

4. $a^2 - 3a - 154 = 0$

5. $4p^2 - 12p - 91 = 0$

6. $5m^2 + 9m = 126$

7. $r^2 - 35r + 70 = 0$

8. $y^2 + 6y - 247 = 0$

9. $x^2 + 12x - 40 = 0$

10. $4n^2 - 81 = 0$

11. $x^2 + 13x + 30 = 0$

12. $a^2 - a = 132$

13. $6w^2 - 23w + 7 = 0$

14. $4x^2 + 33x = 27$

15. $7s^2 - 7 = 0$

16. $x^2 + 5x - 90 = 0$

17. $5b^2 - 20 = 0$

18. $4x^2 - 3x + 6 = 0$

19. $6h^2 + 77h - 13 = 0$

20. $5y^2 = 17y + 12$

21. $g^2 - 15g = 54$

22. $27f^2 = 12$

23. $4x^2 - 52x + 133 = 0$

24. $x^2 + 36x + 60 = 0$

25. $a^2 - 2a - 360 = 0$

26. $x^2 + 10x + 40 = 0$

27. $t^2 - 10t = 39$

28. $4x^2 + 7x - 9 = 0$

29. $2c^2 - 39c + 135 = 0$

30. $4x^2 + 33x + 340 = 0$

31. $m^2 - 40m + 100 = 0$

32. $8x^2 + 25x + 19 = 0$

33. $36w^2 - 289 = 0$

34. $4d^2 + 29d - 60 = 0$

35. $4z^2 + 43z + 108 = 0$

36. $3x^2 - 19x + 40 = 0$

37. $14x^2 = 56$

38. $32x^2 - 18 = 0$

39. $r^2 + r - 650 = 0$

40. $2y^2 = 39y - 17$

41. $5a^2 - 9a + 5 = 0$

42. $x^2 = 9x + 120$

43. $8h^2 - 38h + 9 = 0$

44. $20x^2 = 245$

45. $9h^2 - 72h = -119$

46. $x^2 + 3x + 8 = 0$

47. $6m^2 - 13m = 19$

48. $9x^2 - 81 = 0$

49. $4s^2 + 8s = 221$

50. $6p^2 + 25p - 119 = 0$

51. $2s^2 - 59s + 17 = 0$

52. A rectangular painting has dimensions x and $x + 10$. The painting is in a frame 2 in. wide. The total area of the picture and the frame is 900 in.^{2}. What are the dimensions of the painting?

53. A ball is thrown upward from a height of 15 ft with an inital upward velocity of 5 ft/s. Use the formula $h = -16t^2 + vt + s$ to find how long it will take for the ball to hit the ground.

54. Your community wants to put a square fountain in a park. Around the fountain will be a sidewalk that is 3.5 ft wide. The total area that the fountain and sidewalk can be is 700 ft^2. What are the dimensions of the fountain?

55. The Garys have a triangular pennant of area 420 in.^{2} flying from the flagpole in their yard. The height of the triangle is 10 in. less than 5 times the base of the triangle. What are the dimensions of the pennant?

9-7 • Guided Problem Solving

GPS Exercise 36

Find the base and height of the triangle below. If necessary, round to the nearest hundredth.

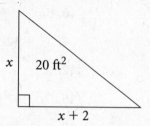

x 20 ft²

$x + 2$

Read and Understand

1. What is the formula for finding the area of a triangle? _____

2. What information can be found from the figure? _____

Plan and Solve

3. Write an equation for the area of the triangle. _____

4. If the area is 20 ft², write your equation in Step 3 in standard form. _____

5. Solve your equation in Step 4. _____

6. What are the base and height of the triangle? _____

Look Back and Check

7. Use the base and height you found in Step 6 to find the area of the triangle. What should it be? Explain.

_____

_____

Solve Another Problem

8. Find the length and width of the rectangle to the right.

_____

15 ft² x

$x + 3$

Practice 9-8

Find the number of solutions of each equation.

1. $x^2 + 6x + 10 = 0$

2. $x^2 - 4x - 1 = 0$

3. $x^2 + 6x + 9 = 0$

4. $x^2 - 8x + 15 = 0$

5. $x^2 - 5x + 7 = 0$

6. $x^2 - 4x + 5 = 0$

7. $3x^2 - 18x + 27 = 0$

8. $4x^2 - 8 = 0$

9. $-5x^2 - 10x = 0$

10. $-x^2 = 4x + 6$

11. $4x^2 = 9x - 3$

12. $8x^2 + 2 = 8x$

13. $7x^2 + 16x + 11 = 0$

14. $12x^2 - 11x - 2 = 0$

15. $-9x^2 - 25x + 20 = 0$

16. $16x^2 + 8x = -1$

17. $-16x^2 + 11x = 11$

18. $12x^2 - 12x = -3$

19. $0.2x^2 + 4.5x - 2.8 = 0$

20. $-2.8x^2 + 3.1x = -0.5$

21. $0.5x^2 + 0.6x = 0$

22. $1.5x^2 - 15x + 2.5 = 0$

23. $-3x^2 + 27x = -40$

24. $2.1x^2 + 4.2 = 0$

25. One of the games at a carnival involves trying to ring a bell with a ball by hitting a lever that propels the ball into the air. The height of the ball is modeled by the equation $h = -16t^2 + 39t$. If the bell is 25 ft above the ground, will it be hit by the ball?

26. You are placing a rectangular picture on a square poster board. You can enlarge the picture to any size. The area of the poster board not covered by the picture is modeled by the equation $A = -x^2 - 10x + 300$. Is it possible for the area not covered by the picture to be 100 in.^{2}?

27. The equation $h = -16t^2 + 58t + 3$ models the height of a baseball t seconds after it has been hit.

   a. Was the height of the baseball ever 40 ft?

   b. Was the height of the baseball ever 60 ft?

28. A firefighter is on the fifth floor of an office building. She needs to throw a rope into the window above her on the seventh floor. The function $h = -16t^2 + 36t$ models how high above her she is able to throw a rope. If she needs to throw the rope 40 ft above her to reach the seventh-floor window, will the rope get to the window?

Find the number of x-intercepts of the related function of each equation.

29. $-16 = x^2 + 10x$

30. $-5 = x^2 + 3x$

31. $7 = x^2 - 2x$

32. $0 = 3x^2 - 3$

33. $0 = 2x^2 + x$

34. $-1 = 3x^2 + 2x$

35. $4 = x^2 - 8x$

36. $-64 = x^2 - 16x$

37. $6 = -2x^2 - 5x$

38. $2 = -4x^2 - 5x$

39. $36 = -x^2 + 12x$

40. $6 = -5x^2 + 11x$

9-8 • Guided Problem Solving

GPS **Exercise 31**

A software company is producing a new computer application. The equation $S = p(54 - 0.75p)$ relates price p in dollars to total sales S in thousands of dollars.

  a. Write the equation in standard form.
  b. Use the discriminant to determine if it is possible for the company to earn $1,000,000 in sales.
  c. According to the model, what price would generate the greatest sales?
  d. **Critical Thinking** Total sales S decrease as p increases beyond the value in part (c). Why does this make sense in the given situation? Explain.

Read and Understand

1. Explain what the equation describes. _____

_____

2. What do the variables S and p represent? _____

Plan and Solve

3. Write the equation in standard form. _____

4. Use the discriminant to determine if it is possible for the company to earn $1,000,000 in sales. _____

5. According to the model, what price would generate the greatest sales? _____

6. Total sales S decrease as p increases beyond the value in part (c). Why does this make sense in the given situation? Explain. _____

_____

Look Back and Check

7. Graph the equation. Use your graph to check the reasonableness of the price that would generate the greatest sales.

Solve Another Problem

8. The height of a firework can be modeled by the equation $h = t(256 - 16t)$, which relates the time t in seconds since the firework was released to height h in feet.

  a. Write the equation in standard form. _____

  b. Use the discriminant to determine if it is possible for the firework to reach 1000 ft. _____

  c. According to the model, at what time would the firework be at its highest? _____

9A: Graphic Organizer

For use before Lesson 9-1

Study Skill To help remember formulas and other important information, use a mnemonic. A mnemonic is a memory device to help us associate new information with something familiar. For example, to remember a formula or equation, change it into something meaningful. To remember the metric terms kilo, hecto, deka, deci, centi, and milli in order, use the first letter of each metric term to represent a word, such as *k*angaroo *h*ops *d*own, *d*rinking *c*hocolate *m*ilk. The key is to create your own; then you won't forget them.

Write your answers.

1. What is the chapter title? _____

2. Find the Table of Contents page for this chapter at the front of the book. Name four topics you will study in this chapter.

   _____   _____

   _____   _____

3. Complete the graphic organizer as you work through the chapter.
   1. Write the title of the chapter in the center oval.
   2. When you begin a lesson, write the name of the lesson in a rectangle.
   3. When you complete that lesson, write a skill or key concept from that lesson in the outer oval linked to that rectangle.
   Continue with steps 2 and 3 clockwise around the graphic organizer.

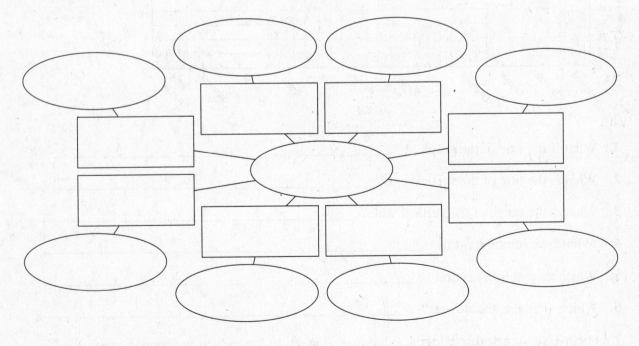

9B: Reading Comprehension

Study Skill Many mathematical applications are related to graphs. Many times you are required to interpret information given in graphs. Being able to identify the specific parts of a graph will help you to answer questions regarding the graph.

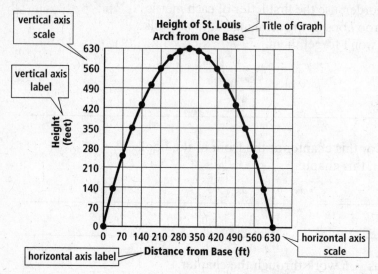

In Exercises 1–6, refer to the graph shown below.

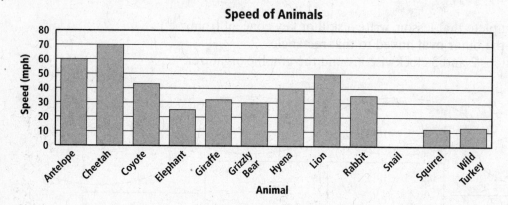

1. What is the title of the graph? _____

2. What is the title of the vertical axis? _____

3. What is the range of the vertical scale? _____

4. What type of graph is this? _____

5. Which animal is the fastest? _____

6. Which animal is the slowest? _____

7. **High-Use Academic Words** What does it mean to *interpret* as mentioned in the study skill?

   a. understand   **b.** verify

9C: Reading/Writing Math Symbols

For use after Lesson 9-7

Study Skill When interpreting mathematical statements, be sure you use the correct words or symbols. Check your written or numerical expressions to make sure you wrote the correct symbols or words.

The graphs below represent the solutions of different linear systems. Some are equations and some are inequalities. The graphs intersect, are parallel, or coincide. Match the graphs with the appropriate system, without actually graphing the systems, by looking for symbols and other indicators (such as slopes and *y*-intercepts).

1. $\begin{cases} x + y = 4 \\ 2x - y = 2 \end{cases}$

   A.
   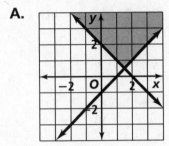

2. $\begin{cases} 3x - 2y = -2 \\ 3x - 2y = 6 \end{cases}$

   B.
   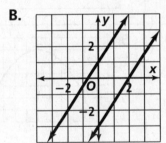

3. $\begin{cases} 2x - 4y \geq 4 \\ x + y < 0 \end{cases}$

   C.
   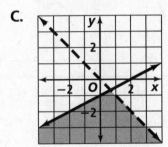

4. $\begin{cases} x + y \geq 2 \\ x - y \leq 1 \end{cases}$

   D.
   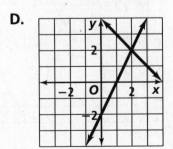

9D: Visual Vocabulary Practice

For use after Lesson 9-8

Study Skill Math symbols give us a way to express complex ideas in a small space.

Concept List

completing the square	discriminant	factor
linear function	parabola	perfect square trinomial
quadratic formula	square root	Zero-Product Property

Write the concept that best describes each exercise. Choose from the concept list above.

1. $x = \dfrac{-b \pm \sqrt{b^2 - 4ac}}{2a}$ _____	**2.** $y = mx + b$ _____	**3.** $x^2 - 5x - 14$ $(x - 7)(x + 2)$ _____
4. The number a if $a^2 = b$. _____	**5.** 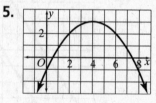 _____	**6.** $x^2 - 12x + n$ $x^2 - 12x + 36$ $(x - 6)^2$ _____
7. For every real number a and b, if $ab = 0$ then $a = 0$ or $b = 0$. _____	**8.** $4x^2 - 4x + 1$ _____	**9.** $b^2 - 4ac$ _____

9E: Vocabulary Check

Study Skill Strengthen your vocabulary. Use these pages and add cues and summaries by applying the Cornell Notetaking style.

Write the definition for each word at the right. To check your work, fold the paper back along the dotted line to see the correct answers.

_____

_____

_____

Quadratic function

_____

_____

_____

Axis of Symmetry

_____

_____

_____

Vertex

_____

_____

_____

Standard form of a quadratic equation

_____

_____

_____

Zeros of a quadratic function

_____

_____

9E: Vocabulary Check (continued)

For use after Lesson 9-6

Write the vocabulary word for each definition. To check your work, fold the paper forward along the dotted line to see the correct answers.

A function that can be written in the form $y = ax^2 + bx + c$.

_____

The fold or line that divides a curve into two matching halves.

_____

The highest or lowest point of a parabola.

_____

A quadratic equation written in the form $ax^2 + bx + c = 0$.

_____

The solutions of the quadratic equation.

_____

9F: Vocabulary Review

For use with Chapter Review

Study Skill When taking notes, make your original notes as easy to read as possible. The amount of time needed to interpret messy notes would be better spent rereading and thinking about them.

Fill in the blanks with the word(s) that best completes the sentence.

1. The function $y = ax^2 + bx + c$ is a _____ function.

2. The function $Ax + By = C$ is written in _____ form.

3. The _____ of a monomial is the sum of the exponents of its variables.

4. When solving a system of linear equations by graphing, any point where all the lines intersect is the _____.

5. A term that has no variable is known as a _____.

6. The "fold" or line that divides a curve into two matching halves is called the _____.

7. The expression $b^2 - 4ac$ is known as the _____.

8. The _____ of a line is its rate of vertical change over horizontal change.

9. The equation $4(5 - 2 + 3) = 4(5) - 4(2) + 4(3)$ represents the _____ property.

10. A relation that assigns exactly one value in the range to each value in the domain is called a _____.

11. Two or more linear equations together form a _____.

12. When a parabola opens upward, the y-coordinate of the vertex is a _____ value of the function.

13. The point at which a parabola intersects the axis of symmetry is called the _____.

Practice 10-1

Simplifying Radicals

Simplify each radical expression.

1. $\sqrt{32}$

2. $\sqrt{22} \cdot \sqrt{8}$

3. $\sqrt{147}$

4. $\sqrt{\dfrac{17}{144}}$

5. $\sqrt{a^2b^5}$

6. $\dfrac{2}{\sqrt{6}}$

7. $\sqrt{80}$

8. $\sqrt{27}$

9. $\dfrac{\sqrt{256}}{\sqrt{32}}$

10. $\dfrac{8}{\sqrt{7}}$

11. $\sqrt{12x^4}$

12. $\dfrac{\sqrt{96}}{\sqrt{12}}$

13. $\sqrt{200}$

14. $\sqrt{\dfrac{12}{225}}$

15. $\sqrt{15} \cdot \sqrt{6}$

16. $\sqrt{120}$

17. $\dfrac{4}{\sqrt{2a}}$

18. $\left(3\sqrt{2}\right)^3$

19. $\sqrt{250}$

20. $\dfrac{\sqrt{65}}{\sqrt{13}}$

21. $\sqrt{84}$

22. $\sqrt{\dfrac{18}{225}}$

23. $\sqrt{48s^3}$

24. $3\sqrt{24}$

25. $\sqrt{15} \cdot \sqrt{35}$

26. $\sqrt{160}$

27. $\dfrac{6}{\sqrt{3}}$

28. $\dfrac{\sqrt{48n^6}}{\sqrt{6n^3}}$

29. $\sqrt{136}$

30. $\sqrt{\dfrac{27x^2}{256}}$

31. $\sqrt{m^3n^2}$

32. $\dfrac{\sqrt{180}}{\sqrt{9}}$

33. $\sqrt{18} \cdot \sqrt{8}$

34. $\left(10\sqrt{3}\right)^2$

35. $\sqrt{\dfrac{17}{64}}$

36. $\sqrt{50}$

37. $\sqrt{48}$

38. $\sqrt{20}$

39. $\sqrt{8}$

40. $\sqrt{25x^2}$

41. $\sqrt{\dfrac{7}{9}}$

42. $\sqrt{\dfrac{13}{81}}$

43. $\dfrac{\sqrt{48}}{\sqrt{8}}$

44. $\dfrac{\sqrt{120}}{\sqrt{10}}$

45. $\dfrac{5}{\sqrt{2}}$

46. $\sqrt{75}$

47. $\sqrt{300}$

48. $\sqrt{49a^3}$

49. $\sqrt{125}$

50. $\sqrt{28x^4}$

51. $\dfrac{7}{\sqrt{3}}$

52. $\sqrt{\dfrac{15}{49}}$

53. $\dfrac{\sqrt{60}}{\sqrt{12}}$

54. $\dfrac{3}{\sqrt{3}}$

55. $\dfrac{4}{\sqrt{8}}$

56. $\sqrt{72x^3}$

57. $\sqrt{50y^3}$

58. $\sqrt{45x^2y^3}$

59. $\sqrt{\dfrac{44x^3}{9x}}$

60. $\dfrac{\sqrt{4}}{\sqrt{3x}}$

61. $6\sqrt{20}$

62. $\sqrt{ab^3}$

63. $\sqrt{a^5b^6}$

64. $12\sqrt{60x^2}$

65. $\left(2\sqrt{3}\right)^2$

66. $\sqrt{12} \cdot \sqrt{27}$

67. $\left(7\sqrt{5}\right)^2$

68. $\sqrt{14} \cdot \sqrt{8}$

69. $\left(5\sqrt{5}\right)^2$

70. $\sqrt{8x^6y^7}$

71. $\sqrt{16a^3} \cdot \sqrt{5a^2}$

72. $\sqrt{8} \cdot \sqrt{7}$

73. $\sqrt{3x} \cdot \sqrt{5x}$

74. $2\sqrt{5} \cdot 2\sqrt{5}$

75. $4\sqrt{3} \cdot 2\sqrt{2}$

76. $6\sqrt{3} \cdot 7\sqrt{8}$

77. $\dfrac{10}{\sqrt{x}}$

78. $\dfrac{\sqrt{9}}{\sqrt{2x}}$

79. $\dfrac{4}{\sqrt{20}}$

80. $\dfrac{\sqrt{12x}}{\sqrt{27x}}$

81. $\dfrac{3\sqrt{7}}{\sqrt{20x}}$

82. $\dfrac{4\sqrt{5}}{\sqrt{8y}}$

10-1 • Guided Problem Solving

GPS **Exercise 74**

A square picture on the front page of a newspaper occupies an area of 24 in.^{2}.

   a. Find the length of each side in simplest radical form.
   b. Calculate the length of each side to the nearest hundredth of an inch.

Read and Understand

1. What formula will you use to find the area of a square? _____

2. What is simplest radical form? _____

Plan and Solve

3. Draw a picture to illustrate this situation.

4. Label the picture with the given information and identify the unknown.

5. Write and solve an equation that relates the side length and area.

6. Find the length of each side in simplest radical form. _____

7. Calculate the length of each side to the nearest hundredth of an inch. _____

Look Back and Check

8. Verify the reasonableness of your answers in Steps 6 and 7 by squaring each answer to see if the area is 24 in.^{2}. Explain why the square of your decimal answer in Step 7 is not exactly 24 in.^{2}.

   _____

   _____

Solve Another Problem

9. The area of a square puzzle is 120 cm^2. What is the length of a side? _____

Practice 10-2

The Pythagorean Theorem

Use the triangle at the right. Find the length of the missing side. If necessary, round to the nearest tenth.

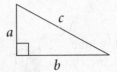

1. $a = 12, b = 35, c = \blacksquare$

2. $a = 10, b = \blacksquare, c = 26$

3. $a = 11, b = \blacksquare, c = 61$

4. $a = 36, b = 15, c = \blacksquare$

5. $a = 8, b = 15, c = \blacksquare$

6. $a = \blacksquare, b = 24, c = 40$

7. $a = 18, b = \blacksquare, c = 35$

8. $a = 17, b = \blacksquare, c = 49$

9. $a = 42, b = 37, c = \blacksquare$

10. $a = \blacksquare, b = 80, c = 90$

11. $a = 8, b = 8, c = \blacksquare$

12. $a = 19, b = \blacksquare, c = 26$

13. $a = \blacksquare, b = 27, c = 33$

14. $a = \blacksquare, b = 13, c = 24$

15. $a = 9, b = \blacksquare, c = 13$

16. $a = 19, b = 45, c = \blacksquare$

17. $a = \blacksquare, b = 24, c = 39$

18. $a = 14, b = 14, c = \blacksquare$

Determine whether the given lengths can be sides of a right triangle.

19. 20, 21, 29

20. 16, 30, 34

21. 24, 60, 66

22. 23, 18, 14

23. 10, 24, 28

24. 45, 28, 53

25. $\frac{4}{5}, \frac{3}{5}, 1$

26. $\frac{2}{3}, \frac{4}{3}, \frac{1}{3}$

27. 3.5, 4.4, 5.5

28. 10.5, 11.3, 13.8

29. 3.3, 6.5, 5.6

30. 24, 70, 74

31. 4.2, 7.0, 5.6

32. 5.2, 6.5, 3.9

33. 2.1, 3.5, 2.8

34. 4.8, 7.5, 5.4

35. 7.5, 4.3, 6.7

36. $\frac{1}{9}, \frac{1}{15}, \frac{1}{18}$

37. $\frac{1}{2}, \frac{6}{5}, \frac{13}{10}$

38. $\frac{1}{5}, \frac{1}{4}, \frac{1}{3}$

Find the missing length to the nearest tenth.

39. A ladder is 25 ft long. The ladder needs to reach to a window that is 24 ft above the ground. How far away from the building should the bottom of the ladder be placed?

40. Suppose you are making a sail in the shape of a right triangle for a sailboat. The length of the longest side of the sail is 65 ft. The sail is to be 63 ft high. What is the length of the third side of the sail?

41. Suppose you leave your house and travel 13 mi due west. Then you travel 3 mi due south. How far are you from your house?

42. A wire is run between the tips of two poles. One pole is 23 ft taller than the other pole. The poles are 37 ft apart. How long does the wire need to be to reach between the two poles?

43. A 20-ft-long wire is used to support a television antenna. The wire is connected to the antenna 15 ft above the ground. How far away from the base of the tower will the other end of the wire be located?

10-2 • Guided Problem Solving

GPS **Exercise 41**

Solar cars use panels built out of photovoltaic cells, which convert sunlight into electricity. Consider a car like the one shown. Not counting the driver's "bubble," the panels form a rectangle.

a. The length of the rectangle is 13 ft and the diagonal is 14.7 ft. Find the width. Round to the nearest tenth of a foot.

b. Find the area of the rectangle.

c. The panels produce a maximum power of about 11 watts/ft^2. Find the maximum power produced by the panels on the car. Round to the nearest watt.

Read and Understand

1. Make a sketch and label it with the known information.

Plan and Solve

2. What relationship can be used to determine the width of the rectangle? _____

3. What is the width of the rectangle rounded to the nearest tenth of a foot? _____

4. Find the area of the rectangle. _____

5. The panels produce a maximum power of about 11 watts/ft^2. Find the maximum power produced by the panels on the car, rounded to the nearest watt. _____

Look Back and Check

6. Check the reasonableness of your answer by verifying that your numbers for the rectangle's dimensions satisfy the Pythagorean Theorem.

Solve Another Problem

7. If the maximum power of the panels is increased to 15 watts/ft^2, what will be the maximum power produced by the panels on the car? _____

Practice 10-3

Operations With Radical Expressions

Simplify each expression.

1. $3\sqrt{7} + 5\sqrt{7}$

2. $10\sqrt{4} - \sqrt{4}$

3. $4\sqrt{2}(2 + 2\sqrt{3})$

4. $\sqrt{45} + 2\sqrt{5}$

5. $12\sqrt{11} + 7\sqrt{11}$

6. $\sqrt{2}(2\sqrt{3} - 4\sqrt{2})$

7. $\sqrt{28} + \sqrt{63}$

8. $3\sqrt{6} - 8\sqrt{6}$

9. $\sqrt{3}(\sqrt{6} - \sqrt{12})$

10. $\sqrt{18} - \sqrt{50}$

11. $4\sqrt{2} + 2\sqrt{8}$

12. $13\sqrt{15} - 11\sqrt{15}$

13. $3(8\sqrt{3} - 7)$

14. $8(2\sqrt{5} + 5\sqrt{2})$

15. $17\sqrt{21} - 12\sqrt{21}$

16. $\sqrt{6}(7 + 3\sqrt{3})$

17. $8(4 - 3\sqrt{2})$

18. $2\sqrt{12} + 6\sqrt{27}$

19. $19\sqrt{3} + \sqrt{12}$

20. $8\sqrt{26} + 10\sqrt{26}$

21. $\sqrt{10}(3 - 2\sqrt{6})$

22. $9\sqrt{2} - \sqrt{50}$

23. $10\sqrt{13} - 7\sqrt{13}$

24. $12\sqrt{6} - 4\sqrt{24}$

25. $5\sqrt{7} + \sqrt{28}$

26. $8\sqrt{13} - 12\sqrt{13}$

27. $13\sqrt{40} + 6\sqrt{10}$

28. $-3\sqrt{3}(\sqrt{6} + \sqrt{3})$

29. $12\sqrt{29} - 15\sqrt{29}$

30. $10\sqrt{6} - 2\sqrt{6}$

31. $8\sqrt{3} - \sqrt{75}$

32. $3\sqrt{6}(2\sqrt{3} + \sqrt{6})$

33. $17\sqrt{35} + 2\sqrt{35}$

34. $\sqrt{19} + 4\sqrt{19}$

35. $12\sqrt{9} - 4\sqrt{9}$

36. $\sqrt{8}(\sqrt{2} - 7)$

37. $\dfrac{1}{\sqrt{2} - \sqrt{3}}$

38. $\dfrac{5}{\sqrt{7} - \sqrt{3}}$

39. $\dfrac{3}{\sqrt{5} + 5}$

40. $(\sqrt{6} - 3)^2$

41. $(3\sqrt{5} + \sqrt{5})^2$

42. $\dfrac{7}{\sqrt{2} - \sqrt{7}}$

43. $\dfrac{3 - \sqrt{6}}{5 - 2\sqrt{6}}$

44. $\dfrac{-12}{\sqrt{6} - 3}$

45. $\dfrac{2\sqrt{3} - \sqrt{6}}{5\sqrt{3} + 2\sqrt{6}}$

Solve each exercise by using the golden ratio $(1 + \sqrt{5}) : 2$.

46. The ratio of the height : width of a window is equal to the golden ratio. The width of the door is 36 in. Find the height of the door. Express your answer in simplest radical form and in inches.

47. The ratio of the length : width of a flower garden is equal to the golden ratio. The width of the garden is 14 ft. Find the length of the garden. Express your answer is simplest radical form and in feet.

48. The ratio of the width : height of the front side of a building is equal to the golden ratio. The height of the building is 40 ft. Find the width of the building. Express your answer in simplest radical form and in feet.

10-3 • Guided Problem Solving

GPS Exercise 53

You can make a box kite like the one at the right in the shape
of a rectangular solid. The opening at each end of the kite is
a square.

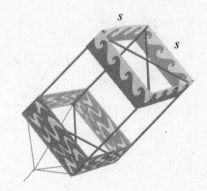

a. Suppose the sides of the square are 2 ft long. How long
are the diagonal struts used for bracing?

b. Suppose each side of the square has length *s*. Find the
length of the diagonal struts in terms of *s*. Write your
answer in simplest form.

Read and Understand

1. What information are you given in the problem? _____

2. What relationship is there between the side lengths and the diagonal? _____

Plan and Solve

3. Write and solve an equation that relates the side lengths of the square and the diagonal.

   _____

4. How long are the diagonal struts used for bracing? _____

5. If each side of the square has length *s*, find
   the length of the diagonal struts in terms of s^2. _____

6. Write your answer from Step 5 in simplest form. _____

Look Back and Check

7. Substitute the answer you found for the length of the diagonal struts into the equation you used
   in step 3 to check the reasonableness of your answer.

   _____

Solve Another Problem

8. A diagonal board is used to brace a wall that measures 8 ft by 8 ft. How long must the board be?

   _____

Practice 10-4

Solve each radical equation. Check your solution. If there is no solution, write *no solution*.

1. $\sqrt{x} + 3 = 11$

2. $\sqrt{x + 2} = \sqrt{3x - 6}$

3. $x = \sqrt{24 - 10x}$

4. $\sqrt{4x} - 7 = 1$

5. $\sqrt{x} = \sqrt{4x - 12}$

6. $x = \sqrt{11x - 28}$

7. $\sqrt{x} = 12$

8. $x = \sqrt{12x - 32}$

9. $x = \sqrt{13x - 40}$

10. $\sqrt{3x + 5} = \sqrt{x + 1}$

11. $\sqrt{x + 3} = 5$

12. $\sqrt{6x - 4} = \sqrt{4x + 6}$

13. $2 = \sqrt{x + 6}$

14. $x = \sqrt{2 - x}$

15. $\sqrt{4x + 2} = \sqrt{x + 14}$

16. $\sqrt{x + 8} = 9$

17. $x = \sqrt{7x + 8}$

18. $\sqrt{3x + 8} = \sqrt{2x + 12}$

19. $\sqrt{2x + 3} = 5$

20. $\sqrt{3x + 13} = \sqrt{7x - 3}$

21. $x = \sqrt{6 + 5x}$

22. $\sqrt{3x} - 5 = 4$

23. $\sqrt{3x + 4} = \sqrt{5x}$

24. $x = \sqrt{x - 12}$

25. $\sqrt{x - 4} + 3 = 9$

26. $x = \sqrt{8x + 20}$

27. $12 = \sqrt{6x}$

28. $x = \sqrt{60 - 7x}$

29. $\sqrt{x + 14} = \sqrt{6x - 1}$

30. $\sqrt{5x - 7} = \sqrt{6x + 11}$

31. $7 + \sqrt{2x} = 3$

32. $\sqrt{x + 56} = x$

33. $5 + \sqrt{x + 4} = 12$

34. The equation $d = \frac{1}{2}at^2$ gives the distance d in ft that an object travels from rest while accelerating, where a is the acceleration and t is the time.

a. How far has an object traveled in 4 s when the acceleration is 5 ft/s^2?

b. How long does it take an object to travel 100 ft when the acceleration is 8 ft/s^2?

35. The equation $v = 20\sqrt{t + 273}$ relates the speed v, in m/s, to the air temperature t in Celsius degrees.

a. Find the temperature when the speed of sound is 340 m/s.

b. Find the temperature when the speed of sound is 320 m/s.

36. The equation $V = \sqrt{\frac{Fr}{m}}$ gives the speed V in m/s of an object moving in a horizontal circle, where F is centripetal force, r is radius, and m is mass of the object.

a. Find r when $F = 6$ N, $m = 2$ kg, and $V = 3$ m/s.

b. Find F when $r = 1$ m, $m = 3$ kg, and $V = 2$ m/s.

10-4 • Guided Problem Solving

GPS **Exercise 47**

a. The equation $v = 8\sqrt{h - 2r}$ gives the velocity v in feet per second of a car at the top of the loop of a roller coaster. Find the radius of the loop when the hill is 150 ft high and the velocity of the car is 30 ft/sec.

b. Find the approximate speed in mi/h for 30 ft/sec. (*Hint:* 1 mi = 5280 ft)

c. **Critical Thinking** Would you expect the velocity of the car to increase or decrease as the radius of the loop increases? As the height of the hill decreases?

d. Explain your reasoning for your answer in part (c).

Read and Understand

1. What information is given to you in the problem? _____

2. What do the variables v, h, and r represent? _____

Plan and Solve

3. Which variable will you be solving for initially? _____

4. Write the formula with numbers substituted for the two variables. _____

5. Solve your equation for r. _____

6. Find the approximate speed in mi/h for 30 ft/sec. _____

7. Would you expect the velocity of the car to increase or decrease as the radius of the loop increases? _____

8. Would you expect the velocity of the car to increase or decrease as the height of the hill decreases? _____

9. Explain your reasoning in your answer for Step 7 and Step 8. _____

_____

Look Back and Check

10. Does your speed in mi/h in Step 6 seem reasonable? Explain. _____

_____

Solve Another Problem

11. What is the height if the velocity of the car is 40 ft/s and the radius is 90 ft? _____

Practice 10-5

Find the domain and range of each function.

1. $f(x) = \sqrt{x - 7}$

2. $f(x) = \sqrt{3x - 12}$

3. $y = \sqrt{4x + 11}$

4. $y = \sqrt{x - 12}$

5. $f(x) = \sqrt{x + 14}$

6. $y = \sqrt{x + 8}$

7. $y = \sqrt{5x + 13}$

8. $y = \sqrt{2x + 3}$

9. $y = \sqrt{6x - 2}$

Make a table of values and graph each function.

10. $y = \sqrt{x} - 12$

11. $y = 3\sqrt{x}$

12. $y = \sqrt{x + 8}$

13. $y = \sqrt{x + 7} - 6$

14. $y = \sqrt{x - 6} - 8$

15. $y = \sqrt{x - 10}$

16. $y = 2\sqrt{x - 2}$

17. $y = \sqrt{x - 8} + 6$

18. $y = \sqrt{x} + 7$

Describe how the graph of each function relates to the graph of $y = \sqrt{x}$.

19. $y = \sqrt{x} - 9$

20. $y = \sqrt{x - 19}$

21. $y = \sqrt{x + 18}$

22. $y = \sqrt{x} + 11$

23. The number of people involved in recycling in a community is modeled by the function $n = 90\sqrt{3t} + 400$, where t is the number of months the recycling plant has been open.

a. Graph the function.

b. Find the number of people recycling when the plant has been open for 6 mo.

c. Find the month when about 670 people were recycling.

24. The time t, in seconds, that it takes for an object to drop a distance d, in feet, is modeled by the function $t = \sqrt{\frac{d}{16}}$. Assume no air resistance.

a. Graph the function.

b. Find the time it takes for an object to fall 1000 ft.

c. How far does an object fall in 10 s?

10-5 • Guided Problem Solving

GPS **Exercise 49**

Last year a store had an advertising campaign. The graph shows
the sales for single-use cameras. The function $n = 27\sqrt{5t} + 53$
models the sales volume n for the cameras as a function of time t,
the number of months after the start of the advertising campaign.

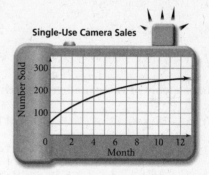

Single-Use Camera Sales

a. Evaluate the function to find how many disposable
cameras the store sold in the seventh month.
b. Solve an equation to find the month in which the
number of single-use cameras sold was about 175.

Read and Understand

1. Describe the information in the graph. _____

2. Explain what the formula describes. _____

_____

Plan and Solve

3. Write the equation you will use to determine how many disposable
cameras the store sold in the seventh month.

_____

4. Simplify your function from Step 3 to determine the number of cameras. _____

5. Write the equation you will solve to determine the month in which
the number of single-use cameras sold was about 175.

_____

6. Solve your equation in Step 5. _____

Look Back and Check

7. Check the reasonableness of your answers in Steps 4 and 6 by estimating
the answers to both questions by reading the graph.

_____

Solve Another Problem

8. The advertising campaign was so successful it was extended an extra six months. Evaluate the
function to see how many cameras were sold after 18 months. _____

Guided Problem Solving

10A: Graphic Organizer

For use before Lesson 10-1

Study Skill After reading a section, recall the information. Ask yourself questions about the section. If you cannot recall enough information reread portions you had trouble remembering. The more time you spend studying the more you can recall.

Write your answers.

1. What is the chapter title? _____

2. Find the Table of Contents page for this chapter at the front of the book. Name four topics you will study in this chapter.

_____   _____

_____   _____

3. Complete the graphic organizer as you work through the chapter.
1. Write the title of the chapter in the center oval.
2. When you begin a lesson, write the name of the lesson in a rectangle.
3. When you complete that lesson, write a skill or key concept from that lesson in the outer oval linked to that rectangle.
Continue with steps 2 and 3 clockwise around the graphic organizer.

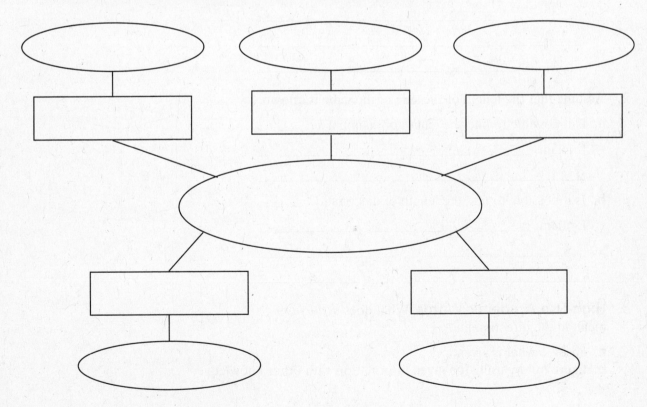

10B: Reading Comprehension

Study Skill Diagrams of three-dimensional objects have solid lines and dashed lines. The dashed lines are the ones that would be hidden from view if you were to look at the object from the perspective that has been drawn.

Answer the question about each figure to practice extracting and deducing information from diagrams.

1. **a.** What is the shape of the base of the figure?

    _____

    b. If you make a slice through the figure from the top of the figure through the center of the base, what is the shape of the slice?

    _____

    c. What figure is formed by the height of the cone, the radius of the base, and the "slant height" of the cone (the distance PQ)?

    _____

    d. How is the slant height of the cone related to the height of the cone and the radius of its base?

    _____

    _____

    _____

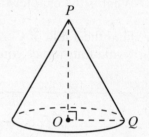

2. Assume that the length of the side of the cube is known.

    a. Is it possible to find the length of diagonal k?_____
    Explain. _____

    _____

    b. Is it possible to find the length of diagonal d?_____
    Explain. _____

    _____

    _____

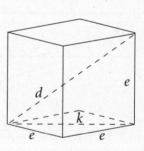

3. **High-Use Academic Words** What does *deducing* mean in the direction line?

    a. observe what is given
    b. figure out by using the given information with other knowledge

10C: Reading/Writing Math Symbols   For use after Lesson 10-3

Study Skill When you take notes in any subject, it helps if you learn to use abbreviations and symbols such as @ (at); #, #s (number, numbers); w/ (with); w/o (without); s/b (should be).

Match each written expression or statement in Column A with its symbolic form in Column B by drawing a line between them.

	Column A		Column B
1.	eight times x equals 40	**A.**	$w \div 6$
2.	the square root of xy	**B.**	$8x = 40$
3.	x divided by y	**C.**	$x^2 y^4$
4.	the square root of the quantity x plus 4 equals 3	**D.**	$5 \le 8$
5.	5 is less than or equal to 8	**E.**	$\frac{x}{y}$
6.	x squared y to the fourth power	**F.**	$\sqrt{xy}$
7.	w divided into 6 equal parts	**G.**	$\sqrt{x} + 4 = 3$

Match each written expression or statement in Column C with its symbolic form in Column D by drawing a line between them.

	Column C		Column D
8.	the quantity x plus four, cubed	**A.**	$\frac{1}{3}x$
9.	2 less than 4 times a number	**B.**	$8 > 5$
10.	one-third of a number x	**C.**	$4x - 2$
11.	three plus x	**D.**	$(x + 4)^2$
12.	eight is greater than 5	**E.**	$2x^2 - 3y$
13.	two times x squared minus three times y	**F.**	$3 + x$
14.	the quantity x plus four, squared	**G.**	$(x + 4)^3$

10D: Visual Vocabulary Practice

For use after Lesson 10-5

Study Skill As you master more vocabulary, more concepts are within your reach.

Concept List

conjugates	Division Property of Square Roots	hypotenuse
leg	like radicals	Pythagorean Theorem
radical equation	square root function	unlike radicals

Write the concept that best describes each exercise. Choose from the concept list above.

1. $3\sqrt{2}$ and $5\sqrt{2}$ _____	**2.**  _____	**3.** $\sqrt{7} + \sqrt{2}$ and $\sqrt{7} - \sqrt{2}$ _____
4. 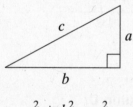 $a^2 + b^2 = c^2$ _____	**5.** $y = \sqrt{2x + 5}$ _____	**6.** $\sqrt{x + 7} = 5$ _____
7. For every number $a \ge 0$ and $b > 0$, $\sqrt{\dfrac{a}{b}} = \dfrac{\sqrt{a}}{\sqrt{b}}$. _____	**8.** 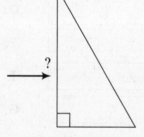 _____	**9.** $2\sqrt{5}$ and $2\sqrt{3}$ _____

10E: Vocabulary Check

For use after Lesson 10-4

Study Skill Strengthen your vocabulary. Use these pages and add cues and summaries by applying the Cornell Notetaking style.

Write the definition for each word at the right. To check your work, fold the paper back along the dotted line to see the correct answers.

_____   Radical expression

_____

_____

_____   Rationalize

_____

_____   Unlike radicals

_____

_____   Conjugates

_____

_____   Extraneous solution

_____

_____

10E: Vocabulary Check (continued)   For use after Lesson 10-4

**Write the vocabulary word for each definition. To check your work, fold
the paper forward along the dotted line to see the correct answers.**

An expression that
contains a radical.   _____

Rewrite as a rational
number. It may be
necessary to obtain the
simplest radical form.   _____

Expressions that do not
have the same radicand.   _____

The sum and difference of
the same two terms.   _____

A solution that does not
satisfy the original
equations.   _____

10F: Vocabulary Review Puzzle

For use with Chapter Review

Study Skill When you read, your eyes make small stops along a line of words. Good readers make fewer stops when they read. The more stops you make when you read, the harder it is for you to comprehend what you've read. Try to concentrate and free yourself of distractions as you read.

Complete the crossword puzzle.

Choose a word from the list below for each of the clues.

binomial	conjugates	converse	discriminant
extraneous	hypotenuse	leg	midpoint
parabola	polynomial	radical equation	radicand
rationalize	vertex		

ACROSS	DOWN
1. the sum or difference of two or more monomials	**1.** the graph of a quadratic function
4. the expression under the radical sign	**2.** reversing the *if and then* parts of a statement
8. a polynomial with two terms	**3.** multiplying the numerator and denominator by the same radical expression to simplify the denominator
11. a type of equation with a variable in the radicand	**5.** the highest or lowest point of a parabola
12. the expression under the radical sign in the quadratic formula	**6.** divides a segment into two equal segments
13. side opposite the right angle in a right triangle	**7.** a solution that does not satisfy the original equation
	9. each of the sides forming the right angle of a triangle
	10. the sum and the difference of the same two terms

Practice 11-1

Simplifying Rational Expressions

Simplify each expression.

1. $\dfrac{6x^4}{18x^2}$

2. $\dfrac{15a^2}{25a^4}$

3. $\dfrac{32h^3}{48h^2}$

4. $\dfrac{12n^4}{21n^6}$

5. $\dfrac{3x-6}{6}$

6. $\dfrac{x^2-2x}{x}$

7. $\dfrac{4t^2-2t}{2t}$

8. $\dfrac{a^3-2a^2}{2a^2-4a}$

9. $\dfrac{21x^2y}{14xy^2}$

10. $\dfrac{32x^3y^2}{24xy^4}$

11. $\dfrac{x^2+3x}{3x+9}$

12. $\dfrac{x^2-5x}{5x-25}$

13. $\dfrac{x^2+13x+12}{x^2-144}$

14. $\dfrac{x^2-9}{x^3-3x^2}$

15. $\dfrac{x^3+x^2}{x+1}$

16. $\dfrac{3x-2y}{2y-3x}$

17. $\dfrac{x^2+x-6}{x^2-x-2}$

18. $\dfrac{x^2+3x+2}{x^3+x^2}$

19. $\dfrac{2x^2-8}{x^2-3x+2}$

20. $\dfrac{2x^2-5x+3}{x^2-1}$

21. $\dfrac{3x+3y}{x^2+xy}$

22. $\dfrac{10+3x-x^2}{x^2-4x-5}$

23. $\dfrac{9-x^2}{x^2+x-12}$

24. $\dfrac{x^2+2x-15}{x^2-7x+12}$

25. $\dfrac{x^2+7x-8}{x^2+6x-7}$

26. $\dfrac{x^2+3x-10}{25-x^2}$

27. Write and simplify the ratio $\dfrac{\text{perimeter of rectangle}}{\text{area of rectangle}}$. The perimeter of
the rectangle is $10w$ and the area of the rectangle is $4w^2$.

28. The ratio $\dfrac{3 \cdot \text{volume of cone}}{\text{area of base}}$ determines the height of a cone. Find the
height when the volume is $4r^3+2r^2$ and the area of the base is $6r^2$.

29. The ratio $\dfrac{2 \cdot \text{area of triangle}}{\text{height of triangle}}$ determines the length of the base of a
triangle. Find the length of the base when the area is $3n^2+6n$ and the
height is $2n+4$.

30. The ratio $\dfrac{\text{volume of rectangular solid}}{\text{area of rectangular base}}$ determines the height of a
rectangular solid. Find the height when the volume is $5s^3+10s^2$ and
the area is $5s^2$.

11-1 • Guided Problem Solving

GPS Exercise 34

a. To keep heating costs down for a structure, architects want the ratio of surface area to volume as small as possible. Find an expression for the ratio of the surface area to volume for each shape.
   i. square prism   **ii.** cylinder

b. Find the ratio for each figure when $b = 12$ ft, $h = 18$ ft, and $r = 6$ ft.

Read and Understand

1. What is the formula for finding the surface area of a prism?

   _____

2. What is the formula for finding the volume of a prism? _____

3. What is the formula for finding the surface area of a cylinder? _____

4. What is the formula for finding the volume of a cylinder? _____

Plan and Solve

5. Write an expression for the surface area of the square prism. _____

6. Write an expression for the volume of the square prism. _____

7. Write an expression for the ratio of surface area to volume for the square prism. _____

8. Write an expression for the surface area of the cylinder. _____

9. Write an expression for the volume of the cylinder. _____

10. Write an expression for the ratio of the surface area to volume for the cylinder. _____

11. Find the ratio for each figure when $b = 12$ ft, $h = 18$ ft, and $r = 6$ ft.

    square prism: _____   cylinder: _____

Look Back and Check

12. Explain why keeping the ratio of surface area to volume as small as possible will help keep heating costs down.

    _____

Solve Another Problem

13. Write an expression for the ratio of surface area to volume for a square prism that has a length and width of 4 and a height of h. _____

Practice 11-2

Multiplying and Dividing Rational Expressions

Multiply or divide.

1. $\dfrac{5}{9} \cdot \dfrac{6}{15}$

2. $\dfrac{8}{3} \div \dfrac{16}{27}$

3. $\left(-\dfrac{3}{4}\right) \div \dfrac{16}{21}$

4. $\dfrac{2}{9} \div \left(-\dfrac{10}{3}\right)$

5. $\dfrac{18m}{4m^2} \div \dfrac{9m}{8}$

6. $\dfrac{8x}{12} \cdot \dfrac{4x}{6}$

7. $\dfrac{9}{15x} \cdot \dfrac{25x}{27}$

8. $\dfrac{12x^3}{25} \div \dfrac{16x}{5}$

9. $\dfrac{6x^3}{18x} \div \dfrac{9x^2}{10x^4}$

10. $\dfrac{4r^3}{10} \cdot \dfrac{25}{16r^2}$

11. $\dfrac{8n^2}{3} \div \dfrac{20n}{9}$

12. $\dfrac{14x^2}{5} \div 7x^4$

13. $\dfrac{4n^3}{11} \cdot \dfrac{33n}{36n^2}$

14. $\dfrac{24r^3}{35r^2} \div \dfrac{12r}{14r^3}$

15. $\dfrac{a^2 - 4}{3} \cdot \dfrac{9}{a + 2}$

16. $\dfrac{4b - 12}{5b^2} \cdot \dfrac{6b}{b - 3}$

17. $\dfrac{2b}{5} \cdot \dfrac{10}{b^2}$

18. $\dfrac{2b}{b + 3} \div \dfrac{b}{b + 3}$

19. $\dfrac{5y^3}{7} \cdot \dfrac{14y}{30y^2}$

20. $\dfrac{4p + 16}{5p} \div \dfrac{p + 4}{15p^3}$

21. $\dfrac{3(h + 2)}{h + 3} \div \dfrac{h + 2}{h + 3}$

22. $\dfrac{a^3 - a^2}{a^3} \cdot \dfrac{a^2}{a - 1}$

23. $\dfrac{h^2 + 6h}{h + 3} \cdot \dfrac{4h + 12}{h + 6}$

24. $\dfrac{n^2 - 1}{n + 2} \cdot \dfrac{n^2 - 4}{n + 1}$

25. $\dfrac{x^2 - x}{x} \cdot \dfrac{3x - 6}{3x - 3}$

26. $\dfrac{5x - 10}{x + 2} \cdot \dfrac{3}{3x - 6}$

27. $\dfrac{x^2 - 16}{x - 4} \div \dfrac{3x + 12}{x}$

28. $\dfrac{x^2 - 1}{3x - 3} \div \dfrac{x + 1}{3}$

29. $\dfrac{x^2 - 2x - 24}{x^2 - 5x - 6} \cdot \dfrac{x^2 + 5x + 6}{x^2 + 6x + 8}$

30. $\dfrac{x^2 + 2x - 35}{x^2 + 4x - 21} \cdot \dfrac{x^2 + 3x - 18}{x^2 + 9x + 18}$

31. $\dfrac{3x^2 + 14x + 8}{2x^2 + 7x - 4} \cdot \dfrac{2x^2 + 9x - 5}{3x^2 + 16x + 5}$

32. $\dfrac{8 + 2x - x^2}{x^2 + 7x + 10} \div \dfrac{x^2 - 11x + 28}{x^2 - x - 42}$

33. $\dfrac{x^2 - x - 6}{3x - 9} \cdot \dfrac{x^2 - 9}{x^2 + 6x + 9}$

34. $\dfrac{6x^2 + 13x + 6}{4x^2 - 9} \div \dfrac{6x^2 + x - 2}{4x^2 - 1}$

35. $\dfrac{x^2 - 2x - 35}{3x^2 + 27x} \div \dfrac{x^2 + 7x + 10}{6x^2 + 12x}$

36. $\dfrac{x^2 - x - 6}{2x^2 + 9x + 10} \div \dfrac{x^2 - 25}{2x^2 + 15x + 25}$

37. $\dfrac{15 - 14x - 8x^2}{4x^2 + 4x - 15} \div \dfrac{4x^2 + 13x - 12}{3x^2 + 13x + 4}$

38. $\dfrac{x^2 - 4x - 32}{x^2 - 8x - 48} \cdot \dfrac{3x^2 + 17x + 10}{3x^2 - 22x - 16}$

39. $\dfrac{9x^2 - 16}{6x^2 - 11x + 4} \div \dfrac{6x^2 + 11x + 4}{8x^2 + 10x + 3}$

11-2 • Guided Problem Solving

GPS **Exercise 41**

Find the volume of the rectangular solid.

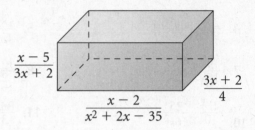

$$\frac{x-5}{3x+2}$$

$$\frac{x-2}{x^2+2x-35}$$

$$\frac{3x+2}{4}$$

Read and Understand

1. What information is given to you in the picture? _____

2. How do you find the volume of a rectangular solid? _____

Plan and Solve

3. Write an expression for the volume of the rectangular solid. _____

4. Explain how you can simplify your expression before multiplying. _____

   _____

5. What is the final product? _____

Look Back and Check

6. Check the reasonableness of your answer by evaluating your original expression for $x = 2$ and then evaluating your final product for $x = 2$ also.

Solve Another Problem

7. Find the volume of a cube if each edge measures $\dfrac{3x}{6x^2 + 9x}$. _____

Practice 11-3

Divide.

1. $\dfrac{10x - 25}{5}$

2. $\dfrac{4x^3 - 3x}{x}$

3. $(3x^2 - 6x) \div 3x$

4. $(10x^2 - 6x) \div 2x$

5. $(-8x^5 + 16x^4 - 24x^3 + 32x^2) \div 8x^2$

6. $(15x^2 - 30x) \div 5x$

7. $(x^2 - 14x + 49) \div (x - 7)$

8. $(2x^2 - 13x + 21) \div (x - 3)$

9. $(4x^2 - 16) \div (2x + 4)$

10. $(x^2 + 4x - 12) \div (x - 2)$

11. $(x^2 + 10x + 16) \div (x + 2)$

12. $(12x^2 - 5x - 2) \div (3x - 2)$

13. $(x^2 + 5x + 10) \div (x + 2)$

14. $(x^2 - 8x - 9) \div (x - 3)$

15. $(3x^2 - 2x - 13) \div (x - 2)$

16. $(x^3 + 3x^2 + 5x + 3) \div (x + 1)$

17. $(5 - 23x + 12x^2) \div (4x - 1)$

18. $(24 + 6x^2 + 25x) \div (3x - 1)$

19. $(2x^2 + 11x - 5) \div (x + 6)$

20. $(x^2 + 5x - 10) \div (x + 2)$

21. $(8x + 3 + 4x^2) \div (2x - 1)$

22. $(3x^2 + 11x - 4) \div (3x - 1)$

23. $(x^3 + x - x^2 - 1) \div (x - 1)$

24. $(10 + 21x + 10x^2) \div (2x + 3)$

25. $(6x^2 - 35x + 36) \div (3x - 4)$

26. $(-2x^2 - 33x + x^3 - 7) \div (x - 7)$

27. The volume of a rectangular prism is $15x^3 + 38x^2 - 23x - 6$. The height of the prism is $5x + 1$, and the width of the prism is $x + 3$. Find the length of the prism.

28. The width of a rectangle is $x + 1$, and the area is $x^3 + 2x^2 - 5x - 6$ cm. What is the length of the rectangle?

Algebra 1 Lesson 11-3 **395**

11-3 • Guided Problem Solving

GPS **Exercise 44**

The volume of a rectangular prism is $2x^3 + 5x^2 + x - 2$. The height of the prism is $2x - 1$, and the length of the prism is $x + 2$. Find the width of the prism.

Read and Understand

1. What is the formula for volume of a prism? _____

2. Explain how you can use the formula to find the width of the prism.

   _____

   _____

Plan and Solve

3. Write an equation for the volume of the rectangular prism. _____

4. Find the product of the length and height. Then rewrite the equation as a long division problem.

   _____

5. What does the quotient represent? _____

6. Write the expression for the width of the rectangular prism. _____

Look Back and Check

7. Substitute the expression for the width of the rectangular prism into your equation from Exercise 3. Check your answer by evaluating for $x = 5$. _____

Solve Another Problem

8. Find the length of a rectangular prism that has a volume of $2x^3 - 2x^2 - 16x + 24$. The height of the prism is $x - 2$ and the width of the prism is twice the height. _____

Practice 11-4

Adding and Subtracting Rational Expressions

Add or subtract.

1. $\dfrac{3x}{4} - \dfrac{x}{4}$

2. $\dfrac{3}{x} + \dfrac{5}{x}$

3. $\dfrac{5x}{6} - \dfrac{2x}{3}$

4. $\dfrac{x}{3} + \dfrac{x}{5}$

5. $\dfrac{3m}{4} + \dfrac{5m}{12}$

6. $\dfrac{4x}{7} - \dfrac{3x}{14}$

7. $\dfrac{6}{7t} - \dfrac{3}{7t}$

8. $\dfrac{d}{3} + \dfrac{4d}{3}$

9. $\dfrac{7}{2d} - \dfrac{3}{2d}$

10. $\dfrac{3}{2d^2} + \dfrac{4}{3d}$

11. $\dfrac{9}{m+1} - \dfrac{6}{m-1}$

12. $\dfrac{3}{x} - \dfrac{7}{x}$

13. $\dfrac{7a}{6} + \dfrac{a}{6}$

14. $\dfrac{4}{k+3} - \dfrac{8}{k+3}$

15. $\dfrac{3}{4z^2} + \dfrac{7}{4z^2}$

16. $\dfrac{6}{x^2-1} + \dfrac{7}{x-1}$

17. $\dfrac{2x}{x^2-1} - \dfrac{3}{x+1}$

18. $\dfrac{3t}{8} + \dfrac{3t}{8}$

19. $\dfrac{4}{3a^2} - \dfrac{1}{2a^3}$

20. $\dfrac{4}{a+4} + \dfrac{6}{a+4}$

21. $\dfrac{4}{x+3} + \dfrac{6}{x-2}$

22. $\dfrac{6}{7t^3} - \dfrac{8}{3t}$

23. $\dfrac{3}{2x+6} + \dfrac{4}{6x+18}$

24. $\dfrac{5}{8a} - \dfrac{3}{8a}$

25. $\dfrac{5}{r^2-4} + \dfrac{7}{r+2}$

26. $\dfrac{6}{a^2-2} + \dfrac{9}{a^2-2}$

27. $\dfrac{5x}{4} - \dfrac{x}{4}$

28. $\dfrac{4}{3x+6} - \dfrac{3}{2x+4}$

29. $\dfrac{4}{c^2+4c+3} + \dfrac{1}{c+3}$

30. $\dfrac{6}{x^2-3x+2} - \dfrac{4}{x-2}$

31. Brian rode his bike 2 mi to his friend's house. Brian's bike had a flat tire, so he had to walk home. His walking rate is 25% of his biking rate.

  a. Write an expression for the amounts of time Brian spent walking and riding his bike.

  b. If Brian's biking rate is 12 mi/h, how much time did he spend walking and riding his bike?

32. Trudi and Sean are on a river canoeing. Because of the current of the river, their downstream rate is 250% of their upstream rate. They canoe 3 mi upstream and then return to their starting point.

  a. Write an expression for the amount of time Trudi and Sean spend canoeing.

  b. If their upstream rate is 2 mi/h, how much time do Trudi and Sean spend canoeing?

  c. If their upstream rate is 3 mi/h, how much time do Trudi and Sean spend canoeing?

11-4 • Guided Problem Solving

GPS **Exercise 41**

A rowing team practices rowing 2 mi upstream and 2 mi downstream.
The team can row downstream 25% faster than they can row upstream.

   a. Let r represent their rate upstream. Write and simplify an expression
   for the amount of time they spend rowing.

   b. Let d represent their rate downstream. Write and simplify an
   expression for the amount of time they spend rowing.

   c. **Critical Thinking** Do the expressions you wrote in parts (a) and
   (b) represent the same time? Explain.

Read and Understand

1. Explain why the team rows faster going downstream than upstream. _____

_____

2. What is the relationship between rate, time, and distance that you will need to use? _____

Plan and Solve

3. Let r represent their rate upstream. Write and simplify
an expression for the amount of time they spend rowing. _____

4. Let d represent their rate downstream. Write and simplify
an expression for the amount of time they spend rowing. _____

5. Do the expressions you wrote in Steps 3 and 4 represent the same time? Explain.

_____

_____

Look Back and Check

6. Check the accuracy of your expressions by verifying that they are equal when $r = 4$ and $d = 5$.

Solve Another Problem

7. Write new expressions for the rowing team's times upstream and downstream
if they can only row downstream 10% faster than they can row upstream. _____

Guided Problem Solving

Name _____ Class _____ Date _____

Practice 11-5 .... Solving Rational Equations

Solve each equation. Check your solution. If there is no solution, write *no solution.*

1. $\frac{1}{x} + \frac{1}{2x} = \frac{1}{6}$

2. $\frac{x}{x+2} + \frac{4}{x-2} = 1$

3. $\frac{1}{3s} = \frac{s}{2} - \frac{1}{6s}$

4. $\frac{x+2}{x+8} = \frac{x-2}{x+4}$

5. $1 - \frac{3}{x} = \frac{4}{x^2}$

6. $\frac{7}{3(a-2)} - \frac{1}{a-2} = \frac{2}{3}$

7. $\frac{n}{n-4} = \frac{2n}{n+4}$

8. $x + \frac{6}{x} = -7$

9. $\frac{2}{r^2-r} - 1 = \frac{2}{r-1}$

10. $\frac{y}{y+3} = \frac{6}{y+9}$

11. $\frac{d}{3} + \frac{1}{2} = \frac{1}{3d}$

12. $\frac{2m}{m-5} = \frac{2m+16}{m+3}$

13. $\frac{1}{m-4} + \frac{1}{m+4} = \frac{8}{m^2-16}$

14. $\frac{5}{x-2} = \frac{5x+10}{x^2}$

15. $\frac{k^2}{k+3} = \frac{9}{k+3}$

16. $\frac{h-3}{h+6} = \frac{2h+3}{h+6}$

17. $\frac{h}{6} - \frac{3}{2h} = \frac{8}{3h}$

18. $4 - \frac{3}{y} = \frac{5}{y}$

19. $\frac{1}{b-3} = \frac{b}{4}$

20. $\frac{1}{t^2} - \frac{2}{t} = \frac{3}{t^2}$

21. $\frac{2}{3n} + \frac{3}{4} = \frac{2}{3}$

22. David and Fiona have a house painting business. It takes Fiona 3 days to paint a certain house. David could paint the same house in 4 days. How long would it take them to paint the house if David and Fiona worked together?

23. Suppose the Williams Spring Water Company has two machines that bottle the spring water. Machine X fills the bottles twice as fast as Machine Y. Working together, it takes them 20 min to fill 450 bottles. How long would it take each machine working alone to fill the 450 bottles?

24. Chao, who is an experienced architect, can draw a certain set of plans in 6 h. It takes Carl, who is a new architect, 10 h to draw the same set of plans. How long would it take them working together to draw the set of plans?

25. For exercise, Joseph likes to walk and Vincent likes to ride his bike. Vincent rides his bike 12 km/h faster than Joseph walks. Joseph walks 20 km in the same amount of time that Vincent rides 44 km. Find the rate that each of them travels.

26. The Ryan Publishing Company has two printing presses. It takes the new printing press 45 min to print 10,000 fliers. Together the two presses can print the 10,000 fliers in 30 min. How long does it take the older printing press by itself to print the 10,000 fliers?

Practice *Algebra 1 Lesson 11-5* **399**

Pearson Education, Inc., publishing as Pearson Prentice Hall. All rights reserved.

11-5 • Guided Problem Solving

Exercise 36

It takes Jon 75 min to paint a room. It takes Jeff 60 min and Jackie 80 min each to paint the same room. How long will the painting take if all three work together?

Read and Understand

1. What is the problem asking you to find? _____

2. Write the rate at which each person paints. _____

Plan and Solve

3. Let n = the time, in minutes, needed to paint the room if the painters work together. Write an equation that represents the problem. _____

4. Using the LCD, clear the fractions on both sides of the equation you wrote in Exercise 3. Write the new equation and solve for n. _____

Look Back and Check

5. What part of the whole painting job will Jon do? Jeff? Jackie? _____

Solve Another Problem

6. Ryan can wash and wax a car in 45 minutes. Carlo can wash and wax the same car in 30 minutes. How long will it take them to wash and wax the car together? _____

11A: Graphic Organizer

For use before Lesson 11-1

Study Skill What do the pages before the first page of Chapter 11 tell you? Keep notes as you work through each chapter to help you organize your thinking and to make it easier to review the material when you complete the chapter.

Write your answers.

1. What is the chapter title? _____

2. Find the Table of Contents page for this chapter at the front of the book. Name four topics you will study in this chapter.

   _____   _____

   _____   _____

3. Complete the graphic organizer as you work through the chapter.
   1. Write the title of the chapter in the center oval.
   2. When you begin a lesson, write the name of the lesson in a rectangle.
   3. When you complete that lesson, write a skill or key concept from that lesson in the outer oval linked to that rectangle.

   Continue with steps 2 and 3 clockwise around the graphic organizer.

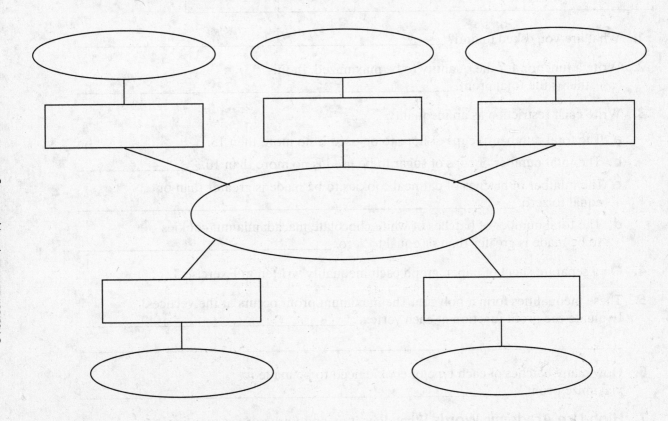

11B: Reading Comprehension For use after Lesson 11-5

Study Skill Some word problems contain so much information it is difficult to know how to deal with it all. Sometimes it helps to organize information in a table.

> Jessica Hernandez bakes and sells gourmet cookies. She bakes two types of cookies: oatmeal and white chocolate macadamia nut. Each batch of oatmeal cookies requires 2 cups of flour and 2 cups of sugar. Each batch of white chocolate macadamia nut cookies requires 3 cups of flour and 1 cup of sugar. Jessica makes a $3 profit on each batch of oatmeal cookies and a $2 profit on each batch of white chocolate macadamia nut cookies. She has 18 cups of flour and 10 cups of sugar on hand. How many batches of each type of cookie should she bake to maximize her profits?

Organize the information you are given into the following table.

	Batches of Cookies	Cups of Flour	Cups of Sugar	Total Profit ($)
Oatmeal	x			
White Chocolate Macadamia Nut	y			
Totals				P

1. What are you asked to find? _____

2. Write a function for the quantity to be maximized. In this case, that is the total profit. _____

3. Write each restriction as an inequality.

   a. The total number of cups of flour to be used is no more than 18. _____

   b. The total number of cups of sugar to be used is no more than 10. _____

   c. The number of batches of oatmeal cookies to be made is greater than or equal to zero. _____

   d. The total number of batches of white chocolate macadamia nut cookies to be made is greater than or equal to zero. _____

4. On a separate sheet of paper, graph each inequality written in Exercise 3.

5. These inequalities form a polygon. The maximum profit occurs at the vertices. Evaluate the profit function at each vertex. _____

   _____

6. How many batches of each type of cookie need to be made to maximize profit? _____

7. **High-Use Academic Words** What does it mean to *organize* as mentioned in the direction line?

   a. write an equation   **b.** categorize

11C: Reading/Writing Math Symbols

For use after Lesson 11-3

Study Skill It is important to read directions carefully before doing any exercises. Sometimes the directions are asking for more than one answer, or something entirely different than what you think at first glance.

Given the formulas below, write out what the formula means in words, and write a brief description of what the formula is used for or what it represents. The first one is done for you.

1. $a^2 + b^2 = c^2$ <u>leg squared plus leg squared equals</u>

<u>hypotenuse squared; Pythagorean</u>

<u>Theorem—used to find a side of a</u>

<u>right triangle</u>

2. $I = prt$ _____

_____

3. $ax^2 + bx + c = 0$ _____

_____

4. $b^2 - 4ac$ _____

_____

5. $d = rt$ _____

_____

6. $m = \dfrac{y_2 - y_1}{x_2 - x_1}$ _____

_____

7. $V = l \times w \times h$ _____

_____

8. $\left(\dfrac{x_1 + x_2}{2}, \dfrac{y_1 + y_2}{2} \right)$ _____

_____

9. $x = \dfrac{-b \pm \sqrt{b^2 - 4ac}}{2a}$ _____

_____

10. $d = \sqrt{(x_2 - x_1)^2 + (y_2 - y_1)^2}$ _____

_____

11D: Visual Vocabulary Practice
High-Use Academic Words

For use after Lesson 11-5

Study Skill Mathematics is like learning a foreign language. You have to know the vocabulary before you can speak the language correctly.

Concept List

apply	consecutive	formula
interpret	methods	notation
simplify	solve	test

Write the concept that best describes each exercise. Choose from the concept list above.

1. $f(x)$ for y	2. The slope of the linear graph is 3, which indicates the class charged $3 per car.	3. n and $n + 1$
4. $V = \dfrac{4\pi r^3}{3}$	5. Expenses are $.90 for printing and mailing a newsletter, plus $600 for writing. The price is $1.50 per copy. Find the number of copies that must be sold to break even.	6. $2(c + 4) - 5c = -3c + 8$
7. 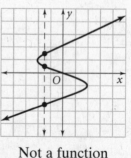 Not a function	8. $\begin{aligned} 2(5x - 3) &= 14 \\ 10x - 6 &= 14 \\ 10x &= 20 \\ x &= 2 \end{aligned}$	9. Solving systems by • Graphing • Substitution • Elimination

Name_____ Class_____ Date_____

11E: Vocabulary Check

For use after Lesson 11-5

Study Skill Strengthen your vocabulary. Use these pages and add cues
and summaries by applying the Cornell Notetaking style.

**Write the definition for each word at the right. To check your work,
fold the paper back along the dotted line to see the correct answers.**

_____

_____

_____

Rational function

_____

_____

_____

Evaluate

_____

_____

_____

Rational expression

_____

_____

_____

Simplify

_____

_____

_____

Coefficient

_____

_____

Vocabulary and Study Skills

Algebra 1 Chapter 11   **405**

11E: Vocabulary Check (continued)

For use after Lesson 11-5

Write the vocabulary word for each definition. To check your work,
fold the paper forward along the dotted line to see the correct answers.

A function that can be
written in the form
$f(x) = \dfrac{\text{polynomial}}{\text{polynomial}}$.

_____

Substitute a given number
for each variable and
then simplify.

_____

An expression which can
be written in the form
$\dfrac{\text{polynomial}}{\text{polynomial}}$.

_____

Replace an expression
with its simplest name
or form.

_____

The numerical factor when
a term has a variable.

_____

11F: Vocabulary Review Puzzle

For use with Chapter Review

Study Skill Read aloud or recite the new terms as you read them. This will help you remember and recall rules, definitions, and formulas for future use.

Unscramble the UPPERCASE letters to form a math word or phrase that completes each sentence.

1. When you divide rational expressions that can be factored, first rewrite the expression using the PRACOLICER before dividing out common factors.

2. An AMPOILLOYN is a monomial or the sum or difference of two or more monomials.

3. An SEVNIER ITVIANARO can be written in the form $xy = k$ or $y = \frac{k}{x}$.

4. A rational expression is in STELIMPS MORF if the numerator and denominator have no common factors except 1.

5. A TAIRNLOA SPINEROXES can be written in the form $\frac{\text{polynomial}}{\text{polynomial}}$.

6. The graph of a quadratic function is a BAAPARLO.

7. The quantity $b^2 - 4ac$ is the RIDNMCITSINA of $ax^2 + bx + c = 0$

8. The highest or lowest point on a parabola is its XTERVE.

9. In a right triangle, the length of the USHEEPONTY is the square root of the sum of the squares of the side lengths.

10. You may TAEZIONILRA the denominator of a radical expression when simplifying the expression.